Advances in Information Security

Volume 90

The purpose of the *Advances in Information Security* book series is to establish the state of the art and set the course for future research in information security. The scope of this series includes not only all aspects of computer, network security, and cryptography, but related areas, such as fault tolerance and software assurance. The series serves as a central source of reference for information security research and developments. The series aims to publish thorough and cohesive overviews on specific topics in Information Security, as well as works that are larger in scope than survey articles and that will contain more detailed background information. The series also provides a single point of coverage of advanced and timely topics and a forum for topics that may not have reached a level of maturity to warrant a comprehensive textbook.

Quanyan Zhu • Zhuo Lu • Paul L. Yu • Cliff Wang
Editors

Foundations of Cyber Deception

Modeling, Analysis, Design, Human Factors, and Their Convergence

Springer

Editors
Quanyan Zhu
New York University
Brooklyn, NY, USA

Zhuo Lu
University of South Florida
Tampa, FL, USA

Paul L. Yu
Army Research Laboratory
Adelphi, MD, USA

Cliff Wang
National Science Foundation
Durham, NC, USA

ISSN 1568-2633 ISSN 2512-2193 (electronic)
Advances in Information Security
ISBN 978-3-031-93866-5 ISBN 978-3-031-93867-2 (eBook)
https://doi.org/10.1007/978-3-031-93867-2

This Springer imprint is published by the registered company Springer Nature Switzerland AG
The registered company address is: Gewerbestrasse 11, 6330 Cham, Switzerland

Preface

Recent years have witnessed a surge of activity in the field of cyber deception across diverse sectors, including academia, industry, and government. Cyber deception has emerged as a transformative paradigm for defending digital assets by creating false information, environments, or signals within a network or system. Its goal is to confuse, delay, or misdirect adversaries, making it more difficult for them to achieve their objectives. This tactic not only protects critical assets but also gathers valuable intelligence about attackers' methods and intentions. Cyber deception has shifted the information advantage, which traditionally favored attackers, back toward defenders by countering the inherent edge attackers often have in terms of information and resources.

The growing interest in this field led to a recent workshop organized at NYU on August 17–18, 2023. The event brought together a distinguished cohort of leading and active researchers from academia, government, and industry. The discussions at the workshop inspired the creation of this edited volume, which aims to address prevailing research issues, precisely identify challenges, discuss new approaches, and advocate for holistic and convergent research in this pivotal field. The volume contains 12 chapters, organized into four coherent parts: (1) Theoretical Foundations, (2) Human Factors, (3) Application Domains, and (4) Roadmaps and Future Challenges. The papers included in this volume attest to the vitality and diversity of ongoing research in cyber deception and provide insights and directions for future advancements in the field.

The first part contains three chapters focusing on the theoretical challenges in analyzing and modeling cyber deception techniques, with trust as the underlying theme. Deception aims to establish and exploit an attacker's trust to understand their behavior and mitigate their impact on networks. Game theory plays a key role in modeling the interactions between adversaries and defenders. Modern AI has introduced new tools for scalable computation and data-driven learning, particularly through foundation models and their associated technologies. The chapters in this section examine how AI, including foundation-model-driven approaches, can enhance the analysis, synthesis, and operational design of cyber deception mechanisms.

The second part of the book comprises five chapters that emphasize the crucial role of human factors in the success of cyber deception. This section examines the psychological and behavioral dimensions of both attackers and defenders, showing how cognitive vulnerabilities, defined as human tendencies that deception seeks to exploit, influence decision-making. In practice, humans often act with bounded rationality, for example, by discounting or ignoring environmental signals and exhibiting risk-averse behavior under uncertainty, particularly when it is difficult to distinguish between anomalous user behaviors and genuine attacks. Such cognitive limitations, including confirmation bias, can be exploited by adversaries, creating opportunities to act before defenders accurately recognize threats or regain effective control. This section surveys recent research on human-centric cyber deception, including studies of psychological barriers to risk assessment; the Tularosa Study, which provides an experimental framework for quantifying the effectiveness of cyber deception; and the application of Structural Equation Modeling to analyze cognitive and behavioral responses. These contributions demonstrate the need to integrate technical and behavioral approaches to cyber deception through multidisciplinary methods spanning computer science, psychology, economics, and statistics.

The third part of the book contains three chapters and examines Convergent Designs and Integration, focusing on the design of deception strategies for specific systems and environments. The application domains covered include enterprise networks, industrial control systems, and cyber-physical systems such as unmanned autonomous vehicle networks. The solutions discussed in this part highlight the unique characteristics of each application and how proactive security measures can be tailored to fit their specific needs. For instance, designing cyber deception for operational technology (OT) systems presents distinct challenges, requiring consideration of legacy equipment in industrial control systems and an understanding of OT performance requirements and standards to develop effective deception mechanisms. This section emphasizes the importance of thoroughly understanding the systems being designed, including their constraints and specifications, to create synergistic solutions that integrate modeling, analysis, human factors, and customized deception strategies for each application.

The final part of the book includes one chapter presenting roadmaps and visions for next-generation deception research. The chapter explores emerging trends in cyber deception and the development of advanced techniques and tools that will shape the future of this field. The section advocates for a more comprehensive understanding of cyber deception, which has garnered significant attention in both research and practical applications. Echoing themes from earlier parts of this book, it emphasizes the continued exploration of how advancements in AI, machine learning, and large language models will play a critical role in the future of cyber deception.

Designed to be a valuable reference, this book is particularly useful for students and early-career researchers who are eager to learn about cyber deception and identify research problems to tackle in the future. The book introduces various application domains, ranging from industrial control systems to AI security, each requiring tailored and context-specific approaches. It recognizes the unique challenges posed by different sectors, emphasizing the importance of developing dynamic and context-aware strategies. These strategies are essential for countering the ever-evolving tactics employed by cyber adversaries, guiding the development of more robust and resilient cybersecurity measures.

Furthermore, the book advocates for a forward-thinking approach, encouraging readers to explore how emerging technologies and interdisciplinary methods can be leveraged to enhance the effectiveness of cyber deception. By addressing both current and future challenges, this book aims to contribute to the ongoing evolution of the field, providing a roadmap for the development of next-generation deception techniques.

We would like to take this opportunity to thank the authors for their outstanding contributions to this volume, the reviewers for their diligent assistance in the evaluation process, and DEVCOM ARL Army Research Office for supporting the workshop that led to the creation of this volume.

New York, NY, USA — Quanyan Zhu
Tampa, FL, USA — Zhuo Lu
Raleigh, NC, USA — Cliff Wang
Adelphi, MD, USA — Paul L. Yu

Contents

Part II Human Factors

Part I
Analysis and Modeling

Proactive Defense Strategy Design in Probabilistic Attack Graphs

Haoxiang Ma, Shuo Han, Charles A. Kamhoua, and Jie Fu

1 Introduction

Proactive defense refers to a class of defense mechanisms for the defender to detect any ongoing attacks, distract the attacker with deception, or use randomization to increase the difficulty of an attack to the system. In this paper, we propose a mathematical framework and solution approach for synthesizing a proactive defense system with deception.

We start by formulating the attack planning problem using a probabilistic attack graph, which can be viewed as a Markov decision process (MDP) with a set of attack target states. Attack graphs(AGs) [12] can be used in modeling computer networks. They are widely used in network security to identify the minimal subset of vulnerability/sensors to be used in order to prevent all known attacks [18, 22]. Probabilistic attack graphs introduce uncertain outcomes of attack actions that account for action failures in a stochastic environment or the effects of moving target defense (MTD). For example, in [10, 11], probabilistic transitions in attack graphs capture uncertainties originating from network-based randomization. Under the probabilistic attack graph modeling framework, we investigate how to optimally allocate intrusion detectors to detect the attackers. Based on the intrusion detector allocation strategy, we dive into using deception mechanisms to prevent the attacker

H. Ma · J. Fu (✉)
University of Florida, Gainesville, FL, USA
e-mail: hma2@ufl.edu; fujie@ufl.edu

S. Han
University of Illinois Chicago, Chicago, IL, USA
e-mail: hanshuo@uic.edu

C. A. Kamhoua
U.S. Army Research Laboratory, Adelphi, MD, USA
e-mail: charles.a.kamhoua.civ@mail.mil

Q. Zhu et al. (eds.), *Foundations of Cyber Deception*, Advances in Information Security 90, https://doi.org/10.1007/978-3-031-93867-2_1

from reaching the real targets, which includes using stealthy sensors to detect the attacker, or allocating decoy resources as fake targets to distract the attacker into attacking the fake targets and modifying the attack action costs to discourage the attacker from reaching the true targets. We show that proactive defense strateg design can be formulated as a bi-level optimization problem, where the defender (at the upper level) designs the defense system, in anticipation of the attacker's (at the lower level) best response, given that the attacker has disinformation about the cyber system due to deception.

Related Work The synthesis of proactive defense strategies studied herein is closely related to the Stackelberg security game (SSG) (surveyed in [23]). In an SSG, the defender is to defend a set of targets with limited resources, while the attacker selects the optimal attack strategy given the knowledge of the defender's strategy. The solution concepts of Stackelberg Equilibrium are employed by [21] to design a mixed strategy for the defender to allocate intrusion detectors and implement the intrusion detectors randomization schedule using moving target defense (MTD). In [17], the authors formulate the security countermeasure-allocation problem as a resource-allocation game, where attack graphs are used to evaluate the security of the network given the allocated resources. A Bayesian attack graph is an empirical attack behavior model constructed from the data and exploitability of the targeted vulnerability [25]. In [15], the authors assume that a Bayesian attack graph [7] represents the attacker's behavior and design optimal defender's strategies under partial observations using solutions of partially observable Markov decision processes. Another related formulation is the plan interdiction problem studied in [14], modeled as a deterministic planning problem where the attacker is to reach a subset of goals with attack actions, and the defender is to mitigate the attack by interdicting or removing the attack actions. They formulated a mixed-integer programming problem to maximize the defender's objective function assuming the optimal plan of the attacker given the interdiction strategy. Regarding using decoy resources to enhance the system's security, the authors in [24] formulate a security game to allocate limited decoy resources to mask a network configuration from the cyber attacker. The decoy-based deception manipulates the adversary's perception of the payoff matrix. In [3], the authors study honeypot allocation in deterministic attack graphs and determine the optimal allocation strategy using the minimax theorem. In [16], the authors study directed acyclic attack graphs that can be modified by the defender using deceptive and protective resources. They propose a mixed-integer linear program (MILP)-based algorithm to determine the allocation of deceptive and protective resources in the graph. In [6], they harden the network by using honeypots so that the attacker can not discriminate between a true target and a fake target.

Compared to existing work, our work makes the following contributions:

- First, we consider the optimal allocation given a "worst-case" attacker who knows about the cyber network structure and the locations of intrusion detectors and plans to evade detection by intrusion detectors. In addition, we allocate stealthy sensors, which are unobservable to the attacker, to decrease the attack success rate further.

- Second, we do not assume any graph structure in the attack graph and consider probabilistic attack graphs instead of deterministic ones. As the attacker can take a randomized strategy in the probabilistic attack graph, it is impossible to construct a payoff matrix and apply the minimax theorem for defense strategy design.
- Third, we consider allocating decoy resources, which can be regarded as fake targets to the attacker. These decoys attract the attackers, so that protect the true target from being compromised.

The following of this chapter is organized as follows: First, we introduce the preliminaries and the basic problem settings of the proactive defense strategy design in probabilistic attack graphs. In Sect. 3, we look into how the defender allocates observable sensors to defend the system. Section 4 discusses how to use deceptive methods to defend the system. Our method includes using stealthy sensors to detect the attacker, and manipulating the attacker's perceived payoff using decoys to distract the attacker. Section 5 shows our numerical experiments to validate our methods. Section 6 concludes this chapter.

2 Preliminaries

Notation Let $\mathbf{R}$ denote the set of real numbers and $\mathbf{R}^n$ the set of real n-vectors. Let $\mathbf{R}^n_{>0}$ (resp. $\mathbf{R}^n_{<0}$) be the set of positive (resp. negative) real n-vectors. We use $\mathbf{1}$ to represent the vector of all ones. Given a vector $z \in \mathbf{R}^n$, let z_i be the i-th component. Given a finite set Z, the set of probability distributions over Z is represented as $\mathsf{Dist}(Z)$. Given $d \in \mathsf{Dist}(Z)$, the support of d is denoted as $\text{Supp}(d) = \{z \in Z \mid d(z) > 0\}$. Let I_B be the indicator function, i.e., $I_B(x) = 1$ if $x \in B$, and $I_B(x) = 0$ otherwise.

We consider the adversarial interaction between a defender (player 1, pronoun she/her) and an attacker (player 2, pronoun he/him/his) in a system equipped with proactive defense (formally defined later). We first introduce a formal model, called the probabilistic attack graph, to capture how the attacker plans to achieve the attack objective. Then, we introduce proactive defense countermeasures with IDS allocation and deception countermeasures.

Definition 1 (Attacker's Planning Problem) Given a system configuration, the corresponding attack graph is represented as a probabilistic transition system

$$M = (S, A, P, \nu, \gamma, F, R_2),$$

where S is a set of states (nodes in the attack graph), A is a set of attack actions, $P : S \times A \to \mathsf{Dist}(S)$ is a probabilistic transition function such that $P(s'|s, a)$ is the probability of reaching state s' given action a being taken at state s, $\nu \in \mathsf{Dist}(S)$ is the initial state distribution, $\gamma \in (0, 1]$ is a discount factor. The attacker's objective is described by a set F of *target states* and a *target reward* function $R_2 : F \times A \to$

$\mathbf{R}_{\geq 0}$, which assigns each state-action pair (s, a) where $s \in F$ and $a \in A$ to a nonnegative value of reaching that target for the attacker.

The probabilistic attack graph characterizes goal-directed attacks encountered in cyber security [13, 19], in which by reaching a target state, the attacker compromises certain critical network hosts. Probabilistic transition dynamics capture the uncertain outcomes of the attack actions and generalize deterministic attack graphs [12].

The attacker is to maximize his discounted total reward, starting from the initial state $S_0 \sim \nu$. A randomized, finite-memory attack policy is a function $\pi : S^* \to \mathsf{Dist}(A)$, which maps a finite run $\rho \in S^*$ into a distribution $\pi(\rho)$ over actions. A policy is called Markovian if it only depends on the most recent state, i.e., $\pi : S \to \mathsf{Dist}(A)$. We only consider Markovian policies because it suffices to search within Markovian policies for an optimal attack policy.

Let $(\Omega, \mathcal{F})$ be the canonical sample space for $(S_0, A_0, (S_t, A_t)_{t>1})$ with the Borel σ-algebra $\mathcal{F} = \mathcal{B}(\Omega)$ and $\Omega = S \times A \times \prod_{t=1}^{\infty}(S \times A)$. The probability measure $\mathbf{Pr}^{\pi}$ on $(\Omega, \mathcal{F})$ induced by a Markov policy π satisfies: $\mathbf{Pr}^{\pi}(S_0 = s) = \mu_0(s)$, $\mathbf{Pr}^{\pi}(A_0 = a \mid S_0 = s) = \pi(s, a)$, and $\mathbf{Pr}^{\pi}(S_t = s \mid (S_k, A_k)_{k<t}) = P(s \mid S_k, A_k)$, and $\mathbf{Pr}^{\pi}(A_t = a \mid (S_k, A_k)_{k<t}, S_t) = \pi(S_t, a)$.

Given a Markovian policy $\pi : S \to \mathsf{Dist}(A)$, we define the attacker's value function $V_2^{\pi} : S \to \mathbf{R}$ as $V_2^{\pi}(s) = \mathbf{E}_{\pi}[\sum_{k=0}^{\infty} \gamma^k R_2(S_k, A_k) | S_0 = s]$, where $\mathbf{E}_{\pi}$ is the expectation given the probability measure $\mathbf{Pr}^{\pi}$.

The defender's objective is defined by a reward function $R_1 : S \times A \to \mathbf{R}_{\geq 0}$ and the he defender's value function given the attacker's policy is $V_1^{\pi} : S \to \mathbf{R}$, defined as $V_1^{\pi}(s) = \mathbf{E}_{\pi}[\sum_{k=0}^{\infty} \gamma^k R_1(S_k, A_k) | S_0 = s]$.

3 Optimal Allocation of Intrusion Detection Systems

In this section, we first define the attacker's perceptual planning problem for a fixed allocation strategy of intrusion detection systems (IDSs). Then we show the design of optimal IDS allocation can be formulated as a bi-level optimization. We investigate the special property of the formulated bi-level optimization problem to develop an optimization-based approach for synthesizing the IDS allocation strategy.

Definition 2 (IDS Allocation) The defender's IDS allocation design is a Boolean-valued vector $\mathbf{x}$, where $\mathbf{x} \in \{0, 1\}^{|S \times A|}$ such that $\mathbf{x}_{s,a} = 1$ if and only if the intrusion detector is placed on state-action pair (s, a).

We introduce false negative rates for intrusion detectors.

Assumption 1 *Given a state-action pair (s, a), if the attack action a is monitored at state s, then with probability $1 - \epsilon(s, a)$, the attack action will be detected. The value $\epsilon(s, a) \in (0, 1)$ is the false negative rate of the detector.*

The defender's IDS allocation strategy changes how the attacker perceives the attack planning problem as follows:

Definition 3 (Attacker's MDP Given IDS Allocation) Given an IDS allocation $\mathbf{x}$, and an attack graph $M = (S, A, P, \nu, \gamma, F, R_2)$. The attacker's model of the attack planning problem is captured by the following MDP:

$$M^{\mathbf{x}} = (S, A, P^{\mathbf{x}}, \nu, \gamma, F, R_2),$$

where S, A, ν, γ, F are the same as those in the attack graph M. Consider $s \in S$, for each action $a \in A$, the transition function $P^{\mathbf{x}}$ is obtained from the transition function P in the attack graph where

$$P^{\mathbf{x}}(s'|s, a) = \begin{cases} 1 - \epsilon(s, a), & \mathbf{x}(s, a) = 1,\ s' = s_{\textsf{sink}}, \\ \epsilon(s, a)P(s'|s, a), & \mathbf{x}(s, a) = 1,\ s' \neq s_{\textsf{sink}}, \\ P(s'|s, a), & \mathbf{x}(s, a) = 0. \end{cases}$$

Given the attacker's MDP, we consider the attacker's objective is to maximize the probability of reaching the set F, which is a stochastic shortest path problem[20]. The optimal attacker's strategy π^* can be computed by solving the stochastic shortest path problem with the following reward function:

$$R_2(s, a) = \begin{cases} 1 & \text{if } s \in F, a \in A \\ 0 & \text{otherwise.} \end{cases}$$

This reward function means that a reward of 1 is received only if the agent reaches a state in F. In this stochastic shortest path problem, the MDP terminates at an absorbing state. The sink state s_{sink} and F are absorbing.

We first review linear program (LP) formulation[5] for solving the optimal attack policy. Later, we will show how this LP formulation facilitates the solution of IDS allocation problems.

Given a MDP $M = (S, A, \mathcal{P}, \nu, \gamma = 1, F, R)$, the optimal value vector be defined as $\mathbf{v}^* = [v_s^*]_{s \in S}$, where v_s^* is the probability of reaching F from s under the optimal attack policy. We introduce a decision vector $\mathbf{v} = [v_s]_{s \in S}$, where v_s is an upper bound on v_s^* for each $s \in S$. Consider the following LP:

$$\min_{\mathbf{v}} \quad \sum_{s \in S} c_s v_s \tag{1}$$

$$\text{s.t.} \quad v_s \geq \sum_{s' \in S} \mathcal{P}(s' \mid s, a) v_{s'}, \quad \forall a \in A,\ \forall s \in S, \tag{2}$$

$$v_s = 0, \quad \forall s \in \{s_{sink}\}, \tag{3}$$

$$v_s = 1, \quad \forall s \in F, \tag{4}$$

$$v_s \geq 0, \quad \forall s \in S, \tag{5}$$

where $\mathbf{c} = [c_s]_{s \in S}$ is a positive vector, termed as state-relevance weights. The state-relevance weights can be selected to be the initial distribution over the states s. It is shown in [5] that any vector $\mathbf{v}$ that satisfies (2) is an upper bound on the optimal value vector $\mathbf{v}^*$. The objective function is equivalent to minimizing a weighted norm of the difference between the upper bound $\mathbf{v}$ and $\mathbf{v}^*$, given the weight vector $\mathbf{c} = [c_s]_{s \in S}$. The solution $\mathbf{v}$ is shown to be equal to the optimal value vector $\mathbf{v}^*$[5]. Using $\mathbf{v}^*$ we can recover the optimal attack policy π^* using the Bellman equation.

The IDS allocation is now formulated as a Stackelberg game, in which the defender designs the allocation, in anticipation of the attacker's best response, in the attacker's MDP with incomplete information.

Problem 1 Assuming zero-sum interaction, that is, $R_1(s, a) = -R_2(s, a)$ for any $s \in S, a \in A$. Let X be the domains of IDS allocation variables $\mathbf{x}$. The IDS allocation design is a bi-level optimization problem:

$$\begin{aligned} \min_{\mathbf{x} \in X}. \quad & V_2^{\pi^*}(\nu; \mathbf{x}) \\ \text{s.t.} \quad & \pi^* \in \operatorname*{argmax}_{\pi} V_2^{\pi}(\nu; \mathbf{x}). \end{aligned}$$

We show that due to the special properties of the IDS allocation problem, an approximately optimal solution can be found by reducing it to a single-level MILP problem. For clarity, we use $x_{s,a}$ to represent $\mathbf{x}_{s,a}$. The MILP for optimal IDS allocation is formulated as follows:

$$\min_{\mathbf{x} \in \mathcal{X}, \mathbf{v}}. \quad \sum_{s \in S} c_s v_s \tag{6}$$

$$\text{s.t.} \quad v_s \geq \sum_{(s' \in S} \big(P^{\mathbf{x}}(s' \mid s, a) v_{s'} (1 - x_{s,a}) + P^{\mathbf{x}}(s' \mid s, a) v_s \cdot x_{s,a} \cdot \epsilon(s, a)\big), \tag{7}$$

$$\forall a \in A, \forall s \in S \setminus (F \cup \{s_{sink}\}),$$

$$\sum_{(s,a) \in S \times A} x_{s,a} \leq k, \tag{8}$$

$$(3), (4), \text{ and } (5),$$

When $x_{s,a} = 1$, the right-hand side of constraint (7) is the value given two cases of the next state: The first case is when the attack action is taken but not detected by the intrusion detector. In this case of detection failure, the attack reaches the next state s' from the current state s by taking action a with a probability obtained by the original probability $\mathcal{P}(s' \mid s, a)$ multiplied with the false negative rate $\epsilon(s, a)$. The second case is when the attack action is taken and detected, the attacker will reach the sink state and the attack terminates at a state with value 0. If $x_{s,a} = 0$, then no intrusion detector is allocated to monitor the state-action pair (s, a), then the value is given by $P^{\mathbf{x}}(s' \mid s, a) v_{s'}$.

The constraint (7) in the optimization problem is nonlinear due to the product between the variable v_s and the integer variable $x_{s,a}$. However, we can introduce new variables to rewrite the problem as an MILP. Note that the constraint (7) is equivalent to

$$v_s \geq \sum_{s' \in S} P^{\mathbf{x}}(s' \mid s, a) w_{s,a,s'}, \quad \forall s \in S, \ \forall a \in A, \tag{9}$$

where for s',

$$w_{s,a,s'} = \begin{cases} v_{s'} \cdot \epsilon(s, a) & \text{if } x_{s,a} = 1, \\ v_{s'} & \text{if } x_{s,a} = 0. \end{cases} \tag{10}$$

Using the big-M method[8], we can rewrite (10) as the following linear constraints:

$$w_{s,a,s'} - v_{s'} \cdot \epsilon(s, a) \leq M \cdot (1 - x_{s,a}), \tag{11a}$$

$$w_{s,a,s'} - v_{s'} \cdot \epsilon(s, a) \geq m \cdot (1 - x_{s,a}), \tag{11b}$$

$$w_{s,a,s'} - v_{s'} \leq M \cdot x_{s,a}, \tag{11c}$$

$$w_{s,a,s'} - v_{s'} \geq m \cdot x_{s,a}, \tag{11d}$$

where M and m are constants to be defined shortly. When $x_{s,a} = 1$, the constraints (11a) and (11b) together recover $w_{s,a,s'} = v_{s'} \cdot \epsilon(s, a)$, whereas the constraints (11c) and (11d) become non-binding as long as M and m are chosen appropriately. For this problem, it is not difficult to verify that it suffices to choose $M = 1$ and $m = -1$. A similar argument can be made for the case when $x_{s,a} = 0$. The final form of the MILP is given as follows:

$$\min_{\mathbf{x} \in \mathcal{X}, \mathbf{v}} \quad \sum_{s \in S} c_s v_s \tag{12a}$$

$$\text{s.t.} \quad (3), (4), (5), (8), (9), (11), \tag{12b}$$

$$w_{s,a,s'} \geq 0, \quad \forall s \in S, \ \forall a \in A, \ \forall s' \in S. \tag{12c}$$

4 Optimal Deception Resource Allocation

In the previous section, we studied how to design IDS allocation strategy that minimizes the attacker's probability of reaching the final state F in the attack graph M. In this section, we look into how to use the deception mechanisms to enhance the system security.

4.1 Deception with Stealthy Sensors

A *steathy* sensor refers to a detector that are unobservable by the attacker prior to the interaction. In practice, stealthy sensors in a cyber network can be realized by honey-patching[4] of a known vulnerability. When the attacker exploits a honey-patching vulnerability, he will be detected. It is noted that adding stealthy sensors does not change the attacker's perceived MDP $M^{\mathbf{x}}$. In this case, the defender's goal is minimizing the attacker's probability of entering the real targets F.

Definition 4 (Stealthy Sensor Allocation) The defender's stealthy sensor allocation design is a pair of Boolean-valued vectors $\mathbf{y}$, where $\mathbf{y} \in \{0, 1\}^{|S\times A|}$ such that $\mathbf{y}_{s,a} = 1$ if and only if the stealthy sensor is placed on state-action pair (s, a).

Assumption 2 *A stealthy sensor has a false negative rate of zero.*

This assumption is due to the nature of honey patching. It can be relaxed, however, to have false negative rates similar to the treatment of intrusion detector.

Definition 5 (The Attack Graph Given Complete Information About Joint IDS and Stealthy Sensor Allocation) Given a stealthy sensor allocation $\mathbf{y}$, and an attack's MDP $M^{\mathbf{x}} = (S, A, P^{\mathbf{x}}, \nu, \gamma, F, R_2)$ with a fixed IDS allocation $\mathbf{x}$, the defender's model of the attack planning problem is captured by the following MDP:

$$M^{\mathbf{x},\mathbf{y}} = (S, A, P^{\mathbf{x},\mathbf{y}}, \nu, \gamma, F, R_1),$$

where S, A, ν, γ, F are the same as those in the MDP without stealthy sensors $M^{\mathbf{x}}$. Consider $s, s' \in S$, for each action $a \in A$, the transition function $P^{\mathbf{x},\mathbf{y}}$ is obtained from the transition function $P^{\mathbf{x}}$ in the attacker's MDP by letting $P^{\mathbf{x},\mathbf{y}}(s' \mid s, a) = P^{\mathbf{x},\mathbf{y}}(s' \mid s, a)(1 - \mathbf{y}_{s,a})$; and $P^{\mathbf{x},\mathbf{y}}(s_{sink} \mid s, a) = \mathbf{y}_{s,a}$. R_1 is the defender's reward function.

Because the stealthy sensor allocation does not change the attacker's perception of the attack graph $M^{\mathbf{x}}$, we assume that the attacker follows the best response strategy π^* computed from $M^{\mathbf{x}}$. Under the assumption of a bounded number of stealthy sensor, we describe the formulation of another optimization problem to determine the optimal stealthy sensor allocation.

We introduce decision variables $\mathbf{v} = [v_s]_{s\in S}$, where v_s is the optimal attack success rate given both intrusion detector and stealthy sensors and new decision variables $\mathbf{q} = [q_{s,a,s'}]_{(s,a,s')\in S\times A\times S}$.

We propose another MILP for computing the optimal stealthy sensor allocation strategy:

$$\min_{q,v,y} \quad \sum_{s\in S} c_s v_s \tag{13a}$$

$$\text{s.t.} \quad v_s = \sum_{(a,s')\in A\times S} q_{s,a,s'}, \quad \forall s \in S, \tag{13b}$$

$$q_{s,a,s'} \leq M \cdot (1 - y_{s,a}), \tag{13c}$$

$$P(s' \mid s, a)\pi^*(s, a)v_{s'} - q_{s,a,s'} \geq m \cdot y_{s,a}, \tag{13d}$$

$$P(s' \mid s, a)\pi^*(s, a)v_{s'} - q_{s,a,s'} \leq M \cdot y_{s,a}, \tag{13e}$$

$$q_{s,a,s'} \geq 0, \forall a \in A, \forall s \in S, \forall s' \in S, \tag{13f}$$

$$\sum_{s,a} y_{s,a} \leq h, \tag{13g}$$

and (3), (4), (5),

where $M = 1$ and $m = -1$ are constants. For this optimization problem, we aim to minimize the weighted sum of attack success rate $\mathbf{v}$ in (13a). Note that if the weights $\mathbf{c} = [c_s]_{z\in s}$ are chosen to be the initial state distribution, the objective function in (13a) is equivalent to minimizing the attack success rate given the initial distribution.

Constraint (13b) enforces that the state value v_s is the summation over state-action-state value $q_{s,a,s'}$ for all actions $a \in A$ and next states $s' \in S$. Constraint (13c) means that if $y_{s,a} = 1$, then the state-action-state value $q_{s,a,s'} = 0$ as the attacker will be detected. If $y_{s,a} = 0$, constraints (13d) and (13e) enforce

$$P(s' \mid s, a)\pi^*(s, a)v_{s'} = q_{s,a,s'}. \tag{14}$$

Substituting $q_{s,a,s'}$ into (13b), we have policy evaluation of π^* given the intrusion detectors allocation. In the end, we consider finite number of stealthy sensors constrained by inequality (13g). Constraint (13f) means that the state-action-state values are non-negative.

By solving this optimization problem, we determine how to allocate stealthy sensors to further reduce the attack success rate, in addition to the detection probability given by the optimal IDS allocation. This defense system with deception exploits the attacker's incorrect knowledge about the sensor allocation in the system.

4.2 Deception with Fake Targets

Allocating fake targets or honeypots is a commonly used cyber deception technique, which manipulates the attacker's perception about the payoff functions. In this subsection, we present an optimization-based approach for fake target allocations in cyber deception.

Assuming that the defender knows the attacker's objective given by the tuple $\langle F, R_2 \rangle$, i.e., the target states and target reward function.

Definition 6 Suppose $D \subset S \setminus F$ is a set of states in the attack graph $M^{\mathbf{x}}$ that can be set to be *fake target states*. A fake target allocation is represented by a vector of fake target rewards $\mathbf{z} \in \mathbf{R}^{|D|}$ that $\mathbf{z}(d)$ is a value that attacker misperceives to receive if the state $d \in D$ is reached.

A state $d \in D$ with $\mathbf{z}(d) = 0$ is not selected to be a fake target state. The defender can determine how to allocate her decoy resource to prevent the attacker from reaching the real targets.

The limited budgetary constraint for allocating fake targets is defined as

$$\mathbf{1}^\mathsf{T}\mathbf{z} \leq h,$$

where $h \geq 0$ is the total budget.

Definition 7 (The Attacker's Perceptual Reward) Given a decoy allocation $\mathbf{z}$, the attacker's *perceptual reward function* is defined by

$$R_2^{\mathbf{z}}(s, a) = \begin{cases} \mathbf{z}(s) & \text{if } \mathbf{z}(s) > 0, \\ R_2(s, a) & \text{if } \mathbf{z}(s) = 0 \text{ or } s \notin D. \end{cases}$$

Assumption 3 *The attack process terminates under two cases: Either the attack succeeds, in which the attacker reaches a target $s \in F$, or the attack is interdicted, in which the attacker reaches a state allocated with a fake target.*

Not only the fake target allocation changes the perceptual reward function for the attacker, it also changes the perceptual attack graph dynamics. To this end, the perceived attack planning problem with a fake target allocation $\mathbf{z}$ is defined as follows.

Definition 8 Let the fake target allocation be $\mathbf{z}$, and the attacker's MDP given IDS allocation $M = (S, A, P^{\mathbf{x}}, \nu, \gamma, F, R_2)$, the perceptual planning problem of the attacker is defined by the following MDP with terminating states:

$$M^{\mathbf{x}}(\mathbf{z}) = (S, A, P^{\mathbf{x},\mathbf{z}}, \nu, \gamma, F \cup D^{\mathbf{z}}, R_2^{\mathbf{z}}),$$

where S, A, ν, γ are the same as those in $M^{\mathbf{x}}$, $D^{\mathbf{z}} = \{s \in D \mid \mathbf{z}(s) \neq 0\}$ are decoy target states and absorbing. The transition function $P^{\mathbf{x},\mathbf{z}}$ is obtained from the original transition function P by only making all states in $D^{\mathbf{z}}$ absorbing. The reward $R_2^{\mathbf{z}}$ is defined based on Def. 7.

The perceptual value for the attacker is

$$V_2^{\pi}(\nu; \mathbf{z}) = \mathbf{E}_{\pi}\Big[\sum_{k=0}^{\infty} \gamma^k R_2^{\mathbf{z}}(S_k, A_k) \mid S_0 \sim \nu\Big],$$

where $\mathbf{E}_{\pi}$ is the expectation given the probability measure $\mathbf{Pr}^{\pi}$ induced by π from the MDP $M(\mathbf{z})$.

The defender's deception objective is given by a reward function $R_1^{\mathbf{z}} : S \to \mathbf{R}$, defined by

$$R_1^{\mathbf{z}}(s) = \begin{cases} 1 & \text{if } s \in D^{\mathbf{z}}, \\ 0 & \text{otherwise.} \end{cases} \tag{15}$$

In other words, the defender would gain a reward of 1 if the attacker reaches a fake target.

Given the probability measure $\mathbf{Pr}^{\pi}$ induced by the attacker's policy π, the defender's value is defined by

$$V_1^{\pi}(\nu; \mathbf{z}) = \mathbf{E}_{\pi}\Big[\sum_{k=0}^{\infty} \gamma^k R_1(S_k) \mid S_0 \sim \nu\Big].$$

With this reward definition, the value $V_1^{\pi}(\nu; \mathbf{z})$ is the discounted probability of the attacker reaching a fake target in $D^{\mathbf{z}}$.

Then the problem of synthesizing an optimal proactive defense strategy $\mathbf{z}$ can be mathematically formulated as

Problem 2

$$\begin{aligned} \max_{\mathbf{z} \in Z}. \quad & V_1^{\pi^*}(\nu; \mathbf{z}) \\ \text{s.t.} \quad & \pi^* \in \operatorname*{argmax}_{\pi} V_2^{\pi}(\nu; \mathbf{z}). \end{aligned}$$

where $Z = \{\mathbf{z} \mid \forall s \in S \setminus D, \mathbf{z}(s) = 0 \text{ and } \mathbf{1}^{\mathsf{T}}\mathbf{z} \le h\}$ is the range for variables $\mathbf{z}$.

In words, the defender decides $\mathbf{z}$ so that the attacker's best response in his perceptual attack planning problem turns out to be an attack policy most preferred by the defender, as it maximizes the defender's value.

Next, we show that when the attacker's policy is proportional to the expected value of the future states' value, the lower-level problem can be formulated as a LP. Thus, the original bi-level optimization is a special case–bi-level LP. Using the

KKT condition of the lower-level problem, the bi-level LP reduces to a single-level optimization with special ordered set (SOS) constraints.

We start with formulating the lower-level LP using occupancy measures [2] as the decision variables. For a given allocation strategy $\mathbf{z}$, the optimal policy perceived by the attacker can be solved using the following LP:

$$\max_{m}. \quad \sum_{s\in S, a\in A} R_2^{\mathbf{z}}(s,a)m(s,a).$$

$$\text{s.t.} \quad \sum_{a\in A} m(s,a) = \gamma \sum_{s'\in S, a'\in A} P(s|s',a')m(s',a') + \nu(s), \forall s \in S, \tag{16}$$

$$m(s,a) \geq 0, \forall s \in S, a \in A. \tag{17}$$

where $m(s,a)$ is the (discounted) occupancy measure that represents the frequency a state s is visited and a is taken. Using the solution of the LP, the optimal attacker policy π is recovered via: $\pi(s,a) = \frac{m(s,a)}{\sum_{a'\in A} m(s,a')}$.

The original bi-level optimization reduces to

$$\max_{\mathbf{z}\in Z}. \quad \sum_{s\in S, a\in A} R_1(s,a)m(s,a)$$

$$\text{s.t.} \quad \max_{m}. \sum_{s\in S, a\in A} R_2^{\mathbf{z}}(s,a)m(s,a), \quad \text{s.t. (16), (17).}$$

By rewriting the lower-level LP using its KKT conditions, we convert the bi-level optimization problem into a single-level optimization problem with SOS1 constraints.

First, we have the lower-level problem:

$$\max_{m}. \quad \sum_{s\in S, a\in A} R_2^{\mathbf{z}}(s,a)m(s,a).$$

$$\text{s.t.} \quad \sum_{a\in A} m(s,a) = \gamma \sum_{s'\in S, a'\in A} P(s|s',a')m(s',a') + \nu(s), \forall s \in S, \tag{18}$$

$$m(s,a) \geq 0, \forall s \in S, a \in A. \tag{19}$$

To derive the KKT condition of the lower-level LP, we first rewrite

$$\sum_{a\in A} m(s,a) = \gamma \sum_{s'\in S, a'\in A} P(s|s',a')m(s',a') + \nu(s), \forall s \in S. \tag{20}$$

to the matrix form, which is equivalent to

$$\mathbf{Cm} - \gamma \mathcal{D}\mathbf{m} - \nu = 0.$$

where $C, \mathcal{D}$ corresponds to the parameters in Equation 20. And $\mathbf{m} \in \mathbf{R}_{\geq 0}^{|S \times A|}$ denotes the vector of discounted state-action visiting frequency.

Thus the Lagrangian function can be written as

$$\mathcal{L}(\mathbf{m}, \mu, \lambda) = (\mathbf{R_2} + \mathbf{z})^T \mathbf{m} + \mu^T \mathbf{m} + \lambda^T (C\mathbf{m} - \gamma \mathcal{D}\mathbf{m} - \nu). \tag{21}$$

where $\mathbf{z}$ is extension of $\mathbf{z}$ to the domain $S \times A$ by defining $\mathbf{z}(s, a) = \mathbf{z}(s)$ for $s \in D$ and $\mathbf{z}(s, a) = 0$ otherwise, and $\mathbf{R_2}$ is the vector form of reward function R_2.

The first-order necessary conditions (KKT) for the solution $\mathbf{m}$ to be optimal are listed as follows:

$$\begin{aligned} & - (\mathbf{R_2} + \mathbf{z}) + \mu + (C - \gamma \mathcal{D})^T \lambda = \mathbf{0}, \\ & C\mathbf{m} - \gamma \mathcal{D}\mathbf{m} - \nu = 0, \\ & - \mathbf{m} \leq \mathbf{0}, \\ & \mu \geq \mathbf{0}, \\ & \mu(i)\mathbf{m}(i) = 0, i = 1, 2, \dots, |S \times A|. \end{aligned} \tag{22}$$

where (22) are special ordered sets of type 1 (SOS1) constraints. We then combine these necessary conditions with the upper-level problem, the bi-level problem can be rewritten as:

$$\begin{aligned} \max_{\mathbf{z} \in Z, \mathbf{m}, \mu, \lambda}. \quad & \mathbf{R_1}^T \mathbf{m} \\ \text{s.t.} \quad & \mathbf{1}^\mathsf{T} \mathbf{z} \leq l_1, \\ & \mathbf{z} \geq 0, \\ & - (\mathbf{R_2} + \mathbf{z}) + \mu + (C - \gamma \mathcal{D})^T \lambda = \mathbf{0}, \\ & C\mathbf{m} - \gamma \mathcal{D}\mathbf{m} - \nu = 0, \\ & - \mathbf{m} \leq \mathbf{0}, \\ & \mu \geq \mathbf{0}, \\ & \mu(i)\mathbf{m}(i) = 0, i = 1, 2, \dots, |S \times A|. \end{aligned} \tag{23}$$

where $\mathbf{R_1}$ is the vector form of reward function R_1. This optimization problem is single-level and can be solved using the Gurobi Optimization toolbox.

Remark 1 In this section, we show how to allocate fake targets with a budgetary constraints in a cyber network equipped with IDSs. If stealthy sensors are to be incorporated as well, it should be allocated after the allocation of fake targets, as the attack strategy will not be affected with the stealthy sensor allocation. In other words, one can compute the attacker's best response to IDSs and fake target allocation π^*, and then design the optimal stealthy sensor allocation using the methods in 5.2.

5 Experiments

To illustrate the effectiveness of our proposed method, we consider several examples.

5.1 Optimal IDS Allocation

We first consider the IDS allocation problem, a cyber system shown in Fig. 1 inspired by [25] is used to illustrate the effectiveness of the proposed method. The system has three hosts: the workstation h_1 handles users' requests, the webserver h_2 handles web service requests, and the database server h_3 houses critical data such as personal credentials. The firewall divides hosts into hosts that internal entities can access and hosts that outside entities can access. In this example, h_1 and h_2 can be accessed by outside entities, and h_3 can only be accessed by internal entities. The attacker is initially outside the network, and the goal is to acquire root privilege on host h_3.

The network is equipped with a proactive redundancy-based MTD strategy; that is, we have replicas of operation system (OS) for network components, and the network configuration is updated dynamically. More specifically, the hosts 1 and 2 probabilistically switch between default OSs and backup OSs. This proactive MTD schedule is captured by a Markov Chain, described as follows: at the state 0 (default), the network MTD controller either switches to backup OSs with probability 0.7 or stay with the default OSs with probability 0.3; at the state 1 (backup), the network system switches back to default OSs with a probability 0.4 or stay with the backup OSs with probability 0.6.

For each network configuration, we generate its corresponding host-based attack graphs [9] based on the vulnerabilities from common vulnerability scoring system (CVSS) [1]. Given the attacker's objective is to gain root privilege in host h_3, the

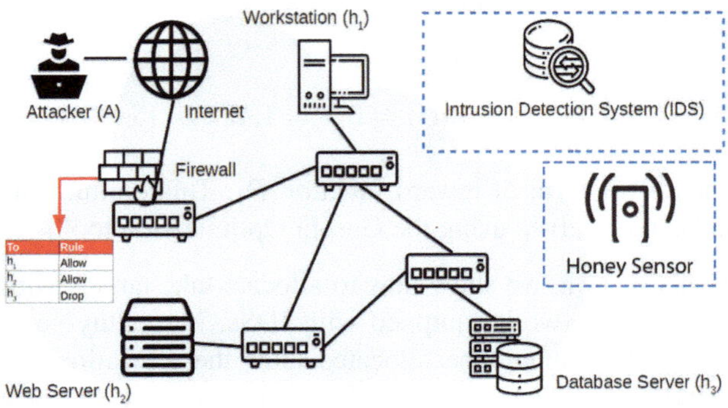

Fig. 1 Network example

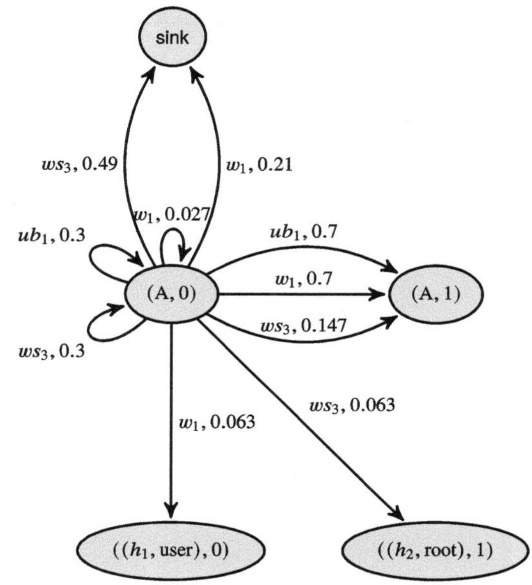

Fig. 2 A fragment of the attacker's MDP

set of goal states in the attack graphs is $\{(h_3, \text{root})\}$ for both attack graphs. The set of final states in the attacker's planning problem is $\{((h_3, \text{root}), 0), ((h_3, \text{root}), 1)\}$.

To illustrate the attack planning problem, we plot a fragment of the attacker's MDP in Fig. 2. The initial state is (A, 0), and the attacker can take action w_1 to reach state $((h_1, \text{user}), 0)$ with probability 0.063, which is calculated based on the product of three quantities: 1) the probability of staying in configuration 0 (0.3); 2) the probability of exploiting the vulnerability w_1 successfully (0.7); 3) the false negative rate $\epsilon = 0.3$ for the intrusion detector is deployed in $((h_1, \text{user}), 0, w_1)$ but missed the detection. We assume for each state except for the target $(h3, root)$, for each attack action, an intrusion detector or a stealthy sensor can be allocated to monitor that state-action pair. The transition probability function is manually assigned. In practice, these transition probabilities are based on the exploitability of vulnerabilities analyzed in CVSS [1].

We first solve the optimal intrusion detector allocation problem, with varying upper bounds on the number of deployable intrusion detectors and varying false negative rates. We assume the same false negative rates for all intrusion detectors to illustrate how the false negative rate affects the effectiveness of the defense. Note that the algorithm allows different intrusion detectors with different false negative rates. Figure 3 summarizes the results. When the false negative rate is fixed, with the more intrusion detectors the system can deploy, the attacker has less chance to achieve the target because although it observes intrusion detectors, due to the randomization he cannot always evade intrusion detectors. When the number of intrusion detectors is fixed, the success rates are monotone and non-increasing as the false negative rate decreases. When the false negative

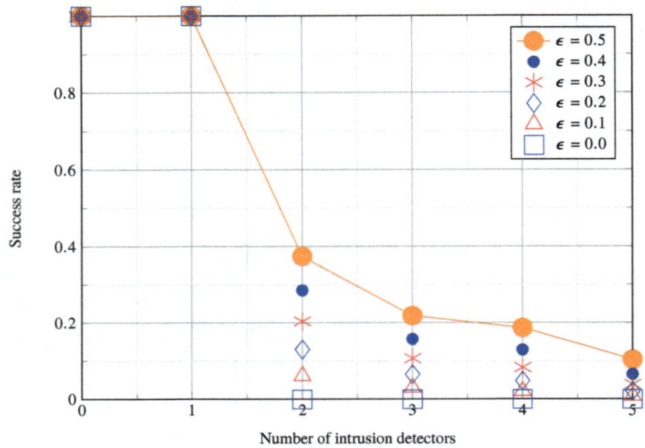

Fig. 3 The number of intrusion detectors versus the attack success rates under different false negative rates ϵ

rate $\epsilon = 0.3$ and the number of intrusion detectors is 4, intrusion detectors should be placed at $\{(\text{A}, r_1), (\text{A}, w_1), ((h_1, \text{root}), b_3), ((h_2, \text{root}), b_3)\}$ at state 0 and $\{(\text{A}, ws_3), ((h_1, \text{user}), b_3), ((h_2, \text{root}), b_1),$ $((h_2, \text{root}), b_3)\}$ at state 1.

5.2 Deception Using Honey-patching Systems

Based on the optimal IDS allocation strategy we obtained in Sect. 5.1, we synthesize the optimal stealthy sensor allocation strategy. We first extract the optimal attacker's policy. Figure 4 summarizes the attack success rates and indicates that, if we fix the number of intrusion detectors and the corresponding policy, the success rates are monotone and non-increasing as the number of stealthy sensors increases.

Furthermore, we compare two cases with a false negative rate $\epsilon = 0.3$: (a) one intrusion detector and one stealthy sensor; (b) two intrusion detectors. For case (a), the attack success rate is 0.167; for case (b), the attack success rate is 0.205. This comparison shows that, for the same number of sensors, deploying stealthy sensors is more effective (with 18.5% reduction in the attack success rate). This is because first, the stealthy sensor has zero false negative rate, and second, the attacker cannot observe these stealthy sensors and plan to evade them. We consider a case when false negative rate is 0.3, and there are 2 intrusion detectors and 1 stealthy sensor available. The solution suggests we deploy intrusion detectors at $\{(\text{A}, w_1), (\text{A}, r_1)\}$ and stealthy sensor at $\{(\text{A}, r_1)\}$ at 0; we deploy intrusion detectors at $\{(\text{A}, w_1), (\text{A}, ws_3)\}$ and stealthy sensor at $\{(\text{A}, r_1)\}$ at 1.

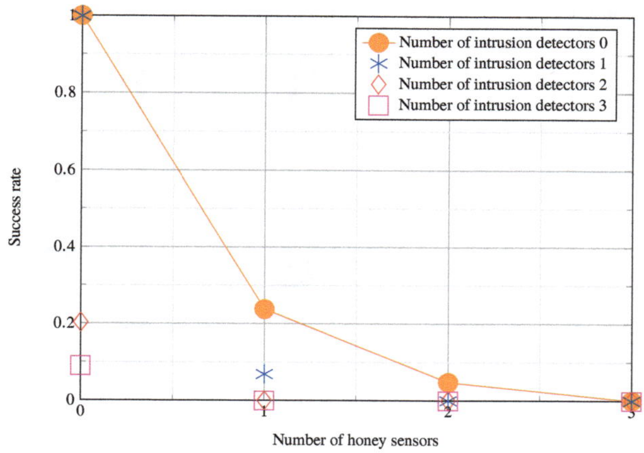

Fig. 4 The number of stealthy sensors versus the attack success rates, where the number of intrusion detectors is $k \in \{0, 1, 2, 3\}$, and false negative rate is $\epsilon = 0.3$

5.3 *Deception Through Fake Target Allocation*

Due to the limited configuration in the cyber network example, we consider different examples for illustrating fake target allocations. We illustrate the proposed methods with two sets of examples, one is a probabilistic attack graph and another is an attack planning problem formulated in a stochastic gridworld.

Figure 5 shows a probabilistic attack graph with the targets $F = \{10\}$. The attacker has four actions $\{a, b, c, d\}$. For clarity, the graph only shows the transition given action a where a thick (resp. thin) arrow represents a high (resp. low) transition probability. For example, $P(0, a) = \{1 : 0.7, 2 : 0.1, 3 : 0.1, 4 : 0.1\}$. The defender can allocate decoy resources at a set $D = \{11, 12\}$ of decoy states and receive a reward of 1 if the attacker reaches the decoy instead of the true targets. If no decoy

Fig. 5 A probabilistic attack graph

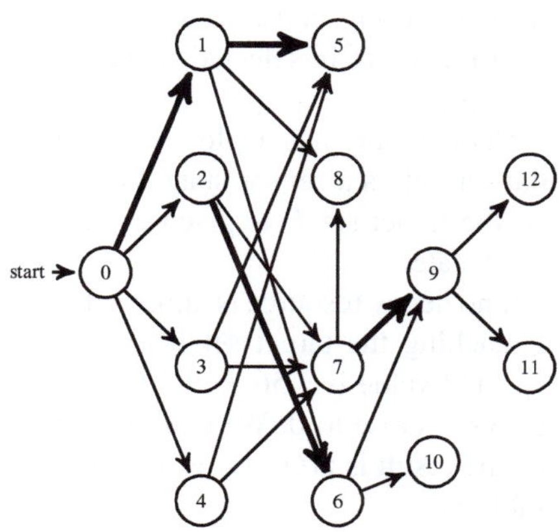

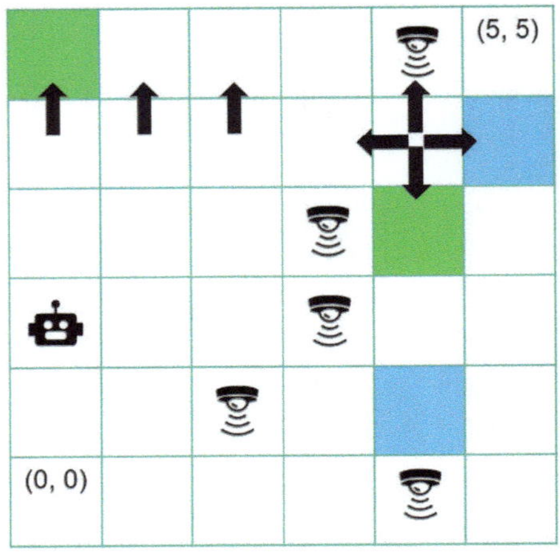

Fig. 6 A 6 × 6 gridworld

resource is allocated, the attacker receives a reward $R_2(s, a) = 1$ for any $s \in F$ and the optimal attack policy has probability 60.33% of reaching the target set F from the initial state 0. In the meantime, the defender's expected value is 0.149. That is, with probability 14.9%, the attacker will reach decoy set D and the attack is terminated.

Consider a defender who has a limited decoy resource constrained by $\mathbf{1}^{\mathsf{T}}\mathbf{z} \leq 3$ and cannot modify the state-action reward. We consider the decoy resource allocation against the attacker, from the bi-level LP solution, the decoy resource allocation is $\mathbf{z}(11) = 1.218$, $\mathbf{z}(12) = 0$. The defender's value is 0.654 given the best response of the attacker in $M^{\mathbf{x}}(\mathbf{z})$.

Next, we consider a robot motion planning problem in attack graphs modeled by stochastic gridworlds. The purpose of choosing such an environment is to make the results more interpretable. Consider first a small 6 by 6 gridworld in Fig. 6. The attacker/robot aims to reach a set of goal states while avoiding detection from the defender. The attacker can move in four compass directions. Given an action, say, "N", the attacker enters the intended cell with $1 - 2\alpha$ probability and enters the neighboring cells, which are west and east cells with α probability. In our experiments, α is selected to be 0.1. A state (i, j) means the cell at row i and column j.

The defender has deployed sensors shown in Fig. 6 to detect an attack. Once the attacker enters a sensor state, his task fails. The decoy set D is given as blue cells and the target set F is given as green cells. The robot icon represents the robot's initial state.

If no decoy resource is allocated, the attacker's policy has a probability of 98.98% of reaching the target set from the initial state. In the meantime, the defender's expected value is 3.56×10^{-6}, which means the attacker's probability of reaching decoys is close to 0. We employ the bi-level LP to solve decoy allocation strategy and the result is $\mathbf{z}((1, 4)) = 1.946$, $\mathbf{z}((4, 5)) = 1.774$, the defender's value is 0.394 (Table 1).

Table 1 Experiment result in 6×6 gridworld given $D = \{(1, 4), (4, 5)\}$

z((1, 4))	z((4, 5))	Attacker's value	Defender's value
0	0	0.99	3.56×10^{-6}
1.946	1.774	0.099	0.394

Table 2 Experiment result in 6×6 gridworld given $D = \{(0, 2), (5, 3)\}$

z((0, 2))	z((5, 3))	Attacker's value	Defender's value
0	0	0.99	7.61×10^{-8}
1.279	1.251	0.003	0.749

In order to test how the decoy set D influences the result. We re-allocate the position of decoys to $\{(0, 2), (5, 3)\}$. If we do not allocate decoy resources, the attacker reaches the target set with 98.97% probability, and the defender's value is 7.61×10^{-8} at the initial state. If the defender can allocate resources to the decoys, the method yields $\mathbf{z}((0, 2)) = 1.279$ and $\mathbf{z}((5, 3)) = 1.251$. The attacker's probability of reaching the target set is 0.3% and the defender's expected value is 0.749. Clearly, the choice of decoy states D influences the attacker's probability of reaching the target set and the defender's expected value: the second set $D' = \{(0, 2), (5, 3)\}$ appears to outperform the first set $D = \{(1, 4), (4, 5)\}$. The defender's value is 0.749 given decoy set D', compared to 0.394 given decoy set D (Tables 1 and 2).

6 Conclusion

We developed a formal method-based modeling and synthesis algorithms for optimally allocating detection and deception resources that minimize the attack success rate or the attacker's payoff. We specifically considered two types of sensors: intrusion detectors that are observable to the attacker and stealthy sensors that are not observable to the attacker. Further, we investigate the bi-level optimization problem where the defender can modify the perceptual reward function of the attacker using fake targets and developed an optimization algorithm for optimal fake target allocation. The deception methods developed herein consider one-time interaction, as the attacker will learn the locations of honeypots after the interaction. Future direction can look into how deception can be effective for long-term interactions and how to achieve robust deception in the presence of uncertainty in the attacker's goal or capability.

References

1. CVSS v3.1 Specification Document. https://www.first.org/cvss/specification-document
2. Altman, E.: Constrained Markov decision processes. Routledge (2021)
3. Anwar, A.H., Kamhoua, C., Leslie, N.: Honeypot allocation over attack graphs in cyber deception games. In: 2020 International Conference on Computing, Networking and Communications (ICNC). pp. 502–506 (2020)

4. Araujo, F., Hamlen, K.W., Biedermann, S., Katzenbeisser, S.: From patches to honey-patches: Lightweight attacker misdirection, deception, and disinformation. In: Proceedings of the 2014 ACM SIGSAC conference on computer and communications security. pp. 942–953 (2014)
5. De Farias, D.P., Van Roy, B.: The linear programming approach to approximate dynamic programming. Operations research **51**(6), 850–865 (2003)
6. Durkota, K., Lisý, V., Bošanský, B., Kiekintveld, C.: Optimal network security hardening using attack graph games. In: Twenty-Fourth International Joint Conference on Artificial Intelligence (2015)
7. Frigault, M., Wang, L.: Measuring Network Security Using Bayesian Network-Based Attack Graphs. In: 2008 32nd Annual IEEE International Computer Software and Applications Conference. pp. 698–703 (Jul 2008)
8. Griva, I., Nash, S.G., Sofer, A.: Linear and nonlinear optimization, vol. 108. Siam (2009)
9. Hewett, R., Kijsanayothin, P.: Host-centric model checking for network vulnerability analysis. In: 2008 Annual Computer Security Applications Conference (ACSAC). pp. 225–234. IEEE (2008)
10. Hong, J., Kim, D.S.: HARMs: Hierarchical Attack Representation Models for Network Security Analysis. In: Australian Information Security Management Conference. p. 9. SRI Security Research Institute, Edith Cowan University, Perth, Western Australia (Dec 2012)
11. Hong, J.B., Kim, D.S.: Assessing the Effectiveness of Moving Target Defenses Using Security Models. IEEE Transactions on Dependable and Secure Computing **13**(2), 163–177 (Mar 2016)
12. Jha, S., Sheyner, O., Wing, J.: Two formal analyses of attack graphs. In: Proceedings 15th IEEE Computer Security Foundations Workshop. CSFW-15. pp. 49–63 (Jun 2002)
13. Lallie, H.S., Debattista, K., Bal, J.: A review of attack graph and attack tree visual syntax in cyber security. Computer Science Review **35**, 100219 (Feb 2020)
14. Letchford, J., Vorobeychik, Y.: Optimal interdiction of attack plans. In: Proceedings of the 2013 international conference on Autonomous agents and multi-agent systems. pp. 199–206 (2013)
15. Miehling, E., Rasouli, M., Teneketzis, D.: Optimal Defense Policies for Partially Observable Spreading Processes on Bayesian Attack Graphs. In: Proceedings of the Second ACM Workshop on Moving Target Defense - MTD '15. pp. 67–76. ACM Press, Denver, Colorado, USA (2015)
16. Milani, S., Shen, W., Chan, K.S., Venkatesan, S., Leslie, N.O., Kamhoua, C., Fang, F.: Harnessing the Power of Deception in Attack Graph-Based Security Games. In: Zhu, Q., Baras, J.S., Poovendran, R., Chen, J. (eds.) Decision and Game Theory for Security. pp. 147–167. Lecture Notes in Computer Science, Springer International Publishing, Cham (2020)
17. Nguyen, T.H., Wright, M., Wellman, M.P., Singh, S.: Multistage Attack Graph Security Games: Heuristic Strategies, with Empirical Game-Theoretic Analysis. Security and Communication Networks **2018**, 1–28 (Dec 2018)
18. Noel, S., Jajodia, S.: Optimal ids sensor placement and alert prioritization using attack graphs. Journal of Network and Systems Management **16**(3), 259–275 (2008)
19. Noel, S., Jajodia, S., Wang, L., Singhal, A.: Measuring security risk of networks using attack graphs. International Journal of Next-Generation Computing **1**(1), 135–147 (2010)
20. Puterman, M.L.: Markov decision processes: discrete stochastic dynamic programming. John Wiley & Sons (2014)
21. Sengupta, S., Chowdhary, A., Huang, D., Kambhampati, S.: Moving Target Defense for the Placement of Intrusion Detection Systems in the Cloud. In: Bushnell, L., Poovendran, R., Başar, T. (eds.) Decision and Game Theory for Security, vol. 11199, pp. 326–345. Springer International Publishing, Cham (2018)
22. Sheyner, O., Haines, J., Jha, S., Lippmann, R., Wing, J.M.: Automated generation and analysis of attack graphs. In: Proceedings 2002 IEEE Symposium on Security and Privacy. pp. 273–284. IEEE (2002)
23. SINHA, A., FANG, F., AN, B., KIEKINTVELD, C., TAMBE, M.: Stackelberg security games: Looking beyond a decade of success. Proceedings of the Twenty-Seventh International Joint Conference on Artificial Intelligence (IJCAI-18),Stockholm, Sweden, July 13-19 pp. 5494–5501 (Jul 2018)

24. Thakoor, O., Tambe, M., Vayanos, P., Xu, H., Kiekintveld, C., Fang, F.: Cyber Camouflage Games for Strategic Deception. In: Alpcan, T., Vorobeychik, Y., Baras, J.S., Dán, G. (eds.) Decision and Game Theory for Security. pp. 525–541. Lecture Notes in Computer Science, Springer International Publishing, Cham (2019)
25. Yoon, S., Cho, J.H., Kim, D.S., Moore, T.J., Free-Nelson, F., Lim, H.: Attack Graph-based Moving Target Defense in Software-Defined Networks. IEEE Transactions on Network and Service Management pp. 1–1 (2020). https://doi.org/10.1109/TNSM.2020.2987085, conference Name: IEEE Transactions on Network and Service Management

Symbiotic Game and Foundation Models for Cyber Deception Operations in Strategic Cyber Warfare

Tao Li and Quanyan Zhu

1 Introduction

Addressing network security challenges is increasingly daunting due to the rise of highly sophisticated attackers, often backed by significant funding and resources from nation-states. These adversaries possess ample resources, including advanced capabilities, dedicated personnel, and deep knowledge, enabling them to pursue their objectives with precision. Traditional defense mechanisms, such as encryption and firewalls, are no longer sufficient in this evolving landscape. In fact, contemporary network security issues have evolved into a form of cyber warfare, wherein adversaries leverage digital technologies to target assets for strategic, political, or military gains. The cyber warfare can be integrated into physical domains. Adversaries can exploit vulnerabilities in both cyber and physical infrastructure in a coordinated fashion to gain a strategic advantage over their opponents.

Through offensive operations, employing tactics like the cyber kill chain, adversaries deploy multiple attack vectors to undermine critical systems in a stealthy and persistent manner. In response, defenders are tasked with safeguarding their assets against cyber threats and attacks. The essence of cyber defense lies in outmaneuvering the attacker through innovative strategies and technologies to thwart malicious activities and preserve the integrity of network infrastructure. To this end, recent trends have focused on automated, proactive, and adaptive defenses that are able to reduce cognitive demands, improve operational tempo and mission speeds, gain information advantage, and achieve decision dominance.

T. Li (✉)
Department of Systems Engineering, City University of Hong Kong, Hong Kong SAR, China
e-mail: li.tao@cityu.edu.hk

Q. Zhu
Department of Electrical and Computer Engineering, New York University, New York, NY, USA
e-mail: qz494@nyu.edu

Q. Zhu et al. (eds.), *Foundations of Cyber Deception*, Advances in Information Security 90, https://doi.org/10.1007/978-3-031-93867-2_2

Cyber deception emerges as one promising class of defenses, involving the creation of traps, decoys, or false information to mislead attackers and divert their attention from valuable assets or genuine security measures [1, 2]. The deployment of cyber deception techniques enables network systems to detect, delay, or disrupt attackers' activities while gathering intelligence about their tactics, techniques, and procedures (TTPs). An automated and adaptive cyber deception strategy can proactively predict and respond to attackers' behaviors by creating further deception to deter the attack or engage attackers to gather information. By minimizing the involvement of human operators in the cyber response workflow and intelligently aligning tactical responses with mission objectives, this approach facilitates faster and more mission-aligned decision-making, enhancing cyber resilience for the mission.

1.1 Role of Game-Theoretic Models

The interaction between defenders and attackers in cyber deception and the cyber warfare in general is often conceptualized as a strategic game, wherein both parties endeavor to outmaneuver the other to achieve their respective goals. In recent literature, many game models (GMs) serve a descriptive framework, wherein a specific attack model, including strategies, objectives, and information structures, is assumed alongside a defender model [3]. Subsequently, the analysis of the game aims to find the equilibria of the game, which include equilibrium payoffs, strategies, and, in dynamic games, equilibrium dynamics or trajectories.

The overarching aim of this analytical endeavor is twofold. Firstly, it seeks to forecast the long-term outcomes of cyber warfare by evaluating the defender's optimal response to repeated attacks orchestrated by adversaries. Secondly, it endeavors to use equilibrium policies as robust defense mechanisms. These strategies are suitable to serve as default approaches in situations where no real-time information about the attackers is accessible, and hence, there is a need for assumptions about worst-case scenarios to ensure performance-guaranteed strategies. However, in scenarios where information is available, albeit incomplete, through intelligence gathering and online observation, a dynamic adaptation of strategies can be implemented to complement these default policies, thereby enhancing the resilience of defensive measures.

This methodological framework finds applications across diverse domains, including jamming games [4–7], authentication games [8–12], routing games [13–15], intrusion detection [16–19], infrastructure protection games [20–24], and insider threat [25–29]. These endeavors yield valuable insights and establish a fundamental understanding of adversarial interactions at a higher level. Typically, the equilibrium analysis of these models plays a crucial role in informing strategic-level decisions, such as risk assessment, investment decisions, and resource planning within organizations and security contexts. Several factors contribute to the significance of equilibrium. Firstly, the credibility of equilibrium forecasts increases

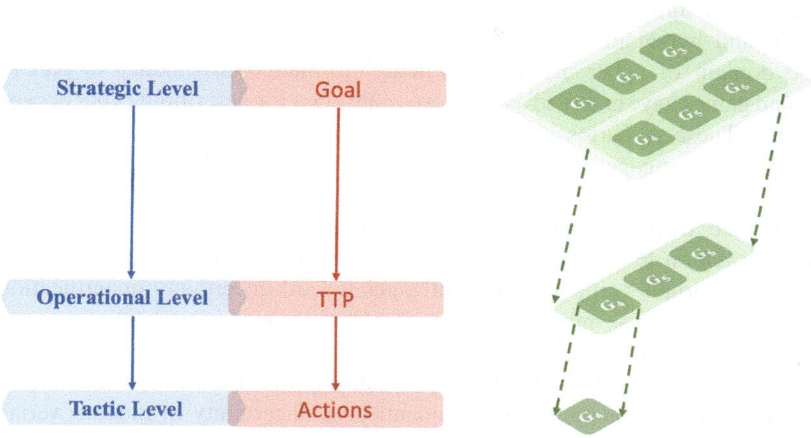

Fig. 1 Multi-level game-theoretic frameworks: strategic level, operational level, and tactical level games. Strategic level games are games that describe high-level decision-making, such as resource allocations and investment planning. The goal of strategic level games is to create long-term planning to achieve overarching objectives of the cyber warefare. Tactical-level games involve specific actions and maneuvers that can be implemented to achieve immediate objectives to support the overarching strategy. Examples of tactics in cyber warfare include the configuration of honeypots and the attacker engagement policies. The operational-level games sit between the strategic and tactical levels, focusing on the planning and coordination of a sequence of defense actions. Examples include the planning of a series of cyber defense strategies starting from intelligence gathering to counter lateral movement to achieve strategic level goals

as games are played repeatedly over an extended period. With time, players tend to figure out the structure and the rule of the game, adopt rational strategies, and make more informed decision-making. Secondly, strategic-level decisions do not mandate a high-level precision of the details of implementation and operations and thus can rely on the equilibrium prediction. A rough estimate of the equilibrium outcomes within the correct magnitude suffices for effective high-level decision-making processes. One area for which game-theoretic frameworks have offered valuable tools is the strategic risk analysis against a variety of adversarial models, each representing contingent goal-driven adversaries [30–32]. This application is particularly vital within cybersecurity contexts, where predicting adversarial behaviors proves challenging, unlike natural events governed by probabilistic distributions. Adversarial TTPs drive these behaviors. Leveraging game theory provides a distinctive framework for cyber risk analysis, with implications spanning domains like cyber insurance [33–36], cyber-physical system integration [37–39], and security investment [40–43].

However, the lack of precision makes it less applicable to tactical scenarios where details of how to act are imperative in the face of an attack (Fig. 1). Obtaining exact models of the game proves challenging, particularly regarding the strategies of attackers and their knowledge. Sometimes, it is also challenging for the defender itself to figure out the knowledge and available strategies. To address this challenge, literature often turns to more intricate modeling approaches, such as Bayesian games [44, 45] and hypergames [46, 47], to accommodate uncertainties. In particular, in the domain of cyber deception, where information asymmetry is prevalent, Bayesian games have emerged as an appropriate class for describing cyber deception scenarios. These scenarios involve various tactics such as honeypot configuration [48–50], attack engagement [37, 51, 52], and information design [53–55], among others.

While the Bayesian approach provides new insights into games of incomplete information by formally modeling imperfect observations and uncertainties about game variables, it shifts the challenges toward uncertainty quantification of underlying unknowns, introducing new complexities to the modeling process. As uncertainties multiply, especially when dealing with numerous uncertain parameters or structures, the model's complexity escalates. For instance, when uncertain parameters are continuous variables, quantifying uncertainty in random variables becomes a formidable task.

Uncertainty quantification often requires a substantial amount of data or repeated interactions between attackers and defenders within the same environment to establish reliable distributions. However, obtaining such data poses challenges, as the game is not time-invariant, and the rounds of interactions between attackers and defenders are limited, which further constrains the observables obtained from these interactions.

Moreover, while this approach is reasonable for handling structured uncertainties (i.e., known unknowns), it encounters difficulties with unstructured uncertainties (e.g., epistemic uncertainties). Furthermore, even with a well-defined model, computing equilibrium concepts like Bayesian equilibrium proves challenging [56] and often lacks predictive power, especially in dynamic tactical environments characterized by nonstationary behaviors and conditions.

It is imperative to go beyond the current approach. Recently, nonstationary reinforcement learning and nonequilibrium solutions have emerged as prominent ways to tackle this challenge. Nonstationary reinforcement learning aims to tackle the nonstationary nature inherent in learning environments. In security games, an agent's game can undergo changes due to the dynamics of the knowledge and behaviors of other players. Additionally, the joint actions taken by the players of the game can lead to shifts in the game environment. It is one type of internalized nonstationarity, which is caused by the players themselves. Externalized nonstationarity refers to changes caused by exogenous factors; for instance, in cyber warfare, the disclosure of vulnerabilities to the public can alter the game dynamics between defenders and attackers due to the change in the information structure.

Learning in a nonstationary environment poses challenges as strategies adapted to earlier games must be re-evaluated for new environments [3]. Unlike in stationary environments, where learning strategies often converge to relevant equilibrium concepts [57], nonstationary games cannot be characterized by equilibrium, and there is a need for a reevaluation of reinforcement learning goals. Learning strategies do not need to aim to converge to an equilibrium outcome [58]; rather, an equilibrium outcome can be viewed as a result of learning behaviors [59]. This perspective can lead to the nonequilibrium solutions that redefine outcomes for nonstationary games [60]. Nonequilibrium solutions are relevant even in stationary games where interactions are limited, meaning players cannot reach equilibrium within short timeframes.

1.2 Role of Foundation Models

Such approaches offer promising avenues to navigate the complexities of dynamic tactical environments where traditional equilibrium concepts may prove insufficient. The advent of foundation models (FMs) introduces a new dimension of possibility to this endeavor. These models enable the encoding of game descriptions through more sophisticated frameworks, offering enhanced precision in capturing detailed aspects of the game. For instance, FMs can encapsulate the knowledge structure of attackers, non-Markov dynamics (e.g., time series data), and diverse attacker types. This granularity holds the potential to provide tactical-level solutions, thereby facilitating improved decision-making processes.

Moreover, FMs facilitate the modeling of flexible learning and reasoning processes of varying styles. Unlike current approaches that are often pre-specified in terms of learning methods and objectives, this adaptability allows for the creation of novel solution concepts capable of describing outcomes within limited interactions, nonstationary environments, and non-Markovian behaviors. Such models are particularly suitable for generating practical, real-time tactics that can achieve decision dominance.

Furthermore, FMs enable not only descriptive modeling but also prescriptive and predictive features. Prescriptive analytics directly yield end-to-end intelligence that informs tactics, bypassing the separate process of modeling the entire game, defining and finding the associated solutions, and creating decision-dominant tactics. This end-to-end approach facilitates the translation of information directly into actionable and adaptive tactics.

Another pivotal aspect of FMs lies in their predictive analytics capability, which plays an important role in warfare scenarios. The ability to anticipate and promptly respond to emerging threats can be a decisive factor. Predictive analytics serves several critical functions in tactical reasoning. Firstly, it enables defenders to forecast the dynamic environment, including the anticipated behaviors of adversaries and the external factors influencing environmental shifts. This foresight enables proactive measures to mitigate risks. Secondly, predictive analytics integrates into the learning and adaptation of strategies, enabling the formulation of look-ahead strategies. These strategies analyze subsequent subgames and anticipate potential counter-strategies from attackers, thereby creating decision-dominant tactics in cyberwarfare. The incorporation of predictive analytics into FMs enhances their adaptability and effectiveness in navigating dynamic and adversarial environments.

1.3 Cyber Deception and Related Game-Theoretic and Foundation Models

Cyber deception is an overt operation. Defenders need to design mechanisms to outsmart attackers, leading them to fall into honeypots or unwittingly disclose information beneficial to the defender's objectives. The application of FMs to cyber deception games is an ideal synergy. FMs can contribute to this goal by improving analytical capabilities crucial for strategic reasoning. A significant challenge in cyber deception lies in the inherent uncertainties. The environment is rife with unknowns, including imprecise knowledge of attacker attributes. It remains unclear whether attackers are aware of the deception and may deploy counterdeception tactics. Additionally, the behaviors of non-attackers, such as normal users, pose another layer of uncertainty. While deceiving normal users is not the intent of cyber deception, their errors can inadvertently diminish its efficacy. FMs offer invaluable tools for addressing these challenges, facilitating hierarchical and predictive reasoning to enhance decision-making processes. For instance, models can anticipate attacker responses to deception and utilize cognitive hierarchies to optimize decisions. Predictive reasoning enables the anticipation of both attacker actions and user behaviors in subsequent steps, thereby preparing defenders to preempt attacks and mitigate user errors effectively.

The essence of cyber deception resonates strongly with game-theoretic models. Cyber deception has essential characteristics that align closely with game-theoretic attributes, including the information asymmetry between the players, multi-stage and multi-phase interactions, the presence of aleatoric and epistemic uncertainties, together with the bounded rational human behaviors. In [61], a taxonomy of cyber deception games is developed to connect each deception scenario with a fundamental class of game-theoretic models. The taxonomy leads to a library of game building blocks that can be used to synthesize multi-round multi-scale dynamic games that capture the cyber kill and defense chains for strategic, operational, and tactic level decision-making, see Figs. 1 and 2. For example, honeypot engagement has been captured by a class of stochastic games with one-sided information. Honeypot deployment problems have been captured by network design games. Intrusion evasion games have been captured by a class of principal-agent detection games. These building blocks enable a divide-and-conquer and modular approach to design cyber defense. These modular games can be fused together with FMs to create function modules that are capable of representing games in the security scenario to provide strengthened learning and computation power. This enables the development of tactical-level applications and the enhancement of cyber deception techniques.

With the aid of game theoretic frameworks, which capture the intricate dynamics of cyber deception, the informed use of FMs becomes possible. Game-theoretic frameworks facilitate the training and adaptation of FMs to suit contextual applications with symbolic representation of the attacker-defender interactions. Integrating game-theoretic models with FMs can play useful roles across different phases of the

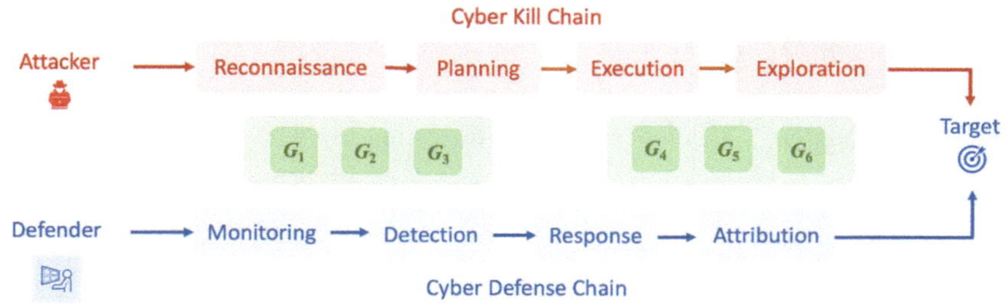

Fig. 2 An example of game modeling: An attacker aims to carry out a cyber kill chain to reach the target while a defender aims to deter and thwart this operation. The goal of the attacker is determined through strategic-level reasoning. It can be viewed as an outcome of a high-level game description. Once the goal is set, the cyber kill chain determines the tactics, techniques, and procedures (TTP) to achieve its goal, while the defender determines the defending TTPs. This operation is composed of a sequence of tactic-level games can provide specific techniques and actions. Each tactic level game corresponds to a stage in the operation. The games will yield tactics that determine the outcome at each stage and, eventually, the outcome of the operation. An adaptive operation is often used to reconfigure the operation when the operation fails at certain stages. In this case, the games will need to be redesigned and synthesized to adapt to the uncertainties in the outcomes

cyber deception process. During the initial design phase, FMs serve as invaluable tools for training and preparation. Subsequently, they enable reinforcement learning, enabling adaptability and refinement as the cyber deception strategy evolves. In the post-implementation phase, FMs support adaptive tuning, ensuring ongoing optimization and effectiveness of cyber deception techniques.

There are several ways to integrate the both. One approach is neurosymbolic learning, where hybrid AI algorithms combine symbolic reasoning with data-driven learning, resulting in robust and trustworthy systems. Symbolic reasoning using game-theoretic models offers the capacity to incorporate sophisticated abstractions grounded in system and game theories and associated formalisms. Supported by advanced tools and methods, neurosymbolic learning enables integrated analysis and assurance, leveraging formal specification and verification technologies. These capabilities can be instrumental in strengthening cyber deception mechanisms. Likewise, meta-reinforcement learning represents another avenue for integrating FMs with game theory. This approach involves developing models capable of learning from a diverse array of game-theoretic security contexts rather than being restricted to a singular context. Meta-reinforcement learning builds on the trained models to create adaptive and self-improving cyber deception systems.

Meta-reinforcement learning and neurosymbolic learning can be integrated to form an iterative process where game-theoretic domain knowledge evolves based on observations, while defense policies adapt using reinforcement learning methodologies. This process intertwines data-driven updates with domain-specific game-theoretic primitives to result in a hybrid neural and symbolic representation. This process can be empowered by FMs, and it will converge towards an optimal combined hybrid neural and symbolic representation.

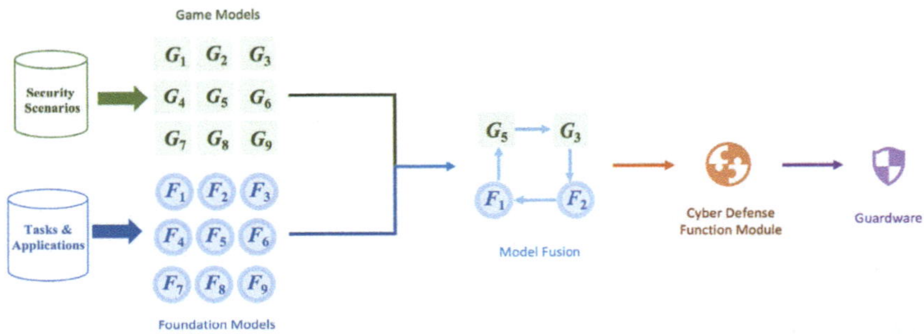

Fig. 3 Game-theoretic models and FMs are fused together to create function modules for cyber defense, which will be built into the guardware. Game-theoretic models are representations of security scenarios while FMs are tailored for different tasks and applications. The guardware is composed of multiple function modules that are enabled different games and FMs. Each function module requires a different architecture to synthesize game and FMs

Large language models (LLMs) stand out as pivotal FMs well known for their proficiency in handling textual and heterogeneous data. Their unparalleled capacity to comprehend extensive textual datasets makes them indispensable for natural language processing tasks, enabling the processing of text, time-series data, and predictive analytics. In cybersecurity, they empower the augmentation of network security through human-like language comprehension and predictive capabilities. Within the domain of cyber deception, LLMs can generate honey files such as counterfeit documents and credentials to entice potential attackers. Moreover, LLMs excel in processing heterogeneous datasets encompassing network traffic, system logs, and user behaviors to detect anomalies, infer potential attacker behaviors, and predict malicious activities. When encountering evolving threats, LLMs adeptly can automate cyber deception policies to mitigate risks by putting together multiple sources of information, including new vulnerability disclosure, defender's service requirements, and the current system state.

This chapter aims to introduce the symbiotic relationship between game-theoretic models and FMs, focusing on their implications in cybersecurity and cyber deception domains. Figure 3 illustrates this relationship. FMs serve as the building blocks for AI applications and research, providing developers and researchers with a solid platform to pioneer and innovate in artificial intelligence and machine learning. Security games stand as building blocks in cybersecurity applications, offering contextual and reasoned frameworks that encapsulate the interactions between attackers and defenders across diverse scenarios. The synergy of these models promises a transformative approach to designing **guardware** that provides autonomous and proactive security measures. In particular, the integration lays the groundwork for designing cyber deception mechanisms that were used to be regarded as cumbersome, limited, or challenging. By leveraging these foundational designs, we can forge a new paradigm of intelligent security mechanisms and win cyber warfare.

1.4 *Organization of the Chapter*

This chapter is organized as follows. Section 2 provides the background on cyber deception and network security games. It discusses the game-theoretic approach to cyber adversarial modeling and the associated analytical, design, and learning approaches. Section 3 provides a background on FMs and their roles in AI, learning, and their relevance in cybersecurity. Section 4 presents the synergy of game-theoretic models and FMs in the context of cyber deception. Section 5 concludes this chapter by presenting several challenges and future directions that need to be addressed to develop transformative security technologies.

2 Cyber Deception and Network Security Games

Security games capture the intricate interactions between attackers and defenders in various contexts. These scenarios span from cybersecurity applications, involving the interaction between intruders and network system administrators, to critical national security applications where safeguarding pivotal assets, such as airports and infrastructures, is paramount against potential terrorist threats. The formalization of security games frequently relies on game-theoretic languages, specifying essential elements like payoffs, players, and action sets.

Cyber deception stands out due to its unique tactics and objectives, which involve the strategic deployment of decoys, honeypots, and false information to manipulate attackers' perceptions of the network and influence their actions. The primary aim of deception is twofold: to deter attacks from exploiting unknown vulnerabilities within our systems and to gain valuable intelligence from attackers' behaviors. Game-theoretic models for cyber deception often revolve around information structures. For instance, asymmetric information games elucidate the information asymmetry between two players. Signaling games serve as a fundamental framework for understanding two-player deception scenarios, where one player observes the true state of the world while the other player can only observe messages or actions. They have been applied to study detection evasion [17], honeypots [62], and insider threats [26].

Stochastic games with one-sided information, e.g., in [63–65], extend this framework into dynamic settings, where one player has complete observation of the state space while the other player navigates with incomplete information, forming beliefs over the state space. Information acquisition games facilitate the trade-off between the cost of gathering information and the quality of decision-making based on such information. Recent literature has been investigating the design of observation kernels [66, 67] and optimal timing for information acquisition [68–70].

2.1 Multi-Level and Multi-Scale Game Models

Decision-making in cybersecurity is multi-scale. We define three levels of modeling, which require distinct levels of granularity. They are, namely, strategic level, operational level, and tactic level. Cybersecurity problems are growing nowadays into a cyber warfare. An attacker plans a kill chain that involves multiple stages of attacks to achieve his planned goals. At the same time, a defender aims to deter and thwart the operation of the attacker to protect the target. The strategic level involves long-term planning and decision-making aimed at achieving overarching goals and objectives. The strategies are concerned with defining the overall goals, allocating resources, and determining the target to attack or protect. The tactical level involves specific actions and maneuvers implemented to achieve immediate objectives and support the overarching strategy. The tactics include the techniques, procedures, and actions that can be taken or implemented to carry out a specific task. Examples include the tactics to engage an attacker in a honeypot and the attacker's tactics to do lateral movement to get to the target. The operational level sits between the strategic and tactical levels, focusing on the planning and coordination of multi-stage tactics to achieve the specified mission from the strategic level. The operation involves planning and replanning the multiple steps of tactics to achieve the goal of compromising a targeted machine.

As illustrated in Fig. 1, the GMs involved at the three levels are multi-scale. At the strategic level, the game is a high-level, coarse-grain description of the adversarial interactions between a defender and an attacker. For example, Blotto-type games, e.g., [71–73] have been classically used to allocate a limited amount of resources to overpower adversaries in cyber warfare by outnumbering their resources. FlipIt games and their variants have also been recently studied in [74–76] to strategically analyze the interplay between attackers and defenders, both striving to assert control over a resource for the maximum duration while minimizing overall move costs. Through strategic reasoning, defenders devise counterstrategies aimed at controlling resources at opportune moments and minimizing downtime and potential compromise. Network games are another class of strategic-level security games. Networks are used to capture the interdependencies and connectivity among the resources. The goal of the defender is to protect or defend essential network assets and minimize the impact of the attacks. For example, the framework proposed by [77] introduces a network design paradigm allowing network designers to fortify links to establish redundant communication pathways between nodes to mitigate potential attacks through resource investment. By proactively considering strategic cyber threats, the framework offers methods to characterize and compute optimal strategies for securing a network within predefined budget constraints. In addition to protective measures, resilient strategies for network recovery following attacks are also essential in network defense. A two-player, three-stage game framework proposed in [23] has aimed to capture both protection and recovery phases. The network designer's objective is to maintain network connectivity both before and after an attack, while the adversary seeks to disrupt the network by compromising specific links. This strategic game framework facilitates analysis of trade-offs not only among nodes and links within the network but also among resources allocated for pre-event protection and post-event recovery.

The game at the operational level decomposes the objective of attacking and defending a selected asset into multiple stages of operations. In accordance with the cyber kill chain, attackers typically execute reconnaissance stages before planning attacks, which involve footprinting, social engineering, and intelligence gathering. Subsequently, after planning, the attack mission is executed through the exploitation of vulnerabilities, privilege escalation, and lateral movement to reach the targeted asset. For this operational sequence, the reconnaissance stage can be modeled as a series of games that delineate the process of information gathering through passive or proactive means. The attacker's planning following reconnaissance can also be modeled through a sequence of games, encompassing multiple stages such as vulnerability exploitation, lateral movement, command and control, and exfiltration. Planning can adapt if the attack fails at any stage, necessitating reevaluation and adaptation of acquired observations and gathered information.

An example of the operation-level games is described in [78]. A multi-phase and multi-stage game is used to capture the attack vectors of advanced persistent threats. Each phase and each stage has distinct characteristics and requires a different form of defense strategy. A dynamic game framework can piece together games at each phase and each stage to capture the whole attack-and-defense operation holistically from the entry point to the target. A more sophisticated dynamic game that incorporates incomplete information and cyber deception has been presented in [37] and [51]. It depicts long-term dyadic interaction between a stealthy attacker and a proactive defender through a multi-stage game of incomplete information. Each player holds private information unknown to the other, and strategic actions are guided by beliefs formed through multi-stage observation and learning processes.

The game at the tactic level is represented by the short-term local interactions between an attacker and a defender. Each stage of the operation involves a distinct type of dyadic interactions. For example, in the social engineering game at the reconnaissance stage, the attacker can exploit the cognitive vulnerabilities of the defenders to gain initial access. The attacker often has an information advantage when it aims to deceive the defender. At the stage of lateral movement, the defender can guide the attacker to a honeypot so that the attack will be detected and revealed. This defensive deception provides the defender information advantage at the stage of the game. Hence, throughout the operation, the game can take different forms depending on the structure of information, interactions, and maneuverability. The survey in [61] explores game theory frameworks designed to model defensive deception strategies in cybersecurity and privacy domains. It introduces a taxonomy comprising six distinct types of deception: perturbation, moving target defense, obfuscation, mixing, honey-x, and attacker engagement. These classifications are characterized by their information structures, agents involved, actions taken, and duration, all of which align closely with game theory concepts. This taxonomy establishes a structured framework for comprehending the diverse strategies of defensive deception. The survey outlined in [79] offers a curated selection of studies that demonstrate the application of game theory in addressing various security and privacy challenges within computer networks and mobile applications. In each domain, we identify security problems, players, and GMs, including security of the physical and MAC layers, security of self-organizing networks, intrusion detection systems, anonymity and privacy, economics of network security, and cryptography. The games that describe the local interaction can be viewed as a building block to synthesize an operational level game, and hence informing the creation of the strategic level games.

The multi-level interdependencies among the three levels of the games are illustrated in Fig. 1. The required granularity of the GMs differs across levels. The strategic-level models are long-term and require a high-level description of potential operation consequences once resources are utilized. The outcome of the strategic-level Blotto game can be predicted by an operational-level game simulator. The tactical-level models require higher precision, as precision is crucial for determining the exact actions to be taken at the focused stage. The tactical-level games are driven by the high-level objectives specified at the strategic level. Hence, inherent interdependencies exist among the three layers of the games. The tactical ones inform the consequences of the strategic ones, while the strategic ones specify the objectives, constraints, and structures of the tactical games. The operational ones reside in the middle layer, serving as an intermediary that interconnects both ends.

It can be observed that cyber warfare games are multi-scale and multi-resolutional. Zooming in from the strategic level to the tactical level is a top-down process that specifies elements of the tactical games. Conversely, zooming out from the tactical level to the strategic level is a bottom-up process. The outcomes of individual tactical games and their compositions lead to the prediction of strategic level interactions and inform strategic level decisions. The zooming-in and zooming-out process can be adaptive. When strategic-level decisions change, the tactical level needs to adapt to the change in an agile manner. If tactics fail due to uncertainties, unexpected events, or errors, resulting in operational-level task failures, there is a need to resiliently adjust strategic-level decisions. This adjustment allows for the design of and adaptation to new missions to recover from the failure and ensure defense.

Accompanied by the ability to zoom in and out, new solution concepts beyond equilibrium are necessary to predict game outcomes across various levels and resolutions. These concepts must be compatible with uncertainties, limited observations, and the non-stationary nature of interactions. Hence, nonequilibrium solutions are essential to address these features, aiming to create a reasonable prediction even though the outcome of the game can be stochastic with limited rounds of interactions. Moreover, solutions for tactical-level games must be consistent with those at the strategic level, despite differences in scales or levels of detail. This consistency represents another dimension of consistency, in addition to conjectural and incentive consistencies (e.g., associated with the solution concepts Berk-Nash equilibrium [80], Nash equilibrium [81]), leading to a holonic solution where localized tactical games consistent with global strategic ones.

The new equilibrium concepts play a crucial role in assessing the risk of the overall mission. Mission risk is inherently multi-scale; risks at the tactical level can impact those at the strategic level. Moreover, planning decisions' risks at the strategic level can influence the selection of tactical level strategies. High-level risks can impose constraints on low-level strategies and guide their decision-making process. Conversely, low-level risks can propagate and manifest as high-level risks. Computational tools associated with solution concepts at each level must be integrated to create a cohesive tool capable of automated, coordinated, zoom-in, and zoom-out risk analysis.

Learning and adaptation are crucial aspects of the solution framework. Rather than viewing equilibrium solutions as defining the learning process, we must reconsider and understand that learning processes shape game outcomes. Learning serves as a natural descriptor of gameplay, alongside strategic and extensive form game descriptions. This description can result in equilibrium and non-equilibrium outcomes depending on the time horizon examined.

The learning description of the game facilitates the development of adaptation schemes for games at multiple levels, as adaptation can be directly and descriptively designed rather than being considered a derivative of equilibrium analysis. Just as solution concepts associated with multilevel learning need to be consistent, adaptation across levels must also exhibit consistency. Firstly, adaptation must exhibit top-down causality, where adaptation at the tactical level may be triggered by uncertainties or unexpected events at its own level and by adaptation at the strategic level. Secondly, adaptation must be coordinated and stable. Multilevel adaptation requires coordination to avoid scenarios where adaptation at one level causes more failures or leads to cyclic or unstable outcomes.

2.2 FM-Enabled GMs

The perspective described above delineates a new research direction aimed at developing programmable and mosaic game-theoretic models along with a range of versatile methods to advance the design of decision-dominant defense tactics and strategies to prevail in cyber warfare. The initial phase involves establishing a library of tactical games as foundational components. These tactic games serve as fundamental building blocks that encapsulate the typical adversarial situations encountered by defenders. They encode the defender's knowledge regarding feasible actions and potential attack responses using various representations, including strategic form games, extensive form games, and learning form games.

Strategic and extensive form games have traditionally been discussed in textbooks. For instance, a simple rock-paper-scissors game can be depicted using a matrix, which is a form of strategic representation. Meanwhile, a stochastic dynamic game with multiple stages of interactions can be represented using a tree structure that illustrates the multi-round interactions among players, their observations, and the uncertainties inherent in decision-making. The learning form game represents a novel approach, specifying how agents respond to and learn from acquired information and knowledge. It eliminates the necessity to utilize utility functions to define players' objectives or incentives. Instead, players' objectives are implicitly conveyed through dynamic learning processes wherein they adapt their strategies toward long-term goals. These goals are expressed through sequences of strategy updates, potentially leading to either equilibrium or non-equilibrium outcomes. The learning representation facilitates the translation of observed player behaviors into learning patterns, which may be nonstationary. The uncertainty quantification of behaviors using learning represents a promising avenue for bridging theory and practice. Furthermore, the GMs offer immediate adaptability, an inherent property of learning dynamics. Moreover, the way in which players learn can also adapt to contextual or environmental changes.

A tactical game is designed to be composable with others. This composability can result in a larger game, leading to a multi-phase and multi-stage operational game that describes a more complex cyber operation [78]. Composability can take on different forms: sequential, expansive, or reinforcing. Sequential composability forms a sequential game where the scenario of one game is followed by that of another. It allows the defender to prepare for forthcoming interactions and make informed defense decisions before the scenario changes, potentially shifting the advantage from the defender to the attacker. Expansive composability involves aggregating two games into one larger game with a more complex structure of action spaces, dynamics, or information structures. It can be viewed as a parallel composition where players engage in two scenarios simultaneously. This enables the defender to confront an attacker with augmented capabilities or multiple attackers coordinating to achieve their goals. Reinforcing composability is a type of feedback composability where the outcome of one game affects the outcome of the other and vice versa. It captures gameplay in which one cyber scenario influences another and eventually returns to itself. When the feedback has a negative impact, the defender faces a vicious cycle where failure leads to further losses in the same scenario.

The canonical forms of composability enable the game framework to be both mosaic and adaptive. By combining two composable games, defenders can effectively analyze and strategize against attackers. Moreover, as contexts or strategic objectives evolve, these games can be reconfigured or recomposed to align with new missions. This flexibility is particularly crucial during operational setbacks, where swift adaptation is vital for strategic resilience. Such adaptability introduces a novel capability for defenders in cyber warfare, and it can be further strengthened by advances in FMs that facilitate online learning and knowledge representation.

The development of tactical games and their ability to compose, reason, and learn is not limited to online response and interactions with adversaries. Another advantage lies in the development of game-theoretic digital twins capable of simulating hypothetical scenarios and predicting outcomes previously encountered [82]. The capabilities of game-theoretic digital twins can inform strategic-level decision-making, allowing comprehensive planning by evaluating risks associated with both familiar and unfamiliar scenarios and the reasoning of an optimal mission-driven strategy. Furthermore, at the tactical level, the game-theoretic digital twin can also be used to create conjectures or predictions of the adversarial behaviors, allowing the defender to gain a preparatory advantage over the attacker and improving the tactical decision dominance.

Learning and adaptation occur at multiple levels, forming several adaptation loops. Strategic-level adaptation must coordinate with associated adaptations at the tactical level. A rapid top-down translation between strategic-level mission goals and tactical-level tactics is necessary to enable agile responses to changes in the continually evolving threat landscape in cyberspace. This translation necessitates different levels of knowledge representation. At the strategic level, knowledge and information are encoded as semantic objectives, rules, constraints, and feasible sets [83, 84]. At the tactical level, knowledge and information are represented by acquired spatio-temporal observations encoded in numerical values, time-series data, and binary outcomes. Neurosymbolic learning, which integrates symbolic reasoning with data-driven learning, is essential to facilitate top-down and bottom-up coordination of responses to heterogeneous knowledge and information generated at different levels and from different sources.

This translation operates in both directions. Apart from the top-down impact of knowledge on tactical decisions, new knowledge generated at the tactical level can significantly influence decisions at operational and strategic levels. The propagation of knowledge, both bottom-up and top-down, requires careful study. It demands symbolic learning mechanisms operating at multiple scales to effectively disseminate insights and optimize decision-making processes. To support these investigations, there is a need to establish new solution concepts along the way. Non-equilibrium and learning-based solution concepts are essential for describing the outcomes of multi-level games. These solutions must demonstrate consistency across levels, while the learning process should be causal, coordinated, and stable.

FMs allow a more powerful way to achieve the above. They enhance the learning capabilities of each game building block, particularly in tactical games where higher resolution payoffs, information, and dynamics are required. FMs excel in understanding information from diverse sources, including textual, semantic, and numerical data, facilitating the fusion of information and enhancing game resolution through FM-enabled analytics.

Moreover, FMs facilitate the synthesis of GMs. FMs can automate the integration and synthesis of operational games by selecting and fusing relevant sets of tactical games. Additionally, they provide a concise and high-level depiction of strategic-level games for decision-making purposes, akin to how LLMs summarize information and grasp its essence.

FMs can also play a role in the coordination of learning and adaptation across the layers. Reinforcement learning enabled by the FMs can provide augmented capabilities for adaptation and learning, leveraging the multi-source and multi-modal time-series information. To achieve this, new architectures involving FMs and GMs are needed to achieve cross-level coordination and adaptation.

Figure 4 illustrates the fundamental architectures of the FMs with GMs. A GM can be supported by an FM to identify the game through the learning of the incentives, information structure, and dynamics of the players and provide a more

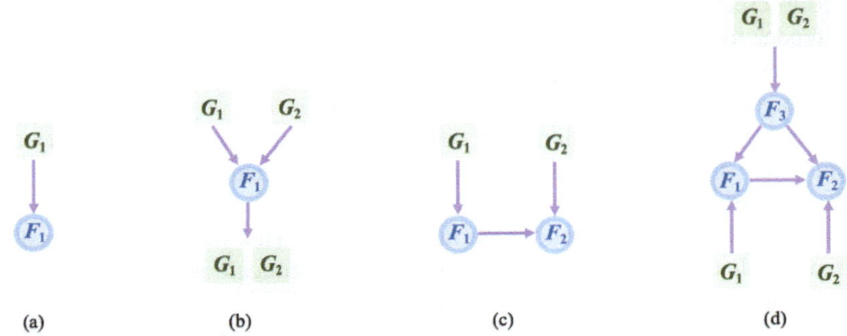

Fig. 4 Examples of Architectures of Symbiotic FMs and GMs: (**a**) FM F_1 enriches GM G_1 by improving the precision of the GM and augmenting its learning capabilities; (**b**) Tactical games G_1 and G_2 are fused together to achieve an operation game through the FM; (**c**) The adaptation of two sequential tactic games G_1 and G_2 is enabled by FM F_1 and G_2. They are coordinated sequentially; (**d**) The operational level game learning F_3 coordinates the learning of F_1 and F_2

accurate representation of the interactions between the players. This relationship has been depicted in Fig. 4a. Two GMs can also be integrated to create a meta-game through an appropriate FM. This process creates operational-level games from the game building blocks at the tactical level. This architecture is illustrated in Fig. 4b. Illustrated in Fig. 4c, the sequential adaptation and coordination between two GMs, each supported by their FMs, are essential to create tactical level resiliency when encountering uncertainties and time-varying environments. The coordination between the two stages at the tactical level improves the efficacy of the operation. When the mission changes, the operation needs to adapts too. The adaptation of an operation meta-game can be enabled by an FM, which not only reacts to the changes in the mission and outcomes of the tactics but also coordinates the learning at the tactical levels. This cross-level architecture is depicted in Fig. 4d.

3 Foundation Models and Large Language Models and the Synergetic Roles in Cybersecurity

FMs refer to machine learning models that are trained on broad data, generally using self-supervision at scale, such that they can be adapted to a wide range of downstream tasks. FMs differ from existing machine learning (ML) models in two aspects: scale and scope. Scale: FMs generally feature large-scale neural network models with an astronomical number of parameters to be determined by self-supervised training over comparable data. For example, GPT-3, an FM in natural language processing, has 175 billion parameters and is trained on 45TB of text data. Scope: FM, as a generalist, aims to handle multi-modal data and perform a wide range of tasks without being explicitly trained to do so. It is observed that FMs

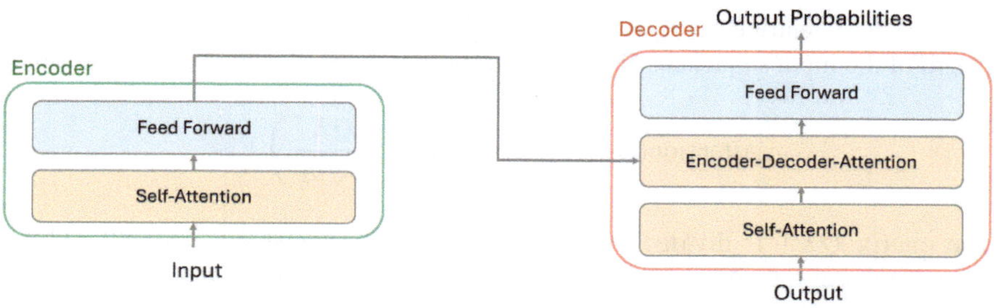

Fig. 5 The encoder-decoder structure of the Transformer architecture, adapted from [89]. Each input datapoint, after embedding and positional encoding, is fed to the attention module in the encoder part (the right half), which extracts temporal correlation (attention scores) across the input datapoint sequence. The attention scores are then passed to the decoder (the left half) to generate an output sequence auto-regressively, together with additional attention within the output sequence. The attention mechanism is instrumental in descriptive, predictive, and perspective analytics in cybersecurity

possess few-show generalizability: a handful of demonstrations from new tasks are sufficient for FMs to adapt. In contrast, ML models are specialists, targeting specific tasks and acting on certain types of data, such as image classification. They typically suffer from poor generalization when transferred to tasks unseen in the training stage. In summary, FMs are large-scale generative models with highly resource-intensive pretraining, capable of learning general features and patterns from diverse data sources. Examples of FMs include large language models (LLM) for natural language processing [85], DALL-E for images[86], MusicGen for music [87], and RT-2 for robotic control [88].

The few-shot generalization ability of FMs stems from the attention mechanism in the transformer architecture [89] shown in Fig. 5, which effectively captures long-range temporal dependencies among inputs. As the building block of FMs, the transformer consists of an encode (on the left half) and a decoder (on the right half). The task of the encoder is to map an input sequence from multi-modal high-dimensional data sources to a sequence of latent representations in a unified vector space, which is then fed to the decoder. Upon receiving the encoder's output, the decoder generates a new output based on its previous outputs, producing an output sequence in an auto-regressive manner. Mathematically, denote the input sequence by $\mathbf{x} = \{x_1, x_2, \ldots, x_n\}$, which, for example, can be a sentence to be translated or a sequence of sensor readings for robot controls. The transformer is a parameterized auto-regressive probabilistic model $\mathcal{P}_\theta$ that consumes the input $\mathbf{x}$ and generates an output sequence $\mathbf{y} = \{y_1, y_2, \ldots, y_m\}$ using previously generated outputs, i.e., $y_t \sim \mathcal{P}_\theta(\cdot|y_{t-1}, \ldots, y_1; \mathbf{x})$.

Each input datapoint x_i to the transformer, which we will call a token, is initially embedded in vectors of a certain embedding dimension with additional positional encoding so that each position in the input sequence acquires a unique representation. Each input embedding generates a query, key, and value vector of dimensions d_k, d_k, and d_v. Vectors of the same type are stacked column-wise to produce three matrices $Q \in \mathbb{R}^{n \times d_k}$, $K \in \mathbb{R}^{n \times d_k}$, and $V \in \mathbb{R}^{n \times d_v}$, with n being the length of the input sequence. The attention score is then calculated with the formula

$$\text{Attention}(Q, K, V) = \text{softmax}\left(\frac{QK^\top}{\sqrt{d_k}}\right)V.$$

The matrix $QK^\top$ is divided by $\sqrt{d_k}$ to prevent the vanishing gradient problem when applying the soft-max row-wise [89]. The entries of the resulting attention matrix represent the correlation among input tokens. Using the translation example, each entry captures how the word to be translated relates to others in the sentence. Both the encoder and decoder rely on the attention mechanism for correlation extraction in the original sentence $\mathbf{x}$ and the translation $\mathbf{y}$, respectively. Yet, their usage of attention bears a subtle difference. The upper off-diagonal triangle part of the resulting matrix $\text{softmax}(QK^\top/\sqrt{d_k}) \in \mathbb{R}^{l \times l}$ is masked with 0s in the decoder part. This causal mask prevents future tokens from influencing the prediction of the current output and is the defining feature of a causal transformer, distinctive from other variations.

To allow the attention mechanism to extract correlation from different representations, FMs often utilize multi-head attention where queries, keys, and values are linearly projected multiple times (one projection corresponds to one head attention) with different learned projections to d_k, d_k, and d_v dimensions, respectively. The attention mechanism reviewed above acts on the projection in parallel, producing d_v-dimensional values to be concatenated into a single final value, as shown in Fig. 5. The positional encoding and generation of Q, K, V matrices, together with feed-forward networks and linear layers in the transformer, are trainable components. The parameter size soars up and easily attains the billion level for recent FMs [85], as the embedding dimension, context length, and number of heads increase.

The attention mechanism is the cornerstone of FM's generalization when performing downstream tasks. The key observation is that the correlation is invariant across various sequential data, and the attention score acquired in pre-training lends itself to a variety of game-theoretic security analytics across various dimensions presented below.

3.1 Descriptive Analytics

FMs demonstrate their use by harnessing historical data to construct a formal description of game scenarios, capturing the dynamics, incentives, and players involved in the interactions. For instance, drawing upon past experiences, these models can create a matrix game that encapsulates the competitive interplay between an inspector, employing randomized examinations to identify attackers, and the agile attacker, adept at evading scrutiny. This descriptive analytics framework captures the essence of the evolving interactions within security games.

Another emerging game-theoretic security paradigm brought by this descriptive analytics is the natural game representation. Unlike the matrix and other standard game representations in the cybersecurity context, the natural representation features an end-to-end treatment of the actual network systems through FMs and, in particular, large language models (LLM) as the prevalent data in cybersecurity are of text type. LLMs are capable of summarizing evidence-based insights from lengthy cyber threat intelligence (CTI) texts and deriving semantic knowledge from CTI [90], which serves as the game state. Thanks to the attention mechanism, LLMs can discover the correlations between vulnerabilities and attack patterns, mapping Common Vulnerabilities and Exposures (CVE) to CommonWeaknesses Enumeration (CWE) [91] and linking CVEs to MITRE ATT & CK techniques [92]. Such LLM-based mapping naturally specifies the attacker strategy space without undergoing mathematical modeling. The end-to-end security pipeline centered around LLMs and FMs is projected to take an increasing share in cybersecurity task automation.

3.2 Predictive Analytics

The predictive capabilities of FMs extend to anticipating the forthcoming games and deciphering the strategies likely to be employed by adversaries. Given the nonstationary nature inherent in many applications, predictive analytics serves as a strategic tool for gaining an intelligence advantage. By inferring patterns and trends from past interactions, FMs facilitate proactive decision-making, ensuring defenders are well-prepared for the next move in the dynamic landscape of security games.

FMs' predictive power proves to be instrumental in predictive reinforcement learning in the cybersecurity context [60], where the policies are updated online according to the defender's forecast of the future consequences and anticipation of the attacker's reactions. Unlike offline or batch reinforcement learning [93], this predictive learning paradigm emphasizes the learning agent's online adaptability to a subjective forecast of future environment evolution and opponent [64]

Two primary challenges arise from the predictive learning paradigm, to which FMs offer a unified data-driven approach. The first is to adapt the policy on the fly to the forecast with lightweight computation. Existing efforts utilize the multistep lookahead idea whereby the agent predicts multiple rounds of possible interactions (trajectories) in the future [60, 94]. A policy improvement is then carried out by seeking the optimal policy maximizing the cumulative utilities within the lookahead horizon. As pointed out in [94], such a lookahead optimization is more involved than vanilla policy optimization. The adapted policy shall only target a set of plausible forecasts, i.e., those close to the actual trajectory evolution, while discarding all other candidates with marginal probabilities. Consequently, the lookahead adaptation boils down to constrained stochastic optimization, requiring sophisticated machinery for efficient computation.

FMs, as a generative model, naturally fit the role of the predictor in generating future trajectories. Unlike the Monte Carlo simulation that is commonly used in existing works [60, 64], FMs can extract the temporal correlation among past interactions via attention scores and apply them to generate new forecasts without explicitly modeling the environment, leading to high-resolution model-free predictions that are indistinguishable from actual trajectories [95, 96]. The high-accuracy predictions pave the way for online planning algorithms, such as Monte Carlo tree search and rollout methods considered in [94] and [60].

The second challenge pertains to the agent's subjective perceptions of the environment and the opponent, based on which it makes forecasts. The agent needs to calibrate its subjective conjecture on the environment dynamics [60] and the opponent's strategy [64] using the online information feedback, e.g., observations. Such a calibration process, performed also online, aims to ensure consistency between the learning agent's subjective perceptions and the objective multi-agent decision-making [64]: what one observes does not contradict what one believes. To ensure consistency, existing works resort to Bayesian learning approaches, inspired by Bayesian parametric statistics [60, 64, 94]. The proposed Bayesian learning begins with a parametric representation of external uncertainties regarding the environment and the opponent: a set of parameterized models is available to the learning agent, each of which represents a possible system dynamics and opponent strategy. Starting with a prior distribution over these models, the agent continuously updates the posterior upon receiving information feedback, which proves to concentrate asymptotically on the models closest to the actual environment dynamics and opponent response [60, 64].

FMs can revolutionize the calibration process in predictive reinforcement learning. To begin with, it is natural to treat different FMs as parametric models in Bayesian learning, with each pre-trained on different data sources capturing various temporal correlations in system trajectories and opponent sequential actions. Beyond such a straightforward extension, FMs can directly cater to the calibration process in a model-free manner, as investigated in [97]. Without building parametric models beforehand, FMs cut straight to the opponent's action sequence predictions (forecasts), which are then fed to FMs again to generate the ego agent's actions conditional on its predictions. The calibration takes place implicitly in the transformer's auto-regressive operation: the updated forecasts depend on the previous predictions and the information feedback. Recall that the transformer corresponds to a probabilistic model $y_t \sim \mathcal{P}_\theta(\cdot|y_{t-1}, \ldots, y_1; \mathbf{x})$. In the context of predictive reinforcement learning, $\mathbf{x}$ denotes the past information feedback and the output $y_t := (\widehat{s}_{t:t+K}, \widehat{a}_{t:t+K}, a_t)$ includes the agent's forecast of future K-step system evolution $\widehat{s}_{t:t+K}$, the opponent's action sequence $\widehat{a}_{t:t+K}$, and the agent's best response a_t against predicted opponent's moves.

More than a forecaster that generates future trajectories, FMs also assume the roles of the actor (policy improvement) and critic (policy evaluation) in reinforcement learning, leading to an integrated forecaster-actor-critic (FAC) pipeline

[64] embodied by the transformer. In contrast to model-based predictive learning [60, 64], FM-powered FAC opens promising avenues to model-free predictive reinforcement learning, exploring a rich class of opponent/system modeling in a data-driven fashion, alleviating the model misspecification in Bayesian learning [60].

3.3 Prescriptive Analytics

The prescriptive analytics in cybersecurity aims to provide targeted recommendations for defense strategies, with the overarching objective of minimizing the impact of potential attacks. FMs serve as a mechanism to generate bespoke recommendations and solutions. These actionable insights become invaluable resources for policymakers and network administrators. By leveraging FMs, prescriptive analytics directly enhances the security intelligence available to end-users and defenders. This strategic augmentation ensures a proactive and informed approach to defense, equipping stakeholders with the foresight and tailored solutions needed to mitigate risks effectively.

The use of prescriptive analytics, together with descriptive and predictive analytics, extends to the design of sophisticated learning algorithms. One emerging paradigm that can benefit from FMs' prescriptive capabilities is the non-equilibrium learning [59, 98, 99] and its associated learning defense. Unlike conventional game-theoretic learning, non-equilibrium learning shifts the focus from long-term equilibrium-seeking to transient strategic interaction characterization. Such a paradigm shift is particularly relevant to cybersecurity, where the defender must acquire an advantageous position within a short window before the attack cyber kill chain materializes [100]. As delineated in [59], the three pillars of non-equilibrium learning are the target set (e.g., advantageous positions), the measurement function, and the time window. A learning process is said to achieve non-equilibrium if the measurement of the learning dynamics falls in the target set within the time window. Compared with equilibrium-focused multi-agent learning, non-equilibrium learning emphasizes finite-time approachability to a set of desired outcomes [101]. Thanks to the measurement function, the approachability evaluation in non-equilibrium learning is much more flexible than the utility-driven one in standard game-theoretic learning, which takes into account broader defense objectives than simply utility-maximization, such as privacy and transparency preserving [56, 61].

The introduction of FMs to the cybersecurity domain enables an offline pre-trained online adaptable prescription for non-equilibrium-based cyber defense. Beginning with the offline pre-training, FMs first digest historical security data, such as CWE, CVE, and system log files, through self-supervised representation learning. The pre-trained FMs provide high-confidence situational awareness of the network systems and adversarial behaviors, which further translates to proper measurement functions producing accurate cyber risk assessment and corresponding desirable outcomes for non-equilibrium learning design.

Naturally, designing learning dynamics from scratch may take a prolonged period, and the defense may completely miss the window of cyber advantage when the defender takes charges before the attack cycle completes. A more viable and effective defense prescription to achieve non-equilibrium is to consider the meta-learning prescription, whereby the FMs first extract common defense strategies or defense response patterns in the offline stage by consuming diverse security data at scale. When deployed online, a handful of online observations on the network system suffices for fast defense policy adaptation, as FMs are decent few-shot learners due to the attention mechanism [85]. The offline pre-trained defense is referred to as the meta-policy, pertaining to a wide variety of security scenarios. As demonstrated in [102, 103], such as meta-learning prescription is scenario-agnostic in the sense that FMs need not examine the exact system configuration. The online adaptation is purely data-driven with marginal computational overhead, leading to effective non-equilibrium defense under system uncertainties.

As we delve into these advanced methodologies, it becomes imperative to reassess traditional equilibrium concepts that underpin our understanding of game outcomes, as motivated by the non-equilibrium concept [59]. The conventional objective has been to compute the equilibrium of the game, where the player's uncertainties regarding the environment and opponents are internalized as incomplete information [104]. However, the advent of FMs, where agents harness data in diverse ways to formulate strategies, challenges the adequacy of solutions that internalize all uncertainties. Instead, practicality dictates the exploration of solutions corresponding to models that externalize uncertainties.

Consider predictive reinforcement learning with parametric models representing internalized system uncertainties. In a case where no external uncertainties are introduced, the firm conclusion is that the learning cannot exceed the optimality under the given uncertainty modeling. Yet, such a claim only holds for closed systems. In real-world applications, many uncertainties are not modeled or are impossible to model precisely, which necessitates an open system model with external uncertainties.

As such, the pursuit of equilibrium defense is no longer legitimate in cybersecurity, due to the presence of externalities. In this context, the need for novel solution concepts arises. As discussed in the preceding subsection, the notion of consistency [64], inspired by the Berk-Nash [80] and self-confirming equilibrium [105], offers a promising avenue for describing game outcomes in models that explicitly externalize uncertainties, achieving superb performance in reinforcement learning [97] and cybersecurity benchmarks [60]. In addition to consistency, another relevant notion is decision dominance [100], where the dominant party refers to one who can extract information from data and learn about external uncertainties. Whoever completes the information acquisition and analysis cycle faster gains an information advantage over the opponent on the external uncertainties. Unlike classical equilibrium defense resting on the steady state of strategic interactions, decision dominance defense focuses on establishing an information advantage within a transient window and acting decisively before losing the initiative. This shift in perspective acknowledges that not all uncertainties need to be explicitly modeled within the game framework.

3.4 Foundation Models for Mechanism Design for Security Games

The design of security games is another domain where FMs can contribute to achieving given security objectives with underlying specifications. The formulation of design problems is facilitated through hyper-FMs, wherein FMs serve as fundamental building blocks for the design process. An illustrative example involves the use of FMs by security game designers to determine optimal game parameters, influencing the course of actions undertaken by the involved agents. This process needs to use additional FMs to anticipate the actions and behaviors of the agents.

Many components of interactions are amenable to design or control, including incentives (player payoffs) [106], game dynamics (course direction shaped by actions), and information disclosed to players during gameplay [53, 107]. The design process itself can take either an offline or online approach. Offline design involves training FMs to ascertain optimal game configurations, while online design employs a reinforcement learning process that dynamically adapts to player actions. Both approaches leverage hyper-combinations of analytics through FMs or the design of hyper-FMs to achieve their objectives.

4 Cyber Deception Game and Foundation Models

There are several quintessential domains in which FMs can play a significant role in cyber deception. Cyber deception operations involve numerous tactical components, including information gathering, detection and response, configuration and deployment of honeypots, and engagement with attacks. In this section, we specifically discuss the connection between FMs and GMs in the use of defensive cyber deception for attack engagement and defensive response. Once an attacker is in the network, the goal of defensive cyber deception is to thwart and mislead the attacker who are attempting to breach or infiltrate the network or systems by deploying techniques such as fake credentials and honeypots to deceive and divert attackers' attention away from valuable assets and towards simulated or less critical targets. Many game-theoretic approaches have been proposed to describe various scenarios, [61, 108]. For instance, a signaling game framework has been used to capture the asymmetric information between the two players [62]. In [63], a one-sided information stochastic game is used to examine the effects of deception on the attacker's belief. The study has explored the sequential nature of attacks and investigates how an attacker's beliefs evolve, influencing their actions. It has demonstrated strategies for defenders to manipulate attacker beliefs effectively, hindering attackers from achieving their objectives and minimizing network damage.

4.1 Challenges in Cyber Deception

One key challenge inherent in cyber deception lies in understanding attacker behaviors through proactive engagements. It is crucial to infer the incentives and motivations driving attackers by leveraging heterogeneous sources of data, including traffic data, log data, and event data. By doing so, defenders can gain insight into TTPs used by the attackers and their objectives. It enables the defender to prescribe the most effective responses to emerging threats.

The following Table 1 is an example of the parsing of PCAP data that captures the scenario when an attacker responds to the patching of network systems and aims for data exfiltration. Their behavior may change as they adapt to the evolving security measures. The attacker initially attempts to exploit known vulnerabilities in the target system. However, as the target system patches these vulnerabilities, the attacker's exploit attempts become unsuccessful. The attacker responds by continuing to probe the target for other potential vulnerabilities and, upon identifying a successful attack vector, exfiltrates data to an external server. This PCAP table illustrates an attacker's adaptive behavior in response to network system patching, highlighting their persistence and ongoing efforts to exploit vulnerabilities and compromise the target environment.

Another example of the attacker's behavior is illustrated using the following PCAP data in Table 2. The attacker interacts with honeypots in a discretionary manner. The attacker initially exhibits hesitant behavior, cautiously interacting with the honeypot to gather information and assess the situation. The honeypot, strategically placed by the defender, maintains the illusion of a legitimate service, effectively attracting and engaging the attacker without raising suspicion. This strategic approach allows the defender to gather valuable intelligence about the attacker's behavior and intentions.

A comprehensive understanding of the attacker's response is pivotal for defenders to formulate effective strategies and implement appropriate defensive measures. Creating a robust strategy involves not only understanding the attacker's immediate actions but also anticipating their potential moves. It requires the ability to agilely analyze the attacker's behavior and determine the most suitable course of action to mitigate the impact of the intrusion.

The defense strategy entails several crucial steps. Firstly, defenders must meticulously map out the attacker's TTPs. This involves gaining insights into the attacker's modus operandi, including their preferred attack vectors, tools, and methodologies. By understanding the attacker's playbook, defenders can proactively identify vulnerabilities and develop countermeasures to thwart potential threats. Moreover, defenders must be adept at estimating the possible trajectories of the attacker's actions. This entails forecasting the potential avenues that the attacker may pursue during the course of the intrusion. By anticipating various scenarios and their associated risks, defenders can better prepare for contingencies and respond effectively to emerging threats. Central to the success of defense strategy is the ability to act quickly and decisively. Defenders must be equipped to make rapid and

Table 1 The presented PCAP table shows the adaptive nature of an attacker encountering patched network systems. Initially, the attacker seeks to exploit known vulnerabilities within the target system. However, as the target's vulnerabilities are patched, the attacker's exploit attempts are thwarted. Undeterred, the attacker adapts by persistently probing the target for alternative vulnerabilities. Upon discovering a successful attack vector, the attacker shifts tactics, opting to exfiltrate data to an external server

Frame	Action	Source	Destination	Protocol	Flags
1	`SYN packet sent`	`Attacker_MAC`	`Target_MAC`	TCP	SYN
2	SYN-ACK response	`Target_MAC`	`Attacker_MAC`	TCP	SYN
3	`Exploitation attempt`	`Attacker_MAC`	`Target_MAC`	TCP	PSH ACK
4	`Exploit attempt unsuccessful`	`Target_MAC`	`Attacker_MAC`	TCP	RST
5	`SYN packet sent`	`Attacker_MAC`	`Target_MAC`	TCP	SYN
6	`SYN-ACK response`	`Target_MAC`	`Attacker_MAC`	TCP	SYN ACK
7	`Data exfiltration attempt`	`Attacker_MAC`	`External_Server_MAC`	TCP	PSH ACK
8	`Data exfiltration successful`	`External_Server_MAC`	`Attacker_MAC`	TCP	ACK

Table 2 The table illustrates a strategic interaction between a cautious attacker and a honeypot deployed by the defender. The attacker initially conducts a cautious scan of the network for potential targets, exhibiting hesitant behavior. The honeypot strategically responds to the attacker's SYN packet with a SYN-ACK, mimicking a legitimate service to attract the attacker. The attacker acknowledges the honeypot's SYN-ACK by sending an ACK packet to establish a connection. Subsequently, the attacker proceeds cautiously, sending probing packets to the honeypot to gather information without revealing their true intentions. The honeypot responds to the attacker's probing, maintaining the illusion of a legitimate service and engaging in interactive communication

Frame	Action	Source	Destination	Protocol	Flags
1	`Reconnaissance by hesitant attacker`	`Attacker_IP`	`Network_Router_IP`	TCP	SYN
2	`SYN packet forwarded to honeypot` response	`Attacker_IP`	`Honeypot_IP`	TCP	SYN
3	`Honeypot responds with SYN-ACK`	`Honeypot_IP`	`Attacker_IP`	TCP	SYN ACK
4	`Attacker sends ACK to establish connection`	`Attacker_IP`	`Honeypot_IP`	TCP	ACK
5	`Honeypot acknowledges connection`	`Honeypot_IP`	`Attacker_IP`	TCP	ACK
6	`Attacker probes honeypot cautiously`	`Attacker_IP`	`Honeypot_IP`	TCP	PSH ACK
7	`Honeypot responds to attacker probing`	`Honeypot_IP`	`Attacker_IP`	TCP	PSH ACK
8	`Attacker engages further with honeypot`	`Attacker_IP`	`Honeypot_IP`	TCP	PSH ACK

well-informed decisions in response to evolving threats. This requires leveraging advanced technologies and methodologies to automate the decision-making process and streamline response efforts.

FMs play a pivotal role in facilitating the learning process and empowering defenders to navigate the complexities of cyber threats effectively. By harnessing FM's capabilities, defenders can gain valuable insights into the attacker's knowledge and intentions, enabling them to map out the cyber landscape and identify potential vulnerabilities. Various types of FMs serve distinct purposes in the intrusion response process. For instance, LLMs excel at parsing and comprehending the nuanced nuances of the attacker's intent, enabling defenders to decipher malicious communications and identify potential threats. Similarly, Decision Transformers [95, 97, 109] leverage sophisticated algorithms and reinforcement learning techniques to predict attacker behaviors and make optimal decisions in real time. By analyzing patterns and trends in attacker activity, Decision Transformers empower defenders to anticipate threats and implement proactive defense measures.

Apart from supporting the ability of the defender to use his knowledge to predict the attacker's paths, FMs can also be used to allow the defender to synthesize and acquire knowledge over time. Understanding the attacker's prior behavior and potential scenarios is crucial for the defender to quickly update its security policies. Proficient knowledge enables the defender to adapt promptly and avoid extensive trial-and-error efforts. This knowledge is typically encoded using symbolic representations of rules, laws, or constraints. For instance, rules may be expressed through first-order or temporal logic statements, while laws can be encapsulated in rule-of-thumb equations, offering approximate responses. Constraints capture feasible directions for updates, which can be weighted to prioritize specific directions. Acquiring knowledge presents a challenge. One immediate method involves knowledge sharing, where insights on unknown attacks can be gleaned from those who have encountered similar incidents. In [110–112], mechanisms for knowledge sharing among intrusion detection systems are explored, introducing an incentive-compatible approach to encourage data sharing and expedite responses to zero-day attacks. Alternatively, knowledge can be synthesized from individual experiences and data. FMs play a pivotal role here, encoding experiences and data into symbolic representations conducive to formal reasoning, computation, and optimization of security policies. Recent works in [113, 114] provide promising approaches of using FMs to synthesize knowledge from datasets.

Another challenging area of cyber deception is the configuration and utilization of honeypots in engaging attackers to acquire information and knowledge. Honeypot games have been used to formalize the deployment and configuration decisions by taking into account the adversarial interactions and the engagement goals. For instance, in [115], a reinforcement learning algorithm is proposed to map out an attacker's behavior. The engagement has to interact with the attacker, making sure that the attacker does not exist in the honeynetwork. By observing and analyzing attacker interactions with honeypots, defenders gain valuable insights into emerging threats and attacker behaviors. There is a tradeoff between learning the attacker's behaviors and removing the attacker directly. The knowledge of attackers can be useful to further protect ourselves from zero-day attacks in the future. However, removing the attackers directly can lead to fewer risks.

Despite extensive research on honeypot games in both academic and practical domains, a noticeable gap persists between the game-theoretic solutions proposed in the literature and the practical requirements for effective defense mechanisms. A significant challenge lies in the necessity for decision dominance in decision-making processes. This means the defender must make faster, better-informed decisions to safeguard the network effectively. To achieve this, it becomes imperative to leverage both offline knowledge databases about the attacker and online observations of attacker behavior to predict their capabilities, moves, and incentives. FMs are capable of generating different attack scenarios. By leveraging these scenarios, the defender can better prepare for potential outcomes and develop proactive deception tactics by simulating them and making decisions based on the simulated outcomes. By doing so, defensive decisions can account for various contingent scenarios, minimizing risks, and maintaining decision dominance.

4.2 A Neurosymbolic Learning Approach to Cyber Deception

In this context, the framework of neurosymbolic learning emerges as a promising approach. This framework integrates multiple FMs to form a cohesive system capable of learning from heterogeneous data sources and making informed decisions regarding attacker engagement strategies. By incorporating neurosymbolic learning techniques, defenders can enhance their ability to adapt proactively to evolving threats and effectively defend against sophisticated cyberattacks. Illustrated in Fig. 6, the defender conjectures the attacker's tactics t_i and policies a_i at each step $i \in T$. Based on the conjectures, the defender designs an optimal policy update d_i to adapt its defense action u_i at each step $i \in T$. The multi-stage rounds of interactions correspond to a sequence of tactical-level games. As the environment and the operational level objective change, the tactical-level games need to adapt. This change is captured through a contextual parameter θ_i, which learns from the heterogeneous sources of data and adapts itself to identify the exact context so that the right set of tactical games can be picked to design the security update policies. The update of θ_i is at an operational level, which has a different time scale from the tactical level. Let $\bar{T}$ be the set of time steps, which leads to a sequence of updates at a slower frequency in comparison with the one associated with T. The contextual update policy is denoted by $D_i, i \in \bar{T}$. Its learning is driven by information from online monitoring of the attack behaviors and network changes, and inputs from the operation and strategic levels. Each context $\theta_i, i \in \bar{T}$ corresponds to a knowledge set $K_i, i \in \bar{T}$, which includes the rules of engagement, system constraints on security policy adjustments, permissible conjectures, and patterns for updating policies. The knowledge set affects the way how the defender conjectures the attacker and adapts the security policy at the tactical level.

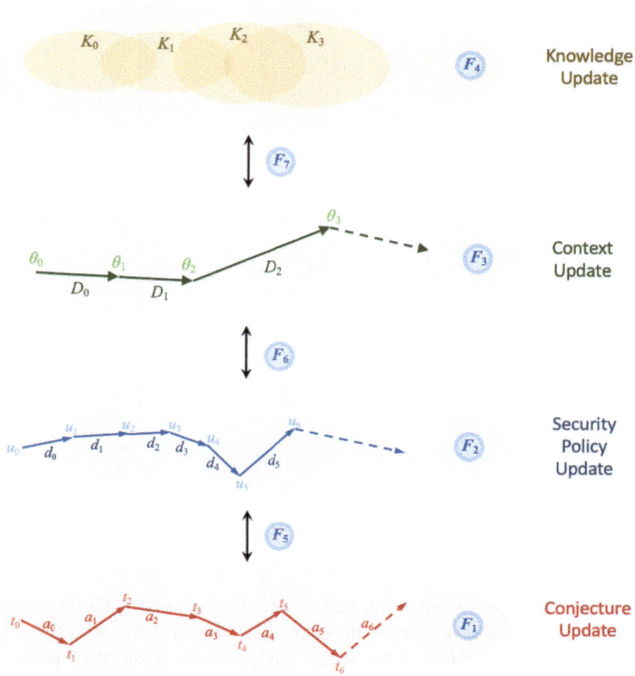

Fig. 6 Multi-agent neurosymbolic learning enabled by GMs and FMs: The defender conjectures the attacker's behavior and policies a and finds the optimal security policy update d at each round of tactical interaction between the two players. The defender updates the context parameter θ, which captures the contextual information, including the operation level information and the environmental information. Each context is associated with a knowledge set, which includes a set of rules of the game, including the system constraints on the security policy updates, the admissible set of conjectures, and learning patterns to update the policy updates. FMs are used for reinforcement learning, knowledge acquisition, conjectural formation, and representation of contextual information. In addition, FMs are used to coordinate the building blocks

FMs serve as pivotal tools across various functions including reinforcement learning, knowledge assimilation, formation of conjectures, and contextual representation. Moreover, they facilitate the coordination of multiple components in neurosymbolic learning. Figure 7 further illustrates the synergy between FMs and GMs for cyber deception. A sequence of tactical games G_1, G_2, G_3 unfold between an attacker and a defender. The defender leverages F_1 to conjecture the attacker's behavior and utilizes F_2 to adapt security measures based on acquired observations. This conjecture and subsequent updates stem from the defender's knowledge, which is symbolically represented using F_4.

Driving the conjectural learning process is F_5, coordinating the evolution of conjectures and policy updates. The tactical game unfolds iteratively, driven by operational-level objectives. Environmental shifts and operational goals require

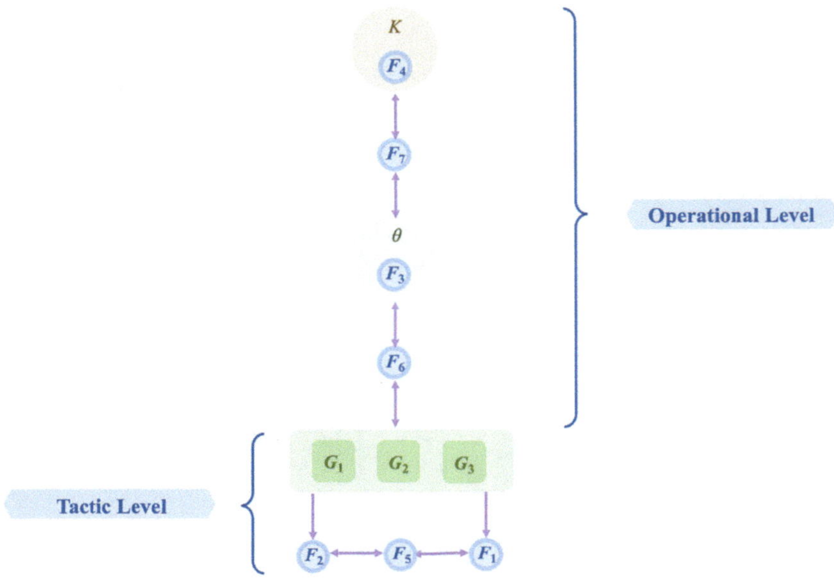

Fig. 7 Interconnections between FMs and GMs for cyber deception: The tactical games are played between an attacker and a defender. A defender uses F_1 to conjecture the attacker's behavior and uses F_2 to update the security knowledge. The conjecture and the update are based on the defender's knowledge. The knowledge is symbolically represented and captured using F_4. The conjectured learning is driven by F_5, which coordinates the conjecture update and the policy update. The tactical game is sequentially played over time to achieve its operational-level objective. The changes in the environment and the operational-level objective can lead to the adaptation of tactical-level games. This change is represented by the contextual parameter θ, which requires F_5 to process heterogeneous data sources to identify the context and F_6 to coordinate between the tactical level games and the contextual changes. Each context has an associated knowledge set K, which updates itself when the context changes. FM F_7 provides a set of rules for policy updates and conjecture formation under a context. FM F_4 is used to figure out the set of relevant knowledge which F_7 can choose from. F_4 can also create new rules for new contexts transferrable from other contexts or learned from datasets

further adaptations in the tactical gameplay. Contextual parameters denoted by θ capture these changes. F_3 processes diverse data sources to identify contextual changes, while F_6 bridges tactical gameplay with contextual shifts. Each context θ has an associated knowledge set K, which dynamically updates in response to contextual changes. FM F_7 provides a set of rules for policy updates and conjecture formation under a context. FM F_4 is used to figure out the set of relevant knowledge which F_7 can choose from. F_4 can also create new rules for new contexts transferrable from other contexts or learned from datasets.

The multi-scale perspective of neurosymbolic learning aligns with the multi-level representation of security games. Contextual and knowledge updates at the broader time scale correlate with operational-level games, which adapt to changes in mission and environment. The symbiotic interaction between GM and FM at this level fosters operational-level resilience. Conversely, security updates and attacker conjectures at the finer time scale correspond to tactical-level games, facilitating comprehensive adversarial reasoning and tactical responses. The symbiotic relationship between GM and FM at this level fosters tactical-level agility. Integrating these elements confers a decision-dominant advantage, providing both agility and resilience for the mission.

4.3 Emerging Challenges

The practical implementation of security games encounters additional system constraints specific to the domain, hardware, and user requirements. Solutions must be tailored to these constraints, considering factors such as response time, ethical defense actions, temporal sequences, and hardware complexity for online learning. To address these constraints, FMs can be imposed during the training or design phase, for instance, hardware-related ones.

For certain constraints, especially logical ones, FMs can be employed to create discriminators capable of vetoing recommendations that do not align with a learned criterion specific to the application setting. This transition from a general-purpose security game to a specific-purpose one is achieved through transfer learning using an appropriate architecture of hyper-FMs.

Despite these promising directions, challenges persist. The foremost challenge is the scarcity of security data, creating the need for the amalgamation of domain knowledge, FMs, and agent simulators to fulfill design goals. The incorporation of system vulnerabilities, application workflows, and common attacker behaviors into the design process becomes crucial.

Another significant challenge revolves around ensuring high confidence in analytics and design. Given that security applications often pertain to mission-critical scenarios, the trustworthiness and reliability of utilizing FMs become paramount concerns. Strategies to address this challenge include the development of adaptive or tunable FMs and the establishment of feedback mechanisms, both contributing to achieving improved reliability in security analytics and design.

Another practical challenge arises from the inference time current FMs consume to output the next token. In the presence of advanced adversarial attacks, and in particular, cyber threats, real-time inference is the prerequisite of a rapid defense response to counteract attackers' swift moves, such as lateral movement within the system. Accelerating the FM's inference with long contexts is imperative for predictive and prescriptive security analytics.

5 Conclusions

Cyber deception operations are increasingly prevalent in today's cyber warfare, aiming to thwart and deter resourceful and intelligent attackers from targeted assets. They utilize decoys, honeypots, and misinformation to manipulate adversaries' behaviors and decision-making processes. This chapter investigates the relationship between game models (GMs) and foundation models (FMs) for cyber deception. On one hand, GMs symbolically encode nominal knowledge of interactions between attackers and defenders. The game-theoretic representation, in strategic, extensive, or learning forms, encapsulates knowledge and experience of attack models and potential defense outcomes. On the other hand, FMs are baseline machine learning models providing powerful tools to process and extract information from heterogeneous data, including unstructured text data such as risk reports, regulatory documents, and incident reports. They enable predictive decision-making by simulating and generating known or unknown scenarios based on historical and current data, facilitating proactive and adaptive responses to attackers online. GMs and FMs can be symbiotically integrated to achieve multiple cyber defense functions, leading to guardware that transforms network security. These building blocks can be integrated through diverse architectures for descriptive, prescriptive, and predictive analytics for applications at tactical, operational, and strategic levels of the mission. This chapter proposes a multi-agent neurosymbolic reinforcement learning paradigm integrating GMs and FMs into one learning-based framework. It advocates for the capabilities of predictive intelligence, symbolic reasoning, and knowledge update in defensive cyber deception. Despite challenges in FMs and their integration with GMs, this chapter provides a promising path toward cyber resilience and decision dominance in cyber warfare.

References

1. Jajodia S, Subrahmanian V, Swarup V, Wang C (2016) Cyber deception. Cham, Switzerland: Springer
2. Al-Shaer E, Wei J, Kevin W, Wang C (2019) Autonomous cyber deception. Springer
3. Li T, Zhao Y, Zhu Q (2022) The role of information structures in game-theoretic multi-agent learning. Annual Reviews in Control 53:296–314, https://doi.org/10.1016/j.arcontrol.2022.03.003
4. Zhu Q, Li H, Han Z, Başar T (2010) A stochastic game model for jamming in multi-channel cognitive radio systems. In: 2010 IEEE International Conference on Communications, IEEE, pp 1–6
5. Zhu Q, Saad W, Han Z, Poor HV, Başar T (2011) Eavesdropping and jamming in next-generation wireless networks: A game-theoretic approach. In: 2011-MILCOM 2011 Military Communications Conference, IEEE, pp 119–124
6. Xu Z, Zhu Q (2017) A game-theoretic approach to secure control of communication-based train control systems under jamming attacks. In: Proceedings of the 1st International Workshop on Safe Control of Connected and Autonomous Vehicles, pp 27–34

7. Nugraha Y, Hayakawa T, Cetinkaya A, Ishii H, Zhu Q (2019) Subgame perfect equilibrium analysis for jamming attacks on resilient graphs. In: 2019 American Control Conference (ACC), IEEE, pp 2060–2065
8. Ge Y, Zhu Q (2023) Gazeta: Game-theoretic zero-trust authentication for defense against lateral movement in 5g iot networks. IEEE Transactions on Information Forensics and Security
9. Rass S, Schauer S, König S, Zhu Q, Rass S, Schauer S, König S, Zhu Q (2020) Cryptographic games. Cyber-Security in Critical Infrastructures: A Game-Theoretic Approach pp 223–247
10. Ge Y, Zhu Q (2022) Mufaza: Multi-source fast and autonomous zero-trust authentication for 5g networks. In: MILCOM 2022-2022 IEEE Military Communications Conference (MILCOM), IEEE, pp 571–576
11. Gupta M, Kumar R, Shekhar S, Sharma B, Patel RB, Jain S, Dhaou IB, Iwendi C (2022) Game theory-based authentication framework to secure internet of vehicles with blockchain. Sensors 22(14):5119
12. Sarıtaş S, Shereen E, Sandberg H, Dán G (2019) Adversarial attacks on continuous authentication security: A dynamic game approach. In: International Conference on Decision and Game Theory for Security, Springer, pp 439–458
13. Zhu Q, Clark A, Poovendran R, Başar T (2012a) Deceptive routing games. In: 2012 IEEE 51st IEEE Conference on Decision and Control (CDC), IEEE, pp 2704–2711
14. Zhu Q, Yuan Z, Song JB, Han Z, Basar T (2012b) Interference aware routing game for cognitive radio multi-hop networks. IEEE Journal on Selected Areas in Communications 30(10):2006–2015
15. Clark A, Zhu Q, Poovendran R, Başar T (2012) Deceptive routing in relay networks. In: Decision and Game Theory for Security: Third International Conference, GameSec 2012, Budapest, Hungary, November 5-6, 2012. Proceedings 3, Springer, pp 171–185
16. Rass S, Alshawish A, Abid MA, Schauer S, Zhu Q, De Meer H (2017) Physical intrusion games—optimizing surveillance by simulation and game theory. IEEE Access 5:8394–8407
17. Hu Y, Zhu Q (2022) Evasion-aware neyman-pearson detectors: A game-theoretic approach. In: 2022 IEEE 61st Conference on Decision and Control (CDC), IEEE, pp 6111–6117
18. Zhu Q, Başar T (2009) Dynamic policy-based ids configuration. In: Proceedings of the 48h IEEE Conference on Decision and Control (CDC) held jointly with 2009 28th Chinese Control Conference, IEEE, pp 8600–8605
19. Zhu Q, Tembine H, Başar T (2010) Network security configurations: A nonzero-sum stochastic game approach. In: Proceedings of the 2010 American control conference, IEEE, pp 1059–1064
20. Chen J, Zhu Q (2019) A game-and decision-theoretic approach to resilient interdependent network analysis and design. Springer
21. Huang L, Chen J, Zhu Q (2018) Factored markov game theory for secure interdependent infrastructure networks. Game Theory for Security and Risk Management: From Theory to Practice pp 99–126
22. Chen J, Touati C, Zhu Q (2019) A dynamic game approach to strategic design of secure and resilient infrastructure network. IEEE Transactions on Information Forensics and security 15:462–474
23. Chen J, Touati C, Zhu Q (2017) A dynamic game analysis and design of infrastructure network protection and recovery: 125. ACM SIGMETRICS Performance Evaluation Review 45(2):128
24. Huang L, Chen J, Zhu Q (2017) A large-scale markov game approach to dynamic protection of interdependent infrastructure networks. In: International Conference on Decision and Game Theory for Security, Springer, pp 357–376
25. Huang L, Zhu Q (2021) Duplicity games for deception design with an application to insider threat mitigation. IEEE Transactions on Information Forensics and Security 16:4843–4856
26. Casey W, Morales JA, Wright E, Zhu Q, Mishra B (2016) Compliance signaling games: toward modeling the deterrence of insider threats. Computational and Mathematical Organization Theory 22:318–349

27. Casey WA, Zhu Q, Morales JA, Mishra B (2015) Compliance control: Managed vulnerability surface in social-technological systems via signaling games. In: Proceedings of the 7th ACM CCS international workshop on managing insider security threats, pp 53–62
28. Feng X, Zheng Z, Hu P, Cansever D, Mohapatra P (2015) Stealthy attacks meets insider threats: A three-player game model. In: MILCOM 2015-2015 IEEE Military Communications Conference, IEEE, pp 25–30
29. Liu D, Wang X, Camp J (2008) Game-theoretic modeling and analysis of insider threats. International Journal of Critical Infrastructure Protection 1:75–80
30. Rass S, Schauer S (2018) Game theory for security and risk management. Springer International Publishing doi 10:978–3
31. Chen J, Zhu Q, Başar T (2021) Dynamic contract design for systemic cyber risk management of interdependent enterprise networks. Dynamic Games and Applications 11:294–325
32. Chen J, Zhu Q (2018) A linear quadratic differential game approach to dynamic contract design for systemic cyber risk management under asymmetric information. In: 2018 56th Annual Allerton Conference on Communication, Control, and Computing (Allerton), IEEE, pp 575–582
33. Zhang R, Zhu Q, Hayel Y (2017) A bi-level game approach to attack-aware cyber insurance of computer networks. IEEE Journal on Selected Areas in Communications 35(3):779–794
34. Zhang R, Zhu Q (2019) FlipIn: A game-theoretic cyber insurance framework for incentive-compatible cyber risk management of internet of things. IEEE Transactions on Information Forensics and Security 15:2026–2041
35. Schwartz GA, Sastry SS (2014) Cyber-insurance framework for large scale interdependent networks. In: Proceedings of the 3rd international conference on High confidence networked systems, pp 145–154
36. Zhang R, Zhu Q (2021) Optimal cyber-insurance contract design for dynamic risk management and mitigation. IEEE Transactions on Computational Social Systems 9(4):1087–1100
37. Huang L, Zhu Q (2020) A dynamic games approach to proactive defense strategies against advanced persistent threats in cyber-physical systems. Computers & Security 89:101660
38. Chen J, Zhu Q (2022) A system-of-systems approach to strategic cyber-defense and robust switching control design for cyber-physical wind energy systems. In: Security and Resilience of Control Systems: Theory and Applications, Springer, pp 177–202
39. Zhu Q, Xu Z (2020) Cross-layer design for secure and resilient cyber-physical systems. Springer
40. Cavusoglu H, Raghunathan S, Yue WT (2008) Decision-theoretic and game-theoretic approaches to it security investment. Journal of Management Information Systems 25(2):281–304
41. Grossklags J, Johnson B (2009) Uncertainty in the weakest-link security game. In: 2009 International Conference on Game Theory for Networks, IEEE, pp 673–682
42. Chen J, Zhu Q (2018) Security investment under cognitive constraints: A gestalt nash equilibrium approach. In: 2018 52nd Annual Conference on Information Sciences and Systems (CISS), IEEE, pp 1–6
43. Chen J, Zhu Q (2019) Interdependent strategic security risk management with bounded rationality in the internet of things. IEEE Transactions on Information Forensics and Security 14(11):2958–2971
44. Harsanyi JC (1968) Games with incomplete information played by "bayesian" players part ii. bayesian equilibrium points. Management science 14(5):320–334
45. Harsanyi JC (1995) Games with incomplete information. The American Economic Review 85(3):291–303
46. Bennett PG (1980) Hypergames: developing a model of conflict. Futures 12(6):489–507
47. Wang M, Hipel KW, Fraser NM (1989) Solution concepts in hypergames. Applied Mathematics and Computation 34(3):147–171
48. La QD, Quek TQ, Lee J (2016a) A game theoretic model for enabling honeypots in iot networks. In: 2016 IEEE International Conference on Communications (ICC), IEEE, pp 1–6

49. La QD, Quek TQ, Lee J, Jin S, Zhu H (2016b) Deceptive attack and defense game in honeypot-enabled networks for the internet of things. IEEE Internet of Things Journal 3(6):1025–1035
50. Boumkheld N, Panda S, Rass S, Panaousis E (2019) Honeypot type selection games for smart grid networks. In: Decision and Game Theory for Security: 10th International Conference, GameSec 2019, Stockholm, Sweden, October 30–November 1, 2019, Proceedings 10, Springer, pp 85–96
51. Huang L, Zhu Q (2019) Dynamic bayesian games for adversarial and defensive cyber deception. Autonomous Cyber Deception: Reasoning, Adaptive Planning, and Evaluation of HoneyThings pp 75–97
52. Caballero W, Cooley J, Banks D, Jenkins P (2024) A behavioral approach to repeated bayesian security games. The Annals of Applied Statistics 18(1):199–223
53. Zhang T, Zhu Q (2023) Stochastic game with interactive information acquisition: A fixed-point alignment principle. In: 2023 59th Annual Allerton Conference on Communication, Control, and Computing (Allerton), IEEE, pp 1–8
54. Zhang T, Zhu Q (2022) Forward-looking dynamic persuasion for pipeline stochastic bayesian game: A fixed-point alignment principle. arXiv preprint arXiv:220309725
55. Zhang T, Zhu Q (2021) On the equilibrium elicitation of markov games through information design. arXiv preprint arXiv:210207152
56. Li T, Zhu Q (2023) On the price of transparency: A comparison between overt persuasion and covert signaling. In: 2023 62nd IEEE Conference on Decision and Control (CDC) 00:4267–4272, https://doi.org/10.1109/cdc49753.2023.10383897, 2304.00096
57. Li T, Peng G, Zhu Q, Baar T (2022) The confluence of networks, games, and learning a game-theoretic framework for multiagent decision making over networks. IEEE Control Systems 42(4):35–67, https://doi.org/10.1109/mcs.2022.3171478
58. Liu S, Li T, Zhu Q (2023) Game-theoretic distributed empirical risk minimization with strategic network design. IEEE Transactions on Signal and Information Processing over Networks 9:542–556, https://doi.org/10.1109/tsipn.2023.3306106
59. Pan Y, Li T, Zhu Q (2023) On the resilience of traffic networks under non-equilibrium learning. In: 2023 American Control Conference (ACC) 00:3484–3489, https://doi.org/10.23919/acc55779.2023.10156139
60. Hammar K, Li T, Stadler R, Zhu Q (2025) Adaptive security response strategies through conjectural online learning. IEEE Transactions on Information Forensics and Security, vol 20, pp. 4055–4070. https://doi.org/10.1109/TIFS.2025.3558600
Automated security response through online learning with adaptive conjectures. arXiv preprint arXiv:240212499
61. Pawlick J, Colbert E, Zhu Q (2019) A game-theoretic taxonomy and survey of defensive deception for cybersecurity and privacy. ACM Computing Surveys (CSUR) 52(4):1–28
62. Pawlick J, Colbert E, Zhu Q (2018) Modeling and analysis of leaky deception using signaling games with evidence. IEEE Transactions on Information Forensics and Security 14(7):1871–1886
63. Horák K, Zhu Q, Bošanskỳ B (2017) Manipulating adversary's belief: A dynamic game approach to deception by design for proactive network security. In: Decision and Game Theory for Security: 8th International Conference, GameSec 2017, Vienna, Austria, October 23-25, 2017, Proceedings, Springer, pp 273–294
64. Li T, Hammar K, Stadler R, Zhu Q (2024) Conjectural online learning with first-order beliefs in asymmetric information stochastic games. In: 2024 IEEE 63rd Conference on Decision and Control (CDC) pp 6780–6785. https://doi.org/10.1109/CDC56724.2024.10886479
65. Anwar AH, Kamhoua C (2020) Game theory on attack graph for cyber deception. In: International Conference on Decision and Game Theory for Security, Springer, pp 445–456
66. Liu S, Zhu Q (2023) Information manipulation in partially observable markov decision processes. arXiv preprint arXiv:231207862
67. Zhang Z, Zhu Q (2020) Deceptive kernel function on observations of discrete pomdp. arXiv preprint arXiv:200805585

68. Huang Y, Kavitha V, Zhu Q (2019) Continuous-time markov decision processes with controlled observations. In: 2019 57th Annual Allerton Conference on Communication, Control, and Computing (Allerton), IEEE, pp 32–39
69. Huang Y, Zhu Q (2021) A pursuit-evasion differential game with strategic information acquisition. arXiv preprint arXiv:210205469
70. Huang Y, Chen J, Zhu Q (2021) Defending an asset with partial information and selected observations: A differential game framework. In: 2021 60th IEEE Conference on Decision and Control (CDC), IEEE, pp 2366–2373
71. Roberson B (2006) The colonel blotto game. Economic Theory 29(1):1–24
72. Hart S (2008) Discrete colonel blotto and general lotto games. International Journal of Game Theory 36(3-4):441–460
73. Golman R, Page SE (2009) General blotto: games of allocative strategic mismatch. Public Choice 138:279–299
74. Van Dijk M, Juels A, Oprea A, Rivest RL (2013) Flipit: The game of "stealthy takeover". Journal of Cryptology 26:655–713
75. Laszka A, Horvath G, Felegyhazi M, Buttyán L (2014) Flipthem: Modeling targeted attacks with flipit for multiple resources. In: Decision and Game Theory for Security: 5th International Conference, GameSec 2014, Los Angeles, CA, USA, November 6-7, 2014. Proceedings 5, Springer, pp 175–194
76. Bowers KD, Van Dijk M, Griffin R, Juels A, Oprea A, Rivest RL, Triandopoulos N (2012) Defending against the unknown enemy: Applying flipit to system security. In: International Conference on Decision and Game Theory for Security, Springer, pp 248–263
77. Chen J, Touati C, Zhu Q (2020) Optimal secure two-layer iot network design. IEEE Transactions on Control of Network Systems 7(1):398–409, https://doi.org/10.1109/TCNS.2019.2906893
78. Zhu Q, Rass S (2018) On multi-phase and multi-stage game-theoretic modeling of advanced persistent threats. IEEE Access 6:13958–13971
79. Manshaei MH, Zhu Q, Alpcan T, Bacşar T, Hubaux JP (2013) Game theory meets network security and privacy. ACM Computing Surveys (CSUR) 45(3):1–39
80. Esponda I, Pouzo D (2016) Berk–nash equilibrium: A framework for modeling agents with misspecified models. Econometrica 84(3):1093–1130
81. Nash J (1953) Two-person cooperative games. Econometrica: Journal of the Econometric Society pp 128–140
82. Li T, Bian Z, Lei H, Zuo F, Yang YT, Zhu Q, Li Z, Chen Z, Ozbay K (2024) Digital twin-based driver risk-aware predictive mobility analytics for real-time situational awareness through cooperative sensing. IEEE Transactions on Intelligent Transportation Systems, Early Access. https://doi.org/10.1109/TITS.2025.3604569
83. Peng G, Li T, Liu S, Chen J, Zhu Q (2021) Locally-aware constrained games on networks. In: 2021 American Control Conference (ACC), pp 4606–4611, https://doi.org/10.23919/ACC50511.2021.9482895
84. Yin M, Li T, Lei H, Hu Y, Rangan S, Zhu Q (2024) Zero-shot wireless indoor navigation through physics-informed reinforcement learning. In: 2024 IEEE International Conference on Robotics and Automation (ICRA), pp 5111–5118, https://doi.org/10.1109/ICRA57147.2024.10611229
85. OpenAI (2023) GPT-4 technical report. URL https://arxiv.org/abs/2303.08774
86. Ramesh A, Pavlov M, Goh G, Gray S, Voss C, Radford A, Chen M, Sutskever I (2021) Zero-shot text-to-image generation. In: Meila M, Zhang T (eds) Proceedings of the 38th International Conference on Machine Learning, PMLR, Proceedings of Machine Learning Research, vol 139, pp 8821–8831, URL https://proceedings.mlr.press/v139/ramesh21a.html
87. Copet J, Kreuk F, Gat I, Remez T, Kant D, Synnaeve G, Adi Y, Défossez A (2024) Simple and controllable music generation. Advances in Neural Information Processing Systems 36
88. Zitkovich B, Yu T, Xu S, Xu P, Xiao T, Xia F, Wu J, Wohlhart P, Welker S, Wahid A, Vuong Q, Vanhoucke V, Tran H, Soricut R, Singh A, Singh J, Sermanet P, Sanketi PR, Salazar G, Ryoo MS, Reymann K, Rao K, Pertsch K, Mordatch I, Michalewski H, Lu Y, Levine S, Lee

L, Lee TWE, Leal I, Kuang Y, Kalashnikov D, Julian R, Joshi NJ, Irpan A, Ichter B, Hsu J, Herzog A, Hausman K, Gopalakrishnan K, Fu C, Florence P, Finn C, Dubey KA, Driess D, Ding T, Choromanski KM, Chen X, Chebotar Y, Carbajal J, Brown N, Brohan A, Arenas MG, Han K (2023) Rt-2: Vision-language-action models transfer web knowledge to robotic control. In: Tan J, Toussaint M, Darvish K (eds) Proceedings of The 7th Conference on Robot Learning, PMLR, Proceedings of Machine Learning Research, vol 229, pp 2165–2183, URL https://proceedings.mlr.press/v229/zitkovich23a.html
89. Vaswani A, Shazeer N, Parmar N, Uszkoreit J, Jones L, Gomez AN, Kaiser L, Polosukhin I (2017) Attention is All you Need. In: Advances in Neural Information Processing Systems, Curran Associates, Inc., NeuriPS, vol 30, https://doi.org/10.48550/arxiv.1706.03762, URL https://proceedings.neurips.cc/paper_files/paper/2017/file/3f5ee243547dee91fbd053c1c4a845aa-Paper.pdf
90. Ranade P, Piplai A, Joshi A, Finin T (2021) Cybert: Contextualized embeddings for the cybersecurity domain. In: 2021 IEEE International Conference on Big Data (Big Data), pp 3334–3342, https://doi.org/10.1109/BigData52589.2021.9671824
91. Das SS, Halappanavar M, Tumeo A, Serra E, Pothen A, Al-Shaer E (2022) Vwc-bert: Scaling vulnerability–weakness–exploit mapping on modern ai accelerators. In: 2022 IEEE International Conference on Big Data (Big Data), pp 1224–1229, https://doi.org/10.1109/BigData55660.2022.10020622
92. Grigorescu O, Nica A, Dascalu M, Rughinis R (2022) Cve2att&ck: Bert-based mapping of cves to mitre att&ck techniques. Algorithms 15(9), https://doi.org/10.3390/a15090314, URL https://www.mdpi.com/1999-4893/15/9/314
93. Bannon J, Windsor B, Song W, Li T (2020) Causality and batch reinforcement learning: Complementary approaches to planning in unknown domains. arXiv preprint arXiv:200602579
94. Li T, Lei H, Zhu Q (2023) Self-Adaptive Driving in Nonstationary Environments through Conjectural Online Lookahead Adaptation. In: 2023 IEEE International Conference on Robotics and Automation (ICRA) 00:7205–7211, https://doi.org/10.1109/icra48891.2023.10161368, 2210.03209
95. Janner M, Li Q, Levine S (2021) Offline reinforcement learning as one big sequence modeling problem. Advances in neural information processing systems 34:1273–1286
96. Li T, Bian Z, Lei H, Zuo F, Yang YT, Zhu Q, Li Z, Ozbay K (2024) Multi-level traffic-responsive tilt camera surveillance through predictive correlated online learning. Transportation Research Part C: Emerging Technologies 167:104804, https://doi.org/10.1016/j.trc.2024.104804
97. Li T, Guevara J, Xie X, Zhu Q (2025) Self-confirming transformer for belief-conditioned adaptation in offline multi-agent reinforcement learning. In: The Seventeenth Workshop on Adaptive and Learning Agents. https://openreview.net/forum?id=kMaYSsEwCT
98. Pan Y, Li T, Zhu Q (2023) Is stochastic mirror descent vulnerable to adversarial delay attacks? A traffic assignment resilience study. In: 2023 62nd IEEE Conference on Decision and Control (CDC) 00:8328–8333, https://doi.org/10.1109/cdc49753.2023.10384003, 2304.01161
99. Pan Y, Li T, Zhu Q (2024) On the variational interpretation of mirror play in monotone games. In: 2024 IEEE 63rd Conference on Decision and Control (CDC), pp. 6799–6804. https://doi.org/10.1109/CDC56724.2024.10885800
100. Li T, Pan Y, Zhu Q (2024) Decision-dominant strategic defense against lateral movement for 5G zero-trust multi-domain networks. In: Chen, Wu Y, Yu J, Wang P, Xiaogang (eds) Network Security Empowered by Artificial Intelligence, Springer Nature Switzerland, Cham, pp 25–76, https://doi.org/10.1007/978-3-031-53510-9_2, URL https://doi.org/10.1007/978-3-031-53510-9_2
101. Li T, Peng G, Zhu Q (2021) Blackwell online learning for markov decision processes. In: 2021 55th Annual Conference on Information Sciences and Systems (CISS) 00:1–6, https://doi.org/10.1109/ciss50987.2021.9400319
102. Ge Y, Li T, Zhu Q (2023) Scenario-agnostic zero-trust defense with explainable threshold policy: A meta-learning approach. IEEE INFOCOM 2023 - IEEE Conference on Computer Communications Workshops (INFOCOM WKSHPS) 00:1–6, https://doi.org/10.1109/infocomwkshps57453.2023.10225816, 2303.03349

103. Pan Y, Li T, Li H, Xu T, Zheng Z, Zhu Q (2023) A first order meta stackelberg method for robust federated learning. In: Adversarial Machine Learning Frontiers Workshop at 40th International Conference on Machine Learning, https://doi.org/10.48550/arxiv.2306.13800
104. Michael M, Eilon S, Shmuel Z (2020) Game Theory. Cambridge University Press, Cambridge, https://doi.org/10.1017/cbo9780511794216, URL https://www.cambridge.org/core/books/game-theory/B0C072F66E027614E46A5CAB26394C7D
105. Fudenberg D, Levine DK (1993) Self-Confirming Equilibrium. Econometrica 61(3):523, https://doi.org/10.2307/2951716
106. Huang L, Jia S, Balcetis E, Zhu Q (2022) Advert: an adaptive and data-driven attention enhancement mechanism for phishing prevention. IEEE Transactions on Information Forensics and Security 17:2585–2597
107. Yang YT, Li T, Zhu Q (2023) Designing policies for truth: combating misinformation with transparency and information design. 2023 21st International Symposium on Modeling and Optimization in Mobile, Ad Hoc, and Wireless Networks (WiOpt) 00:127–134, https://doi.org/10.23919/wiopt58741.2023.10349848
108. Kamhoua CA, Kiekintveld CD, Fang F, Zhu Q (2021) Game theory and machine learning for cyber security. John Wiley & Sons
109. Chen L, Lu K, Rajeswaran A, Lee K, Grover A, Laskin M, Abbeel P, Srinivas A, Mordatch I (2021) Decision transformer: Reinforcement learning via sequence modeling. In: Ranzato M, Beygelzimer A, Dauphin Y, Liang P, Vaughan JW (eds) Advances in Neural Information Processing Systems, Curran Associates, Inc., vol 34, pp 15084–15097, URL https://proceedings.neurips.cc/paper_files/paper/2021/file/7f489f642a0ddb10272b5c31057f0663-Paper.pdf
110. Fung C, Zhu Q, Boutaba R, Başar T (2011) Smurfen: A system framework for rule sharing collaborative intrusion detection. In: 2011 7th International Conference on Network and Service Management, IEEE, pp 1–6
111. Zhu Q, Fung C, Boutaba R, Başar T (2011) A game-theoretic approach to rule sharing mechanism in networked intrusion detection systems: Robustness, incentives and security. In: 2011 50th IEEE Conference on Decision and Control and European Control Conference, IEEE, pp 243–248
112. Zhu Q, Fung C, Boutaba R, Basar T (2012) Guidex: A game-theoretic incentive-based mechanism for intrusion detection networks. IEEE Journal on Selected Areas in Communications 30(11):2220–2230
113. West P, Bhagavatula C, Hessel J, Hwang J, Jiang L, Le Bras R, Lu X, Welleck S, Choi Y (2022) Symbolic knowledge distillation: from general language models to commonsense models. In: Carpuat M, de Marneffe MC, Meza Ruiz IV (eds) Proceedings of the 2022 Conference of the North American Chapter of the Association for Computational Linguistics: Human Language Technologies, Association for Computational Linguistics, Seattle, United States, pp 4602–4625, https://doi.org/10.18653/v1/2022.naacl-main.341, URL https://aclanthology.org/2022.naacl-main.341
114. Wu X, Li YL, Sun J, Lu C (2023) Symbol-llm: Leverage language models for symbolic system in visual human activity reasoning. In: Oh A, Neumann T, Globerson A, Saenko K, Hardt M, Levine S (eds) Advances in Neural Information Processing Systems, Curran Associates, Inc., vol 36, pp 29680–29691, URL https://proceedings.neurips.cc/paper_files/paper/2023/file/5edb57c05c81d04beb716ef1d542fe9e-Paper-Conference.pdf
115. Huang L, Zhu Q (2019) Adaptive honeypot engagement through reinforcement learning of semi-markov decision processes. In: Decision and Game Theory for Security: 10th International Conference, GameSec 2019, Stockholm, Sweden, October 30–November 1, 2019, Proceedings 10, Springer, pp 196–216

The Game-Theoretic Symbiosis of Trust and AI in Networked Systems

Yunfei Ge and Quanyan Zhu

1 Trust in Networked Systems

The rapid development of network systems has been a catalyst for innovations such as 5G communications, edge computing, and network slicing [6], driving the transformation of Industry 4.0 [18] and introducing new services for critical infrastructures. This has led to a more interconnected and expansive network environment, where Information Technology (IT) and Operational Technology (OT) networks converge, creating large, hybrid systems with heterogeneous devices [40]. However, this evolution has also expanded the attack surface, with threats becoming more sophisticated and stealthy. Techniques such as Advanced Persistent Threats (APTs) pose significant challenges, making the security of these complex, connected systems increasingly difficult to manage. Despite the transformative benefits of these advancements, ensuring the security and resilience of networked systems remains a critical concern.

At the core of network security is trust. When trust is compromised, it can lead to devastating consequences, including security breaches, data loss, and a loss of confidence in the integrity of systems and services [14]. Trust permeates every phase of a network's lifecycle—from its initial setup to its operational outcomes, as illustrated in Fig. 1. It manifests across multiple dimensions [5]. Firstly, trust in network policy is paramount, particularly when it comes to penetration testing and vulnerability assessments [16]. Poorly constructed or untrustworthy policies can result in security gaps or malfunctions in network operations. Secondly, trust in identity is crucial, as it underpins access control mechanisms [10, 13]. Without confidence in the identity of entities within the network, malicious actors could easily infiltrate, making it

Y. Ge (✉) · Q. Zhu
New York University, New York, NY, USA
e-mail: yg2047@nyu.edu; qz494@nyu.edu

Q. Zhu et al. (eds.), *Foundations of Cyber Deception*, Advances in Information Security 90, https://doi.org/10.1007/978-3-031-93867-2_3

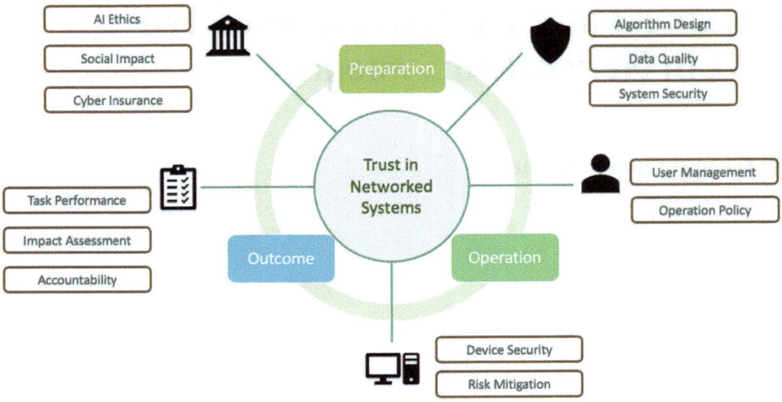

Fig. 1 Trust is integral to all stages of a networked system. A trustworthy network system ensures reliability from preparation and operation through to the outcomes

impossible to ensure that only legitimate users or devices are granted access. Lastly, trust in system performance is vital, especially in critical infrastructures where reliability and accountability are non-negotiable [9]. If a system's performance falters, users may lose trust in its reliability, discouraging adoption and threatening its long-term viability. Thus, addressing and comprehensively understanding the dimensions of trust in modern networked systems is vital for safeguarding them.

Existing approaches to establishing trust in networked systems are often inadequate. Trust in network policy, for example, frequently relies on perimeter-based security models, which are insufficient for addressing insider threats [53]. Trust in identity typically hinges on rule-based checks and encryption techniques, leaving systems vulnerable to identity fraud, credential theft, and other manipulations [37, 56]. Moreover, trust in system performance is under constant threat from increasingly sophisticated attacks, such as APTs [22], which can manipulate system behavior undetected, as exemplified by attacks like Stuxnet [27]. These limitations point to the urgent need to rethink how trust is utilized, measured, and protected in networked environments. The central research question thus becomes: How can we redefine trust in a way that better accounts for the dynamic, strategic nature of interactions in modern network systems to improve security?

1.1 Deception and Trust

Trust and deception are inherently intertwined. Cyber deception, by design, seeks to manipulate trust—either by instilling a false sense of trust where there should be none or by fostering distrust where trust is warranted [45]. The goal of deception is often to create a misleading narrative that either encourages the deceivee to place trust in a compromised entity or distracts them from recognizing legitimate threats [61, 63]. Defensive cyber deception, for instance, frequently employs techniques like honeypots [20], designed to lure attackers into engaging with decoy systems that mimic production environments. This misleads the attacker into believing that they have infiltrated a valuable target when, in reality, they are interacting with a controlled system. Conversely, attackers may deploy deceptive tactics, such as generating false alerts to overwhelm system operators, thereby obscuring legitimate threats within a sea of noise. This exploits human cognitive vulnerabilities, particularly their limited attention, to erode the operator's ability to effectively trust the validity of alerts [26].

Trust lies at the heart of deception. To fully understand deception in networked systems, it is essential to examine trust not just as a static or random variable but as a strategic interaction that can be shaped, manipulated, and exploited [8]. Current models of trust in computing systems often treat it as an exogenous factor—something that exists outside the system, randomly determined, and subject to estimation [52]. However, this view fails to capture the strategic nature of trust interactions in environments where adversarial behaviors and deceptions are prevalent. Trust can be manipulated, forged, or undermined, and thus requires a more nuanced approach that considers its strategic dimensions [14].

1.2 A Strategic Approach to Trust in Networked Systems

We propose reframing trust as a dynamic and controllable interaction, rather than a static variable. This shift in perspective is critical for addressing challenges in zero-trust architectures, cyber deception, misinformation campaigns, and evasion tactics used by attackers. Trust is not merely something to be estimated or passively observed—it is an interactive process that can be deliberately shaped by the entities that control it. By understanding trust as a strategic component, we can begin to develop models that account for adversarial behaviors and the manipulation of trust. This includes both recognizing when trust is being falsified and understanding how to foster rightful trust in networked environments.

To advance this understanding, we first examine traditional approaches to modeling trust in computing systems. Then, we introduce the of trust as a strategic interaction—one that requires models that endogenize the behaviors of both trusted and untrusted entities, as well as those who seek to manipulate or exploit trust. This strategic approach diverges from existing models by recognizing that trust is exogenous to the system and that it is not just a variable shaped by the entities outside the system. Understanding the endogenized strategic framework is essential for developing more robust cybersecurity strategies that can adapt to the increasingly complex and deceptive nature of modern networked environments.

The strategic understanding of trust is directly applicable to several critical areas, including zero-trust systems, cyber deception, combating misinformation, and attack evasion. In each of these contexts, trust is not merely a static attribute but a dynamic element that can be manipulated, forged, or strategically withheld, depending on the entities controlling it. Let's explore how this strategic approach to trust applies to each of these areas:

Zero-Trust Systems

In zero-trust architectures, the traditional model of implicit trust based on network boundaries is abandoned. Instead, every user, device, and application is continuously authenticated and validated, regardless of their location within or outside the network perimeter [53]. The strategic nature of trust plays a key role here, as trust is not automatically granted but must be earned through continuous verification.

When trust is viewed as strategic and controllable, zero-trust systems can be designed to dynamically adjust trust levels based on contextual information. For instance, behavioral analytics, adaptive authentication, and risk-based access control can be employed to assess the trustworthiness of users or devices in real-time [13]. The entity controlling trust in this scenario—the system administrator or security mechanism—must constantly evaluate whether trust should be granted, reduced, or revoked based on the observed behavior of the network's participants [17]. This strategic adjustment of trust helps to prevent both internal and external threats, ensuring that no entity within the system is blindly trusted.

Cyber Deception

In cyber deception, attackers attempt to manipulate trust to gain unauthorized access or influence the target's perception of the system. For example, an attacker may use phishing techniques to forge trust by impersonating a legitimate user or entity [23]. Similarly, defensive cyber deception uses techniques like honeypots [30] to mislead attackers into trusting decoy systems.

A strategic understanding of trust is crucial in cyber deception, as it allows for the design of systems that can both detect and exploit the adversary's manipulation of trust. In a defensive context, security teams can manipulate the trust perceptions of attackers by creating deceptive environments that appear legitimate. For attackers, the challenge is in controlling trust in ways that can evade detection while gaining access to critical resources. Understanding trust as a manipulable element on both sides of the deception equation provides deeper insights into how to defend against or employ deception more effectively.

Combating Misinformation

Misinformation campaigns thrive on the manipulation of trust. False information is often designed to appear trustworthy, aiming to mislead audiences or undermine confidence in reliable sources [55]. Whether it's disinformation spread through social media, fake news websites, or deepfakes, the central tactic involves forging a false sense of trust in misleading content.

When trust is viewed strategically, combating misinformation involves identifying and disrupting the mechanisms by which false trust is established. This includes using algorithms to verify sources, flagging inconsistencies, and providing contextual information to restore rightful trust in legitimate sources. Strategic trust models can also help to identify patterns of misinformation dissemination and predict how trust in certain types of content is manipulated. Moreover, defensive strategies can be devised to reinforce trust in accurate information while delegitimizing untrustworthy content.

Attack Evasion

In attack evasion, attackers attempt to manipulate the trustworthiness of their activities to bypass security mechanisms, such as intrusion detection systems (IDS) or antivirus software. For example, attackers may use techniques such as polymorphic malware, which alters its appearance to evade detection, or low-and-slow attacks that operate under the radar of traditional security tools.

From a strategic trust perspective, security systems must continuously adapt their trust evaluations to anticipate and respond to such evasive techniques. Trust in system behavior must be continuously reassessed based on the detection of anomalies, unusual patterns, or contextual data. By strategically controlling trust, systems can be designed to detect subtle deviations in normal behavior that might indicate an attack. For attackers, the challenge is to manipulate trust in such a way that their actions remain undetected while avoiding suspicion.

2 Symbiotic Relationship Between AI and Trust

Artificial Intelligence (AI) is changing how we analyze trust in networked systems by tackling the complexity, scale, and constant evolution of modern infrastructures. AI can process large volumes of log files and security alerts, improving both the speed and accuracy of trust assessments across networks. With advancements in processing power, AI now handles vast amounts of historical and real-time data, making it possible to assess the trustworthiness of users and devices more precisely.

AI systems also integrate expert knowledge from established security frameworks, such as OWASP, MITRE ATT&CK, and the CVE database, which provides them with reliable insights into network vulnerabilities. This combination of expert knowledge and real-time data allows AI to make trust evaluations that are both robust and nuanced, surpassing traditional methods that rely on static, manual updates.

AI's adaptability and automation are crucial in a field where network configurations, users, and topologies change constantly. By monitoring networks around the clock and responding rapidly to threats, AI supports continuous trust management. Effective trust assessment goes beyond evaluating current actions to predict future behavior and intentions. For example, game-theoretic models [31, 47, 65] allow AI to anticipate possible interactions between users, attackers, and defenders within a network, making trust management adaptive and forward-looking rather than solely reactive.

Machine learning methods like reinforcement learning and meta-learning further strengthen AI's ability to adapt trust mechanisms in cybersecurity [17]. These approaches help AI analyze past incidents to automatically adjust security policies, moving away from manual, reactive processes typical in Security Operations Centers (SOC). Reinforcement learning, in particular, allows AI to evolve trust policies in real-time, creating a self-sustaining security framework where systems continuously refine their defenses without waiting for human input [1].

Despite its benefits, AI in trust analysis also presents challenges, particularly around transparency and ethics. Many AI models operate as "black boxes", meaning their decision-making processes aren't easily understood, which can be risky when trust decisions impact critical infrastructure, such as power plants. Additionally, AI-driven decisions can inadvertently carry biases from training data, raising fairness and accountability concerns.

Trust in AI systems is essential for their adoption in security applications. Strong governance frameworks that define clear standards for AI development and deployment can help build this trust [15]. These frameworks should be flexible and evolve alongside technological advancements. Tools like liability measures and insurance can address errors or unintended consequences, while transparent accountability mechanisms help ensure that ethical concerns are responsibly managed.

The relationship between AI and trust is mutually reinforcing. AI improves trust analysis in network security by driving strategic security enhancements and autonomous resilience, while the trustworthiness of AI affects its safe and effective application. This relationship can be seen as a "meta-game", where the capabilities of AI and the trust placed in it influence each other. In a positive equilibrium, AI strengthens trust in network security, and high trust in AI accelerates its integration. Conversely, low trust can limit AI's role in security applications, emphasizing the need for strong governance and ethical oversight as AI becomes central to security and trust analysis.

In this chapter, we explore the synergy between AI and trust, aiming to achieve a balanced point where they positively reinforce each other. By focusing on AI and trust in networked cybersecurity, we investigate their interdependence and propose methods such as game theory and learning theories to provide new insights into trust in networked systems. Additionally, we propose governance frameworks that enhance the responsible use of AI systems, providing a foundation for strategic network security, autonomous resilience, and responsible AI governance.

The chapter is organized as follows. Section 2 explores the symbiotic relationship between AI and trust, examining how AI transforms trust management through data processing, integration with established frameworks, and real-time adaptability. Section 3 discusses the use of game theory and AI for trust modeling and evaluation, reviewing techniques that focus on metrics, target entities, and evaluation methods. It covers policy-based and reputation-based approaches, as well as game-theoretic frameworks, to demonstrate how trust can be modeled as a strategic game. This approach enables systems to respond dynamically to adversarial behaviors, using Bayesian updates and strategic incentives to support resilience in zero-trust environments. Section 4 addresses the vulnerabilities of AI algorithms and the role of game theory in enhancing AI trustworthiness. It includes a case study on an AI-driven traffic management system, illustrating how game-theoretic principles and red teaming strengthen trust and resilience in critical infrastructures. Section 5 concludes the chapter, summarizing key insights and future directions.

3 Role of Game Theory in Trust and AI

Game theory serves as the crucial link that bridges the gap between trust and AI, offering a structured approach to integrate these two domains. First, the strategic trust framework is inherently compatible with game-theoretic models. In a network environment, trust evaluation often involves adversarial agents who strategically manipulate the system to achieve their goals. Game theory allows us to model these agents' behaviors, motivations, and interactions, enabling a deeper understanding of how trust can be established or undermined [36, 64, 65]. By incorporating incentives, strategies, and objectives into the trust evaluation process, game theory provides a more targeted approach. Instead of evaluating trust by examining every possible scenario, which can be overwhelming, this framework directs attention toward the most relevant strategic interactions, making trust management more efficient and focused.

Second, game theory is not just a theoretical and analytical tool in economics but also an integral part of AI, and AI systems themselves can be leveraged extensively in trust management [24]. AI enables the transformation of raw data, past experiences, and domain-specific knowledge into actionable models for evaluating trust. With AI, decisions about trust management can become more data-driven and context-aware. AI algorithms can adapt to new information and identify patterns that humans might miss, making them invaluable for dynamically managing trust in complex and dynamic networks.

However, AI systems are not infallible. They are prone to errors, particularly when faced with unexpected inputs, adversarial attacks, or shifts in data distributions. This vulnerability makes it critical to develop robust AI methods that can defend against uncertainties and adversarial manipulation. Game-theoretic approaches have been used to address this challenge by framing the problem as a zero-sum game between the AI system and potential adversaries. In this context, the AI must maximize its robustness against data distribution shifts and adversarial inputs, while the adversary seeks to exploit weaknesses. These game-theoretic

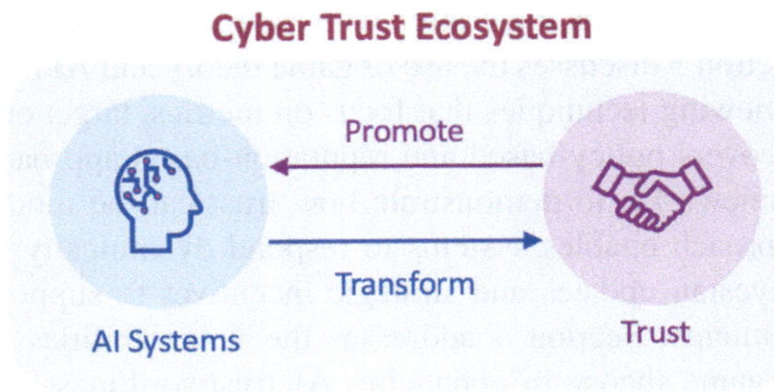

Fig. 2 The symbiotic relationship between AI and Trust forms a cyber trust ecosystem, with each reinforcing the other

methods help in building more resilient AI systems that not only perform well in trusted environments but can also withstand attempts to undermine them.

At a higher level, as illustrated in Fig. 2, there is a symbiotic relationship between AI and trust. AI technologies are transforming the way we evaluate and manage trust, and at the same time, trust is essential for the wider adoption and acceptance of AI as a reliable tool. This dynamic interaction can be modeled as a best-response scenario, where advancements in AI prompt improvements in trust management, and vice versa. When the two fields evolve in isolation, we risk falling into an equilibrium where distrust in AI limits its potential, stifling its role in transforming trust management systems. This is particularly dangerous in critical domains like network security or autonomous systems, where a lack of trust could delay the adoption of powerful AI-driven solutions.

To avoid this unfavorable equilibrium, it is essential to create an ecosystem where trust and AI mutually reinforce each other. This involves establishing governance mechanisms that promote the responsible use of AI in trust management, ensuring that AI tools are transparent, accountable, and reliable. When trust in AI is elevated, it, in turn, enhances AI's ability to transform trust management, creating a virtuous cycle. The design of such an ecosystem can be informed by game theory, which offers a framework for understanding and optimizing strategic interactions. By using game-theoretic insights, we can craft policies that drive a positive equilibrium—one in which AI and trust grow hand-in-hand, reinforcing each other's strengths, and leading to more secure and resilient systems.

This chapter focuses on the game theory-centric role in trust assessment and the trustworthiness of AI. Game theory aids in formalizing the adversarial interactions AI systems face from potential attackers while managing the trust mechanisms used by defenders. We use AI-driven traffic management as a case study, where game theory models the dynamics between the adversaries (who seek to disrupt traffic flow through data poisoning and model evasion) and defenders (who implement adversarial training and anomaly detection to maintain system integrity). By strategically assessing trust at every interaction, game theory enables us to optimize how AI systems manage vulnerabilities and how they respond to dynamic, adversarial threats.

In this section, we review the trust model and methods. In the first part, we examine trust modeling, focusing on the key attributes that define trust in networked systems, such as the target of trust, metrics used for evaluation, and how trust information is collected and assessed. We discuss how trust-based decision-making is critical in environments where adversaries may deceive or mislead, especially in cybersecurity scenarios where entities may try to gain unauthorized access by manipulating trust metrics.

In the second part, we analyze trust management methods, exploring both policy-based and reputation-based approaches. We describe how policies can be defined to enforce trust through credentials, attribute checks, and incentive mechanisms, ensuring that only trusted entities can access system resources. Similarly, reputation-based methods use historical behaviors and third-party recommendations to establish trustworthiness, but these approaches are vulnerable to false data, making them less reliable in dynamic environments.

At the last subsection of this review, we introduce game-theoretic trust evaluation. This approach models trust as a strategic game between adversaries and defenders, where both parties adjust their strategies dynamically. Game theory allows us to model trust relationships in more complex, adaptive environments, enabling systems to anticipate adversarial behaviors and optimize trust management processes based on the evolving interaction between trusted and untrusted entities. This section will also explore how Bayesian updates and strategic incentives contribute to a more resilient trust framework, especially in zero-trust environments.

3.1 Trust Modeling and Management

Trust plays a pivotal role in networked system security. It has been extensively studied in various fields such as psychology, economics, political science, sociology, and computer science [5]. Essentially, trust refers to the degree of confidence an entity has in the expected behavior of another entity [54]. The trust-based decision-making is significant when there is a possibility of deception by the adversary, as in the case of cyber security. In such scenarios, attackers may intentionally mislead or conceal information to gain strategic advantage. Therefore, it is essential to understand the definition, metrics, and evaluation techniques of trust to create an efficient framework. Table 1 illustrates the necessary attributes to design a trust-based framework in networked systems.

Target of Trust

Different from transitional perimeter-based security, we expands the target of trust to every component in the network. Trust decisions will be based on not only the trustworthiness of the requiter but also on the device and environment where the data flow takes place. The granularity of the target depends on the computational capability and the need of the system.

Table 1 Trust definition attributes in computer networks

Attributes	Explanation
Target	Who is the entity that will be evaluated
Metric	What is the metric that is used to measure trust
Collection	What information is collected to calculate trust
Evaluation	How to evaluate trust
Purpose	How trust will be used in decision-making
Management	How to manage the trust information in the system

Metric of Trust

Trust-based decisions adopt a metric to measure the trustworthiness of the entity and provide risk analysis for policy decisions. In this chapter, we refer to this metric as the trust score (TS). To be specific, we formalize the trust score of an entity at the current time as the probability that the entity is non-adversarial to the system. Let $\theta \in \Theta$ be the attributes of the entity i, and denote the non-adversarial attributes set as Θ_T. Formally,

Definition 1 (Trust Score) The Trust Score (TS) of the entity i at time t is defined as the probability that the entity is non-adversarial to the system:

$$TS^t(i) := \Pr(\theta_i^t \in \Theta_T) \in [0, 1], \tag{1}$$

where θ_i^t is the attributes of entity i at time t.

It should be noted that in practice, trust is multi-faceted and the attribute θ can be a multi-dimensional vector where each entry represents different trust attributes.

Collection and Evaluation of Trust

We adopt the categories from Bonatti et al. [2] and discuss two common approaches to trust collection and evaluation: policy-based and reputation-based trust management. Then, we propose our approach of Bayesian trust evaluation, which is a combination of policy-based and reputation-based methods.

Policy-based Method

Policy-based methods enable the system to manage trust based on a set of predefined policies. These policies may include rules that specify the types of users or devices that are allowed to access certain resources, the level of access that is granted, and the conditions under which access is granted or denied. We provide several examples under this category.

- **Network credential.** The access request can be granted based on the given credentials of the entity. The trust information of the entity is encrypted in the credential as we assume only the trusted entity will process the credential. Kerberos [41] is one example of authenticating service requests between trusted hosts across an untrusted network, such as the Internet. The underlying requirement for this method is that the system needs to ensure that the credential is private and not revealed to the attacker.
- **Ad-hoc attributes check.** The system can configure a set of qualified attributes that must be met before access is allowed. These attributes may include the device configuration, network environment security, application permission, etc. Identifying the necessary security attributes requires extensive knowledge of the system vulnerabilities. Poor security checks can result in inaccurate estimation of TS along with unresolved security vulnerabilities.
- **Promise and incentive compliance.** Trust can be influenced by promises and penalties. To encourage desirable safe behaviors of the entity, the system can create a set of rules or contracts that promote incentive-compatible actions. A reward and penalty mechanism can also be strategically designed to elicit such behaviors. For instance, trust-based collaborative intrusion detection systems use incentive-compatible mechanisms to ensure no free-riding and facilitate cooperative network defense [7, 66]. Similarly, strategic trust frameworks based on evaluating the incentives of the opponents are used to guide the integration of IoT into communication networks [44, 46].

Reputation-based Method

Reputation-based methods estimate the trustworthiness of an entity and adjust access permissions based on interactions or observations from past experiences, either directly (e.g., using historical behaviors) or indirectly (e.g., using third-party recommendation). This method can integrate more information but is also more vulnerable to false positives or false negatives. evaluation. We provide some examples under this category.

- **Historical behaviors.** If the system has had direct interactions with the entity, the TS of the entity at this request can be developed based on the history of their encounters. The behavior characteristics of the entity can be multi-dimensional that involve login information, operational habits, abnormal behavior record, etc. The system needs to find proper risk measures that achieve the security goals. In addition, expired experiences should be excluded from the trust evaluation due to the dynamic features of modern networks. The out-of-date interaction record contributes little to the current trustworthiness of the entity and it is important to consider the attenuation in the data history.
- **Social Reputation.** Reputation from third parties or society can also serve as a source for trust evaluation. Reputation may be defined as the global perception of the entity as being trustworthy. In other words, it is a collective trust opinion of other systems about the behavior of a subject node. The system prefers to

grant access to a well-reputed entity. This information is helpful when the entity aims to enter the system for the first time.

- **Recommendation.** Recommendation is the simplest case of trust propagation. For instance, a recommendation from a trusted neighbor will increase the TS of the new entity. Reliable recommendation reduces information overload, uncertainties, and risk of the access attempt. It is important to provide a trust inference model to find a reliable recommendation that could improve trust evaluation accuracy.
- **Supply Chain.** Supply chain contains inter-organizational relationships among interdependent companies contributing to the final components in the target system. The trust in the suppliers also influence the trust evaluation of the device they provided. This type of trust propagation is multi-hop due to the multi-tier structure in the supply chain. Accountability investigation and cyber insurance in the supply chain [9] could encourage truth-telling and information transparency to support trust evaluation.
- **Third-party Evaluation.** Besides the trust information propagated from others, the security system can also leverage third-party evaluation results (e.g., Intrusion Detection System (IDS) [66], Security Information and Event Management (SIEM) [38], etc.) to develop a more reliable measure of trust score of the entity. The trace of the user provides a sequence of events that can be used for security analysis. It should be noted that the reliability of the side evidence largely impacts trust propagation. The system needs to incorporate reliable side evidence for an accurate trust measure.

Bayesian Trust Evaluation

Under the dynamic network environment, it is important for zero-trust security to continuously adjust the TS after the initial trust evaluation. The system needs to respond to changes in trust by investigating and orchestrating responses to potential incidents. The dynamic update should take account of previous knowledge about the entity as well as currently observed behaviors. In this chapter, we propose a Bayesian trust model to update the trust score. This model offers a quantitative way to combine policy-based trust with reputation-based evidence and update the TS subject to the perceived strategies of the entity.

Definition 2 (Bayesian Trust Update) The Trust Score (TS) of the entity i at time $t+1$ is the probability that the entity is non-adversarial ($\theta_i^{t+1} \in \Theta_T$) based on the prior knowledge, side evidence, and observed strategies of the entity:

$$\begin{aligned} TS^{t+1}(i) &= \Pr(\theta_i^{t+1} \in \Theta_T | a^t, e^t, \pi^t) \\ &= \frac{h(e^t|a^t, \theta_i^t \in \Theta_T)\sigma(a^t|\theta_i^t \in \Theta_T)\pi^t(\theta_i^t \in \Theta_T)}{\sum_{\hat{\theta}_i \in \Theta} h(e^t|a^t, \hat{\theta}_i)\sigma(a^t|\hat{\theta}_i)\pi^t(\hat{\theta}_i)} \end{aligned} \tag{2}$$

where $a^t \in \mathcal{A}$ is the observed action of the entity, $e^t \in \mathcal{E}$ is the received side evidence, and π^t is the system's prior knowledge about the entity up to time t. σ

is the observed strategy of the opponent and h is the evidence-generating function given by the third party. Note that the relationship between TS and π is: $TS^t(i) = \pi^t(\theta_i^t \in \Theta_T)$.

- **Prior Knowledge** π^t: Prior knowledge is the ex-ante likelihood of the entity being non-adversarial before taking into consideration any new (posterior) information. This information can be collected through various sources through policy-based methods or reputation-based methods. The initial trust score $TS^0(i) = \pi^0$ is usually constructed based on some kind of experience with, or firsthand knowledge of, the other party. For instance, attributes check, historical behaviors, reputation, etc. can all contribute to the prior computation. The system can establish an initial trust estimation of the entity at $t = 0$ and compute the probability of the agent being trusted, i.e., $TS^0(i) \in [0, 1]$.
- **Side Evidence** $e^t \in \mathcal{E}$: The system can also incorporate side security evidence during trust updates. The side evidence may involve real-time network detection, system monitoring information, intelligent risk analysis, security alerts, etc. Reliable evidence helps establish a fast and accurate trust evaluation [10]. For instance, the external evidence is additional information taking binary value $e^t \in \mathcal{E} = \{0, 1\}$, where $e^t = 1$ indicates a security alarm, and $e^t = 0$ means no alarm. The security alarm warns the defender when the agent is more likely to be malicious. In general, the evidence is generated based on the probability that the agent with type θ^t takes an action a^t at the current time t. Observing the evidence e^t, the defender can further update the trust of the agent via Bayes' rule.
- **Observed Strategies** $\sigma(a^t|\theta^t)$: The trustworthiness of an agent is determined by various factors, with their observed strategies playing a major part in trust updates. A strategy is a plan of actions that an agent intends to take to achieve its objectives. It also takes into account how an agent with a different type would behave in the current security state. Abnormal behaviors of the agent, such as attempting to access sensitive or restricted information in the system, could indicate that the agent has been compromised by an attacker. In such cases, the trust score of the agent should be decreased. To ensure the security of the system, it is essential to monitor the agent's behavior regularly and update or re-evaluate its trustworthiness as needed.

Purpose of Trust

In this thesis, the TS is used to assist trust-based security policies. It plays a key role in establishing secure communication between different systems, networks, and individuals. Depending on the needs of the system, each situation places different requirements on trust. For instance, in data communication, the trust requirements would focus on the security level of the transmission environment. In contrast, in supply chain security, the trust of the supplier depends more on the supplier's reputation and compliant behaviors.

Trust Management

Two major approaches to managing trust in cyber security are centralized and distributed trust management. Centralized trust management involves a central authority or entity that is responsible for managing and enforcing trust policies across a system or network [11, 17]. It is typically used in environments where there is a clear hierarchy of trust relationships. Distributed trust management, on the other hand, involves a decentralized network of entities that are responsible for managing and enforcing trust policies. In this approach, trust decisions are made based on consensus among multiple entities, rather than by a single central authority. Each entity in the network may have its own trust policies and evaluation criteria, and trust decisions are made based on the collective evaluation of these policies and criteria.

Both centralized and distributed trust management approaches have their advantages and disadvantages. Centralized trust management can provide a clear hierarchy of trust relationships and centralized enforcement of trust policies, but it may also be vulnerable to single points of failure and may require significant resources to maintain. Distributed trust management can be more resilient and adaptable to changing trust relationships, but it may also be more difficult to manage. The choice between centralized and distributed trust management in zero trust depends on the specific needs and requirements of the system or network.

3.2 Game-Theoretic Trust

Game theory plays a critical role in risk assessment by offering a structured framework to analyze and predict the outcomes of strategic interactions between attackers and defenders [48, 64]. In cyber resilience, traditional risk assessment approaches often fall short because they focus on probabilistic measures without considering the intelligent and adaptive behaviors of adversaries. Game theory fills this gap by introducing the of strategic cyber risk, where risks are not merely quantified by the likelihood of certain events but also by the actions, goals, and adaptive strategies of both attackers and defenders. By modeling these interactions as a game, defenders can better predict likely attack strategies, optimize their defense mechanisms, and allocate resources more effectively.

In this context, game theory allows defenders to model risk using dynamic interactions [21, 22, 63]. Cyber threats evolve over time, making static risk assessments insufficient. Game theory addresses this issue by using dynamic game models that capture the ongoing interaction between attackers and defenders. For instance, repeated games model persistent threats where adversaries continuously probe a system for weaknesses, while sequential games capture how both attackers and defenders adjust their strategies over multiple stages of interaction. In these models, resilience mechanisms can be deployed in three stages: proactive measures to prevent attacks, responsive mechanisms to react in real-time, and retrospective strategies to recover from damage already done. Each stage is modeled in terms of payoffs (the consequences of actions) and transition dynamics (how actions change the system's state). This dynamic perspective enables defenders to adapt their strategies based on observed behaviors and real-time threats, enhancing overall cyber resilience.

A key feature of game theory in risk assessment is its ability to handle situations with asymmetric information [4, 28, 29, 32]. Often, attackers have more information about certain vulnerabilities, or defenders may not fully understand the attacker's capabilities. In such cases, game theory uses models like Bayesian games and signaling games. Bayesian games are particularly useful in scenarios where players have incomplete information about each other's actions and intentions. For example, a defender may not know the exact nature of an attacker's capabilities or targets, but they can infer these based on the prior information. More formally let's consider that each agent i has a private type θ_i, which reflects characteristics relevant to trustworthiness (e.g., history of reliable behavior). The set of all possible types for agent i is Θ_i. The joint distribution over types for all agents is denoted by $p(\theta)$, where $\theta = (\theta_1, \theta_2, \ldots, \theta_N)$ represents the type profile of all agents. Since each agent is unaware of the exact types of others, they rely on their beliefs about the type distribution, denoted by $p(\theta_{-i}|\theta_i)$, where θ_{-i} represents the types of agents other than i. In a trust evaluation framework, agent i forms a strategy based on their beliefs about others' types, aiming to maximize their expected utility given the probabilistic nature of their beliefs. Agent i's utility function $u_i(a, \theta)$ depends on both the action profile $a = (a_1, a_2, \ldots, a_N)$ and the type profile θ. Agent i's expected utility, given their type θ_i and belief $p(\theta_{-i}|\theta_i)$, is calculated as:

$$\mathbb{E}[u_i(a, \theta)|\theta_i] = \sum_{\theta_{-i} \in \Theta_{-i}} p(\theta_{-i}|\theta_i) u_i(a, \theta).$$

This expectation integrates over all possible types of other agents, weighted by agent i's belief in each type, providing a trust-informed utility estimate.

In game-theoretic trust settings, Bayesian Nash Equilibrium (BNE) represents a stable outcome where each agent i chooses a strategy σ_i^* that maximizes their expected utility given their type and their beliefs about other agents' strategies and types. Formally, a BNE for agent i with type θ_i is achieved when:

$$\sigma_i^*(\theta_i) \in \arg\max_{a_i} \sum_{\theta_{-i} \in \Theta_{-i}} p(\theta_{-i}|\theta_i) u_i \left(a_i, \sigma_{-i}^*(\theta_{-i}), \theta\right).$$

Recent research has explored the use of Bayesian-based beliefs and strategies to differentiate legitimate users from potential attackers. The GAZETA framework [13] proposes a game-theoretic, zero-trust authentication schema that employs dynamic game models to enable zero-trust defense in networked systems. This framework supports a robust, resilient, and efficient zero-trust model, leveraging game theory and trust for enhanced cybersecurity.

Signaling games are a class of dynamic Bayesian games. They are essential for trust evaluation scenarios where agents must decide whether to trust others based on observed signals and prior beliefs. In these games, agents act as either senders or receivers of signals, and their strategies involve both sending and interpreting signals to maximize expected utility under conditions of incomplete information. In a signaling game for trust evaluation, a sender with type θ_i chooses a signal $s \in S$ to send to a receiver. The receiver, who does not know the sender's type, updates their belief about θ_i using Bayes' rule based on the observed signal s. If $p(\theta_i)$ is the prior probability of the sender's type, then the receiver's posterior belief after observing s is:

$$p(\theta_i|s) = \frac{p(s|\theta_i)p(\theta_i)}{\sum_{\theta_i' \in \Theta_i} p(s|\theta_i')p(\theta_i')}.$$

This updated belief $p(\theta_i|s)$ reflects the receiver's revised confidence in the sender's intentions or trustworthiness based on the signal received. Once the receiver updates their belief about the sender's type, they must decide whether to trust the sender by taking an action a_j (where j denotes the receiver) that maximizes their expected utility. The receiver's expected utility, conditional on the updated belief $p(\theta_i|s)$, is:

$$\mathbb{E}[u_j(a_j, s)|\theta_j] = \sum_{\theta_i} p(\theta_i|s)u_j(a_j, \theta_i),$$

where $u_j(a_j, \theta_i)$ is the utility the receiver gains from taking action a_j given their belief about the sender's type θ_i. This framework allows the receiver to weigh the benefits of trusting the sender against the potential risks.

In signaling games, the sender anticipates how the receiver will interpret signals and selects a signal s to maximize their own expected utility. The sender's strategy, $\sigma_i^*(\theta_i)$, is chosen to optimize their outcome by influencing the receiver's trust decision. The sender's optimal strategy is:

$$\sigma_i^*(\theta_i) = \arg\max_s \sum_{a_j} p(a_j|s)u_i(s, a_j, \theta_i),$$

where $u_i(s, a_j, \theta_i)$ is the utility for the sender given their type θ_i, the chosen signal s, and the receiver's action a_j. The equilibrium in signaling games is often referred to as a Perfect Bayesian Equilibrium (PBE), in which (i) The sender's signal s is optimally chosen based on their type θ_i; (ii) The receiver's action a_j is optimal given the posterior belief $p(\theta_i|s)$ and their expected utility.

In the context of cyber deception, signaling games can be applied to scenarios where defenders (senders) send misleading signals to manipulate attackers' (receivers) beliefs and actions, steering them toward suboptimal choices. For example, a defender may deploy a honeypot—a deceptive signal intended to appear as a vulnerable system. The attacker observes this signal s = "honeypot" and updates their belief about the system's risk level [42]. If the attacker perceives the system as low-risk, they may proceed with an attack, revealing themselves and wasting resources. In a Perfect Bayesian Equilibrium (PBE), both the sender's and receiver's strategies are optimal and consistent with their beliefs and the observed actions of the other party. This equilibrium framework in signaling games enables robust trust evaluation and effective cyber deception by aligning agents' actions with their updated beliefs, allowing them to balance potential rewards and risks effectively.

Game theory enhances trust and risk assessment in cybersecurity through payoff functions that quantify the costs and benefits of actions for both attackers and defenders. For defenders, payoffs account for the costs of implementing security measures, such as network segmentation or cyber deception, and the potential financial or reputational damage from a successful attack. For attackers, the payoff represents the value they gain from exploiting system vulnerabilities. The overall cyber risk can be dynamically assessed by calculating the expected payoff, which is often modeled as the product of the attack's success probability and the impact magnitude. This dynamic risk profile evolves as both attackers and defenders adjust their strategies, capturing the adaptive nature of cyber conflict rather than relying on static risk probabilities.

Another essential contribution of game theory to trust and risk assessment is mechanism design [62], where defenders proactively shape the rules of engagement to influence attacker behavior. Mechanism design frequently utilizes Stackelberg games [35], where the defender (acting as the leader) anticipates the attacker's (follower's) responses and designs the system to channel the attacker towards less harmful actions. An example is cyber insurance [34], where game theory aids in evaluating network compromise risks and designing policies that incentivize organizations to adopt stronger security measures. Similarly, in zero-trust architectures [13], game theory supports adaptive access control by continuously monitoring user behavior and adjusting authentication requirements, thereby minimizing the attacker's advantage and enhancing system resilience.

Game theory can also incorporate bounded rationality and learning algorithms [49], recognizing that attackers and defenders often operate with limited information and computational resources. In practical settings, adversaries may not act with full rationality, and defenders may lack complete models of attacker behavior. Game theory addresses these limitations with models of bounded rationality and reinforcement learning [31], allowing both sides to learn and adjust their strategies over time. For example, conjectural learning [32] enables defenders to form hypotheses about future attacker actions based on observed past behavior, allowing continuous refinement of defense strategies. These adaptive learning models create a robust framework for trust and risk assessment, accommodating the evolving strategies and imperfect information typical in real-world cybersecurity scenarios.

4 Role of Game Theory in Strengthening AI Trustworthiness

The main issues with AI security revolve around the growing vulnerabilities created by the integration of AI into a wide range of systems, significantly increasing the attack surface. Traditional cyber defenses are often not equipped to handle these new attack vectors, particularly in machine learning (ML)-based AI systems, which are highly susceptible to adversarial attacks. In these attacks, inputs are intentionally manipulated to deceive the AI models, causing them to make incorrect predictions or decisions [12]. These manipulations can target various AI-enabled systems, including those used in facial recognition, healthcare, and autonomous vehicles. Real-world case studies have shown that adversarial attacks can result in severe financial damage, such as a notable case where a facial recognition system suffered millions in losses due to an adversarial attack.

One of the most pressing challenges in AI security is bias. AI models can inadvertently learn biases from the datasets they are trained on, leading to unsafe, unfair, or discriminatory outcomes [15]. Bias is not only a social concern but also a security risk because it can be exploited by adversaries to degrade the performance of the system or manipulate its behavior. Ensuring the trustworthiness of AI models is crucial for making them reliable in high-stakes scenarios, particularly where fairness, accountability, and transparency are critical.

A major concern exacerbating AI security issues is the increased attack surface. The integration of AI into existing infrastructure expands the number of possible entry points for attackers. AI systems interact with vast data sets and complex networks, making them more vulnerable to both traditional cyberattacks and AI-specific exploits. These expanded attack surfaces include the data pipelines feeding into AI models, the models themselves, and the environments in which these models operate. This introduces new vectors for attacks, such as data poisoning and model inversion, which can compromise the integrity and confidentiality of AI systems.

4.1 Robust Adversarial Training

One of the most effective ways to counter adversarial attacks is through adversarial training. This approach involves training AI models on adversarial examples—inputs that have been intentionally manipulated to test the model's robustness. By exposing models to these adversarial examples during the training phase, the AI can learn to recognize and resist such manipulations in real-world scenarios. Adversarial training helps build a model's resilience to deceptive inputs, improving its performance in the face of malicious attacks.

Game theory plays a foundational role in adversarial training by modeling the ongoing strategic conflict between adversaries (attackers) and machine learning models (defenders). This framework facilitates understanding how machine learning systems can be made more resilient to adversarial attacks, particularly those that seek to exploit weaknesses in AI models by introducing deceptive inputs. Game theory allows researchers to model this as a dynamic, multi-step interaction between two competing agents, leading to better defense strategies and increased robustness of the models.

Adversarial Training as a Min-Max Game

In adversarial training, the goal is to harden models against adversarial perturbations—small, imperceptible changes to input data that can lead models to make incorrect predictions. This process is typically modeled as a min-max optimization problem [50, 51], where the adversary seeks to maximize the model's classification error (or loss), and the defender (the model) seeks to minimize this error under worst-case perturbations. Specifically, the adversary creates adversarial examples to fool the model, while the defender tries to adapt by learning from these examples and improving the model's resilience. This iterative optimization can be described as a two-player zero-sum game, where the adversary's gain is directly proportional to the model's loss.

Game theory helps formalize this relationship and structure the learning process. By modeling the training as a game, it becomes possible to assess the effectiveness of the model in withstanding worst-case adversarial attacks. The game-theoretic approach allows for the exploration of equilibrium points—where neither the attacker nor the defender can further improve their position without changing their strategy—helping to identify optimal defense mechanisms.

Furthermore, game theory allows for the analysis of more sophisticated attack-defense dynamics, such as scenarios involving multiple adversaries or defenders, each with their own objectives and constraints. This multi-agent framework can be extended to incorporate distributional adversarial training, where the defender learns to counter a broad distribution of potential attacks rather than focusing on a specific type of adversarial example [25, 57].

Recent research has sought to provide a unified game-theoretic interpretation of adversarial perturbations and robustness, helping to explain the behavior of adversarially trained models and offering insights into why certain defense strategies succeed. This framework suggests that adversarial perturbations primarily affect high-order interactions in deep neural networks, while adversarial training helps models build resilience by focusing on low-order interactions that are more robust to attack [57].

Stackelberg Games in Adversarial Learning

A common game-theoretic framework used in adversarial training is the Stackelberg game [3, 33, 35, 43]. In this framework, the adversary is modeled as the "leader" who makes the first move by crafting adversarial examples, and the defender is the "follower" who responds by updating the model to minimize the impact of these examples. The Stackelberg model is particularly useful because it accounts for the sequential nature of attacks and defenses, capturing the dynamic, iterative nature of adversarial learning.

In a Stackelberg game, the leader (the adversary) optimizes their strategy with full knowledge that the follower (the defender) will react to their move. The defender then optimizes their strategy based on the adversary's action. This setup provides a way to formally analyze the adversary's behavior and design more effective defense strategies. The Nash equilibrium of the Stackelberg game represents a point where neither the adversary nor the defender can improve their outcome by changing their strategies, making it a stable state for the defense process.

Dynamic Interactions in Adversarial Training

Adversarial training often involves alternating between generating adversarial examples and updating the model [58–60]. In game-theoretic terms, this is called an alternating best-response strategy. The adversary first generates an example that maximizes the model's loss, and then the model updates its parameters to minimize this loss. This process continues in a loop until an equilibrium is reached. The defender's updates correspond to minimizing the loss over a worst-case adversarial distribution, which can be viewed as solving a min-max game at each iteration.

However, challenges arise because this adversarial process may not always converge smoothly. As noted in some studies, alternating best-response strategies can lead to non-converging behavior, especially when the game is not convex-concave [50]. This non-convergence can make it difficult to find robust solutions, as the iterative game between the attacker and the defender might cycle indefinitely without reaching an equilibrium. Game theory helps in understanding these dynamics and suggesting conditions under which convergence can be achieved, as well as identifying Nash equilibria that guarantee robust solutions .

4.2 *Red and Blue Teaming*

Another crucial domain in AI security is red teaming and threat emulation. AI red teaming simulates adversarial behavior to rigorously test system defenses, identifying vulnerabilities before real-world attackers can exploit them. Frameworks like MITRE's ATLAS equip AI developers with insights to anticipate potential threats and refine defenses. Through threat emulation techniques, security teams mimic real-world attack scenarios to evaluate an AI system's resilience against complex, evolving threats.

Game theory forms the backbone of red and blue teaming dynamics, where red teams adopt an offensive role as attackers and blue teams defend the system. Integrating these approaches into a purple teaming strategy enables organizations to simulate a comprehensive, cyclical attack-defense process, bolstering system resilience by operationalizing adversarial insights. Innovations like PenHeal [19] showcase how game theory and agent-based LLM solutions can strategically design and execute security defenses through simulated adversarial and defensive interactions. Combined with foundation models—large, pre-trained AI models—these solutions operationalize complex threat detection and mitigation strategies in real-time.

The recently proposed ADAPT framework [20] provides a powerful example of game-theoretic principles in action. ADAPT is designed to tackle vulnerabilities in AI-driven systems, especially within complex, high-stakes infrastructures like healthcare. Leveraging meta- and micro-games, ADAPT facilitates automated penetration testing that simulates adversarial scenarios at different levels, making it foundational to advanced AI red teaming and enhancing the security posture of AI systems against real-world threats.

Case Study: Securing AI-Driven Traffic Management System Using the MITRE ATLAS Framework

A large metropolitan city deployed an AI-driven traffic management system to optimize traffic flow, reduce congestion, and enhance public safety. This system integrates machine learning algorithms, sensor data from vehicles and cameras, and GPS information to make real-time adjustments to traffic signals and manage road congestion. However, given the critical role of this system in the city's infrastructure, it became a prime target for adversarial cyberattacks aimed at disrupting traffic patterns and creating chaos, particularly during emergency situations.

During a routine red teaming exercise, a simulated cyberattack was executed, targeting the traffic management AI system. The goal was to manipulate the system's decision-making process through data poisoning. The red team fed the AI system corrupted sensor and GPS data, leading the AI to misclassify traffic conditions. This misinterpretation resulted in improper traffic signal adjustments, causing gridlock at major intersections, delays in emergency response times, and widespread traffic disruption throughout the city.

Moreover, the attackers employed model evasion techniques, where subtle modifications to input data allowed them to bypass the AI system's security mechanisms. These adversarial perturbations were designed to be undetectable but effective enough to influence the system's decisions. This type of attack was based on real-world adversarial tactics cataloged by the MITRE ATLAS framework [39], which documents vulnerabilities specific to AI systems in critical infrastructures.

Attack Techniques

The red team utilized several advanced techniques outlined in the MITRE ATLAS framework, including:

- Data poisoning is one of the most impactful attacks on AI systems, where adversaries inject malicious data into the training set, leading the AI to learn incorrect patterns. This can cause severe misclassifications in real-time operations. The red team in this case study introduced corrupted GPS and sensor data, causing the AI to misinterpret traffic conditions, ultimately resulting in traffic mismanagement. For example, the Common Vulnerabilities and Exposures (CVE) system includes vulnerabilities like CVE-2021-28370, which highlights a weakness where poisoned datasets could cause AI models to misbehave. The MITRE ATLAS framework helps in understanding how to detect and mitigate these data poisoning attacks by ensuring that training data is properly verified and tested before being applied in real-world AI models.
- Adversarial perturbations involve introducing small modifications to input data, which cause AI systems to make erroneous decisions. In the traffic management case study, the red team slightly altered the sensor and GPS inputs in such a way that the system incorrectly interpreted traffic patterns. The perturbations were designed to evade basic security checks but still manipulate the system's behavior. MITRE ATLAS emphasizes this technique by categorizing such attacks under adversarial examples that deceive models into making false predictions. For instance, CVE-2020-14472 describes how adversarial examples can be created to evade detection, which is closely aligned with this attack method. Mitigation strategies include defensive distillation, which makes the model less sensitive to such minor modifications.
- Model evasion refers to attacks that allow adversaries to bypass the AI system's security defenses without detection. The red team in the traffic management scenario used this technique to adjust inputs in a way that avoided triggering alarms while still influencing the AI's decision-making process. The adversaries employed evasion strategies to manipulate the traffic light timing and create gridlocks. Model evasion attacks are well-documented in MITRE ATLAS and are also referenced in specific CVE entries, such as CVE-2020-10713, which outlines vulnerabilities where evasion techniques can bypass AI security checks. Mitigation involves improving anomaly detection systems and employing stronger model verification processes.

These adversarial techniques are precisely mapped in the MITRE ATLAS framework, which categorizes attack vectors like data poisoning, adversarial examples, and model evasion under a structured set of Tactics, Techniques, and Procedures (TTPs). MITRE ATLAS serves as a critical tool for AI developers and security professionals to better understand and anticipate adversarial behaviors, helping to enhance the defense posture of AI systems. By utilizing such frameworks, AI-driven systems, like the one in the case study, can anticipate and defend against sophisticated adversarial threats.

In this case study, red teaming and threat emulation played a critical role in testing and securing the AI-driven traffic management system. Red teaming involves simulating adversarial behaviors to identify vulnerabilities before real-world attackers can exploit them. By using tools from the MITRE ATLAS framework, the red team anticipated potential threats and developed attack strategies such as data poisoning and model evasion. These techniques allowed the team to feed corrupted data into the system, causing disruptions in traffic management decisions, such as improper signal timing and gridlocks.

The threat emulation approach, which mimics real-world attack scenarios, enabled the red team to explore how small, seemingly innocuous perturbations in data could bypass security mechanisms, leading to widespread system failure. This process provided valuable insights for the blue team (defenders), who responded by applying countermeasures such as adversarial training and defensive distillation. These AI-specific defenses hardened the system, making it more resistant to adversarial manipulations in the future. The use of game theory is fundamental in underpinning the adversarial dynamics between red and blue teams. Game theory models the interaction as a strategic game where both teams adapt their strategies in response to the actions of the other. The red team (attackers) continuously seeks to maximize disruption, while the blue team (defenders) aims to minimize damage and maintain system integrity. Through game-theoretic modeling and simulations, both teams were able to anticipate each other's moves and optimize their strategies.

In this case, we can adopt a purple teaming approach, where red and blue teams collaborate to simulate a comprehensive attack-defense cycle. Purple teaming enables the organization to test and refine both offensive and defensive strategies iteratively, creating a feedback loop that continuously improves system resilience. By simulating realistic attack scenarios and assessing defenses in real-time, the organization can operationalize these strategies more effectively. Further reinforcing this approach, game-theoretic models can be used to strategically plan security defenses, combining agent-based solutions with game theory to simulate both adversarial and defensive scenarios. These simulations allowed for more precise planning of responses to potential attacks, ensuring that both red and blue teams could adjust their strategies dynamically during the exercise.

Finally, the integration of foundation models, large pre-trained AI models, operationalized the system's real-time defense. These models enhanced the system's capability to detect and respond to adversarial threats as they evolved. The foundation models analyzed incoming traffic and sensor data, detected unusual patterns indicative of attacks, and automatically adjusted traffic signals and routes to mitigate the impact of the adversarial inputs. This combination of game theory, red and blue teaming, and the use of foundation models ensured a resilient AI system capable of defending against increasingly sophisticated threats.

5 Conclusion

In conclusion, the chapter underscores the intertwined nature of AI and trust in achieving secure, resilient networked systems. AI enables advanced trust management through real-time adaptability and strategic insight, yet its deployment requires a strong foundation of trust in the technology itself. Game theory emerges as a vital tool, modeling the adversarial dynamics and guiding adaptive trust mechanisms that allow AI to respond effectively to evolving cybersecurity threats. While AI advances trust evaluation, a governance framework that addresses transparency, accountability, and ethical use is essential to foster a positive feedback loop. By reinforcing trust in AI and leveraging AI to enhance network security, organizations can achieve a sustainable equilibrium that supports the long-term adoption and resilience of AI-powered systems.

References

1. Giovanni Apruzzese, Pavel Laskov, Edgardo Montes de Oca, Wissam Mallouli, Luis Brdalo Rapa, Athanasios Vasileios Grammatopoulos, and Fabio Di Franco. The role of machine learning in cybersecurity. *Digital Threats: Research and Practice*, 4(1):1–38, 2023.
2. Piero Bonatti, Claudiu Duma, Daniel Olmedilla, and Nahid Shahmehri. An integration of reputation-based and policy-based trust management. In *W9: The Semantic Web and Policy Workshop (SWPW)*, page 136. Citeseer, 2007.
3. Michael Brückner and Tobias Scheffer. Stackelberg games for adversarial prediction problems. In *Proceedings of the 17th ACM SIGKDD international conference on Knowledge discovery and data mining*, pages 547–555, 2011.
4. Juntao Chen and Quanyan Zhu. A linear quadratic differential game approach to dynamic contract design for systemic cyber risk management under asymmetric information. In *2018 56th Annual Allerton Conference on Communication, Control, and Computing (Allerton)*, pages 575–582. IEEE, 2018.
5. Jin-Hee Cho, Kevin Chan, and Sibel Adali. A survey on trust modeling. *ACM Computing Surveys (CSUR)*, 48(2):1–40, 2015.
6. Xenofon Foukas, Georgios Patounas, Ahmed Elmokashfi, and Mahesh K Marina. Network slicing in 5g: Survey and challenges. *IEEE communications magazine*, 55(5):94–100, 2017.
7. Carol J Fung and Quanyan Zhu. Facid: A trust-based collaborative decision framework for intrusion detection networks. *Ad Hoc Networks*, 53:17–31, 2016.
8. Yunfei Ge. *The Symbiosis of Trust and AI: Scientific Foundations for Strategic Network Security, Autonomous Resilience, and Prescriptive Governance.* PhD thesis, New York University Tandon School of Engineering, 2024.
9. Yunfei Ge and Quanyan Zhu. Accountability and insurance in iot supply chain. *arXiv preprint arXiv:2201.11855*, 2022a.
10. Yunfei Ge and Quanyan Zhu. Mufaza: Multi-source fast and autonomous zero-trust authentication for 5g networks. In *MILCOM 2022-2022 IEEE Military Communications Conference (MILCOM)*, pages 571–576. IEEE, 2022b.
11. Yunfei Ge and Quanyan Zhu. Trust threshold policy for explainable and adaptive zero-trust defense in enterprise networks. In *2022 IEEE Conference on Communications and Network Security (CNS)*, pages 359–364. IEEE, 2022c.
12. Yunfei Ge and Quanyan Zhu. Ai liability insurance with an example in ai-powered e-diagnosis system. *arXiv preprint arXiv:2306.01149*, 2023a.
13. Yunfei Ge and Quanyan Zhu. Gazeta: Game-theoretic zero-trust authentication for defense against lateral movement in 5g iot networks. *IEEE Transactions on Information Forensics and Security*, 2023b.
14. Yunfei Ge and Quanyan Zhu. Zero trust for cyber resilience. *arXiv preprint arXiv:2312.02882*, 2023c.
15. Yunfei Ge and Quanyan Zhu. Attributing responsibility in ai-induced incidents: A computational reflective equilibrium framework for accountability. *arXiv preprint arXiv:2404.16957*, 2024a.

16. Yunfei Ge and Quanyan Zhu. Mega-pt: A meta-game framework for agile penetration testing. In *International Conference on Decision and Game Theory for Security*, pages 24–44. Springer, 2024b.
17. Yunfei Ge, Tao Li, and Quanyan Zhu. Scenario-agnostic zero-trust defense with explainable threshold policy: A meta-learning approach. *arXiv preprint arXiv:2303.03349*, 2023.
18. Morteza Ghobakhloo. Industry 4.0, digitization, and opportunities for sustainability. *Journal of cleaner production*, 252:119869, 2020.
19. Junjie Huang and Quanyan Zhu. Penheal: A two-stage llm framework for automated pentesting and optimal remediation. *arXiv preprint arXiv:2407.17788*, 2024.
20. Linan Huang and Quanyan Zhu. Adaptive strategic cyber defense for advanced persistent threats in critical infrastructure networks. *ACM SIGMETRICS Performance Evaluation Review*, 46(2):52–56, 2019a.
21. Linan Huang and Quanyan Zhu. Dynamic bayesian games for adversarial and defensive cyber deception. *Autonomous Cyber Deception: Reasoning, Adaptive Planning, and Evaluation of HoneyThings*, pages 75–97, 2019b.
22. Linan Huang and Quanyan Zhu. A dynamic games approach to proactive defense strategies against advanced persistent threats in cyber-physical systems. *Computers & Security*, 89: 101660, 2020.
23. Linan Huang and Quanyan Zhu. Advert: Defending against reactive attention attacks. In *Cognitive Security: A System-Scientific Approach*, pages 67–83. Springer, 2023.
24. Charles A Kamhoua, Christopher D Kiekintveld, Fei Fang, and Quanyan Zhu. *Game theory and machine learning for cyber security*. John Wiley & Sons, 2021.
25. Minseon Kim, Jihoon Tack, and Sung Ju Hwang. Adversarial self-supervised contrastive learning. *Advances in neural information processing systems*, 33:2983–2994, 2020.
26. Yeongwoo Kim, György Dán, and Quanyan Zhu. Human-in-the-loop cyber intrusion detection using active learning. *IEEE Transactions on Information Forensics and Security*, 2024.
27. David Kushner. The real story of stuxnet. *ieee Spectrum*, 50(3):48–53, 2013.
28. Tao Li and Quanyan Zhu. Commitment with signaling under double-sided information asymmetry. *arXiv preprint arXiv:2212.11446*, 2022.
29. Tao Li and Quanyan Zhu. On the price of transparency: A comparison between overt persuasion and covert signaling. In *2023 62nd IEEE Conference on Decision and Control (CDC)*, pages 4267–4272. IEEE, 2023.
30. Tao Li and Quanyan Zhu. Symbiotic game and foundation models for cyber deception operations in strategic cyber warfare. *arXiv preprint arXiv:2403.10570*, 2024.
31. Tao Li, Yuhan Zhao, and Quanyan Zhu. The role of information structures in game-theoretic multi-agent learning. *Annual Reviews in Control*, 53:296–314, 2022.
32. Tao Li, Kim Hammar, Rolf Stadler, and Quanyan Zhu. Conjectural online learning with first-order beliefs in asymmetric information stochastic games. *arXiv preprint arXiv:2402.18781*, 2024a.
33. Tao Li, Henger Li, Yunian Pan, Tianyi Xu, Zizhan Zheng, and Quanyan Zhu. Meta stackelberg game: Robust federated learning against adaptive and mixed poisoning attacks. *arXiv preprint arXiv:2410.17431*, 2024b.
34. Shutian Liu and Quanyan Zhu. On the role of risk perceptions in cyber insurance contracts. In *2022 IEEE Conference on Communications and Network Security (CNS)*, pages 377–382. IEEE, 2022.
35. Shutian Liu and Quanyan Zhu. Stackelberg risk preference design. *Mathematical Programming*, pages 1–39, 2024.
36. Mohammad Hossein Manshaei, Quanyan Zhu, Tansu Alpcan, Tamer Bacşar, and Jean-Pierre Hubaux. Game theory meets network security and privacy. *ACM Computing Surveys (CSUR)*, 45(3):1–39, 2013.
37. Sara N Matheu, Jose L Hernandez-Ramos, Antonio F Skarmeta, and Gianmarco Baldini. A survey of cybersecurity certification for the internet of things. *ACM Computing Surveys (CSUR)*, 53(6):1–36, 2020.

38. David R Miller. *Security information and event management (SIEM) implementation.* McGraw-Hill Higher Education, 2011.
39. MITRE Corporation. Mitre atlas framework, 2024. URL https://atlas.mitre.org. Accessed: 2024-11-17.
40. Glenn Murray, Michael N Johnstone, and Craig Valli. The convergence of it and ot in critical infrastructure. 2017.
41. B Clifford Neuman and Theodore Ts'o. Kerberos: An authentication service for computer networks. *IEEE Communications magazine*, 32(9):33–38, 1994.
42. Jeffrey Pawlick and Quanyan Zhu. Deception by design: evidence-based signaling games for network defense. *arXiv preprint arXiv:1503.05458*, 2015.
43. Jeffrey Pawlick and Quanyan Zhu. A stackelberg game perspective on the conflict between machine learning and data obfuscation. In *2016 IEEE International Workshop on Information Forensics and Security (WIFS)*, pages 1–6. IEEE, 2016.
44. Jeffrey Pawlick and Quanyan Zhu. Strategic trust in cloud-enabled cyber-physical systems with an application to glucose control. *IEEE Transactions on Information Forensics and Security*, 12(12):2906–2919, 2017.
45. Jeffrey Pawlick and Quanyan Zhu. *Game Theory for Cyber Deception: From Theory to Applications*. Springer Nature, 2021.
46. Jeffrey Pawlick, Juntao Chen, and Quanyan Zhu. istrict: An interdependent strategic trust mechanism for the cloud-enabled internet of controlled things. *IEEE Transactions on Information Forensics and Security*, 14(6):1654–1669, 2018.
47. Jeffrey Pawlick, Edward Colbert, and Quanyan Zhu. A game-theoretic taxonomy and survey of defensive deception for cybersecurity and privacy. *ACM Computing Surveys (CSUR)*, 52(4): 1–28, 2019.
48. Stefan Rass and Stefan Schauer. Game theory for security and risk management. *Springer International Publishing. doi*, 10:978–3, 2018.
49. Stefan Rass, Stefan Schauer, Sandra König, Quanyan Zhu, Stefan Rass, Stefan Schauer, Sandra König, and Quanyan Zhu. Bounded rationality. *Cyber-Security in Critical Infrastructures: A Game-Theoretic Approach*, pages 99–114, 2020.
50. Meisam Razaviyayn, Tianjian Huang, Songtao Lu, Maher Nouiehed, Maziar Sanjabi, and Mingyi Hong. Nonconvex min-max optimization: Applications, challenges, and recent theoretical advances. *IEEE Signal Processing Magazine*, 37(5):55–66, 2020.
51. Jie Ren, Die Zhang, Yisen Wang, Lu Chen, Zhanpeng Zhou, Yiting Chen, Xu Cheng, Xin Wang, Meng Zhou, Jie Shi, et al. Towards a unified game-theoretic view of adversarial perturbations and robustness. *Advances in Neural Information Processing Systems*, 34:3797–3810, 2021.
52. Avani Sharma, Emmanuel S Pilli, Arka P Mazumdar, and Poonam Gera. Towards trustworthy internet of things: A survey on trust management applications and schemes. *Computer Communications*, 160:475–493, 2020.
53. VA Stafford. Zero trust architecture. *NIST Special Publication*, 800:207, 2020.
54. Zheng Yan and Silke Holtmanns. Trust modeling and management: from social trust to digital trust. In *Computer security, privacy and politics: current issues, challenges and solutions*, pages 290–323. IGI Global, 2008.
55. Ya-Ting Yang, Tao Li, and Quanyan Zhu. Designing policies for truth: Combating misinformation with transparency and information design. In *2023 21st International Symposium on Modeling and Optimization in Mobile, Ad Hoc, and Wireless Networks (WiOpt)*, pages 127–134. IEEE, 2023.
56. Zheng Yang, Jun He, Yangguang Tian, and Jianying Zhou. Faster authenticated key agreement with perfect forward secrecy for industrial internet-of-things. *IEEE Transactions on Industrial Informatics*, 16(10):6584–6596, 2019.
57. Haotian Ye, Chuanlong Xie, Tianle Cai, Ruichen Li, Zhenguo Li, and Liwei Wang. Towards a theoretical framework of out-of-distribution generalization. *Advances in Neural Information Processing Systems*, 34:23519–23531, 2021.

58. Rui Zhang and Quanyan Zhu. Security of distributed machine learning: A game-theoretic approach to design secure dsvm. *Adversary-Aware Learning Techniques and Trends in Cybersecurity*, pages 17–36, 2021a.
59. Tao Zhang and Quanyan Zhu. A dual perturbation approach for differential private admm-based distributed empirical risk minimization. In *Proceedings of the 2016 ACM Workshop on Artificial Intelligence and Security*, pages 129–137, 2016a.
60. Tao Zhang and Quanyan Zhu. Dynamic differential privacy for admm-based distributed classification learning. *IEEE Transactions on Information Forensics and Security*, 12(1):172–187, 2016b.
61. Tao Zhang and Quanyan Zhu. Hypothesis testing game for cyber deception. In *Decision and Game Theory for Security: 9th International Conference, GameSec 2018, Seattle, WA, USA, October 29–31, 2018, Proceedings 9*, pages 540–555. Springer, 2018.
62. Tao Zhang and Quanyan Zhu. Informational design of dynamic multi-agent system. *arXiv preprint arXiv:2105.03052*, 2021b.
63. Tao Zhang, Linan Huang, Jeffrey Pawlick, and Quanyan Zhu. Game-theoretic analysis of cyber deception: Evidence-based strategies and dynamic risk mitigation. *Modeling and Design of secure Internet of Things*, pages 27–58, 2020.
64. Quanyan Zhu. Foundations of cyber resilience: The confluence of game, control, and learning theories. *arXiv preprint arXiv:2404.01205*, 2024.
65. Quanyan Zhu and Stefan Rass. Game theory meets network security: A tutorial. In *Proceedings of the 2018 ACM SIGSAC conference on computer and communications security*, pages 2163–2165, 2018.
66. Quanyan Zhu, Carol Fung, Raouf Boutaba, and Tamer Basar. Guidex: A game-theoretic incentive-based mechanism for intrusion detection networks. *IEEE Journal on Selected Areas in Communications*, 30(11):2220–2230, 2012.

Part II
Human Factors

The Beginning of the End of Security Awareness Training: How AI Marks a New Era in Cybersecurity

Arun Vishwanath

On August 10, 2024, an email landed in my inbox from Disney+. It reminded me to renew my subscription—something I've routinely done without a second thought. But in today's world, where spearphishing has evolved into a sophisticated art form, I've trained myself—and countless others—to scrutinize such requests. So, I took a closer look.

I checked the email headers, scrutinized the sender's address, and examined the domain name. I delved into technical details like the legitimacy of the server from which the email originated, looking for SPF (Sender Policy Framework) and DKIM (DomainKeys Identified Mail) compliance. Everything appeared legitimate.

But it wasn't.

A hacker had managed to abuse Proofpoint's email relay system, bypassing both SPF and DKIM protections. The email was a flawless replica of a genuine Disney+ message. Clicking on the link led me to a webpage that was, at first glance, indistinguishable from the actual Disney subscription page. But something felt off—tiny print at the bottom of the page asked for my credit card information in a way that triggered my suspicion. Upon closer inspection, the deception unraveled.

This was no ordinary phishing attempt. It was part of a larger campaign that had been exploiting Proofpoint's email protection, which shields 87 of the Fortune

Author Note Earlier versions of this paper were presented at the NSF Workshop on LLMs and Network Security, held at NYU in October 2024, and at ConnectCon 2024 in Las Vegas, Nevada. This article is a forthcoming chapter in *Large Language Models for Network Security*, edited by Quanyan Zhu and Cliff X. Wang, Springer-Nature, Boston, MA.

For correspondence regarding this manuscript, please contact Arun Vishwanath at arun@cyberhygieneacademy.com

A. Vishwanath (✉)
Cyber Hygiene Academy Inc., Buffalo, NY, USA
e-mail: arun@cyberhygieneacademy.com

Q. Zhu et al. (eds.), *Foundations of Cyber Deception*, Advances in Information Security 90, https://doi.org/10.1007/978-3-031-93867-2_4

100 companies. Over 6 months, these attackers dispatched around three million impeccably spoofed emails daily, targeting consumers of brands like IBM, Coca-Cola, Nike, and Best Buy before their activities were fully uncovered [1]. This incident is a harbinger of a grim future. When an email has all the trappings of legitimacy—when it looks like the real thing, comes from the real source, and behaves like the real thing—then we must confront a harsh truth: it is the real thing.

This is the reality we face, even before Large Language Models (LLMs) and AI-generated media begin synthetically recreating reality in ways so authentic that we can't discern what's real and what's fabricated. AI-created deepfakes have already shown us what's possible—voices and images reproduced with such precision that they're virtually indistinguishable from the real thing. In such a world, what role can traditional security awareness play?

This chapter delves into the unsettling future that LLMs are ushering in—a future where AI-driven social engineering attacks become the norm. We'll explore how attackers might exploit LLMs for phishing and other malicious purposes, and consider the broader consequences, including the shift from today's technology-driven equality of opportunity to an equality of outcomes, where any hacker, regardless of skill, can generate incredibly persuasive attacks.

1 Implications of LLMs on Social Engineering

Social engineering isn't new. Its roots trace back to ancient India, where the Thuggee cult exploited asymmetric information for their gain [2]. This practice has appeared throughout history—from the French Revolution to the American Civil War and the World Wars—whenever the uninformed could be preyed upon by the informed with ill intent. In the absence of shared information between nations and among people in neighboring regions, criminal groups thrived, luring victims with promises of quick riches, only to trap them. This manipulation persists today in the form of pretexting—exemplified by the notorious Nigerian scams and their many revisions—and in spear phishing emails, IRS scam calls, social media impersonations, and various messaging attacks. The tactics remain consistent: pretending to be credible; leveraging threats, rewards, or intrigue; and baiting the unsuspecting into clicking a malicious link or handing over sensitive information. Today's hackers, much like their historical counterparts, weaponize trust.

The Internet exacerbates this problem. It thrives on a system where identity is reduced to credentials—login names, passwords, and digital handles—which, once replicated, make it difficult to distinguish the authentic from the fraudulent. This foundational flaw in computing dates back to the mainframe era and persists despite layers of modern security measures like biometrics and multi-factor authentication. Each layer ultimately converts to a digital format, stored behind another set of credentials, each susceptible to the same vulnerability.

Given these intrinsic flaws, the industry's focus has shifted towards strengthening the user—arming them with vigilance to counteract these threats. From the early days of AOL to the present, creating awareness among users has been the front-line defense against social engineering. As attacks have multiplied and technical defenses have failed, the demand for creating security awareness has grown.

The vendor community has responded with "security awareness" products that promise to create resilience in users against social engineering. Often marketed as cure-alls to CISOs and IT professionals desperate for solutions, these products usually center around pen-testing, where users are sent mock spear-phishing attacks to gauge their detection abilities. Pen-tests are repeated periodically, with the idea that repetition reinforces learning and builds lasting resilience.

In practice, however, these approaches yield short-term results that quickly fade—often hours after training ends. They offer minimal security resilience—defined here as the ability to resist a variety of phishing and social engineering attacks. Many pen-tests are contrived, presenting scenarios that range in quality and applicability to the user. Users, particularly those in organizations where training is mandated, often comply with tests or ignore them, rendering the resulting data from pen-tests highly unreliable.

Yet, this is the primary data available on users. CISOs and cybersecurity insurers take it at face value, often overestimating their users' awareness and resilience. When social engineering attacks inevitably succeed, users are blamed for not learning, perpetuating the myth that people are the problem in cybersecurity. This self-perpetuating loop—where training leads to more training—has primarily benefited the vendor community, with many commanding valuations in excess of a billion dollars.

Rather than reinvesting these profits into research and improvement, security awareness vendors have funneled resources into lobbying and cementing their market dominance. Consequently, instead of evolving to meet the changing threat landscape, they have remained stagnant. Little has changed in the realm of pen-testing—whether in approach or the data it yields—since its inception. This complacency is troubling, as the industry has shifted its focus from advancing user security to evangelizing the need for more security awareness.

Security awareness programs, originally designed to inform the uninformed, are, therefore, woefully inadequate against present-day social engineering threats. The advent of Generative AI has fundamentally transformed the capabilities of hackers worldwide, tipping the scales significantly in their favor. It has altered the playing field, rendering current approaches to security awareness obsolete in at least three critical ways.

1.1 From Equality of Opportunity to Equality of Outcomes

Imagine your cellphone rings. The caller ID shows a familiar number—perhaps it's your parent or a trusted friend. You answer it. A foreign-sounding voice on the other end demands payment for some outstanding bill.

Such phone-spoofing robocalls are a global plague. They started with hard-to-recognize numbers that many users learned to block, evolving into "neighborhood spoofing," where the number appears to be from your local area code or from contacts in your address book [3]. Most originate from outside the U.S., using VoIP and other internet-based technologies to mask their origin. Americans receive close to 4.5 billion robocalls monthly, totaling around 54 billion annually [4]. Even though many users know to block these calls, some still fall victim. In 2021, an estimated 60 million Americans lost money to phone scams, with total losses exceeding $29.8 billion [5].

The phone-spoofing phenomenon is driven by Internet-based technologies that democratize deception. VoIP and caller ID spoofing, which are available to anyone with an internet connection, anywhere in the world, provide *equal opportunity for exploitation*. But GenAI shifts this.

Now, consider the same scenario again: Your phone rings; the number is familiar; but so is the voice on the line. The impersonation is perfect—it sounds like your parent or your friend, and it responds just as they would. This isn't some dystopian future—it's today's reality, enabled by tools from OpenAI and others, accessible to hackers at minimal cost.

This is the *Equality of Outcomes*—a world where anyone can convincingly become anyone else, whether through a phone call or, soon, through video—enabled by GenAI. Email, messaging, and social media, already easy to spoof, become even more convincing with voice and video in the mix.

The implications are profound. Traditional security awareness, which focused on identifying "tells" or signs of deception—foreign accents, odd phrasing, suspicious requests—fails in a GenAI-enhanced landscape. As the saying goes, "If it quacks like a duck and walks like one, it probably is a duck." In that vein, if you receive a call from your spouse's number, the voice on the other end sounds like them, and the conversation flows just as theirs would, how can you train users to distinguish the deception?

Voice impersonations now have latency measured in milliseconds. The barrier isn't technology—it's processing speed, which continues to accelerate. This dark future isn't decades away; it's merely days.

1.2 Hyper-Personalized Attacks

In August 2024, news broke about a massive breach involving National Public Data (NPD), a company responsible for conducting background checks for employers across the globe [6]. Hackers managed to steal the personal information of over three billion individuals, encompassing everything from Social Security numbers to entire employment histories.

NPD is just one in a long string of breaches that date back to at least 2014. In a 2015 CNN op-ed, I remarked that everyone in the U.S. had likely lost their data to some breach and just weren't aware of it [7]. This wasn't hyperbole. Back then, breach notification requirements were minimal, leaving many unaware of their compromised information. Today, breach notifications are mandatory, and most of us have received at least one letter informing us that our data was part of a hack.

Reams of compromised information, now scattered across the internet, are a goldmine for malicious actors. Most of it cannot be repudiated—it's immutable, static data that cannot be changed or revoked by the user. Details like birth dates, mother's maiden names, and places of birth are permanent identifiers that can be repeatedly used to craft convincing phishing emails.

The data are fodder for organizations and nation-states. Companies like Zhenhua, reportedly working for the Chinese government, have been scraping and organizing such data on a massive scale. Zhenhua's operations, exposed in a significant data leak, revealed their global collection efforts, encompassing personal details from individuals across the world [8]. These activities highlight how data stolen in one breach can be aggregated to build comprehensive profiles on individuals.

It doesn't take much imagination to figure out how this data can be used to target someone using social engineering. Even a teenager with a modicum of ingenuity could use these details to manipulate or deceive. As AI systems continue to evolve, they will perform these actions at scale.

Imagine a scenario where an AI-driven attack uses information from prior breaches to enhance its credibility—creating phishing emails that not only appear to be from someone you know but also reference past interactions, making the deception nearly flawless. These attacks could adapt in real-time based on users' recent online actions, utilizing information gleaned from websites visited, people communicated with, or other activities performed using their devices. All of this could be done at scale, across millions of endpoints. This trajectory underscores the urgent need to rethink our approach to preparing users to counter such threats.

1.3 Multimodal Attacks at Scale

Hackers have historically stuck to just one modality—whether it's email, phone, or another channel—to execute their schemes. IRS scammers predominantly use VoIP spoofing, while others rely on email as their weapon of choice. Mastery over a single modality allowed attackers to streamline their efforts, focusing on refining their techniques within that channel to maximize their success rate. It is practical choice in a world where resources and human-expertise is still needed to craft compelling attacks. A classic case in point is the North Korean hackers' incursion into the SWIFT interbanking system, where they deployed a series of meticulously crafted emails—each serving a distinct purpose: gathering intel, authorizing transactions, managing money transfers, and covering their tracks.

But AI, particularly large language models (LLMs), is set to shatter this single-modality approach. LLMs can process and generate text, voice, and even visual content with astonishing accuracy and speed, eliminating the barriers that once made multimodal attacks cumbersome and difficult to execute.

Now, attackers can effortlessly deploy a combination of modalities—such as email, phone calls, and text messages—all tailored and synchronized to create a seamless and convincing narrative. LLMs enable this by automating the creation and coordination of these multimodal attacks, ensuring that each interaction builds upon the previous one to enhance credibility and deception. The result is a more sophisticated and persistent attack strategy that can overwhelm traditional defenses, rendering the old single-modality approach obsolete.

This shift is not just a technical evolution but a strategic one, where the ability to launch multimodal attacks at scale becomes a game-changer in the landscape of cyber threats. Here again, our current security awareness training remains woefully inadequate. Most programs still focus on a single modality—primarily email—leaving users vulnerable to the sophisticated, persistent, and multimodal nature of AI-driven attacks. This isn't merely an evolution of existing threats; it marks a fundamental change in the nature of social engineering.

The future of user-targeted cyber-attacks will be not only multimodal but also hyper-personalized, relentless, and synthetically authentic, making them increasingly difficult to distinguish from genuine interactions. They will not only transform the nature of cyber threats but will also have far-reaching impacts on how we interact with and use the Internet itself.

2 Consequences of AI-Driven Attacks

2.1 The Mafia Code

John Gotti, the notorious head of the Gambino crime family, remains a legendary figure in American Mafia history. At his peak in the 1980s, he was reportedly pulling in over $500 million annually—equivalent to approximately $1.6 billion today—through various criminal enterprises. The FBI had long kept a close watch on him, dedicating agents to surveil him around the clock and installing electronic bugging devices in his "office" in Little Italy. Yet, for years, Gotti managed to evade capture, earning the nickname "Teflon Don."

He had learned to outsmart the technology used by law enforcement. Aware that his offices were bugged, Gotti avoided saying anything incriminating on the phone or inside his office. Instead, he took his associates on long walks through the streets of Little Italy, conducting "business" during these walk-and-talks. This practice persists among many criminal enterprises today, born out of a deep distrust of technology and the pervasive reach of law enforcement.

A lack of trust in internet-based technologies will likely lead to similar outcomes for users. Already, with the rise of incessant phone spoofing, many users–87% of people apparently [5]—no longer answer calls on their phones. Entire generations are abandoning platforms like Facebook due to privacy concerns and the distrust fueled by data scandals. As email, messaging, and other communication methods become unreliable due to deep fakes and synthetic forgeries, people may eventually stop using them entirely. This does not bode well for organizations or society as a whole, where we have come to rely on these modes of communication for efficiency and connectivity.

2.2 AI Pilots and Data Passengers

Han van Meegeren, a Dutch painter, is one of history's most infamous forgers. In the 1930s and 40s, he produced forgeries in the style of Johannes Vermeer and other Dutch masters that sold for enormous sums of money. The forgeries were so convincing that even the leading art experts of the time were deceived. Some of his most famous works were purchased by high-ranking Nazis, including Hermann Göring, who believed he was acquiring a genuine Vermeer.

It wasn't until after World War II, when van Meegeren was arrested and charged with collaborating with the Nazis, that he confessed to the forgeries, claiming he had swindled the Nazis rather than assisted them. Modern forensic techniques, including X-ray analysis and chemical testing, eventually confirmed his claims. These tests revealed that he had painted over older, less valuable canvases and used synthetic resins that did not exist in Vermeer's time, definitively proving the works were forgeries. Today, an army of sophisticated forensic scientists, art conservators, restorers, appraisers, and researchers work with advanced technologies such as lasers and chemical analysis to identify art forgeries. This is likely what deepfakes and synthetic AI fakes will require in the future.

Given the scale of attacks, it is unlikely that the average end-user will be capable of detecting synthetic attacks. We will likely need AI programs built into endpoints and servers that work on detecting deception from other AI programs. AI will become both the perpetrator and the protector. This will lead to an upward cascade of sophistication, where, much like an average museum visitor is incapable of discerning fake art, the only mechanism for detecting deception will be another technology. All of us would become like museum visitors or simply passengers on our devices, using them under the supervision of AI programs that function as pilots, directing our responses.

In this scenario, the balance of power shifts from users making informed decisions to simply following automated directives, much like how modern pilots must rely on their instruments due to the overwhelming complexity of their tasks. End-users would effectively become passengers, surrendering all technical control to AI systems that function as pilots. Security awareness training would become obsolete, fading into irrelevance.

2.3 *Increased Centralization and Mono-Technology Culture*

As AI becomes more pervasive and formidable, CISOs—who currently operate within rigid, binary frameworks of administrative control—will gain unprecedented capabilities to manage endpoints. Given their longstanding view of users as the weakest link in cybersecurity, the advent of AI-driven attacks will only reinforce their rationale for tightening control over user access to networks and devices. This shift will further concentrate power in the hands of IT administrators.

Concentration of power appears to also be inherent to AI's development. AI, by its nature, is resource-intensive, demanding vast computational power, specialized expertise, and massive training datasets. This makes it challenging for smaller organizations to develop AI systems. It fosters increased concentration of AI development and deployment in the hands of a few dominant technology companies. These companies not only possess the resources to build and train advanced AI models but also control the vast datasets necessary to optimize these systems, creating a de facto monopoly over the technology.

The rise of a mono-technology culture is a direct consequence of this. In such a culture, a handful of dominant AI systems will control extensive networks of endpoints, leading to a homogenized technological landscape where diversity and innovation are stifled. Users, stripped of their ability to troubleshoot, innovate, or engage in independent problem-solving, will find themselves increasingly guided—and controlled—by AI systems. This deepens the power imbalance between human operators and the AI "pilots" steering our digital lives, ultimately leading to a more homogenized IT environment, where a few large players dictate the infrastructure and usage of technology across organizations.

The risks of this increased centralization are already evident. Consider the July 2024 CrowdStrike incident, where a poorly coded patch crippled computers, leaving users powerless to revert to a previous, stable state. The patch was auto-installed on millions of Microsoft endpoints, giving users limited control over the process. Because Microsoft is the dominant operating system used at the enterprise level and CrowdStrike provides security management services for the majority of Fortune 500 companies, all were crippled [9]. And due to organizational IT admin rules, users in many organizations had limited control and even less knowledge of how to revert systems to an older state. The recovery process was needlessly prolonged—a scenario likely to become more common as AI-driven centralization tightens its grip.

In a future dominated by AI and centralized systems, security awareness training, which once focused on empowering users to protect themselves, risks becoming obsolete, if it fails to evolve. Users may find themselves in passive roles, with AI making critical decisions while their agency diminishes. The concept of security awareness could soon become a relic—something we practiced back in the early days of computing, before AI changed everything.

3 Solutions Against Obsolescence

As AI-driven cyber threats become more advanced, the static, one-size-fits-all security awareness solutions of today will no longer be sufficient. In this section, we explore innovative security awareness solutions that go beyond conventional methods, focusing on adaptive, real-time solutions that align with the evolving digital environment. Drawing on insights from "*The Weakest Link*" [2], we'll delve into how these approaches can be leveraged to fortify security awareness in the face of an ever-changing threat landscape.

3.1 Adaptive Security Awareness

Driven by the vulnerabilities of the users, the industry has long clung to a one-size-fits-all approach, where products come first, and the user—along with their specific risks and proclivities—comes second. This approach is fundamentally flawed. In The Weakest Link, I argued for replacing this with a cognitive-behavioral risk analysis of users, where solutions are tailored to individuals, much like how the medical field diagnoses and treats patients.

The concept is straightforward and outlined in the book: identify where the user's risk lies. Is it in their thinking patterns, behaviors, reactions, or responses? More precisely, where does the risk manifest—during the attack, in how they cognitively process it, or in the cognitive factors that influence their decisions? A finite set of predictors—ranging from cognitive processing styles to cyber risk beliefs and habits—determines the likelihood of someone falling for a social engineering attack. By employing various penetration tests, we can measure these vulnerabilities in each user. My book also explains how to assess user vulnerability using this approach in a clear, practical manner, and how different types of security awareness methods—from knowledge reinforcement to habit correction—can be applied based on the data.

AI and large language models (LLMs) have the potential to scale this approach, enabling the creation of individualized risk profiles before an incident occurs, followed by AI-driven security training personalized to each user's specific vulnerabilities. Imagine a system that not only identifies a user's unique risks but also tests them in real-time, providing immediate feedback and corrective actions. This goes beyond mere education; it's about continuous, adaptive training that evolves in step with the threat landscape.

3.2 Dynamic Security Policies

Currently, most security policies are binary, lacking the nuance necessary to address the diverse range of user behaviors and risks. These policies typically impose blanket restrictions on access to sites and systems, without considering individual needs or the specific context in which a user operates. I have proposed developing risk-based security policies that leverage individual risk profiles to create more personalized and effective security measures.

With the advent of large language models (LLMs), security policies can be dynamically adjusted based on real-time analysis of user behavior in conjunction with their risk profiles. For example, consider a user traveling outside the office. Based on their cognitive-behavioral risk profile and their current location, they might need access to certain Wi-Fi networks or web pages that would typically be blocked within the organization's network. Another scenario could involve a high-risk user who is granted access to sensitive data only when connected to a secure, monitored network, while a low-risk user might enjoy broader access privileges.

Moreover, these dynamic policies could extend to other security aspects, such as adjusting the strength of authentication requirements based on the user's behavior and location. For instance, a user logging in from an unfamiliar location might be required to undergo additional verification steps, whereas the same user logging in from their usual workspace might experience a more streamlined process. This level of flexibility not only enhances security but also improves the user experience, reducing the friction that often leads to security fatigue.

3.3 Creation of Private Modalities

As AI and LLMs continue to advance, the need for organizations to establish secure, private communication channels has never been more critical. Just as the mafia historically developed clandestine methods to avoid detection, today's organizations must adopt similar strategies to combat the growing threat of synthetically authentic attacks, such as deep fakes.

One promising approach is to move beyond the current two-factor authentication (2FA) model toward a multi-modality verification process. Imagine a scenario where a person's voice is confirmed through a phone call, followed by entering a 2FA code sent to a separate device. This layered security makes it significantly harder for attackers to breach the entire communication chain, adding a robust layer of protection.

In my book, I highlighted the importance of user suspicion in responding to social engineering attacks. Building on this, organizations could implement "suspicion scores" for emails and other forms of communication. These scores would flag messages with a high likelihood of deceit, drawing attention to suspicious elements. They could add flags or markers within emails, pointing out content that is suspicious, so as to allow users to spend time reviewing the email's content for deception. Such systems could complement existing techniques, such as marking external emails, and be seamlessly integrated with AI-driven tools that continuously analyze communication patterns, enhancing detection capabilities.

Additionally, organizations should explore the use of AI-generated personalized encryption keys that adapt dynamically to the context of each communication. By generating unique encryption for every interaction, this approach would make it nearly impossible for attackers to predict or replicate the security measures in place. Leveraging AI in this way not only secures communication channels but also ensures they evolve in tandem with the growing threats posed by LLMs.

4 Conclusion

The rise of large language models (LLMs) marks the beginning of the end for traditional security awareness—a product-centric industry that has long thrived on a superficial sense of security. This has left a dangerous gap, deepened by complacency and a lack of innovation.

As AI and LLMs introduce new, sophisticated threats, the security awareness community must evolve. The old methods are no longer sufficient in a landscape where attacks are increasingly personalized, persistent, and multimodal. However, the same technologies that pose these threats can also be harnessed to protect users. By embracing adaptive security awareness, dynamic security policies, and innovative private communication methods, we can create a more resilient and secure digital environment. It's time for the security awareness industry to break free from the status quo and embrace a future where AI not only challenges us but also serves as a critical safeguard in our digital lives.

References

1. Guardio Labs. (2024, August 10). EchoSpoofing: A massive phishing campaign exploiting Proofpoint's email protection to dispatch spoofed emails. *Guardio*. https://labs.guard.io/echospoofing-a-massive-phishing-campaign-exploiting-proofpoints-email-protection-to-dispatch-3dd6b5417db6
2. Vishwanath, A. (2023). *The weakest link: How to diagnose, detect, and defend users from phishing*. MIT Press. https://mitpress.mit.edu/9780262047494/the-weakest-link/
3. NordVPN. (n.d.). What is neighbor spoofing? *NordVPN*. https://nordvpn.com/blog/what-is-neighbor-spoofing/
4. Better Business Bureau. (n.d.). A new kind of phone scam: Neighbor spoofing. https://www.bbb.org/article/news-releases/16670-a-new-kind-of-phone-scam-neighbor-spoofing
5. Truecaller Insights. (2021). Truecaller insights 2021 U.S. spam & scam report. *Truecaller.*https://www.truecaller.com/blog/truecaller-insights/truecaller-insights-2021-us-spam-scam-report

6. Coyer, C. (2024, August 12). *Background check data of 3 billion stolen in breach, suit says. Bloomberg Law*. https://news.bloomberglaw.com/privacy-and-data-security/background-check-data-of-3-billion-stolen-in-breach-suit-says
7. Vishwanath, A. (2015, June 8). Stopping hacking starts with you. *CNN*. https://www.cnn.com/2015/06/08/opinions/vishwanath-stopping-hacking/index.html
8. Vishwanath, A. (2020, July 10). China data leak points to massive global collection effort. *VOA News*. https://www.voanews.com/a/east-asia-pacific_voa-news-china_china-data-leak-points-massive-global-collection-effort/6196030.html
9. Vishwanath, A. (2024, August). CrowdStrike meltdown: Wake-up call for cybersecurity. *Dark Reading*.https://www.darkreading.com/vulnerabilities-threats/crowdstrike-meltdown-wake-up-call-for-cybersecurity

Social Psychological Barriers to Accurate Risk Assessment in Cyber Security

Nalanda Ray, David Chun, June Van De Graaff, and Emily Balcetis

1 Introduction

Google and Facebook, two of the biggest technology companies in the world, lost over $100 million dollars in total between 2013 and 2015 [1, 2]. Some attacks waged against these titans were, in fact, so convincing and nefarious that these companies continued to succumb to the ploys for years after the initial attack, paying out fraudulent invoices from supposed top suppliers for 2 years until they finally realized that they had been duped [1]. Belgian banking company, Crelan Bank, was cheated out of approximately $75.8 million dollars in 2016 [3]. Valley View Hospital in Colorado saw over 21,000 patient and employee records compromised in 2022 [4]. Each of these cases–and many more like them–have a singular common thread. They arose because of a single employee who engaged with a fraudulent phishing email.

Cybercrime that targets individuals working inside of organizations' networks continues to be one of the greatest global threats [5]. Despite technological advances, the scope of cyber attacks is growing rather than declining. The Federal Bureau of Investigation's Internet Crime Report [6] identified losses from internet crime surpassing $12.5 billion last year. By 2024, predictions indicate that cyber-crime will amount to $9.5 trillion USD [7]. By 2031, Cybersecurity Ventures [8] estimates that the annual financial loss from attacks will surpass $265 billion.

The success of these attacks, importantly, stems not only from technological challenges of protecting infrastructure from attempts to get inside it but from individual users' responses to the bait put out there by hackers. About 91% of all cyber attacks originate with malicious phishing and spear phishing emails directed

N. Ray · D. Chun · J. Van De Graaff · E. Balcetis (✉)
Department of Psychology, New York University, New York, NY, USA
e-mail: emilybalcetis@nyu.edu

Q. Zhu et al. (eds.), *Foundations of Cyber Deception*, Advances in Information Security 90, https://doi.org/10.1007/978-3-031-93867-2_5

at individuals inside networks [9], surmounting to roughly 3.4 billion scam emails distributed daily [10]. Spear phishing emails are particularly damaging because of their narrowly targeted intentions, focusing personalized appeals on deceptive tactics to extract sensitive information from a single individual or group within a larger organization [11]. In fact, the Federal Bureau of Investigation's Internet Crime Report [6] identified phishing as the top internet crime type in terms of the number of complaints received.

Moreover, these attempts to coerce individuals are successful. In fact, a 2014 IBM report found that 95% of attacks are caused by human error [12]—a trend that continues [13]. Investigative probes inside infected companies found that it is often employees who click on fraudulent email links or download malicious email attachments that ultimately result in successful cyber breaches [13]. Proofpoint, a leading cybersecurity protection firm, surveyed 7500 end users and found that of the 71% engaged with unknown links and disclosed private credentials with unfamiliar sources [14]. Likewise, MGM Resorts International experienced a massive data breach in 2023 that stemmed from a single fake reservation [15]. Attackers reserved a room, and then sent a series of messages about the urgency of their request and some personal information designed to evoke pity. A hotel worker responded to these emails by clicking a link that allowed criminals to gain entry into networked records and steal hotel and client profiles, resulting in a $100 million theft. Director of Technology Programs for Norwich University, Dr. Henry Collier, and his colleagues go so far as to state that humans are the weakest link in information security sectors [16].

In this chapter, we dive into the psychological conditions of human users that allow the scope of cyber attacks to, in fact, be so massive. While cybersecurity companies implement approaches to bring awareness to organizations about their unique and individualized vulnerabilities, we discuss the human psychology that may undermine the efficacy of this approach. We discuss security pentests, their intended purpose, and the holes in their efficacy given individual users' psychology. Specifically, we discuss individuals' psychological reactions to the threat posed by cyber crime including their perceived illusion of invulnerability. We discuss cognitive biases including self-enhancement and the illusion of invulnerability that increase the effectiveness of attackers' targeted attempts to coerce individuals into taking the bait including base rate neglect. Finally, we also probe the sociocultural orientations that exaggerate and perhaps could mitigate the impact of cyber threats.

2 Penetration Testing as a Protection Against Cyber Crime

To combat the rising threat of phishing attacks, companies rely on breach tests—known in the cyber community as penetration (or pen) testing. They may cost anywhere between $2500 to $50,000, a pricing structure determined by factors including timeline, a pentester's expertise, or the type of pentest deployed [17]. Pentesting is estimated to become a $5 billion industry by 2031 [18]. Though a large figure, it pales in comparison to the cost of a successful attack. Equifax, one of America's most prominent consumer credit reporting companies, suffered a massive cyber attack in 2017 [19]. Felonious cyberattackers exfiltrated social security numbers, addresses, and other personally identifying records of approximately 143 million customers. Two years post-breach, Equifax reported having spent $1.4 billion on cleanup including on technological advances to improve infrastructure and data security. Moody's though still downgraded the company's financial ratings because of anticipated continued costs, including the record-breaking settlement with the Federal Trade Commission and a class action lawsuit which amounts to at least $1.38 billion to resolve consumer claims [20].

Cybersecurity companies engage pentests by deploying skilled cyber-technicians to simulate an attack within an organization [21]. They employ ethical hackers to find and exploit vulnerabilities in a computer system [22]. This approach bears similarities to a bank hiring someone to dress as a burglar to try to break into their building and gain access to the vault. If the burglar succeeds and gets into the bank or the vault, the bank will gain valuable information on how they need to tighten their security measures.

The implementation of pentests may be categorized into four stages [23]. It starts with a phase of reconnaissance, during which an ethical hacker spends time gathering information that they will use to plan their simulated attack [24]. They then identify system vulnerabilities that may be exploited, which could range from employee-level to company-level weak spots. At this stage, they may also test how a system's present cybersecurity measures respond to simulated attacks, which could look like sending a dubious email to the system's firewall and observing its reaction. To this extent, some ethical hackers, depending on the purpose and style of pentesting, may even choose to carry out a physical pentest by disguising themselves as delivery people to gain physical access to a building to deploy hardware or software internally to a network [25].

In the next phases, ethical hackers devise techniques to then override any security measures that are in place during their simulated cyber attack. This helps them gain and maintain access to the target system, which requires a broad set of tools and specialized hardware, including credential-cracking tools, vulnerability scanners, and port scanners [26]. They might also plug inconspicuous boxes into a computer to garner remote access to that network.

Ethical hackers also engage in social engineering tools [26, 27]. Hackers try to coax individuals on the inside of networks into providing sensitive information. In general, an attacker sends an email to a victim which appears to come from someone in the victim's contact list. In these simulated phishing scams, an attacker baits users online with links that claim to be downloads of popular movies or software, but in reality, these downloads contain a malicious script that launches after someone clicks on the link.

In the following stages, hackers work to exfiltrate data. The tester identifies things like points of access and determines how private data and communication channels are affected. They use this insight for vulnerability chaining [24], exploiting one vulnerability to the next one, thereby inserting themselves deeper into the system's cyber network. They then work to restore the network configurations to their pre-testing state [28] before reporting of test results. This information can then be used to implement security upgrades. Pentesting is a proactive and preventative measure to assess potential security weaknesses.

3 Human Vulnerabilities in Pentesting

Pentests produce reports of the identified security weaknesses in a company's cyber structure along with suggested improvements to remedy such weaknesses. One crucial piece of information that pentesting returns to companies is the percentage of individuals within an organization who succumbed to the simulated phishing attack. These are base rates on the true prevalence of specific behaviors. In turn, this information is shared with executives, security teams, and sometimes individuals within the organizations themselves with the aim of mitigating risk.

In particular, companies may share back the base rates with employees to, in part, instill fear, increase engagement with the content, and most importantly increase employees' awareness about their own susceptibility to phishing attacks [29]. For example, Proofpoint uses prevalence rates to advertise their services. They state that 71% of their survey respondents reportedly engaged in risky cyber action [14], and Terranova Security reports that over two-thirds of those who click on a phishing link are likely to disclose private information on a phishing website [30]. Lawfare, a multimedia publication that specializes in national security issues holds that such measures of information sharing are crucial to increasing situational awareness [31]. Information sharing is key to enhancing threat detection abilities and defense measures.

However, on their own, these cyber security measures, including disseminating base rates gathered from pentests, to employees and other insiders in an organization, will not increase security resilience [32]. This is in part because of basic fallacies in human cognition. In what follows, we review human cognitive biases that contribute to the ineffectiveness of this preventative measure.

4 Base Rate Neglect

Companies spend extensive time, effort, and expense in trying to gather information about responses to phishing attacks, and may share back the prevalence rates with organizations' leadership teams. Those teams might themselves share the prevalence rates with members of the firm, employees, or other company insiders in order to increase awareness and curtail risky behavior. However, a common human cognitive bias may undermine the utility of such efforts. Sharing back base rate statistics about the prevalence of succumbing to simulated attacks is ineffective at mitigating risk because of base rate neglect. People give less weight to objective, statistical information, in favor of anecdotal accounts. People place less value on relevant statistical information including prior probabilities of events in favor of case-specific information including personal stories or case histories [33–36]. In finance, for instance, evidence suggests investors pour heavily into a particular stock based on anecdotal news they receive, and ignore statistics relevant to base rates regarding the current market [37]. In general, prefer vivid, rich accounts even if it is a less accurate source of information relative to data-driven, distributional information describing prevalence rates.

Such disregard for distributional information describing the prevalence of specific outcomes occurs to an even stronger degree when forecasting one's own future outcomes. When predicting one's own behavior, people seem to rely on specific self-knowledge they possess, leading them to disregard population base rates that might otherwise enhance the accuracy of their predictions [38, 39]. Even when individuals can accurately articulate the true likelihood of an outcome occurring, and can incorporate that information into projections about others' behaviors suggesting they understand its utility in this task, they do not do so when forecasting their own [40].

In the context of cybersecurity, people place relatively less weight on diagnostic base rate information when forecasting their own compared to others' likelihood of succumbing to a phishing attack. To demonstrate this directly, we presented individuals within an organization emails designed to look like phishing scams that are known to be effective at luring individuals into providing sensitive information or downloading content that could prove malicious. For instance, we presented emails that looked to originate from Bank of America and included requests for individuals to click a link to determine if their account had been compromised. Participants indicated the likelihood that they, or someone from their institution, would do as requested. Importantly, as they made these forecasts, they had access to true and accurate information describing the percentage of people from inside a relevant peer institution who had responded as the email requested, by for instance, clicking on the link sent by the bank. Across four studies and over 1300 participants, we found that the predictive ability of base rates was two to three times lower when forecasting one's own likelihood of victimization compared to others' [41]. Individuals did not use the base rate information to inform their personal predictions to nearly the same degree that they could and did use it when estimating others' risk profiles. While base rate neglect is a common cognitive error, it is particularly deleterious to the accurate assessment of one's own personal risk. Cybersecurity companies' attempts to mitigate risk by presenting distributional information from pentests may prove more futile than anticipated.

5 Illusion of Invulnerability

People maintain an illusory and erroneous belief that they are invulnerable to threat [42] because they misuse relevant base rate information in cognitive processing, but also because they are motivated to maintain such inflated positive beliefs. People are biased towards believing that their futures will be better off than could possibly be true [43]. For example, about 90% of U.S. adults believe they would never fall for a cyber scam, but 27% do every year [44]. Moreover, such biases are common. On average, 80% of the general public displays this form of self-enhancement [45]. People want to believe that good things are more likely to happen to them than to other people [46]; as a result, they enhance the likelihood they will experience positive outcomes.

They also believe themselves to be relatively less vulnerable to future negative life events than are other people [47]. For example, they tend to underestimate their own likelihood of experiencing negative outcomes like falling prey to phishing emails [41, 48]. American university students believed their chances of being stalked or harassed online, having passwords or credit card information stolen, or having compromised personal information sold were much lower than others' chances [49]. They believe that they are far less likely to click on a malicious cyber link than another person [41, 50]. In addition, Generation Z Americans believe that older generations are more susceptible to scams, when in reality, their own generation has fallen victim to them more than any other generation [51]. But Gen Zers are not alone. In fact, on average, 80% of the general public holds these and other types of self-enhancing beliefs [45].

Such self-enhancement is more common in scenarios that seem preventable by individual action, scenarios in which the hazard is infrequent, and in scenarios that people have not previously experienced [52]. These factors in fact account for 57% of the variance in the amount of unrealistic optimism and self-enhancement elicited [52]. Importantly, these are all features of the cyber context.

Self-enhancing beliefs are difficult to undo, as the tendency to underestimate personal risk occurs despite evidence that contradicts the positive illusion. Even when presented with accurate and relevant information that informs on self-assessments of risk, people update their forecasts about their future less in response to negative information about the future than positive information [45]. In fact, such resistance to integrating negative information into forecasts may, in fact, have contributed to the 2008 stock market crash. Financial analysts, government officials, banks, and other actors all shared the unrealistic expectation that the market would continue growing, despite mountains of evidence to the contrary [53].

Self-enhancing beliefs are not easily undone or updated by base rate information either. Illusions of invulnerability arise in the cybersecurity space, for example, despite base rate information about the prevalence of victimization because people find little value in such diagnostic information [41]. In our own research, we used covert eye-tracking and found that people rarely even looked at base rate information when they were considering the likelihood they would fall prey to attempts at cyber exploitation [41]. When predicting others' future risk, they looked 14% more frequently at base rates than when predicting their own risk, though the information was equally relevant and diagnostic in both cases.

Even more alarming is that people do not recognize that they are ignoring base rates when forecasting their own actions and forming self-enhancing conclusions about their risk profile. There were no correlations between self-assessments of eye gaze patterns and actual eye gaze patterns when thinking about one's own actions [41]. People fail to realize that they were weighting the diagnostic value of base rates differently when the target of risk assessment shifted. They were poorer at diagnosing their own risk profile than they were others' and they did not even realize the source of such accuracy differences.

Self-enhancement bias does not simply impact one's outlook on life. It also impacts consequential behaviors. If people underestimate their risk, they may fail to take proper precautions to protect themselves against harm. Self-enhancing beliefs increase people's actual vulnerability to a threat because it discourages them from taking protective measures [47]. People who underestimate the odds they will develop lung cancer in the future or that they are unlikely to get into a car accident are more likely to engage in harmful behaviors such as smoking or refraining from wearing a seatbelt [45]. However, when people feel more susceptible to negative life events, they are more likely to engage in preventative measures [54]. The problem is that people do not believe that they in fact are susceptible to attack, at least not to the degree that they may actually be, when it comes to cybersecurity.

6 Human Informed Technology Solutions to Threat Assessment

CEOs or CISOs typically respond to data breaches by enhancing their security technology; however, they tend to neglect the role their employees played in generating that vulnerability in the first place [55]. We believe technological solutions to technical problems will not solve cyber security challenges because of individuals' cognitive biases. Instead, we advise investing in the development of security-assistive technologies. Such technologies can be trained to monitor individuals' behaviors, scan the content of what they are engaging with online, and present solutions to forewarn users of potential harm. This technological solution learns to deploy in response to, and with, the goal of serving alongside human experience. Specifically, such solutions can deter and adaptively correct sources of user error resulting from the innate cognitive vulnerabilities of individual thinking. For example, visual aids (e.g., warning flags, educational messages, etc.) that pop up over browser tabs or within computer software can interact with and manipulate human cognition and behavior.

We have applied our thinking of security-assistive technologies with the goal of addressing the lack of regard individuals tend to engage in when assessing cyber security threats. As we found [41], people orient visual attention disproportionality across sources of information that could inform on the propensity for risk when predicting their own future susceptibility. This could happen as well when reading emails and determining whether and how to engage with them. While nefarious emails sent as hacking attempts do often contain clues to their duplicitous nature like misspellings, emotional demands, and suspicious reply addresses, people may not orient visual attention to these features that could signal the potentiality for harm. But what if they did? Would their decisions about whether to click, download, or respond to the email shift in ways that better protect themselves and the networks they are embedded in change for the better?

Using covert eye-tracking, we monitored users' eye movements while they reviewed scam emails, and leveraged that behavior to generate a human-informed technological solution [56]. Specifically, we recorded the user's eye-gaze locations and pupil sizes, as an index of cognitive engagement. We identified areas of interest within the emails, including subject titles, hyperlinks, attachments, and other components, that could signal that this email presents a threat.

Next, we developed adaptive learning algorithms to generate visual aids as feedback and signals aimed at bringing awareness to the threat this email could pose, that users may not have had without such aids. We created an adaptive technology called ADVERT to counteract visual attentional biases and improve the human recognition of phishing attacks. In probing this process, we found that visual aids can engage attention, towards diagnostic contents, and improve the accuracy of phishing recognition from 74.6% to a minimum of 86% and even at rates exceeding 90%. ADVERT, as one example of human-informed technological solutions to security challenges, enables an adaptive visual-aid generation to guide and sustain the users' attention to the right content of an email and consequently makes users less likely to fall victim to phishing.

7 Social Context Effects in Base Rate Neglect

Sharing back base rate information gathered from pentests as a means to increase awareness of cyber risk profiles may be less effective in some social contexts and more effective in others. Specifically, base rate neglect may be more common in individualist contexts relative to collectivist ones. For example, the inefficiencies of gathering and sharing back base rates gathered through pentesting may be particularly exaggerated in the United States and other individualistic countries. Such countries emphasize autonomy, personal achievements and individual rights, prioritization of one's own needs, and emotional independence [57, 58]. Similarly, in loose cultures, individuals are permitted to engage in atypical behaviors that do not align with standard, common actions and practices without serious repercussions [59, 60]. Loose cultures do not require close monitoring of other members' behaviors, nor do they require awareness of social norms [61]. For instance, schools in the United States select class valedictorians, rewarding one single person for their outstanding academic achievements relative to those of peers. In American workspaces, meritocratic values motivate individuals' proactive, competitive drive. Sayings like "early bird that gets the worm" encourage top, peak, and first performance. Companies commonly identify an "Employee of the Month." These practices of American individualism prioritize individual-level goals ahead of team ones [62].

In contrast, collectivist cultures emphasize interdependence, group achievements, and prioritization of social needs that best serve the group [57, 58]. Similarly, in tight cultures, individuals are discouraged through social mechanisms to engage in non-normative practices [59, 60]. Similarly, tight cultures require individuals within them to follow societal rules and regulations [63]. Social norms are explicit and are strictly enforced [61]. Consequently, tight cultures require individuals to pay attention to their social environment and the activities of others in their social environment [64].

These social contexts shift cognitive processing styles. People in individualist, loose social contexts hold more analytical, context-independent cognitive processing styles, where focus is directed on singular targets rather than surroundings, on individual people rather than the social contexts they are embedded in [65]. Individualist cultures discourage directing attention toward the actions and thoughts of others [66]. In contrast, collectivist cultures promote a holistic, context-dependent processing style that leads to interdependent thinking [67]. Collectivists attend to targets and the environments in which they are embedded [68, 69].

All of these features of individualistic cultures, particularly juxtaposed against collectivist cultures, may combine to contribute to even greater levels of base rate neglect. Base rates reflect information about larger social contexts individuals are embedded in, information again that individualistic cultures find less value in. Such fundamental differences in cognitive processing among members of these two cultural orientations may lead to lower levels of base rate base neglect in collectivist cultures. Indeed, American participants underestimated the probability of events given base rate information significantly more than did Chinese participants ([70], Study 1). Moreover, given differences in the focus on awareness of social norms, tight and loose cultural values may differentially affect the salience of base rate information. People embedded in tight cultures may find base information more salient in decision-making than people embedded in loose cultures. Such differences in base rate saliency can shift the prevalence of base rate neglect. Indeed, when base rates are more relevant or more salient, base rate neglect is attenuated or even eliminated [70, 71]. While research has not directly tested the psychological impact of sharing pentest prevalence results on individuals' awareness of cyber threats, or the accuracy of their cyber risk assessments, it is possible that individualistic social contexts mitigate the efficacy of this security tactic, while collectivist social contexts might increase it.

8 Shifting Organizational Values to Reduce Base Rate Neglect

Organizations, institutions, and companies are capable of creating their own subcultures that preserve the basic tenets of tight collectivism, which may hold implications for cybersecurity efforts. Molding organizational values may shape individuals' cognitive styles and shift the magnitude of base rate neglect when predicting personal cyber risk.

In fact, when individuals within an organization find their cognitions better aligned with each other, cyber security improves. Proofpoint [14] stated in their annual report that one of the reasons that users expose themselves to risky behavior online is the lack of agreement on accountability and responsibility. The majority of respondents (52%) were uncertain about whether they held any personal responsibility for cybersecurity in their workplace and 7% believed themselves to hold no responsibility. In contrast, 85% of security professionals assert that employees already know that they are responsible for these security measures. In other words, there is a disconnect between what information security officers think individuals embedded in networks believe to be their role in protecting infrastructure security and what those individuals themselves believe. This discrepancy highlights a discrepant cognitions and lack of mutual accountability and shared responsibility, with very few individuals seeing how their behaviors connect to the safety of the bigger institution within which they are embedded.

Institutions may benefit from shifting towards a more tight, collectivist value system if they wish to increase employees' sense of shared responsibility. It is possible for institutional values to change even within a country that does not typically promote that value system strongly. Organizations can incorporate interdependent themes from linguistic styles; they can use "we" or "us", instead of "I" and "me" in their memos, company newsletters, and business templates [29]. These linguistic cues increase interdependent cognitions and promote an emphasis on group identities, which influence subsequent judgment [72].

Companies can create a teamwork culture, or an organizational environment characterized by shared beliefs that success hinges upon collaboration and cooperation. Companies can encourage consensus decision-making models whereby each team member feels responsible for the collective success of the organization [73]. Moreover, they can increase employees' sense of mutual accountability and amenability which increases receptiveness to organizational norms. Gallup, a multinational analytics company, reported [74] that 26% of employees receive feedback less than once annually, while less than one-half of the employees surveyed felt that their manager held them accountable for their goals in the workplace. To increase perceived accountability, leaders need to connect with their employees [75]. Replace mandatory and mundane quarterly check-in meetings with discussions about asking employees what they learned this month or to report on what they felt most proud of accomplishing. Leaders can encourage conversations about the milestones that employees meet.

Taken together, fostering tighter, collectivist organizational cultures by encouraging individuals to reflect on shared experiences within a larger group may amplify the perceived significance of base rate information related to that group, especially when it comes to likelihood judgments of oneself versus others in the context of threat assessment to cyber attacks. Castaneda and Ramírez [76] suggest that collective values such as having an interest in what relevant others do are crucial for ensuring knowledge-sharing and the longevity of organizations.

9 Conclusion

The solution to cybersecurity threats cannot lie in only technological solutions, as human cognition is complicit in producing human behavior, including behavioral responses to cyber threats. To mitigate risk, technology and psychology need to partner together. Psychological states serve as barriers to accurate risk assessment as people consider the threat posed by cyber attackers. Pentesting as an approach to cybersecurity, as a means to bringing awareness about individualized vulnerabilities, likely fails to increase how well-calibrated individual risk assessment is against the actual threat posed because of several cognitive challenges individuals experience. People are motivated to maintain the belief that they are invulnerable to risk. Attempts to correct that misperception often involve sharing back prevalence rates of risk to individuals within institutions. However, sharing back such prevalence rates may lack efficacy because of basic human cognitive tendencies to underweight diagnostic, normative, and distributional information, particularly when assessing personal risk. While these biases may emerge to a stronger degree in the United States and other loose, individualistic countries, it is possible for institutions to shape the values that undergird employees' cognitions, beliefs, and behaviors. Moreover, the development of adaptive technology to forewarn individuals of cyber risk may shift what information they consider, weigh, and use when deciding how to respond to potentially malicious attempts to breach security. Addressing cyber threats must integrate both technological and psychological solutions.

Acknowledgements This work has been supported by a grant from the National Science Foundation (BCS 2122060) awarded to Balcetis.

References

1. Huddleston, T. (2019, March 27). *How this scammer used phishing emails to steal over $100 million from Google and facebook*. CNBC. https://www.cnbc.com/2019/03/27/phishing-email-scam-stole-100-million-from-facebook-and-google.html
2. Tessian. (2023, February 7). *15 examples of real social engineering attacks - updated 2023*. https://www.tessian.com/blog/examples-of-social-engineering-attacks/
3. Zorz, Z. (2016, January 26). *Belgian bank Crelan loses €70 million to Bec Scammers*. Help Net Security. https://www.helpnetsecurity.com/2016/01/26/belgian-bank-crelan-loses-e70-million-to-bec-scammers/
4. Brad. (2023, January 4). *Notable phishing attacks of 2022*. PhishProtection.com. https://www.phishprotection.com/phishing-awareness/notable-phishing-attacks-2022
5. Gravrock, E. von. (2019, March 4). *Here are the biggest cybercrime trends of 2019*. World Economic Forum. https://www.weforum.org/agenda/2019/03/here-are-the-biggest-cybercrime-trends-of-2019/
6. Federal Bureau of Investigation. (2023). (rep.). *Internet Crime Report 2023*.
7. Cybersecurity Ventures. (2023b, October 25). *Cybercrime to cost the world $9.5 trillion USD annually in 2024*. Cybercrime Magazine. https://cybersecurityventures.com/cybercrime-to-cost-the-world-9-trillion-annually-in-2024/

8. Cybersecurity Ventures. (2023c, July 07). *Global Ransomware Damage Costs Predicted To Exceed $265 Billion By 2031*. Cybercrime Magazine. https://cybersecurityventures.com/global-ransomware-damage-costs-predicted-to-reach-250-billion-usd-by-2031/
9. Deloitte. (2020, January 09). 91% of all cyber attacks begin with a phishing email to an unexpected victim. *Deloitte*. Retrieved from https://www2.deloitte.com/my/en/pages/risk/articles/91-percent-of-all-cyber-attacks-begin-with-a-phishing-email-to-an-unexpected-victim.html.
10. Palatty, N. J. (2023, December 22). *81 phishing attack statistics 2024: The ultimate insight*. Astra Security Blog. https://www.getastra.com/blog/security-audit/phishing-attack-statistics/
11. IBM. (n.d.-b). What is spear phishing? https://www.ibm.com/topics/spear-phishing
12. IBM Global Technology Services. (2014). (rep.). *IBM Security Services 2014 Cyber Security Intelligence Index*. Retrieved from https://i.crn.com/sites/default/files/ckfinderimages/userfiles/images/crn/custom/IBMSecurityServices2014.PDF.
13. Verizon. (2023). (rep.). *2023 Data Breach Investigations Report*.
14. Proofpoint. (2024). (rep.). *2024 State of the Phish*.
15. Positive Technologies. (2024, February 20). *Trends in phishing attacks on organizations in 2022–2023*. ptsecurity.com. https://www.ptsecurity.com/ww-en/analytics/trends-in-phishing-attacks-on-organizations-in-2022-2023/
16. Collier, H., Morton, C., Alharthi, D., & Kleiner, J. (2023). Cultural influences on information security. *University of Colorado Colorado Springs*.
17. Keshri, A. (2024, February 23). *How much does a penetration testing cost on average?*. Astra Security Blog. https://www.getastra.com/blog/security-audit/penetration-testing-cost/
18. Cybersecurity Ventures. (2023a, August 14). *Global penetration testing market to exceed $5 billion USD annually by 2031*. Cybercrime Magazine. https://cybersecurityventures.com/global-penetration-testing-market-to-exceed-5-billion-usd-annually-by-2031/
19. Odom, C. (2023, July 06). *Penetration testing unveiled: Real-World Case Studies and lessons learned*. Emagined Security. https://www.emagined.com/blog/penetration-testing-unveiled-real-world-case-studies-and-lessons-learned
20. Fruhlinger, J. (2020, February 12). *Equifax Data Breach FAQ: What happened, who was affected, what was the impact?*. CSO Online. https://www.csoonline.com/article/567833/equifax-data-breach-faq-what-happened-who-was-affected-what-was-the-impact.html
21. Alhamed, M., & Rahman, M. H. (2023). A Systematic Literature Review on Penetration Testing in Networks: Future Research Directions. *Applied Sciences*, *13*(12), 6986.
22. Shinde, P. S., & Ardhapurkar, S. B. (2016). Cyber security analysis using Vulnerability Assessment and penetration testing. *2016 World Conference on Futuristic Trends in Research and Innovation for Social Welfare (Startup Conclave)*, 1–5. https://doi.org/10.1109/startup.2016.7583912
23. Shah, S., & Mehtre, B. M. (2014). An overview of vulnerability assessment and penetration testing techniques. *Journal of Computer Virology and Hacking Techniques*, *11*(1), 27–49. https://doi.org/10.1007/s11416-014-0231-x
24. IBM. (n.d.-a).What is penetration testing? https://www.ibm.com/topics/penetration-testing
25. ISACA. (2023, September 5). *Physical penetration testing: The most overlooked aspect of security*. https://www.isaca.org/resources/white-papers/2023/physical-penetration-testing
26. Yasar, K. (2022). *What is penetration testing?: Definition from TechTarget*. TechTarget. https://www.techtarget.com/searchsecurity/definition/penetration-testing
27. Allen, J. (2019, November 10). *Social engineering penetration testing: Attacks, methods, & steps*. PurpleSec. https://purplesec.us/social-engineering-penetration-testing/
28. Mitnick Security. (2023, September 12). *The 4 phases of penetration testing*. Mitnick Security Consulting. https://www.mitnicksecurity.com/blog/phases-of-penetration-testing
29. Weiss, A., & Balcetis, E. (2022). Sociocultural Orientation and Perceived Utility of Base Rates in Self and Social Judgments of Cyber Risk. *Current Research in Psychology and Behavioral Science (CRPBS)*, *3*(5), 1–6. https://doi.org/10.54026/crpbs/1059
30. Jones, C. (2022, Nov. 24). *Theory, practice and application: Tackling phishing in three steps*. Expert Insights. https://expertinsights.com/insights/theory-practice-and-application-tackling-phishing-in-three-steps/

31. Turetsky, D., Nussbaum, B., & Tatar, U. (2020, July 15). *Cybersecurity Information Sharing Success Stories*. Lawfare. https://www.lawfaremedia.org/article/cybersecurity-information-sharing-success-stories
32. Sharma, T., & Bashir, M. (2020). An analysis of phishing emails and how the human vulnerabilities are exploited. *Advances in Intelligent Systems and Computing*, 49–55. https://doi.org/10.1007/978-3-030-52581-1_7
33. Bar-Hillel, M. (1980). The base rate fallacy in probability judgments. *Acta Psychologica*, *44*(3), 211–233. https://doi.org/10.1016/0001-6918(80)90046-3
34. Epley, N., & Dunning, D. (2000). Feeling "holier than thou": are self-serving assessments produced by errors in self-or social prediction?. *Journal of personality and social psychology*, *79*(6), 861.
35. Pronin, E. (2008). How we see ourselves and how we see others. *Science*, *320*(5880), 1177–1180. https://doi.org/10.1126/science.1154199
36. Pronin, E., Gilovich, T., & Ross, L. (2004). Objectivity in the eye of the beholder: Divergent perceptions of bias in self versus others. *Psychological Review*, *111*(3), 781–799. https://doi.org/10.1037/0033-295x.111.3.781
37. Cuofano, G. (2024, February 24). *What is base rate fallacy and why it matters in business*. FourWeekMBA. https://fourweekmba.com/base rate-fallacy/
38. Balcetis, E., & Dunning, D. (2013). Considering the situation: Why people are better social psychologists than self-psychologists. *Self and Identity, 12,* 1-15.
39. Epley, N., & Dunning, D. (2006). The mixed blessings of self-knowledge in behavioral prediction: Enhanced discrimination but exacerbated bias. *Personality and Social Psychology Bulletin*, *32*(5), 641-655.
40. Balcetis, E., Dunning, D., & Miller, R. L. (2008). Do collectivists know themselves better than individualists? Cross-cultural studies of the holier than thou phenomenon. *Journal of Personality and Social Psychology, 95*(6), 1252–1267. https://doi.org/10.1037/a0013195
41. Cox, E. B., Zhu, Q., & Balcetis, E. (2020). Stuck on a phishing lure: differential use of base rates in self and social judgments of susceptibility to cyber risk. *Comprehensive Results in Social Psychology, 4*(1), 25–52. https://doi.org/10.1080/23743603.2020.1756240
42. Perloff, L. S. (1987). Social comparison and illusions of invulnerability to negative life events. In *Coping with negative life events: Clinical and social psychological perspectives* (pp. 217-242). Boston, MA: Springer US.
43. Shepperd, J. A., Klein, W. M., Waters, E. A., & Weinstein, N. D. (2013). Taking stock of unrealistic optimism. *Perspectives on Psychological Science, 8*(4), 395–411.
44. Citi. (2023, November 30). *Citi Survey finds overconfidence may leave Americans exposed to financial scams*. Citi. https://www.citigroup.com/global/news/press-release/2023/citi-survey-finds-overconfidence-may-leave-americans-exposed-to-financial-scams
45. Sharot, T. (2011). The optimism bias. *Current biology*, *21*(23), R941-R945.
46. Balcetis, E., & Dunning, D. A. (2008). A mile in moccasins: How situational experience diminishes dispositionism in social inference. *Personality & Social Psychology Bulletin, 34*(1), 102–114. https://doi.org/10.1177/0146167207309201
47. Perloff, L. S. (1983). Perceptions of vulnerability to victimization. *Journal of Social Issues*, *39*(2), 41-61.
48. Perloff, L. S., & Fetzer, B. K. (1986). Self-other judgments and perceived vulnerability to victimization. *Journal of Personality and Social Psychology*, *50*(3), 502–510. https://doi.org/10.1037/0022-3514.50.3.502
49. Campbell, J., Greenauer, N., Macaluso, K., & End, C. (2007). Unrealistic optimism in internet events. *Computers in human behavior*, *23*(3), 1273-1284.
50. Balcetis, E. (2009). Claiming a moral minority, saccades help create a biased majority: Tracking eye movements to base rates in social predictions. *Journal of Experimental Social Psychology*, *45*(4), 970-973.
51. Steinbach, M. (2024, February 9). *Americans think their older loved ones are more vulnerable to scammers–but Gen Zers report having fallen for scams more than any other generation*. Fortune. https://fortune.com/2024/02/09/americans-vulnerable-scammers-gen-z-scams-generation-personal-finance/

52. Weinstein, N. D. (1987). Unrealistic optimism about susceptibility to health problems: Conclusions from a community-wide sample. *Journal of behavioral medicine, 10*(5), 481–500.
53. Shefrin, H. (2009). Ending the management illusion: preventing another financial crisis. *Ivey Business Journal, 73*(1), 7.
54. Haefner, D. P., & Kirscht, J. P. (1970). Motivational and behavioral effects of modifying health beliefs. *Public Health Reports, 85*(6), 478–484. https://doi.org/10.2307/4593885
55. Alnifie, K. M., & Kim, C. (2023). Appraising the manifestation of optimism bias and its impact on human perception of Cyber Security: A Meta Analysis. *Journal of Information Security, 14*(02), 93–110. https://doi.org/10.4236/jis.2023.142007
56. Huang, L., Jia, S., Balcetis, E., & Zhu, Q. (2022). Advert: an adaptive and data-driven attention enhancement mechanism for phishing prevention. *IEEE Transactions on Information Forensics and Security, 17*, 2585-2597.
57. Gouveia, V. V., & Ros, M. (2000). Hofstede and Schwartz s models for classifying individualism at the cultural level: their relation to macro-social and macro-economic variables. *Psicothema, 12*(Su1), 25-33.
58. Hofstede, G. (1984). Culture's consequences: International differences in work-related values. Beverly Hills, CA: Sage Publications
59. Gelfand, M. J., Raver, J. L., Nishii, L., Leslie, L. M., Lun, J., Lim, B. C., Duan, L., Almaliach, A., Ang, S., Arnadottir, J., Aycan, Z., Boehnke, K., Boski, P., Cabecinhas, R., Chan, D., Chhokar, J., D'Amato, A., Subirats Ferrer, M., Fischlmayr, I. C., ... Yamaguchi, S. (2011). Differences between tight and loose cultures: A 33-nation study. *Science, 332*(6033), 1100–1104. https://doi.org/10.1126/science.1197754
60. Price, R. H., & Bouffard, D. L. (1974). Behavioral appropriateness and situational constraint as dimensions of social behavior. *Journal of Personality and Social Psychology, 30*(4), 579–586. https://doi.org/10.1037/h0037037
61. Carpenter, S. (2000). Effects of cultural tightness and collectivism on self-concept and causal attributions. *Cross-cultural research, 34*(1), 38-56.
62. Alikhani, A. (2019, July 1). Is American individualism hurting our teams at work? Medium. https://medium.com/hackernoon/is-american-individualism-hurting-our-teams-at-work-cdad9c591577
63. Aktas, M., Gelfand, M. J., & Hanges, P. J. (2016). Cultural tightness–looseness and perceptions of effective leadership. *Journal of Cross-Cultural Psychology, 47*(2), 294–309. https://doi.org/10.1177/0022022115606802
64. Baldwin, M., & Mussweiler, T. (2018). The culture of social comparison. *Proceedings of the National Academy of Sciences, 115*(39). https://doi.org/10.1073/pnas.1721555115
65. Kitayama, S., Karasawa, M., Grossmann, I., Na, J., Varnum, M. E. W., & Nisbett, R. (2019). East-West differences in cognitive style and social orientation: Are they real? PsyArXiv. https://doi.org/10.31234/osf.io/c57ep
66. Kitayama, S., Markus, H. R., Matsumoto, H., & Norasakkunkit, V. (1997). Individual and collective processes in the construction of the self: Self-enhancement in the United States and self-criticism in Japan. *Journal of Personality and Social Psychology, 72*(6), 1245–1267. https://doi.org/10.1037/0022-3514.72.6.1245
67. Markus, H. R., & Kitayama, S. (1991a). Culture and the self: Implications for cognition, emotion, and motivation. *Psychological Review, 98*(2), 224–253. https://doi.org/10.1037/0033-295X.98.2.224
68. Markus, H.R., Kitayama, S. (1991b). Cultural variation in the self-concept. In J. Strauss, & G. R. Goethals (Eds.), *The self: Interdisciplinary approaches* (pp. 18–48). Springer. https://doi.org/10.1007/978-1-4684-8264-5_2
69. Verplanken, B., Trafimow, D., Khusid, I. K., Holland, R. W., & Steentjes, G. M. (2009). Different selves, different values: Effects of self-construals on value activation and use. *European Journal of Social Psychology, 39*(6), 909–919. https://doi.org/10.1002/ejsp.587
70. Wu, S., & Emery, C. (2021). American base-rate neglect: It is not the math, but the context. *Journal of Behavioral Decision Making, 34*(1), 116–130. https://doi.org/10.1002/bdm.2182

71. Hsee, C. K., Yang, Y., & Li, X. (2019). Relevance insensitivity: A new look at some old biases. *Organizational Behavior and Human Decision Processes*, *153*, 13-26.
72. Gardner, W. L., Gabriel, S., & Lee, A. Y. (1999). "I" value freedom, but "we" value relationships: Self-construal priming mirrors cultural differences in judgment. *Psychological Science, 10,* 321-326. https://doi.org/10.1111/1467-9280.00162
73. Jopson, L. (2019, May 22). *How individualism and collectivism impact team success.* Medium. https://medium.com/design-and-tech-co/how-individualism-and-collectivism-impact-team-success-f29e4a2dc04c
74. Wigert, B., & Harter, J. (2017). (rep.). *Re-Engineering Performance Management.* Gallup.
75. Carucci, R. (2020, November 23). *How to actually encourage employee accountability.* Harvard Business Review. https://hbr.org/2020/11/how-to-actually-encourage-employee-accountability
76. Castaneda, D. I., & Ramírez, C. A. (2021). Cultural values and knowledge sharing in the context of sustainable organizations. *Sustainability*, *13*(14), 7819.

The Tularosa Experiment: A Foundational Study for Cyber Deception

Andi Rogers, Temmie Shade, Maxine Major, Chelsea K. Johnson, and Kimberly Ferguson-Walter

1 Introduction

The study of deception in kinetic warfare is well-known, dating at least as far back as the fifth century B.C.E. with Sun Tzu's *The Art of War*. While most modern countries exhibit deceptive tactics in kinetic space, very little attention had been put into employing similar strategies in the fast-growing cyberspace of our modern era. Around 2013, this gap in defensive strategy was noted by our group, the Laboratory for Advanced Cybersecurity Research (LACR). We have since strived to explore and grow this field, starting with a promising new defensive capability we identified.

The state of cyber deception in the early 2010s was almost exclusively honeypots, honeynets, honeytokens, and other applications of the 'honey' strategy: luring adversaries to some deceptive network object with attractive bait, typically in the form of a weak-looking node, appetizing file, or system. While such traps were useful in tracking cyber adversaries and making them waste time and other resources on false assets, there were many downsides to these technologies. They consumed defenders' physical resources such as power and rack space. Mental energy and time were required to keep the false nodes looking realistic and active on the network. Honeypots and honeynets were typically resigned to separate segments of networks to decrease the risk to defended assets; Oftentimes, their placement and role on the network did not look or act convincing. Even if a honey device blended in well, there was no guarantee that it would attract adversaries, making the expenditure

A. Rogers (✉) · T. Shade · C. K. Johnson · K. Ferguson-Walter
National Security Agency, Fort Meade, MD, USA
e-mail: avroger@uwe.nsa.gov

M. Major
Department of Cyber Science and Technology, Naval Information Warfare Center Pacific, San Diego, CA, USA
e-mail: maxine.m.major.civ@us.navy.mil

Q. Zhu et al. (eds.), *Foundations of Cyber Deception*, Advances in Information Security 90, https://doi.org/10.1007/978-3-031-93867-2_6

of resources to keep these nodes active appear wasteful for stakeholders. Overall, the drain on resources for upkeep typically far outweighed the security gains from managing honey tools, especially for defense teams already spread too thin.

LACR took a different spin on the idea of the typical honeypot. Instead of making monolithic, expensive nodes to host deceptive environments, we used a prototype defense tool that created lightweight network nodes, deemed 'decoys', that focused more on being high-confidence tripwires appearing alongside real assets than being separate, sophisticated fake environments to fool adversaries.

Decoys were small, required little to no maintenance, sat in the same IP space as real machines, and took far fewer physical resources to run. Though they were unable to fully engage adversaries as honeypots did, these unique decoys could still waste adversaries' resources via hosting fake services on open ports. More importantly, the decoys utilized a strategy that honeypots had not specifically concentrated on: a tripwire effect. Since these machines were not supposed to be visited by authorized users, any activity directed to them was an indicator of potential malicious reconnaissance activity. Moreover, since they were within normal IP space and were deployed in large numbers for a modest deployment cost, defenders' networks could quickly become minefields filled with high confidence alerting traps. While the presence of activity could similarly act as an indicator of malicious activity on honeypots, the low resource requirement and large-scale deployment of decoys inside user space made them a utilitarian, novel development.

However, compared to honeypots with their years of use and experimentation, these novel decoys had no published operational experiences to guide deployment practices and no controlled testing to give confidence that they would have a measurable effect. There were no studies to prove they were effective. Indeed, even honeypots themselves had a notable absence of true scientific rigor in their studies to date. Most experimentation with honey devices collected data from unknown adversaries with undetermined skill sets [1–3]. To remedy this, LACR started planning a series of experiments to rigorously test and evaluate not only the efficacy of decoys but the fundamentals of existing cyber deception practices as a whole.

To attain ecologically valid results from experimentation, however, we needed a participant pool who best matched the group we wanted to understand. One of the major problems with holding an experiment to test effectiveness against cyber attackers is that we needed to perform the test on those attackers, a diverse mixture of hackers, insiders, and nation-state cyber warriors. None of these parties are typically willing to cooperate or easy to bring into a controlled testing environment for data collection. LACR instead opted to utilize the closest available substitutes: red teams. These trained professionals are skilled in offensive cyber operations, typically acting as for-hire network defense testers for industry or government entities.

2 Case Study

2.1 A Four-Phase Study

LACR decided to start with a case study, utilizing a small red team to see if the group's novel deployment of cyber deception was worth the investment in a larger participant pool [4]. A group of three red teamers from a U.S. Defense Contractor were selected to be the participants for the duration of the study. The experiment was conducted on a real, operational network. The team's mission objective was to perform reconnaissance, exploit vulnerable assets, and exfiltrate any items of interest. The case study ran four 2-day phases, each with a unique condition, at 6-month intervals. We chose these intervals to reduce confounding variables through memory decay so the red teamers would be less likely to remember details of the previous phase. Each successive phase increased awareness and understanding of the deployed cyber deception tool.

Perhaps the most insightful part of the dataset collected during the case studies was the dialogue between the red team members, who were tasked to speak aloud to describe their thoughts and actions while attempting to exploit the network. These thoughts revealed direct evidence of cyber deception's effects on their operations, be it through confusion, misunderstanding, fear, or other cognitive changes. Additionally, post-experiment interviews were conducted to assess overall feelings experienced during the studies. A key result in these experiments was correlating red teamers' communication to direct network activity, noting how their observations changed their perceptions of the environment and altered their path forward.

In the first phase, cyber deception was applied on the first day via the inclusion of decoys without informing the red team. The team experienced difficulties when they attempted to connect to and attack the decoys; this was by design, as the decoys had no functional interfaces to exploit. It was observed through conversation and decisions on attack strategy that the red teamers believed the issue was with themselves or their tools, not that the targets may be false. On the following day, decoys were removed from the network. The team briefly spent time looking for the missing assets, and at the end of the day they assumed the experiment was to test a new cloaking capability. At the conclusion of the study the group was debriefed on the inclusion of deceptive decoys in the network. Remarkably, decoys made up 19% of the network on day one but consumed 38% of the team's time and received 83% of their launched exploits.

The second phase was set up identically to phase one except that the red team was informed prior to the exercise that decoys had been deployed. This awareness caused the team to neglect their stated objectives, instead focusing on trying to identify which nodes were real and which were fake. This appraisal activity significantly slowed down their operations, caused them to act much more cautiously, and introduced confusion to their attacks and results. Even when participants were specifically looking for deceptive nodes, only 13% of the decoys were correctly identified as fake, while 4% of the decoys were mistakenly identified as real.

The third phase tested psychological deception. The red team was again told decoys were on the network, but this time no decoys were actually present. Despite everything in the environment being real, the team again wasted a significant amount of resources trying to identify deceptive versus real nodes. In this case, the natural messiness of the network was a benefit to the defenders, as mundane traits such as odd-looking usernames or nonstandard banner sizes led the team to mistakenly believe that certain nodes were fake.

Finally, the last phase aimed to emulate a future where cyber deception tools are available and readily deployed on networks, meaning they are likewise available for attackers to study and learn to evade. A week before the final phase, the user guide for the decoy tool was given to the red team, allowing them to understand the exact details of what was deployed on the network. Again, the decoys were launched on the network. This time, the team acted extremely cautious toward all nodes, as they did not want to create any alerts from their activities. As a result, they strictly conducted passive reconnaissance, collecting and studying packets sent on the network while refusing to send a single packet themselves. This slowdown greatly diminished the operations of the team, causing the proctors near the end of the day to step in and request the team at least attempt to identify what they thought was real and what was a decoy.

2.2 Case Study Analysis: Investigating Cyber Attack Team Cognition

The group's transcripts in the case study were a perfect place to study team dynamics and observe shifts in operational strategy. We sought to specifically examine team-level and team-influencing cognitive biases [5]. Team-level biases only occur in interactions between teammates while team-influencing biases result when one member's biased decision-making influences the team to pursue a less–than-optimal action together. The investigation cited examples of two main biases: team-level escalation of commitment, which is the tendency for the group to continue to support a failing course of action, and team-influencing confirmation bias, or the tendency to interpret new evidence as confirmation of one's existing beliefs.

In one instance during the phase when the team was unaware that decoys were on the network, red teamer C identified a false target as real and tasked red teamer A to exploit it. Red teamer A complied and wasted hours trying different attacks. Even though the team discussed the possibility that the target was a decoy and exploit attempts failed, they decided to execute a very high-risk and unsuccessful "hail Mary" exploit. This sequence illustrates confirmation bias when red teamer C assumed the network would match their preformed beliefs about networks. It also displays escalation of commitment as the team continued to try to attack an unexploitable decoy target.

In another example, the team was deceptively informed that decoys were present when they were not. This information resulted in a strategy change. Instead of trying to exploit the network, they focused all efforts on trying to identify the decoys. These actions show that cognitive biases, both team and individual, can impede and disrupt cyber-attacks.

2.3 *Case Study Conclusions*

In the end, results from the case study showed that cyber deception, either its presence or merely the idea of its presence, incurred a considerable cost on the operations of cyber attackers. Fewer legitimate targets were successfully attacked, the attackers were often confused or extremely cautious, and there were frequent deviations from the attackers' goals, mostly resulting from attempts to identify decoys. Even when trying to classify nodes, the team was frequently uncertain of their own determinations or even confidently wrong in their appraisals. Overall, the case study provided ample evidence that an experiment with a larger participation count was warranted.

3 The Tularosa Experiment

Due to the success of the case study, we were confident in pursuing a much more rigorous experiment to prove cyber deception's effectiveness on cyber attackers. This new study required a sufficiently large sample size to provide adequate power to its conclusions. Its design was similar to that of the case study with a few notable differences that provided stronger evidence both within- and between-subjects.

3.1 *Research Questions and Hypotheses*

We framed the experiment's hypotheses around testing different levels of deception awareness and the many effects it may have on cyber attackers:

- Hypothesis H1: Defensive cyber and psychological deception tools impede an attacker who seeks to penetrate computer systems and infiltrate information.
- Hypothesis H2: Defensive deception tools are effective even if an attacker is aware of their use.
- Hypothesis H3: Defensive deception is effective when the attacker merely believes it may be in use, even when it is not.

- Hypothesis H4: Defensive cyber and psychological deception causes increased confusion and surprise in the attacker.
- Hypothesis H5: There is an observable correlation between cyber deception and physiological measures.

Data sources to answer each of these hypotheses were planned, with network-based capture to test H1, H2, and H3, psychological tests for H4, and a device to collect physiological data for H5. The meaning of 'effectiveness' here could manifest in several ways; this key point inspired different approaches to our follow-on data analyses.

3.2 Participants and Resources

Unlike the case study, participants in this experiment worked alone instead of in groups. Though operational cyber tasks are often worked in team environments, we made this decision for several reasons. Proctoring groups, as had been done in the case study, would have been too difficult with the sheer number of participants. There is uncertainty in group cohesion, a confounding variable introduced when mixing different skillsets among red teamers. Additionally, the difficultly in measuring an individual's behaviors and cognitive state in group tasks causes problems in identifying effects brought on by the experimental variable.

Participants were provided with two computers. One was connected to the experimental network that was disconnected from any outside networks. The other provided internet access and housed a chat client for testers to provide their thoughts, track their attacks, and report useful information about target systems during their operations. Use of a chat client was chosen both for recording purposes and to keep participants' communications from introducing bias to each other. The only direct communication allowed on the client was with experiment proctors to ask for aid if a problem was found with their system.

Special care was taken to ensure each participant had the same tools and resources so differences in performance were more likely due to the added deception instead of trade secret tools or scripts. To accomplish this, a common toolset was built using Kali Linux as a base. Each participant's organization was asked prior to the experiment to supply any additional tools their employees wanted with the caveat that all participants would have access those tools. Unsurprisingly, few were supplied, as the groups were likely competitive in the commercial red team market. Those that did submit tools simply submitted easily-accessible Kali Linux modules. This restriction unfortunately meant red teamers with heavy reliance on custom tools in their operations were likely less effective as a result, but that a necessary tradeoff to standardize the participants' toolboxes.

In order to most closely align with real-world cyber events, participants were told to gather as much information as possible and exploit what they could to pass off to a fictional partnered red team, all without compromising future network operations. This goal is notably different from a traditional Capture the Flag (CTF) event. CTF competitions are designed to be engaging, no-holds-barred competitions which provide several short-term goals to participants. Feedback is provided with each cyber success, giving a measureable indication of team progress. Real-world cyber events, unlike CTF events, can be long and drawn-out, with ambiguous goals and successes.

Tularosa aimed to strike a balance between internal and external experimental validity, keeping participants within the bounds of the experiment without being prescriptive. Human Subjects Research (HSR) data was managed through random assignment to experimental groups. This made the groups comparable and ensured any differences between them would be due to semi-random factors and not research biases, such as selection or sampling bias. We also wanted to evaluate cognitive effects but needed to ensure that only the conditions influenced participants' answers, not the information we gave or the questions we asked. All of these considerations are not normally part of CTF events, which instead are competitions measuring entrants' personal technical skills and knowledge.

3.3 Environments

Three environments were crafted for the experiment. Participants were placed on a different environment for each of the 2 days they participated. Two of the networks had 50 nodes each, while the last had 50 nodes and 50 decoy nodes. The network with decoy nodes was used for all Present conditions, while the two without decoys were used for Absent conditions. Two Absent networks were needed as the condition testing psychological deceptive persistence used two successive Absent networks.

Each environment was emulated with a wide array of operating systems, patch levels, and services. Decoy nodes were configured with similar operating system and service heterogeneity. We chose emulation to allow for easily deployable, uniform experiences for participants, granting more comparable activity between subjects. Of the available nodes, subsets were configured to be servers, clients, and other network roles. Domain users were created for the network, including some domain administrators.

The participants were split into four different conditions, each of which had different combinations of existence of decoys (Present or Absent) and awareness (Informed or Uninformed) of the possibility of deception (see Fig. 1). Participants in the Informed groups were provided with an additional note in their instructions, stating "There may be deception on the network" [6]. Participants experienced different networks on each of the 2 days they attended, giving insight into within-subjects differences.

Research Question	Day 1	Day 2	Day 1 to Day 2 Investigates
Is just belief effective? / Effective if known / Effectiveness	Decoys Absent, Subjects Uninformed CONTROL (AU)	Decoys Present, Subjects Uninformed (PU)	Reaction when deceptive defense is added to known network
	Decoys Present, Subjects Uninformed (PU)	Decoys Absent, Subjects Uninformed (AU)	Persistence of cyber deceptive influence without prior awareness
	Decoys Present, Subjects Informed (PI)	Decoys Absent, Subjects Uninformed (AU)	Persistence of cyber deceptive influence with prior awareness
	Decoys Absent, Subjects Informed (AI)	Decoys Absent, Subjects Uninformed (AU)	Persistence of psychological deceptive influence

Fig. 1 Participants' conditions throughout the 2-day experiment. Each participant was assigned to a condition-unique environment on Day 1 and 2. Each combination investigated one of four possible questions

Table 1 A subset of psychological scales and inventories implemented in the Tularosa experiment

Scale name	Description
Big Five Inventory [7]	5 aspects of personality: openness, conscientiousness, extraversion, agreeableness, and neuroticism
General Decision-Making Style Inventory [8]	How individuals approach and make decisions
Indecisiveness Scale [9]	Tendency toward intuitive speeded decisions or gathering as much information as possible before making a decision
Need for Cognition [10]	Tendency to pursue and enjoy the process of thinking
Remote Associates Task [11]	Convergent creative thinking (i.e., generating atypical links between concepts in order to generate a solution to a problem)

Participants completed these and other similar tasks to characterize their personalities, ways of thought, and cognitive capabilities

3.4 Collected Data

The Tularosa experimental range was outfitted with several network taps and data capturing tools to give our analysts as much information as possible about the participants' activities. Packet capture and netflow gave a perspective of what was crossing the wire, while the hosts themselves recorded console logs, keylogs, and full video capture. These traditional data supplied insight into attacker methodologies and decisions made on choosing nodes to attack. Susceptibility to deception was easily observable, as any command sent to a decoy was an indication that there was a belief that the node was real.

Several psychological scales were used in the experiment to baseline participants' cognitive ability and measure changes in mental states and perception due to deception. A subset of the scales employed appear in Table 1. Each measurement captured a different aspect of cognition, intelligence, and problem solving.

Physiological data was captured during the experiment using wristbands that measured heartrate, galvanic skin response, acceleration, blood volume pulse, and temperature. These measurements were captured to observe participants' biological changes during the experiment to identify moments of stress, surprise, or excitement.

3.5 Execution

The experiment ran for several months and data was gathered on over 130 red teamers. The data collected was vast and offered potential to be studied in many ways, from its intended goal to identify cyber deception's effects to studying cyber attacker methodologies. Over the next few years, we utilized this dataset as a basis to discover evidence in support of a multitude of post-hoc hypotheses.

The first paper from the study [12] debuted at the Hawai'i International Conference on System Sciences in 2019. It was the foundation for future analyses on the extensive data collected during the study. The experiment was outlined in great detail, explaining the design, implementation, subject pool, collected data, and other structural elements. The publication additionally included statistical analyses on a small selection of the data.

Overall, takeaways from the prior case study were confirmed with the larger number of participants in Tularosa: defensive cyber deception had a tangible effect on cyber attackers whether or not it was known to be deployed. It invoked greater negative affect, specifically suspicion, frustration, and surprise, and caused substantial slowdowns in operations. These conclusions represented only a small piece of the collected dataset, however; there were many other observations and viewpoints left to analyze. Over the next few years, we published findings in several publications and presentations to the computer science community. These findings are reviewed below; for full details, the reader is encouraged to reference those publications.

4 Network-Derived Impacts and Effectiveness

Each of Tularosa's data sources outline interesting effects from cyber deception. Through them, understanding was gained about how an attacker's composure and mental state is affected by their interactions with decoys. This information could give defenders insight into how to best influence their adversaries' operations. Ultimately, we sought to discover what changes can be reliably measured to reveal cyber deception's effects on an attacker, both to understand the data collected during the experiment and to inform live cyber response strategy.

4.1 Exploring Measures of Effectiveness

Historically, there has been little community agreement on measures of effectiveness for cyber defense tools and technologies and little support to define such measures, so assessments of effectiveness are still somewhat subjective. Many potential indicators of success depend on defender goals, attacker motivation, attacker strategy, and the details of the network environment. Participant stealth, speed of completing tasks, and success in exfiltration are all measureable metrics that may signify success. Evasion of decoy systems is a key consideration that not only measures a degree of success for the participant but also provides insight into decoys' overall effectiveness. For the Tularosa experiment, we looked at a variety of possible measures of success in order to compare participant progress across experimental conditions. These measures were explored in-depth in Ferguson-Walter et al. [13].

Given the instructions provided to the participants, there was no clear indication of an end-goal or final successful action. This allowed the individual motivations and incentives of participants to be displayed, although the documentation of each participant's individual strategies and motivations varied in level of detail. However, it also made trying to rate the success of each participant in our data analysis more difficult.

Ferguson-Walter et al. [13] examined different measures of success from the first day of the experiment. A subset of data was missing or unusable for some participants, requiring them to be excluded from specific analyses. After their removal, the following numbers of participants were included for this analysis: 35 for Absent Uninformed, 28 for Absent Informed, 30 for Present Uninformed, and 30 for Present Informed, making a total of 123 red teamers. This analysis mostly focused on between-group comparisons across the conditions. To contrast performance on the cyber task between these conditions, we not only had to define the attacker's success in exploiting the network, we also had to quantify the attacker's time and resources expended on decoys. Metrics examined included alerting, forward progress, wasted resources, and altered perception. The data supported Tularosa hypothesis H1 for all of these metrics, each proving deception impeded attackers in their own way.

4.2 Alerting

Adversarial cyber success is often greatly dependent on remaining undetected to avoid discovery and removal from compromised targets. To our knowledge, little research has been done to understand loud versus stealthy attacker behavior or the characteristics of the attackers who display each. Increasing the detectability of a cyber attacker is another potential benefit to cyber defenders deploying cyber deception.

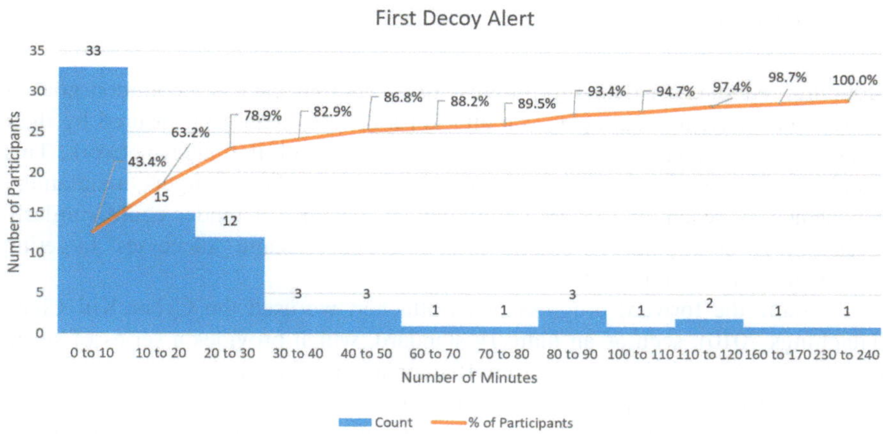

Fig. 2 Time to first decoy system alert. Each participant on day 1 with decoys present was binned by the amount of time it took them to cause an alert from the decoy system. The solid line represents the cumulative percentage of participants that triggered an alert at each time period

The decoys deployed in the experiment served as tripwires, sending alerts when any packets were sent to them. Many were first tripped from typical reconnaissance tactics, such as nmap scans. As reconnaissance is one of the first actions an attacker must do to gain a foothold in a network, these alerts are vital in early identification of malicious activity. Over 63% of the participants triggered a decoy alert within the first 20 min of the experiment, and over 93% caused alerts after an hour and a half (Fig. 2). This added visibility, alongside the high confidence that comes from the decoys' alerts, gives defenders a head-start in identifying suspicious behavior so they can take action to stop attackers or mitigate the damage they incurred.

While first contact gave an estimation of time to identify adversarial activity, the decoy system alerted on other activity as well based on the number of decoys targeted in a span of time and the number of packets sent to each decoy. These alerts were studied in depth by Ferguson-Walter et al. [13]. The Present-Informed condition had significantly more touch alerts (a single packet sent to a decoy) and scan alerts (packets sent to more than one decoy in a short time period) than the Present-Uniformed condition, but fewer probe alerts (multiple packets sent to one decoy).[1] We theorized that the increased touch alerts in the Present-Informed condition demonstrated an attempt to discover the nature or location of the deception. Later support for this explanation was provided in Ferguson-Walter et al. [14].

[1] touch $p = 0.006$, scan $p = 0.005$, probe $p < 0.0001$

4.3 Forward Progress

Stopping, reducing, or delaying progress of a cyber attacker is a common goal of many cyber defense techniques. An attacker's progress can be measured by their strategic gains (or lack thereof) as they progress through the target network. This could include escalating privileges, compromising a number of targets, maintaining persistence, or reaching a desired end goal. A deceptive defender could similarly measure their own impact by enumerating an attacker's same "successes" targeting decoys instead of real infrastructure.

To frame the forward progress of an attacker, we used the Cyber Kill Chain (Hutchings 2010), seen as an industry standard, which provides a series of seven high-level cyber-attack stages, from Reconnaissance to Actions on Objectives. The Tularosa data uniquely positioned us to allow visibility into an attacker's strategies and beliefs through the collection of self-reports, log files capturing attack preparation, and screen recordings.

One representation of forward progress is participants' interactions with the network's nodes. Participants in the Present-Informed condition targeted significantly more decoys than those in the Present-Uninformed condition,[2] supporting Tularosa hypothesis H2 that information on the presence of decoys does not reduce their impact. While this result may seem counter intuitive, this may be because participants in the Present-Informed condition made the least forward progress, which forced them to remain in the reconnaissance stages longer and spend more time targeting machines. Uninformed participants generally took less time to target their first real machine than those in Informed conditions, further demonstrating that knowledge of decoys can impact the time and effort attackers expend in their operations. Interestingly, participants in the Present-Uninformed condition took significantly longer to initiate an interaction with a decoy than those in the Present-Informed condition.[3]

We additionally measured the number of keystrokes participants performed throughout the day to serve as a metric of progress. While individual attackers can be more or less verbose in their commands, we expected to see a correlation between the number of keystrokes and increased forward progress, as participants cannot progress very far without interacting with the attack client. There are limitations in this metric, however, such as possible overcounting from keystrokes not related to progress and undercounting due to performing tasks with Graphical User Interfaces. Despite these caveats, total keystroke counts mirrored the results of other data sources: participants in the Absent conditions had significantly more keystrokes than those in the Present Conditions.[4]

[2] Kruskal-Wallis chi-squared $= 4.4416$, $p = 0.035$

[3] $H(1) = 4.44$, $p = 0.035$

[4] Kruskal-Wallis chi-squared $= 2.7079$, $p = 0.015$

Access to key terrain is another metric we considered, specifically the identification of, access to, and exfiltration from the domain controller (DC). While not significant due to the low number of participants who reached this stage, we noted that less than half (48%) of the participants in the Present conditions correctly identified the DC, while more than half (57%) of participants in the Absent condition did, suggesting that decoys may impede forward progress.

Significantly fewer participants in the Present-Informed condition leveraged stolen admin credentials than in the Absent-Uninformed condition.[5] This demonstrated that those in the control condition, in general, made more progress in terms of privilege escalation and lateral movement. In terms of exploitation, a specific protocol exploit was commonly used by all participants. It was novel at the time of the experiment and frequently successful when launched. Participants in the Present condition used this exploit significantly less than those in the Absent condition,[6] which demonstrated further progress made by those in the conditions without decoys. It is noteworthy that we did not see a significant difference in mentions of this exploit across conditions. This implies participants initially discovered the vulnerability and searched for the exploit equally across conditions, but those affected by deception had their progress impeded later in the Cyber Kill Chain (prior to exploitation). It is thus unsurprising that in self-reports, participants in the Present conditions reported significantly fewer exploit successes,[7] which is consistent with results from analysis of the cyber data.

We see this pattern continue through later stages of the Kill Chain as well. For example, fewer than half the number of participants exfiltrated valuable files in the Present condition than in the Absent condition.

4.4 Wasted Resources

Cyber deception techniques, such as decoys, contribute to a unique defender goal of wasting attacker resources. Since the Tularosa experiment provided a limited amount of time to perform tasks, time investment on decoys can signify a level of effort and waste of resources on deception. This investment also acts as a representation of decoy effectiveness, essentially revealing how convincing the decoys were. To investigate this metric, we examined the commands containing an IP address that were typed by the participant. Significantly fewer real machines were targeted in Present conditions than in the Absent conditions,[8] indicating attacker resources were wasted on the decoys. Results also indicated that significantly fewer bytes were sent to real machines than decoys in Present conditions.[9] While the fact

[5] $\chi^2 = 4.48$, $p = 0.0034$
[6] $H(1) = 3.97$, $p = 0.046$
[7] $H(3) = 6.48$, $p = 0.011$
[8] $H(1) = 4.58$, $p < 0.01$
[9] $H(1) = 5.28$, $p = 0.022$

that fewer targets were available on the networks without decoys (50) than with decoys (100) complicates interpretation of this metric, the participants' inability to distinguish decoy nodes from real ones is clearly demonstrated.

An Intrusion Detection System (IDS) alert can serve as a simple proxy for an attempted attack against a decoy or real machine. Any participant activity that generates an IDS alert on a decoy is considered wasted effort, not only for lost network resources, labor, and time, but that particular action also loses value because a defender is now more likely to be aware of the attacker's activity and their potential target. When decoys were present, 42% more IDS alerts per person were triggered. At face value, this may just appear to be because there were more target nodes on the present conditions. However, of those alerts in the present conditions, decoys garnered 30% more IDS alerts than real assets, effectively reducing the number of alerts on real assets by 44% per person. This is a concrete example of effort wasted on decoys, as all effort would be focused on real machines if decoys were not present.

4.5 Altered Perception

While altering the perception of the cyber attacker may not be the ultimate goal of using cyber deception techniques, it is a beneficial effect for defenders nonetheless. In terms of impacting impressions on overall network security, significantly more participants in the Present-Uninformed condition assessed the network as secure versus insecure in their end-of-day reports when compared to the Absent-Uninformed condition.[10] Half as many cyber task failures were reported by participants in the Present-Informed condition in the end-of-day reporting as well, despite being the least successful condition. This potentially indicates that being informed about deception made participants no longer blame themselves for their failures. Particularly in a deception scenario, an attacker's perception of success may not reflect true progress toward their goals.

The presence of decoys caused many misidentifications of target machines. Chat data logs for day 1 of the experiment revealed 248 instances of misidentifying a node across the 109 participants who supplied chat logs of their endeavors. The data indicate 95% of these misidentifications were the result of mistaking decoys with real machines, based on participants either rating a target as high-value or attempting to exploit it. Figure 3 reveals the average misidentification by condition. Both the presence of decoys and information about deception's presence caused an increase in misidentifications, with Present Informed conditions showing the strongest effects.

Perception may also be impacted by knowledge about the network. Being informed of deception had a measurable impact on the red teamers' productivity

[10] $\chi^2 = 4.30$, $p = 0.030$

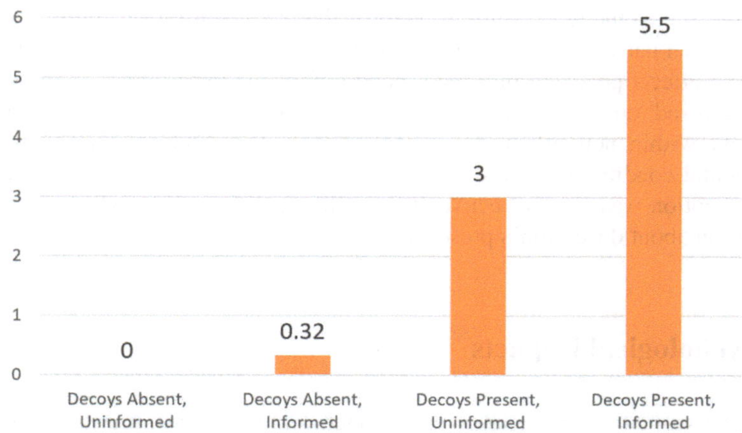

Fig. 3 Average misidentifications of targets per participant. Identifications of nodes were collected from participants' chat data, using valuations and exploit attempts as evidence of a target being perceived as real. Being informed of deception and having decoys present both increased the average number of target misidentifications

[12]. Overall, informed participants suspected deception more frequently whether it was present or not. Merely being told that there may be deception deployed caused participants a great deal of self-doubt and loss of confidence. This confidence loss was reported by participants far more when deception was not actually present, likely due to the participants being unable to find clear evidence of it. These findings confirm Tularosa hypothesis H3, which states defensive deception is effective if the attacker believes it may be in use, whether it is or not.

When deception was present, however, Informed participants expressed a slight boost in confidence in thinking they could navigate around it. Red teamers that were uninformed of deception while it was present, though, assumed any unsuccessful operations were due to their own skills being faulty rather than attributing it to a deceptive defense. This finding matches the case study's results, perhaps explained by deception being an uncommon obstacle for red teams at the time.

4.6 *Timing of Offensive Actions*

A unique analysis of the network data was performed in Senft [15]. This in-depth work took a unique approach by exploring the impact of defensive cyber deception on the timing of offensive cyber actions using the PCAP dataset. A graph database was used to identify the role of latency, duration, and frequency of actions in the PCAP data toward explaining variances in attacker behavior. This included analyzing the impact of experimental conditions on the timing of attack behavior, initial interactions, frequency of interactions, and the duration of these interactions.

Senft [15] concluded through his analysis that decoy-based deception was more effective when participants were informed about it, supporting Tularosa hypothesis H2. These effects persisted into the second day of the experiment, as the greatest effect occurred on the Present-Informed condition. Overall, temporal patterns of activity within network traffic supported our other findings that each of the experimental conditions had a distinct impact on cyber attacker behavior and that cyber deception was most effective at degrading attack activity when paired with information about deception's presence.

5 Psychological Impacts

The cognitive battery, personality assessment, and cyber task questionnaire were the first data analyzed to identify the effect of deception on participant behavior and performance [12]. These measurements aimed at understanding the participants' personalities, cognitive abilities, and beliefs. Impact of the experimental manipulations themselves could additionally be determined through reports of difficulty and confusion while comparing experiences between different groups.

5.1 Psychological Scales

Psychological measurements, unlike the network data, could not be collected passively throughout the experiment. To uncover perspectives on the human actors in the experiment, many classical psychological measurements were employed that had years of testing, refinement, and vetting. The collection of data retrieved from these tests could be utilized to answer many questions about participants and their cognitive processes during their cyber operations, as described in the Collected Data section of the Tularosa Experiment section above. This was done to attain a characterization of industry red teamers. Other measurements were used to assess the potential to predict performance in network penetration tasks from psychological profiles.

The participants' performance on these scales was first analyzed to pinpoint differences based on their experimental group. As expected due to semi-random assignment, no group differences were found. Next, the scores were analyzed to determine differences from the general populace as reflected in several studies with large sample sizes. Tularosa's participants scored similarly to this sample on overall cognitive ability, fluid intelligence, working memory, and the ability to distinguish reality from fiction. The scales on which Tularosa participants differed from the general populace are listed in Table 2. The professional red teamers were assessed as more agreeable and conscientious and as less neurotic than the average person. In a study of host-based deception using computer specialists as participants, Shade et al. [16] noted similar results on the Big Five Inventory (BFI).

Table 2 Differences in psychographics between Tularosa participants and the general public

	Tularosa			Larger sample			Mean difference	Effect size	Statistical test	
Task	Mean	SD	N	Mean	SD	N	TR-CS	Cohen's d	t-Statistic	Significance
GDMSI rational	21.39	2.86	120	20.34	2.84	1919	1.05	0.37	3.91	$p < 0.001$
GDMSI avoidant	10.57	4.83	120	12.68	4.81	1919	-2.11	−0.44	4.65	$p < 0.001$
Indecisiveness	26.24	6.86	123	30.65	3.15	291	-4.41	−0.88	6.83	$p < 0.001$
Need for cognition[a]	76.7	10.5	114	68.95	15.3	1919	7.66	0.6	7.43	$p < 0.001$
Remote associates test RT[b]	7060.09	1721.42	113	7566.09	1684.3	76	-506	−0.3	2.01	$p < 0.05$
BFI-44 agreeableness[a]	70.8	15.7	124	66.4	17.79	132, 515	4.4	0.26	3.12	$p < 0.002$
BFI-44 conscientiousness[a]	70.6	17.1	124	63.84	18.02	132, 515	6.76	0.38	4.4	$p < 0.001$
BFI-44 neuroticism[a]	34.5	17.2	124	51.02	21.34	132, 515	−16.52	−0.86	10.68	$p < 0.001$

Shown are the measurements that returned statistical significance, with means and differences to show how strongly the groups differed

[a] POMP transformed

[b] RT for accurate trials only

The Tularosa participants scored higher in rational decision-making and in the Need for Cognition. They additionally scored lower in the tendency to avoid making decisions, indecisiveness, and creativity. Given that red teamers work on tasks that require the ability to think systematically about problems, to make rational decisions, and engage in deliberative decision-making, these results are not surprising.

The Big Five Inventory's results showed the red teamers had higher agreeableness, higher conscientiousness, and lower neuroticism. These trends indicated the group was more trusting and organized, which matched the other collected test results. These traits undoubtedly help in operations, as red teams must trust their members, prepare attacks ahead of time, and leave minimal traces of activity to avoid being discovered by defense teams. Lower neuroticism means less irritability, which helps them stay calm in high-pressure situations such as meeting unexpected results or making mistakes during operations. The red teamers additionally showed higher Need for Cognition scores, which indicate an affinity for debate, difficult problem solving, and making sense of the world through structured understanding. With the vast amount of attack vectors that must be understood for exploitation and different network architectures that must be derived through observations, there is no shortage of tough problems to solve in their line of work.

Overall, the participants scored higher in conscientiousness and lower in avoidance and neuroticism compared to a larger sample. People with this type of profile, combined with years of experience as a red teamer, would be expected to stick with difficult problems and would be less likely to doubt themselves or their abilities when encountering difficulties.

5.2 *Task Specific Questionnaire*

Following the completion of the experiment each day, a series of questions were asked about the level of confusion, surprise, frustration, self-doubt, and confidence felt during the task [17]. Likert responses to experienced levels of confusion, frustration, etc. (negative affect) were grouped into 3 categories: Low (scores of 1 or 2), Medium (scores of 3), and High (scores of 4 or 5). General trends indicated that the percentage of participants reporting negative affect rose when decoys were present (Fig. 4). Fewer participants reported low confusion and more indicated medium confusion when decoys were present. Both medium and high ratings increased for surprise, and a higher percentage of red teamers also claimed experiencing high ratings of frustration with deception present. The difference in ratings was greatest in self-doubt, where the percent rating high self-doubt was 38% higher with decoys present.

Confidence is a positive emotion and thus is interpreted differently from the others: high scores are seen as more advantageous than low. Scores for confidence were shown in a separate graph and sorted in the reverse order to make levels comparable with the negative affect ratings. As noted earlier, unlike the other

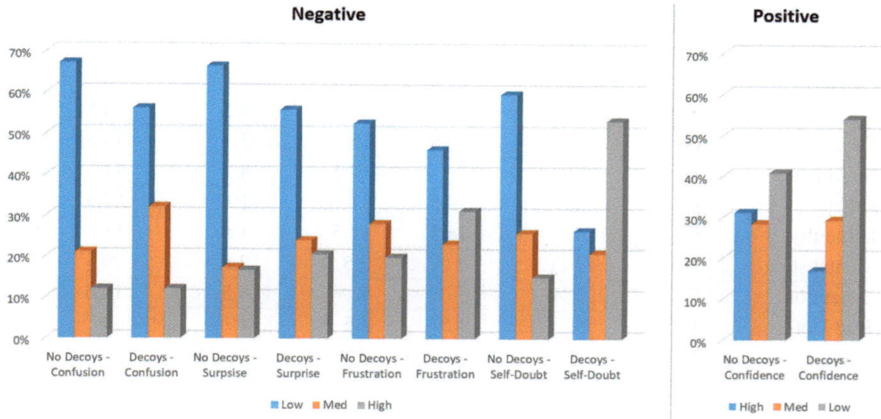

Fig. 4 Levels of affect across all conditions. Ratings of negative affect were grouped into low, medium, and high ratings and compared between group with and without decoys. Negative affect increased when decoys were present, manifesting as fewer low ratings and more medium and high ratings

affective responses, confidence was higher in the present condition. Overall, these differences in ratings support Tularosa hypothesis H4, as most groups with decoys reported higher levels of confusion and surprise.

In addition to identifying levels of affect, a thematic analysis examined the free-text responses provided by the participants when asked to explain the Likert rating they chose for each category. Participants identified ten labeled themes accounting for the scores given. The most frequently occurring theme was related to the experimental design itself. That theme accounted for 29% of the coded responses (Table 3). It was followed by "lack of progress" (14%), "deviation" (13%), "self-blame" (12%), and "other" (11%). The remaining reasons each accounted for less than (10%) of the responses. That is, responses on confidence were only 10% of the total comments, while each of the other reactions ranged from 21% to 24%.

5.3 Attitudes Toward Deception

To better understand expert red teamers' experience, expectations, and opinions regarding cyber deception, participants were asked to respond to a questionnaire following the completion of the task on the second day. The major points of interest addressed by this questionnaire were identifying what attackers expected from deception, how attackers would respond to it, and what defenders might do to maximize its effectiveness. Results from studying this data appear in Ferguson-Walter et al. [14].

Table 3 Count of themes averaged between two raters

	Confusion	Self-doubt	Surprise	Frustration	Confidence	Total	%
Exp design	50.5	32	29.5	42.5	13	167.5	29
Lack of progress	20.5	22.5	7	24	9.5	83.5	14
Deviation	19	6.5	30.5	15.5	3	74.5	13
Self-blame	12.5	34	3	13.5	8	71	12
Other	8	8.5	20.5	11	19.5	67.5	11
Difficulty	8	6	24.5	11.5	1.5	51.5	9
Mental state	7	7	4	8.5	2.5	29	5
Deception	5	3	3	7	0.5	18.5	3
Trad Def	4	5	1.5	2.5	1	14	2
Teams	2	4	0	2	2	10	2
Total	136.5	128.5	123.5	138	60.5	587	

Each Likert rating had a free text box for participants to explain their answer. Responses were grouped based on common themes

An inductive approach to a thematic analysis based on guidelines by Braun and Clarke [18] was conducted on the participants' answers to 12 open-ended questions in order to derive succinct characterizations of their beliefs about deception. Approximately 70% of the participants provided answers to the questions. A detailed description of the process can be found in [14]. Table 4 provides a brief summary of some of the open-ended questions. Answers were grouped by common themes mentioned by participants with minor themes that reoccurred within those broad groupings. Themes mentioned by small portions of participants (less than 10%) were not included, as those answers were deemed to be non-representative. Additionally, note that individual participant responses or explanations could contain multiple themes, so percentages may not add to 100%.

Participants were first asked about what generally made them suspicious and how they usually respond. Most answered that deviations in the network rouse suspicion, such as unexpected or unusual behavior, conflicting or changing results, attacks that were too easily executed, or due to a non-cyber answer (i.e. "shady people"). Participants typically interpret suspicious network behavior to be related to defenses, either from cyber deception or traditional defenses.

Other questions related to participants' thoughts about deception being deployed and their investigation into it. Overall, most did not think deception would be present and did not look for it. When they did suspect or confirm deception was in a network the red teamers typically changed their activities, either in frequency or strategic direction.

While these questions were presented at a time when cyber deception was not a widespread defense tactic, it was interesting to note that even after completing two 6-h days working in systems with deception present, many respondents did not recognize it as a technology they needed to be concerned about.

Table 4 Sample of open-ended questions given on beliefs about deception

Major theme	%	Descriptions (% of minor theme answers)
5. How do you respond when you suspect deception is in the system?		
Increase Activity	38%	Investigate (59%), Validate Data (25%), Countermeasures (14%)
Decrease Activity	21%	Exercise Caution (62%), Backtrack (33%), Cover Tracks (19%)
Redirect activity	18%	Avoid (53%)
6. How do you respond when you confirm the system is utilizing deception?		
Redirect Activity	26%	Avoid Deception (53%)
Increase Activity	22%	Investigate (41%), Counter Deception (23%)
Decrease Activity	18%	Exercise Caution (48%)
8. If you attacked a system where deception was used, how likely is it that you will attack the system again? (both)		
Negative answer	65%	(Few explanations given)
Depends on the context	41%	Mission/Job (33%), Target Value (32%)
Positive answer	21%	(Few explanations given)
10. If the system explicitly warned you that deception is present, how likely are you to believe the message?		
Negative answer	45%	Message was Deceptive (64%), No Activity Change (32%)
Context Dependent	18%	Nature of Deception (54%), Network Owner (35%)
Positive answer	37%	Seek Deception (14%), Grab and Run (2%)

A thematic analysis was done and common themes (10% or higher of participants' answers) were reported. Minor themes exhibited within the major themes give further insight into provided answers

5.4 *Cognitive Biases in Chat Data*

Drawing from the text reports of chat client communications, report data were examined for evidence that decision-making heuristics were present and measurable biases could be identified. Two biases were evaluated: the confirmation bias and goal framing effects. The confirmation bias is the tendency to seek information that confirms existing beliefs and hypotheses and to underweight or disregard disconfirming evidence [19]. Decision makers also tend to misinterpret ambiguous information as confirming their current hypothesis [20]. Goal framing reports the impact of a persuasive message and is dependent on the strength of a message's effectiveness in stressing either the positive consequences of a goal or activity or the negative consequences of not performing the goal or activity [21]. In truth, both positive and negative conditions promote the same act. Research indicates the emphasis on the negative consequences is more influential than emphasizing the positive [22–24].

Evidence of decision-making biases was evaluated via text reports generated as part of attacker activities. Post-hoc hypotheses sought to determine a few aspects of these biases [25]. Firstly, we tested if confirmation bias could be empirically observed within the text report data. Secondly, we explored the initial assessment of IP addresses, specifically presuming that participants in the informed conditions were more likely to rate IP addresses as uncertain, both when decoys were present and within the informed condition overall.

A major contribution of this publication to cybersecurity research was the qualitative analysis performed on the text. The text reports contained both evaluative and technical information. For example, some participants reported nmap scan results by enumerating the systems, services, and other details (operating system, ports) in the network along with their subjective evaluation of the vulnerability for attack. Some simply listed their network discoveries without further insight into value. Others indirectly inferred the utility of findings.

To analyze these data, cyber and cognitive subject matter experts iteratively reviewed and thematically coded over 4000 rows of text. To identify cases of confirmation bias or goal framing, these data were analyzed to determine the effects of the technical and psychological deception on the belief that network systems were real or decoys. The text reports were codified according to (1) explicit statements of value for future attack activities; (2) inferred statements of value; (3) cyber activity; and (4) suspected deceptive systems or services. Table 5 is a portion of the methodology developed to classify each statement; additional classifications such as inferring value and types of behavior based on actions taken are included in the paper.

Table 5 Explicitly stated value, thematic coding definitions, and interpretation for scoring

Score	Definition	Interpretation
Low value	Participant states low or 'slight' value	Low belief the system was real
Moderate value	Participant states medium or moderate value	Medium belief the system was real
High value	Participant states high value	High belief the system was real
No value	Participant clearly states "no value" or specifically indicated they wanted to exclude or ignore an IP. These could have been for various reasons	System or service had no value for attacker goals
Uncertain	Participant specifically indicated uncertainty about the value of an IP	Uncertainty about system or service
Lack of statement	IPs are simply reported, with no attached information or judgment that indicates an explicit value of any sort. Examples included simple enumeration of IPs, or simply saying they had been scanned	System or service reported in the network
Deception/deceptive practice	An IP reported as falling into any category of interaction and reporting, which indicated the participant believed deception may be present	Belief the system or service were deception related

5.5 Key Findings

Confirmation bias was identified within the textual data. Both decoy-present conditions and psychologically informed groups demonstrated more confirmation bias than absent conditions. Framing worked similarly on decoy and real systems and was more effective when decoys were also present. Providing information about the possibility of deception on a network increased the occurrence of the confirmation bias and the effects of goal framing. This suggests that cyber attackers confirmed rather than disconfirmed their beliefs about systems and services following initial phases in the Cyber Kill Chain (e.g., reconnaissance).

These findings are operationally relevant for network defenses and demonstrate that the presence of the confirmation bias was associated with more decoy targeting, delay in forward progress, and reduced likelihood of a successful attack. In addition, providing information about possible deception created a negative goal frame that increased uncertainty, reducing interaction with machines suspected to be deceptive, irrespective of whether deception was actually present. Thus, decision-making heuristics can be leveraged by specifically designing network architecture, such as adding decoys, to affect attackers' cognition. Such designs can bias attackers' perceptions during their campaigns and affect their subsequent behavior.

5.6 Physiological Data

Wymbs et al. [26] explored what could be learned about Tularosa participants from the physiological data collected by the wristband devices worn during the study. Out of several physiological data types collected, heart rate variability (HRV) and electrodermal activity (EDA) were used to measure stress response during the exercise. The results from this paper support the original Tularosa hypotheses H5: There is an observable correlation between cyber deception and physiological measures.

Heart rate variability measures stress levels by evaluating the intervals between heartbeats. "Increased emotional stress... leads to an overall reduction in HRV because the timing between consecutive heartbeats becomes increasingly uniform. This decrease in HRV is further associated with negative emotional events, including states of confusion, surprise, and frustration." Essentially, low HRV typically indicates higher levels of stress, while high HRV correlates to a more relaxed state. Conversely, electrodermal activity measures sweat gland function via skin conductance response, where emotionally arousing events result in higher conductance. Higher EDA correlates to a higher stress response.

While they were performing reconnaissance, we found that Day 1 psychological deception (Absent-Informed) participants showed increased stress with

HRV compared to the Absent-Uninformed and Present-Uninformed[11] conditions. Day 1 deception-Present participants showed increased stress with EDA during reconnaissance events.[12]

Day 2 analyses demonstrated persistence of the effects of the experimental conditions from Day 1. For example, day 2 HRV data showed that participants who were only informed of deception on Day 1–despite there being no cyber deception–showed more stress on Day 2 when deception was absent and they were not informed, compared to other groups that were not informed of deception on Day 1.[13] This demonstrates that indictors of physiological stress associated with information about deception can persist from 1 day to the next.

HRV and EDA were also evaluated against TSQ survey results, showing that stress levels during cyber tasks were related to the type of cyber activity participants were doing. For instance, participants who reported greater feelings of confusion and surprise at the end of each experiment day also experienced lower HRV (higher stress)[14] during intrusion events. Similarly, participants self-reporting confusion had lower HRV (higher stress) and higher EDA (higher stress)[15] during targeted reconnaissance events.

Participants who self-reported greater confusion on the second day of testing also exhibited greater stress in HRV during exploit activities.[16] HRV analysis showed that lower self-reported confidence on the second day was correlated with lower HRV (higher stress) during exploit activities.[17] These results show that physiological data can be used during HSR experimentation to measure participant stress levels during cyber tasks, and it may be used to measure the cognitive effects of cyber and psychological deception.

6 Recommendations and Lessons Learned

As the first of its kind and scale, Tularosa presented an opportunity to evaluate the effectiveness of cyber deception. Conducting an experiment at this scale with cyber expert participants provided several valuable lessons that can be unique to this type of research. In this section, several aspects of the Tularosa experiment are described, including setup, design, recruitment, data collected, the value of chosen approaches,

[11] Absent-Uninformed: $T(39) = -2.201$, $p = 0.034$; Present-Uninformed: $T(35) = -2.540$, $p = 0.016$

[12] Deception-Informed: $F(1,77) = 5.033$, $p = 0.028$; Deception-Present: $F(1,57) = 4.403$, $p = 0.040$

[13] $T(15.32) = -2.482$, $p = 0.025$

[14] confusion: $r = -0.290$, $p = 0.007$; surprise: $r = -0.285$, $p = 0.008$

[15] confusion: $r = -0.221$, $p = 0.042$; surprise: $r = 0.252$, $p = 0.046$

[16] $r = -0.290$, $p = 0.007$

[17] $r = 0.437$, $p = 0.018$

and some challenges unique to cyber experimentation. While Tularosa was a great first step into this field of study, additional rigorous HSR experimentation is needed to fully understand cyber deception's role and strengths in cybersecurity. We hope our lessons learned, enumerated in Table 6, will benefit future experimental designs.

7 Conclusions

Overall, Tularosa supported all of its hypotheses. Our many measures of effectiveness exhibited varying evidence of impeding cyber attackers, such as high IDS alert counts, fewer exploits launched, and more target misidentifications. Data analyses on number of decoys targeted suggested decoys were still effective when adversaries were knowledgeable of their deployment. The mere suggestion that deception may be present caused measurable effects in adversaries' operations, such as higher command latency and lower system interaction. Our psychological studies revealed cyber deception brought more confusion, surprise, and frustration to the red teamers' operations, which slowed down their activities and caused them to deviate from their goals. Further, cognitive biases in human operators, such as confirmation bias and goal framing effects, were demonstrably present in deceptive environments. Finally, we observed that knowing cyber deception was deployed as a defense caused higher physiologically-measured stress, and that stress persisted into a second day of work, even if deception was removed from the network. These findings are compelling evidence for cyber deception's effectiveness and utility in any modern cyber defense system.

We additionally derived psychological profiles to explore the differences between cyber attackers and normal users. These profiles showed highly rational, decisive, agreeable, and conscientious experts who were less neurotic and decision-avoidant than average people. These forward thinkers and strategic planners are also great at thinking outside the box, which lend them to several interesting issues in using them as experimental participants. Through the experiences and data analyses performed on Tularosa, numerous lessons were learned about handling these experts in an experimental setting. These lessons were shared to help future research in cyber deception so this immensely promising new field of cyber defense can grow even richer in the coming years.

8 Final Thoughts

For many years, honeypots were the primary form of cyber deception tradecraft. Though they were effective when deployed correctly, they were expensive to maintain and situational for defense teams. The use of decoys built upon those foundational ideas and restructured them into a more practical, usable format. Though their tripwire effects and relatively low upkeep set them apart from their

Table 6 A lengthy list of lessons learned while performing the tularosa experiment and during its data analysis phase

Pilot study lessons	
Pilot study	Pilot studies should encompass every part of your experiment, from participant interaction with your systems to the timing of any tests you conduct or feedback you gather. Though a critical component of the main study, our pilot study did not test the data collection process, and data collection issues were found much later, rendering some data unusable
	A pilot should also test the full data pipeline, from data collection to validation. Good pilot data could possibly even give the data analysis process a head start for testing scripts and analysis tools before experimental data is ready, although this is not typically the purpose of a pilot
	A cyber experiment (and pilot) should anticipate cyber expert actions that sometimes leak over into the experimental environment. Pilot experiments should have good guardrails in place against out-of-bounds-behavior, such as participants changing their own host IP address or attacking off-limits experiment resources such as the Network Time Protocol server
Participant lessons and task execution	
Recruitment	Professional cyber contractors can be expensive but are a similarly-skilled proxy for cyber attackers. This pool of potential participants is made up of a fairly small community, so be aware of the risks of double-recruitment of the same participants
	Experience in several domains of cyber expertise do not always correlate to expertise in the particular skills needed for a cyber task. For example, a recruit with years of experience managing a cyber team may not be adept at the basic suite of Kali Linux tools
	Cyber expertise is incredibly diverse, and so the recruitment criteria need to be based on suitability for the cyber task to appropriately test the experimental hypotheses
Rules of engagement	Clear Rules of Engagement must be established for the participants before the study to help clarify which resources are off-limits and determine which behaviors will dismiss the participant from the study. Clearly communicate those behaviors at the time of contracting and at the start of each day
	Plan in advance how to handle cyber or HSR data if participants are excluded, both during and after the experimentation is complete. Be aware that technical issues not caused by the performers may still alter their experience and pollute the data collected, though HSR data collected prior to the technical issues may still be valid
Task clarity and realism	During both recruitment and onboarding, make it clear whether the cyber exercise will resemble a capture the flag (CTF) type of event or a more realistic cyber campaign in which success and goals are not always certain. This will help ensure that participants are approaching the task with realistic expectations and strategies
	To improve engagement, it may help for HSR experimentation to capitalize on some of the more interesting aspects of CTFs that do not tamper with the experimental controls. For example, present participants with an engaging cyber narrative where ambiguous goals can create a fun investigative journey, even if successes are unclear

(continued)

Table 6 (continued)

Pilot study lessons	
Cyber data	
Packet capture data (PCAP)	PCAP can be used to recreate data sources after the experiment (Netflow, TCP streams, byte counts, IDS alerts, and some experimentally-planned cyber-attacks)
	PCAP logging directly from a Kali attack host can use considerable resources. Plan ahead to stress-test PCAP data collection to minimize resource impact during the experiment. Data processing over PCAP data will also require high performance processing for most analyses
Screen recordings	Screen recordings are valuable as a sanity check for uncertain participant activities, such as when the cyber data collected does not provide a clear picture of events. For example, we used the screen recordings to validate participant claims of Domain Controller compromise which were not backed by cyber data
	Optical Character Recognition (OCR) over the screen recordings is very difficult for cyber experiments. It is common for an attacker to use multiple terminal windows simultaneously and to constantly rearrange them. Graphical user interface (GUI)-based attack tools may be leveraged, which are difficult for OCR tools to properly represent or parse. Additionally, the participant may not be aware that information displayed on the screen is there. Any research insights that could be obtained from OCR, such as attack success messages, are likely more easily obtained by logging those messages from the source while the experiment is running
Terminal history (e.g., bash, zsh)	Terminal logging should include all common shells available on that host. Even if one particular shell is mandated, participants may accidentally default to their favorite shell out of habit
	Log all active terminal windows, not just the first one opened
	Log which terminal window a command was typed into so commands can also be ordered by task
	Enable timestamping of each terminal command
	Note that terminal histories do not record commands typed into terminal-based attack tools
Keylogger data	Remove "unnecessary" keystrokes (e.g., single versus double spaces, <CAPS LOCK>)
	It may be difficult, if not impossible to know the outcome of other keyboard shortcuts, such as <CTRL> + C and <CTRL> + V (copy + paste), <ALT> + <TAB>, etc., without additional instrumentation
	Take into account that <UP> followed by <BACKSPACE> was likely used to make key changes to prior terminal commands. <BACKSPACE> is not universally indicative of mistakes

	Pair the keylog with terminal histories to create a more complete log of what the participant intended to type. This makes it valuable to ensure these corrections are accurate
	Keylogs cannot be used reliably to determine if certain commands were typed into GUI applications
Attack tool logging	Process logs may be valuable for troubleshooting and determining if certain attacks or tools were used by participants. Plan ahead to determine which processes will be valuable to monitor, if any
	Processes launched from each tool or activity do not always indicate what actions are taking place
	Process logs for GUI tools may not indicate if the tool is being actively used
	The number of running processes does not correspond with the number of actions. For example, a single attack may spawn multiple processes
Malicious files	Be aware that collecting cyber participant files can present a risk to the machines they are stored on. PCAPs may contain payloads; these pose little risk at rest; however these files may also trigger antivirus software
	Plan management of two datasets if one version must be sanitized of malicious files
	Validate that the risks of collecting malicious data is outweighed by the research benefits from analyzing the dataset
Physiological data	Physiological devices are very sensitive by nature and prone to data loss. For example, the wristbands that Tularosa participants wore generated artifacts based on hand/wrist movement from typing
	Test physiological devices early and pre-analyze sample data before live experimentation to resolve any issues that arise
Data collection, curation and analysis	
Data collection	Abnormally high resource consumption on Kali hosts may cause PCAP files to be missing on the host
	Enable logging for each of the experiment data collection processes. If a process does crash, document each event cleanly in a log explicitly designated for this purpose
	Automate data collection at the end of each experiment. Validate that every expected file is collected, that no files are empty or of unexpected sizes, and that no files are duplicated (this can be done via checksums)
	Store files in both primary and backup locations. Preserve the backup as read only. When data needs to be accessed, it can be pulled from a copy, mitigating any risks to the original data. Automate the data transfer, but manually verify that the scripts ran cleanly and that data has been collected before deleting the original data from the source
Data curation, analysis, and wrangling	Before data analysis begins, make a plan for how to process each type of data collected. For example: • How will each second of the keylog be pieced together to tell a story? • Which IDS alerts are we collecting, and what format will they be exported into? • What do you want to learn from the self-reports, and how do you pull that data out?

(continued)

Table 6 (continued)

Pilot study lessons	
	Determine a common format for analyzing and comparing data across sources
	Avoid difficult or proprietary data processing tools where possible and utilize tools that your team is equipped to manage. Ensure your team can maintain tools you select and that they are not too expensive for the value you would get out of using them
	Data will need to be converted into a common format
	Check for gaps in data collection, timestamp inconsistencies, and extraneous content
	Develop data cleaning and analysis scripts prior to the experiment to ensure that the entire pipeline from data collection to hypothesis testing is effective. This step requires the expertise of multiple disciplines
	Pre-planning of data analysis is critical. Not instrumenting methods to easily identify performer activities beforehand can result in a slow, difficult analysis process
Free text data collection	
Self-reports	Use minimally invasive methods to prompt self-reporting to reduce interruptions, and thus impacts, on the timing measurements needed to evaluate different success measures across conditions
	Measurements may not contain ground truth due to human limitations of memory, awareness, or ability
	How people report they will behave oftentimes differs from how they actually behave
	Reports may vary in verbosity
	Reports can be hard to enforce, especially when participants are focused on a cyber task
Codebook analysis	Interdisciplinary Subject Matter Experts must collaborate to develop a codebook for labeling textual data. These experts should independently and manually code participant data, regroup as a team, and iterate over the process to produce agreement over the codebook and labels for cognitive events in the text
	It is time-consuming to perform multiple iterations of teamwork to agree on a rubric for evaluating and labeling cyber and cognitive events in the dataset
	It may be beneficial to produce an early draft of a codebook prior to the experiment's execution based on established procedures for this type of analysis. Although the exact features of the freeform fields will not be known in advance, methods do exist to prepare for textual analysis

predecessors, it was the Tularosa study's quantification of resources wasted and cognitive affect that truly inspired many others throughout academia, government, and industry to seriously consider and invest in cyber deception as a new strategic tool for cyber defense. For example, prior to 2020 before the first Tularosa paper was published, the market share for deception technologies was under \$1 billion. As of the publishing of this book, that same share is at \$16.3 billion with an anticipated growth to \$36.5 billion in the next 10 years [27]. In terms of academic investment, academic research publications on cyber deception have grown with more total publications in the last 3 years (1243 publications) than in the 5 years prior to the Tularosa experiment (453 publications) based on a search in Google Scholar.

The combination of cyber defense and psychology is proving to be a fruitful avenue for new research in the cyber security realm. The results compounded from Tularosa's participants reveal as much–the added frustration, confusion, and surprise are added stressors to cyber adversaries that hold promising leads for follow-up studies. Humans are the driving force behind programming offensive tools, choosing targets, executing operations on computer systems, and understanding the attack surface of any target network. They are key players in the attacker-defender model that have been overlooked, as more focus has been traditionally put on more technological, tool-oriented solutions.

Deception has always been a major factor of warfare and exploitation and continues to be an important strategic part of attack and defense throughout the world. As consumer spaces, social hubs, and battlegrounds extend further into the cyber realm, it becomes increasingly important to implement cyber deception defensively to protect the multitude of assets connected to the space. With the push given from the Tularosa experiment's results, the computer security community is starting to seriously invest in defenses against the exploitable human actors that have typically gone relatively uncontested. As cyber deception tools mature and gain newfound capabilities in the coming years, cyber defenders may finally gain the upper hand over their adversaries in the ever-evolving arms race that is cybersecurity.

References

1. Nicomette, Vincent & Kaaniche, Mohamed & Alata, Eric & Herrb, Matthieu. (2011). Set-up and deployment of a high-interaction honeypot: Experiment and lessons learned. *Journal in Computer Virology*. 7. 143–157. https://doi.org/10.1007/s11416-010-0144-2.
2. Rowe, Neil & Custy, E. & Duong, Binh. (2007). Defending Cyberspace with Fake Honeypots. *Journal of Computers*. 2. https://doi.org/10.4304/jcp.2.2.25-36.
3. Yuill, Jim & Denning, Dorothy & Feer, Fred. (2006). Using deception to hide things from hackers: Processes, principles, and techniques. *Journal of Information Warfare*. 5. 26–40.
4. Ferguson-Walter, Kimberly & Lafon, Dana & Shade, Temmie. (2017). Friend or Faux: Deception for Cyber Defense. *Journal of Information Warfare*. 16(2). 28–42.
5. Johnson, Craig & Ferguson-Walter, Kimberly & Gutzwiller, Robert & Scott, Dakota & Cooke, Nancy. (2022). Investigating Cyber Attacker Team Cognition. Proceedings of the Human Factors and Ergonomics Society Annual Meeting. 66. https://doi.org/10.1177/1071181322661132.

6. Ferguson-Walter, Kimberly & Shade, Temmie & Rogers, Andrew & Trumbo, & Nauer, Kevin & Divis, Kristin & Jones, Aaron & Touva, Angela & Abbott, Robert. (2020). Appendix to The Tularosa Study: An Experimental Design and Implementation to Quantify the Effectiveness of Cyber Deception.
7. John, O.P. & Srivastava, S. (1999). The Big-Five trait taxonomy: History, measurement, and theoretical perspectives. Handbook of Personality: Theory and Research. 2. 102–138.
8. Scott, Susanne & Bruce, Reginald. (1995). Decision-Making Style: The Development and Assessment of a New Measure. Educational and Psychological Measurement. *EDUC PSYCHOL MEAS*. 55. 818–831. https://doi.org/10.1177/0013164495055005017.
9. Rassin, Eric & Muris, Peter & Franken, Ingmar & Smit, Maartje & Wong, Maggie. (2007). Measuring General Indecisiveness. *Journal of Psychopathology and Behavioral Assessment*. 29. 60–67. https://doi.org/10.1007/s10862-006-9023-z.
10. Cacioppo, John & Petty, Richard & Kao, Chuan. (1984). The efficient assessment of NFC. *Journal of Personality Assessment*. 48. 306–7. https://doi.org/10.1207/s15327752jpa4803_13.
11. Cropley, Arthur. (2006). In Praise of Convergent Thinking. *Creativity Research Journal - CREATIVITY RES J*. 18. 391–404. https://doi.org/10.1207/s15326934crj1803_13.
12. Ferguson-Walter, Kimberly & Shade, Temmie & Rogers, Andrew & Niedbala, Elizabeth & Trumbo, Michael & Nauer, Kevin & Divis, Kristin & Jones, Aaron & Touva, Angela & Abbott, Robert. (2019). The Tularosa Study: An Experimental Design and Implementation to Quantify the Effectiveness of Cyber Deception.
13. Ferguson-Walter, Kimberly & Major, Maxine & Johnson, Chelsea & Muhleman, Daniel. (2021). Examining the Efficacy of Decoy-based and Psychological Cyber Deception. 30th USENIX Security Symposium (USENIX Security 21). 1127–1144.
14. Ferguson-Walter, Kimberly & Major, Maxine & Johnson, Chelsea & Johnson, Craig & Scott, Dakota & Gutzwiller, Robert & Shade, Temmie. (2023). Cyber Expert Feedback: Experiences, Expectations, and Opinions About Cyber Deception. *Computers & Security*. https://doi.org/10.1016/j.cose.2023.103268.
15. Senft, Michael. (2023). Exploratory Data Analysis of Defensive Cyber Deception Experimentation. https://hdl.handle.net/10945/72260
16. Shade, Temmie & Rogers, Andrew & Ferguson-Walter, Kimberly & Elson, Sara & Fayette, Daniel & Heckman, Kristin. (2020). The Moonraker Study: An Experimental Evaluation of Host-Based Deception. https://doi.org/10.24251/HICSS.2020.231.
17. Gutzwiller, Robert & Gilbert, Madison & Drescher, T. & Ferguson-Walter, Kimberly & Mikanda, Noella & Johnson, Craig & Scott, Dakota. (2023b). Frustration, Confusion, Surprise, Confidence, And Self-Doubt: Cyber Operators' Affects During A Realistic Experiment. Proceedings of the Human Factors and Ergonomics Society Annual Meeting. 67. https://doi.org/10.1177/21695067231192883.
18. Braun, Virginia & Clarke, Victoria. (2006). Using thematic analysis in psychology. *Qualitative Research in Psychology*. 3. 77–101. https://doi.org/10.1191/1478088706qp063oa.
19. Mynatt, C. R. & Doherty, M. E. & Tweney, R. D. (1977). Confirmation Bias in a Simulated Research Environment: An Experimental Study of Scientific Inference. *Quarterly Journal of Experimental Psychology*. 29(1). 85–95. https://doi.org/10.1080/00335557743000053
20. Rabin, Matthew & Schrag, Joel L. (1999). First Impressions Matter: A Model of Confirmatory Bias. *The Quarterly Journal of Economics*. 114(1). 37–82.
21. Levin, I. P. & Schneider, S. L. & Gaeth, G. J. (1998). All frames are not created equal: A typology and critical analysis of framing effects. *Organizational Behavior and Human Decision Processes*. 76(2). 149–188.
22. Brewer, M. B., & Kramer, R. M. (1986). Choice behavior in social dilemmas: Effects of social identity, group size, and decision framing. *Journal of Personality and Social Psychology*. 50(3). 543.
23. Ganzach, Yoav & Karsahi, Nili. (1995). Message framing and buying behavior: A field experiment, *Journal of Business Research*. 32(1). 11–17. https://doi.org/10.1016/0148-2963(93)00038-3.

24. Kahneman, D. & Knetsch, J. L. & Thaler, R. H. (1990). Experimental tests of the endowment effect and the Coase theorem. *Journal of Political Economy*. 98(6). 1325–1348.
25. Gutzwiller, Robert & Rheem, Hansol & Ferguson-Walter, Kimberly & Lewis, Christina & Johnson, Chelsea & Major, Maxine. (2023a). Exploratory Analysis of Decision-Making Biases of Professional Red Teamers in a Cyber-Attack Dataset. *Journal of Cognitive Engineering and Decision Making*. https://doi.org/10.1177/15553434231217787.
26. Wymbs, Nicholas & Major, Maxine & Gabrys, Ryan & Ferguson-Walter, Kimberly. (2024). Physiological Response to Cyber and Psychological Deception. Proceedings of the 57th Hawaii International Conference on System Sciences. 964–973.
27. GlobeNewswire. (2024). https://www.globenewswire.com/news-release/2024/02/05/2823228/0/en/Endpoint-Security-Market-Surges-to-USD-36-5-Billion-by-2033-Fueled-by-Robust-Adoption-of-Advanced-Threat-Protection-Solutions.html

Modeling Human Behavior in Cybersecurity: Leveraging Structural Equation Modeling to Address Cognitive Biases and Enhance Defense Strategies

Nikolos Gurney, Peggy Wu, Kylie Molinaro, Fred Jones, Beau Schelble, and Quanyan Zhu

1 Introduction

The field of cybersecurity has become increasingly important throughout the last two decades, with critical breaches of security resulting in the extortion of millions of dollars within the United States and the crippling of infrastructure [1]. Thus, improving the defenses of existing and new cyber systems is imperative to ensure the safe use of networked systems. Traditional efforts at cyber defense have focused on intrusion detection systems, intrusion prevention systems, and anti-virus software. However, recent research has studied the potential for approaches to oppositional human factors [2]. These techniques complement traditional cyber defense practices by implementing cyber deception techniques, such as decoy systems, to mislead cyber attackers [3]. This form of cyber deception has already been empirically

N. Gurney (✉)
Institute for Creative Technologies, University of Southern California, Los Angeles, CA, USA
e-mail: gurney@ict.usc.edu

P. Wu · F. Jones
Raytheon Technologies, Arlington, VA, USA
e-mail: Peggy.Wu@rtx.com; Frederick.Jones@rtx.com

K. Molinaro
Bulls Run Group, Bethesda, MD, USA
e-mail: kmolinaro@bullsrungroup.com

B. Schelble
Department of Industrial and Systems Engineering, University of Tennessee Knoxville, Knoxville, TN, USA
e-mail: bschelbl@utk.edu

Q. Zhu
Department of Electrical and Computer Engineering, New York University, New York, NY, USA
e-mail: qz494@nyu.edu

Q. Zhu et al. (eds.), *Foundations of Cyber Deception*, Advances in Information Security 90, https://doi.org/10.1007/978-3-031-93867-2_7

demonstrated to have significant potential to reshape the cybersecurity landscape [4–6], providing a novel approach to strengthen existing cyberinfrastructure moving forward that easily coincides with existing practices. However, the deception utilized by such techniques necessitates modeling human behavior and decision-making, specifically within the realm of cybersecurity. This modeling of human behavior and decision-making is not as widespread within the cybersecurity context, as a great deal of work remains left to do in this space before cyber deception techniques become widespread. As such, the current chapter argues for cyber deception techniques in cybersecurity and how human behavior and decision-making can be modeled using the powerful modeling technique known as structural equation modeling (SEM).

1.1 The Utility of Modeling Human Behavior in Cyber Defense

Military strategists have championed the strategic offensive principle of war (SOP) from Sun Tzu to Mao Zedong and Niccolo Machiavelli to George Washington. Many readers will recognize this strategy from the adage, "The best defense is a good offense." Historically, applying the SOP in cyber realms was not feasible as hackers easily obfuscate their identity and blend in with regular network traffic. However, the fortune of defenders may be changing with the emergence of a more effective class of cyber defense approaches based on the SOP: cyber deception [3, 7–12]. Cyber deception attacks hackers' cognition via misinformation and manipulations of network environments to erode their situational awareness, influence their beliefs and perceptions, and sabotage their decision processes. The venerable honeypot [13], a sacrificial system that serves as a decoy to hackers, and decoy systems [10], essentially less sophisticated honeypots, are some of the most widely studied cyber defenses. Insights from the behavioral sciences have uncovered a new crack in red teamers' fortress: their cognitive biases [14–17]. This chapter introduces structural equation modeling (SEM) [18] as an approach to capturing the vulnerabilities inherent to the biased decision-making of hackers—their cognitive vulnerabilities—and suggests how to leverage these models in defensive systems.

Even the most rational of humans can suffer from lapses of judgment and shortcomings in their reasoning. Herbert Simon famously noted that humans are boundedly rational or subject to constraints on their rationality [19]. Trying to understand these constraints spawned an entire scientific discipline committed to studying human judgment and decision-making, a core theme of heuristics and biases. The heuristics and biases research agenda is well into its fifth decade of prominence in the behavioral sciences. Early work on human judgment in the face of uncertainty from Daniel Kahneman and Amos Tversky [20] triggered a landslide of research documenting how minor reasoning shortcuts can either undermine our decision-making (i.e., a bias) [21] or make us smart (i.e., a heuristic) [22]. A cognitive bias is typically considered a systematic deviation in either thought or behavior from the predictions of a rational model. In contrast, a heuristic is a cognitive shortcut that helps a person realize a desirable outcome without processing all the relevant data. The list of named cognitive biases and heuristics is long, varied, and still in flux, thanks to differing perspectives on what *is* rational and how to model it. There are, however, some recurring themes, such as resistance to realizing losses (e.g., the sunk cost fallacy [23] and loss aversion [24]), pattern-seeking (e.g., the gambler's fallacy [25] and sample size insensitivity [26]), and overreliance on memory (e.g., the availability heuristic [27] and context effects [28]), to name a few. As the heuristics and biases research agenda continues to grow and develop, these themes will undoubtedly change and become more concrete.

Application of the fundamental science insights generated from the heuristics and biases research agenda are far reaching. Perhaps the most famous applied example is the simple nudge or a choice architecture that predictably alters decision-making without limiting options or changing the incentive structure [29]. At their core, nudges rely on cognitive heuristics and biases to direct human behavior or decision-making. For example, setting a default response to "yes" for organ donation decisions can lead to significantly more people agreeing to be donors [30]. Cyberdefense researchers have recently begun applying such insights to the cyber domain [16]. Analysis of data from a small experiment in which members of a red team completed multiple phases of a deception experiment suggested that they used the take-the-best-heuristic (using the first differentiating cue to make a choice between two options [31]) plus the availability heuristic (assessing the likelihood of something based on how easily relevant examples come to mind) [32] and possibly fell victim to an anchoring bias (when a judgment or decision is heavily influence by a reference bit of information [20]). This preliminary evidence suggests that insights from the heuristics and biases research agenda also have application in cyber defense settings, particularly to achieve effective cyber deception.

Anticipating what *cognitive vulnerabilities* (CVs), such as a heuristic or bias, an attacker is subject to is one of the biggest challenges cyber defenders face when they deploy cyber deceptions. Doing so requires a deep understanding of CVs, the attacker, *and* the attack environment (i.e., a network). Behavioral science provides extensive insights about modeling the various CVs that cyber defenders might want to target. For example, a defender may recognize that attackers are unusually cautious after obtaining a credential. Such caution may reflect *loss aversion*, a bias in which people are overly sensitive to losses relative to gains [24]. The classic (albeit contested) example of loss aversion involves giving study participants a mug they can later sell to other participants. Economic theory predicts that roughly half of the mugs should change hands. However, the empirical observation is that sellers typically have a higher strike price than buyers, meaning that their willingness to part with the mug, despite being randomly endowed with it, is not in line with economic theory.

The tendency to overvalue a network asset or credential in this way can be captured using a hypothesized utility function for a hacker. The classic formulation for such utility functions relies on the S-curved function from Prospect Theory [33]. The origin is a person's reference point when projected on a two-dimensional plane. An increase (decrease) in utility, i.e., a gain (loss), is captured by moving right (left) along the x-axis. From the origin, the line representing gains is shallower than the line representing losses. The metric *lambda*, defined as the derivative of the loss slope divided by the derivative of the slope of the gain for a person's utility function, captures a person's relative degree of loss aversion. A model incorporating insights about a hacker's utility function and any tendency to overvalue current assets could guide a cyber defender's efforts, possibly allowing them to trap or capture a hacker on a network.

Operationalizing the SOP using CVs requires a modeling approach that can account for network variables, model a hacker's decision-making, and predict how a cyber deception approach will impact a hacker's future behavior; that is, an approach that can account for the causal links between these items. Structural equation models (SEMs) are one method for accomplishing such a task. SEMs facilitate connecting latent variables (those that cannot be directly observed, such as a hacker's degree of loss aversion) with observable variables (such as network traffic) via postulated causal links. These links are typically captured in some functional form. Consider a case in which a hacker gains access to a network device after securing the necessary credentials. An SEM could describe how the hacker's behavior changed after obtaining access by modeling their future behavior according to the loss aversion CV. Before gaining access, the hacker may have risked revealing themselves in an attack on another network device. Afterward, the relative cost of losing access to the device might lead them to be more cautious. The current chapter will present the following three sections: (1) A brief review of the cyber deception space and the need for modeling human behavior and decision-making within cybersecurity; (2) Structural equation modeling in brief; (3) Applying structural equation modeling to cyber defense and deception. In doing so, this chapter defines the structural equation modeling process for researchers in the cybersecurity domain, details the benefits of deception within cyber defense, and provides examples of structural equation modeling applied to the modeling of human behavior and decision-making within cyber security contexts. These contributions increase awareness of novel methods that improve the cybersecurity space, expand the methodology toolkit available to cybersecurity researchers, and provide concrete examples for the field to work from when undergoing similar modeling efforts in the future.

2 Structural Equation Modeling for Human Behavior and Decision-Making

Structural equation modeling has been utilized for decades in cognitive science to understand and model human behavior and decision-making [34]. This technique goes beyond well-known techniques (i.e., ANOVA) by simultaneously incorporating and testing multiple independent and dependent variables. By testing all these variables simultaneously, structural equation models characterize direct and indirect effects across the entirety of the model. They also enable researchers to showcase cause and effect from a linear time perspective and/or theoretical perspective, offering enhanced flexibility for researchers and the research questions they wish to pursue.

Structural equation modeling is a form of factor analysis that regresses the factors onto one another and the independent variables of the experiment. It has several advantages compared to other methods, such as ANOVA or t-tests, because structural equation modeling simultaneously tests the measurement model and all the hypotheses (structural model) [35]. The measurement model is defined as the relationship between the observed variables, such as survey items or behavioral observations, and latent variables, also known as factors [36]. These latent variables are any unobservable metric of interest to researchers that influences multiple observable measures, causing a correlation between the observed measures because they are affected by the same latent variable. Examples of latent variables include IQ, trust, satisfaction, and team cohesion. As such, latent variables must be indirectly defined by identifying and characterizing the covariance among observable metrics known as indicators to create a measure of the unobservable latent variable, or factor, causing the covariance among the indicators [36]. Others have detailed the specific statistical definitions of structural equation modeling and, thus, will not be covered in detail here (see [34, 35, 37]).

When first engaging in structural equation modeling, the first step is defining the research questions and experimental design. Once research questions and the experimental design are defined, that will allow for identifying latent variables. The latent variables will be the unobservable variables of interest based on the specific research questions of interest (e.g., trust, anxiety, propensity to be persuaded). Upon identifying the latent variables relevant to the research question, the observed variables, or indicators, will be used to define the latent variable through factor analysis. As such, the observed variables must be defined ahead of time, using at least three observable measures (as a latent variable cannot be made from less than 3). Generally, if an existing set of observed measures exists to characterize a latent variable (e.g., existing validated survey measure), it is best to use the existing measures. Developing new measures for an experiment should be reserved for cases where the latent variable has no established observable metrics available or the research questions demand a novel factor, as much more work will be needed to develop and ensure the new measures' validity.

Once the question of latent variables and their measurement is settled, developing a hypothesized structure for the structural equation model is necessary. For example, if the experiment is interested in three dependent variables (satisfaction, trust, and technology acceptance) and includes a single independent variable, then the hypothesized structural equation model would need to organize all three of the dependent variables in cause-and-effect order, starting with the independent variable because it is a manipulated variable within an experiment (though not all structural equation models are used for experiments). Referencing the same hypothetical experiment with three dependent variables and one independent variable, one

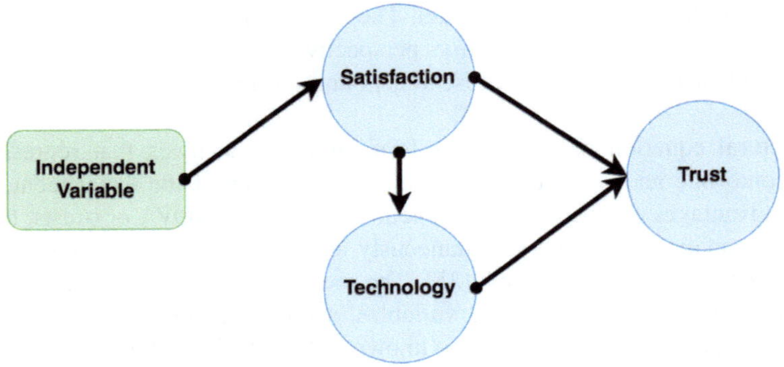

Fig. 1 Example structure of structural equation model

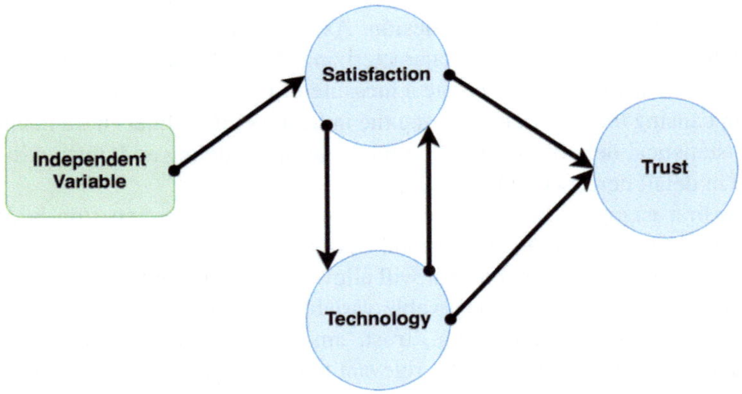

Fig. 2 Recursive structural equation model

possible structure can be seen in Fig. 1 and described using the following notation: (Independent Variable > Satisfaction > Technology > Trust).

The hypothesized paths of structural equation models can, in theory, fit whatever the researcher believes is the correct flow of cause and effect among the variables of interest. The hypothesized organization of factors and regression paths should always be driven by existing theory to ensure it is validated and reduce the potential for a model failing to achieve adequate fit. However, there is a significant difference in the level of effort in analysis when examining models with feedback loops and those without feedback loops. Specifically, models with feedback loops are recursive (see Fig. 2), while those without are non-recursive (see Fig. 1). As stated, non-recursive models are exceedingly more common as they are far simpler to analyze than recursive models.

After hypothesizing the flow of cause and effect for the variables of interest within the model, the data collection, cleaning, and analysis process can begin. Several programs can analyze structural equation models, but some of the most common include R (using lavaan), MPlus, Amos, and LISREL. Regardless of the software used, the data analysis steps remain the same. This involves cleaning the data for input into the software and validating the measurement model using confirmatory factor analysis. The confirmatory factor analysis establishes convergent and discriminant validity in creating the latent variables. Convergent validity states that the indicators of a factor measure the same thing, and discriminant validity states that no two factors measure the same thing [35]. Several different benchmarks are said for both validity types; however, this chapter will reiterate the benchmarks conveyed by Knijnenburg and Willemsen [35]. Specifically, convergent validity is met if the average variance extracted for all indicators of a factor exceeds 0.50, which can be found by averaging all the R^2 values for each indicator within a factor. Discriminant validity can be achieved when the correlation between two factors is greater than or equal to the square root of the average variance extracted from both factors. Indicators can also be removed to improve these metrics and ensure validity for the various latent variables tested by the confirmatory factor analysis. Once the validity of the measurement model has been determined, the next step of structural equation modeling can occur. The final steps to developing a structural equation model begin with defining a fully saturated model, which is a model with all possible regression paths in place (excluding recursive paths). The fully saturated model's regression paths are then iteratively trimmed until only significant paths remain. The process of trimming paths also involves several rules; however, these rules can vary, and defining them is outside the scope of this brief overview. Once trimming the model is complete, its fit can be determined using statistical tests, which determine the amount of misfit between the model and the reality of the data. These tests include the Chi-square test of Model Fit, comparative fit index (CFI), Tucker-Lewis index (TLI), and root mean square error of approximation (RMSEA). Traditionally, the Chi-square test is overly sensitive and has fallen out of favor in lieu of the CFI, TLI, and RMSEA metrics. When determining the adequacy of model fit, the cutoff values proposed by Hu and Bentler are popular [38], which propose the following cutoff values: CFI > 0.96, TLI > 0.95, and RMSEA <0.05. Furthermore, many structural equation modeling programs provide a 90% confidence interval for the RMSEA value, which should remain below 0.10 [35].

This section briefly introduces and overviews the development of a structural equation model. However, this chapter does not discuss many other factors to consider when hypothesizing, cleaning, analyzing, and testing a structural equation model. Several excellent resources are available to dive more deeply into the topic (see [18, 39]).

Deploying structural equation modeling has several advantages and disadvantages that must be considered when determining whether the technique suits a specific research question. Several of the benefits stem from the ability of structural equation models to test the measurement model and structural model at the same time. In doing so, the structural equation modeling technique provides additional precision in analysis by allowing the measurement model to be corrected through the confirmatory factor analysis (i.e., dropping indicators with a low R^2). Further on this line of accuracy, modeling human behavior often utilizes metrics that are rarely validated in a robust manner, which is not something that a researcher must be concerned with when using structural equation modeling as it is a requirement to validate the measurement model to establish the latent variables that define such models. Structural equation models are also an excellent analysis technique for understanding the direct and indirect effects across a cause-and-effect series. For example, in Fig. 1, the impact of the independent variable on technology acceptance is fully mediated by satisfaction. Furthermore, the effect of satisfaction on trust is partially mediated by technology acceptance. Being able to model and visualize these complex relationships all at one time within the same analysis provides an excellent opportunity to understand and model the complexities of human behavior and decision-making, which can be directly leveraged to develop more intelligent machine learning models that also reduce the amount of time spent on feature selection [40]. Machine learning models developed in this manner also benefit from enhanced explainability, which can increase adoption across users and developers. However, there are disadvantages to note regarding structural equation modeling. Namely, there is a need for a great deal of data to achieve adequate power for the analysis, which is a notably tricky effort when human subjects research is involved. While there is no exact number of participants required to achieve adequate power, a rough minimum of 200 is typically recommended by other sources [35]. Structural equation models can also be exceptionally tricky to fit the measurement model when utilizing entirely new indicators for latent variables; in fact, many published papers are dedicated entirely to validating a new factor through multiple rounds of exploratory and confirmatory factor analysis [41]. Finally, interpreting structural equation models is not always straightforward, as the final model can include many factors with complex mediated relationships that are difficult to interpret and act upon meaningfully. Considering these limitations and advantages when deciding whether or not to utilize structural equation modeling is crucial to ensuring the results align with the overall goals of the research. Finally, the benefits of this technique emphasize its utility in effectively modeling complex relationships between factors that influence human behavior and decision-making, which ensures its place within the cybersecurity research toolkit.

3 Applying Structural Equation Modeling to Cyber Defense and Deception

The utility of structural equation modeling to cybersecurity research is significant. The ability to model direct and indirect effects along temporal cause-and-effect timelines enhances researchers' and cybersecurity developers' ability to understand attacker actions throughout the cyber kill chain. The following section will discuss an example of such an application of structural equation modeling to understanding attacker behavior and decision-making during a simulated attack sequence. Specifically, the following cyber defense scenarios and structural equation models are meant to understand the characteristics of an individual, network, and environmental variables that make an attacker susceptible to cognitive vulnerabilities. Cognitive vulnerabilities are the biases and heuristics stemming from the brain's propensity to take mental shortcuts in decision-making in lieu of expending more resources on deeper analysis [42]. Common cognitive vulnerabilities in the following example application of structural equation modeling include representativeness bias and loss aversion; however, there are many more, such as availability heuristic, confirmation bias, and sunk cost fallacy. These cognitive vulnerabilities have long been a topic in cognitive science fields such as economics, psychology, and finance. However, they are beginning to spread to other fields as concepts, such as oppositional human factors, demonstrate their utility.

3.1 Representativeness Bias (Base Rate Neglect)-Early Stage

Definition: Representativeness bias, also known as base rate neglect, is a cognitive bias where individuals overemphasize the representativeness of a piece of evidence, often ignoring how frequently that evidence occurs [26]. In cybersecurity, this bias can be particularly influential in the decision-making of attackers. For instance, an attacker might generalize their understanding of a network based on a limited set of observable data points. A common example involves a server showing both Windows and Linux service ports, leading attackers to misidentify it as a fake host. Similarly, attackers may focus on user login names that appear representative of high-value accounts, such as "username-admin," while neglecting the actual base rate of such admin accounts in a typical network. This misjudgment can lead attackers to pursue high-value targets based on faulty assumptions.

Cyber Implementation: In practice, attackers often fall into the trap of representativeness bias by overgeneralizing their understanding of a network's structure or valuable data. When attackers see accounts or files that appear representative of high-value targets, such as admin accounts or files with valuable-sounding names, they may ignore how atypical such targets actually are. For instance, attackers might prioritize "username-admin" logins, believing these accounts represent valuable access points. However, they might disregard the fact that, in many networks, admin accounts make up only a small percentage—typically around 3%. By contrast, a network that contains 80% admin accounts would be highly unusual. Attackers who fail to account for this base rate are more likely to misallocate their resources, targeting accounts that are designed to mislead them, such as decoy accounts in a honeypot environment.

Vignette Design: The goal of the vignette design is to simulate an environment where attackers are incentivized to target high-value assets based on misleading or incomplete information. In this scenario, the attacker's main goal is to navigate the network undetected while selecting targets, such as admin logins, to escalate privileges. Their efforts are at risk of being detected if they attempt too many failed logins or generate anomalous traffic.

In this vignette, attackers are primed to overvalue admin accounts through manipulations in the environment, such as a high number of accounts with the "-admin" suffix, or by presenting filenames indicative of valuable data. However, these targets are often decoys designed to exploit representativeness bias. The network environment contains a large number of active accounts that appear valuable based on activity and login status, and high percentages of files with enticing filenames. The cyber kill chain stage involved is reconnaissance, and the relevant MITRE ATT&CK techniques are Privilege Escalation and Account Manipulation.

Bias Trigger and Manipulation: To encourage representativeness bias, attackers are rewarded for gaining access to admin accounts or for extracting files that appear valuable. The vignette incorporates a base rate manipulation, where attackers are informed that typical organizations in the industry have around 3% admin accounts. In contrast, the simulated network contains a much higher, atypical percentage of admin accounts, which primes the attacker to target these accounts. The environment is designed to mislead the attacker into overvaluing these targets while disregarding the improbability of such high concentrations of valuable resources in a real-world network.

Hypothesized Behavioral Manifestation: In a rational scenario, an attacker would retain the base rate information and distribute their access attempts based on a typical network environment. They would attempt to access both valuable and non-valuable data points in a more calculated manner, optimizing their chances of gaining access to valuable assets without raising suspicion. On the other hand, a biased or irrational attacker, influenced by representativeness bias, would disproportionately focus on high-value targets like admin accounts. They might invent justifications for attempting more access attempts than rational behavior would dictate, rationalizing, for instance, that the organization is unusually lax with admin privileges.

Bias Sensors and Observables: The activation of representativeness bias can be observed through several network metrics. The number of attempts to access accounts with the "-admin" suffix or other higher-level access accounts provides insight into whether the attacker is overvaluing these accounts. Another key observable is the number of false target files accessed or attempted to be extracted from the network. Attackers influenced by representativeness bias would disproportionately attempt to access these decoy assets, providing measurable evidence of the bias in action.

Confounding Factors: There are several potential confounds or moderator variables that might influence the attacker's behavior. For example, the sheer number of "-admin" accounts in the network might cause an attacker to make more attempts than usual, even if they are aware of the base rate. Additionally, attackers might have a default association between "-admin" logins and high-value accounts, which could cloud their judgment. Other variables that could impact behavior include the attacker's experience with network administration, their general expertise in infiltrating networks, and any specific knowledge they have of the fictional industry being simulated.

Ground Truth Validation: To validate the presence of representativeness bias, pre- and post-session surveys can be administered to measure the attacker's base rate perception of admin accounts in the network. This would provide a baseline for assessing how well the attacker understands the typical distribution of admin privileges and whether their behavior during the task deviated from this understanding.

Potential CyphiD Defense: A successful defense against representativeness bias could involve injecting fake accounts that mimic admin logins. Attackers targeting these decoy accounts could be redirected to a honeypot, where their actions can be monitored or neutralized. This method would have minimal impact on benign users but would effectively trap attackers who rely on faulty assumptions about the network's structure.

This structured approach to representativeness bias demonstrates how cognitive vulnerabilities can be systematically exploited in cyber deception to mislead attackers. Through careful manipulation of the environment and the attacker's expectations, defenders can induce attackers to make irrational decisions, increasing the likelihood of detection while protecting the network's true assets.

Hypothesized Cyber Behavior Impacts

The following table (Table 1) outlines the hypothesized impacts on attacker behavior within a cyber environment, using various behavioral metrics to measure the effectiveness of deception strategies and defenses. Each row focuses on a specific cyber behavior and provides corresponding metrics that can be used to track and quantify these impacts during experiments or real-world tests.

Decrease in Rate of Attack Success: The first row examines the impact of defenses on reducing the overall success rate of an attacker. The key metric used here is the number of goals completed by the attacker, specifically the number

Table 1 Hypothesized cyber behavioral impacts and corresponding metrics

Cyber behavioral impact	Reference behavioral metric	Instantiated behavioral metric	Experimental measures
Decrease rate of attack success	Number of goals completed	Number of true admin accounts with sensitive information privileges accessed successfully	Number of admin account credentials captured
Decrease in time until detection	Time until first alert	Time until at least three decoy accounts are attacked	Time spent undetected/time spent detected
Increase time to task completion	Duration of time to complete task	Duration of time spent attacking false-admin level accounts	Duration of time spent attacking fake admin accounts/duration of time spent attacking network

of successful accesses to admin accounts that hold sensitive information. In this context, the instantiation of this behavioral metric is the number of valid admin account credentials that the attacker successfully captures during their infiltration. The corresponding experimental measure tracks how many admin credentials are acquired, providing insight into how well the defense mechanisms prevent attackers from achieving their goals.

Decrease in Time Until Detection: The second row focuses on reducing the time it takes to detect an attacker within a network. The reference metric is the "time until first alert," which captures how quickly the system can identify malicious activity. The instantiated metric further specifies that detection is considered effective when the attacker interacts with at least three decoy accounts. This behavior can be measured by comparing the amount of time the attacker remains undetected versus the time spent detected, providing a clear indicator of how effectively deception strategies speed up the detection process.

Increase in Time to Task Completion: The third row evaluates how defenses affect the time attackers spend attempting to complete their objectives. The behavioral metric measures the total time required for attackers to finish their tasks, focusing on the time they waste interacting with false or decoy accounts (e.g., attacking accounts with "-admin" in the name that are actually decoys). By measuring the duration attackers spend interacting with fake admin accounts compared to the total time they spend on the network, this metric offers insight into how well the defense strategies delay the attacker, thereby decreasing their efficiency and increasing the chances of detection or failure.

These metrics allow for a detailed analysis of attacker behavior in response to cyber defenses, focusing on their success rate, detection time, and the amount of time they spend being misled or delayed by deceptive tactics. Each measure provides a way to quantify the effectiveness of deception strategies in slowing down or deterring attackers while increasing the likelihood of early detection.

Graphical Representation(s) of Hypothesized Relationships Between CogVulns, Behavioral Impacts, Bias Sensors and Bias Triggers (Hypothesized SEM)

In the context of cyber deception, the use of Structural Equation Modeling (SEM) provides a powerful tool for understanding the relationships between cognitive vulnerabilities (CogVulns), behavioral impacts, bias sensors, and bias triggers, as depicted in Fig. 3. By applying SEM to model these interactions, we can hypothesize how cognitive biases affect attacker decision-making, sensemaking, and inference-making processes. This allows cyber defenders to anticipate attacker behavior and implement defenses that exploit these vulnerabilities.

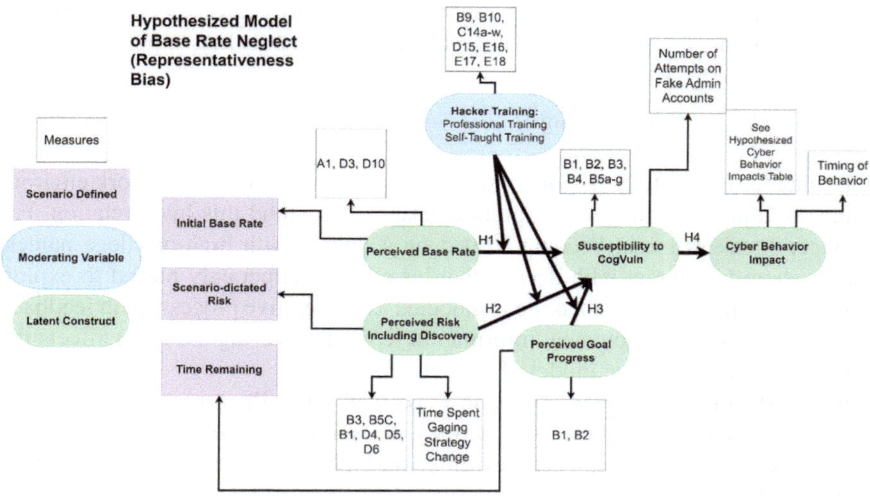

Fig. 3 Hypothesized structural equation model (SEM) of attacker behavior influenced by base rate neglect

SEM Model of Attacker Behavior

The SEM framework is designed to map out the flow of decision-making, sensemaking, and inference-making, considering how cognitive biases distort an attacker's understanding of the network. The model visualizes how different elements, including moderating variables (e.g., **Hacker Training** and **Scenario-defined Base Rates**), interact with cognitive vulnerabilities and ultimately lead to cyber behavior impacts (see Fig. 3).

Model of Attacker Decision-Making

Attacker decision-making is shaped by both rational analysis and irrational biases. Ideally, a rational attacker would evaluate the network environment based on the observable data, such as login credentials and the structure of access control systems. However, cognitive biases such as representativeness bias often skew this process. For example, attackers might overestimate the importance of an "admin" login due to its appearance, ignoring the actual base rate of admin accounts in the network. In the SEM, this is captured by linking **Perceived Base Rate** to **Susceptibility to CogVuln**, with the number of **Attempts on Fake Admin Accounts** serving as a key observable behavior impacted by bias.

These decision-making processes are influenced by moderating factors, such as the attacker's level of training and the perceived risk of discovery. As shown in the model, attackers with formal training may have a better grasp of typical base rates, making them less susceptible to certain biases. The model hypothesizes that training and scenario-defined risks moderate how biases affect decision-making, either reinforcing or mitigating the cognitive distortions attackers experience.

Model of Attacker Sensemaking

Sensemaking is the attacker's ongoing process of interpreting the network environment and adjusting strategies. Cognitive biases often cloud this interpretation. For instance, attackers might become fixated on accounts with high-privilege names, leading them to interact with decoys that have been deliberately placed to exploit these biases. In SEM, sensemaking is modeled as an iterative process, with feedback loops that account for how new information (e.g., discovering a decoy) affects the attacker's evolving mental model of the network.

In the diagram, **Perceived Risk** and **Perceived Goal Progress** play significant roles in how attackers adjust their actions. If attackers believe they are making progress (e.g., by capturing what they think are high-value admin credentials), they are more likely to continue on their current path, even if they are being misled by cognitive vulnerabilities. Sensors such as the **Time Spent Attacking Fake Admin Accounts** provide real-time data on how attackers misinterpret the network, further influencing their sensemaking process.

Model of Attacker Inference-Making

Inference-making involves the conclusions attackers draw from their actions and observations. For example, after repeatedly encountering accounts with "admin" in the name, an attacker might infer that the network is poorly secured or that gaining full control is within reach. However, these inferences are often driven by cognitive distortions, such as overconfidence or anchoring bias, leading attackers to overestimate their progress and underestimate the risk of discovery.

In SEM, this inference-making is represented by causal paths that connect **Perceived Base Rate** and **Perceived Goal Progress** to the actual **Cyber Behavior Impact**. The SEM predicts that biased inferences, influenced by faulty sensemaking and decision-making, will lead attackers to interact with false targets more frequently, extending the time until task completion and increasing the likelihood of detection.

Hypothesized Relationships Between Cognitive Vulnerabilities, Behavioral Impacts, Bias Sensors, and Bias Triggers

The SEM ties together several layers of relationships:

- **Cognitive Vulnerabilities (CogVulns):** These latent constructs represent the cognitive biases (e.g., representativeness bias, loss aversion) that shape attacker behavior. In the model, attackers with a high **Susceptibility to CogVuln** are more likely to be influenced by misleading cues (e.g., high numbers of admin-

sounding accounts) and to engage in irrational behavior, such as targeting decoys.

- **Behavioral Impacts:** These are the observable outcomes of the attacker's actions, such as the number of fake admin accounts attacked or the time spent interacting with false targets. The model links these impacts to attacker decision-making, sensemaking, and inference-making, demonstrating how biases distort these processes.
- **Bias Sensors and Bias Triggers:** These are environmental manipulations or defenses embedded in the network to detect and exploit cognitive biases. For example, introducing a large number of decoy "admin" accounts serves as a **Bias Trigger** for representativeness bias, while monitoring the number of failed login attempts provides a **Bias Sensor** to measure the activation of this bias.

Bias sensors provide measurable outputs that indicate when cognitive biases are affecting attacker behavior, allowing defenders to track and respond to attacker actions in real time. For instance, a spike in failed login attempts on decoy admin accounts would suggest that the attacker has fallen victim to representativeness bias, and defenders could adjust their strategies accordingly.

Graphical Representation of the SEM

The graphical SEM model represents latent variables (e.g., cognitive biases, perceived risk) connected to observable variables (e.g., attack behaviors, time spent on tasks) through hypothesized causal paths. **Bias Triggers** act as external stimuli designed to activate cognitive vulnerabilities, while **Bias Sensors** capture real-time data that reflect the attacker's biased behavior. In the model, **Perceived Base Rate** influences the attacker's decision-making, sensemaking, and inference-making processes, which in turn affect their actions on the network. As the attacker interacts with decoy accounts or other traps, the SEM tracks how these interactions alter their mental model of the network and influence their next steps. The feedback loops in the diagram emphasize the dynamic nature of these processes, showing how each stage informs the next in an ongoing cycle of bias-driven behavior.

3.2 Loss Aversion-Endowment Effect, Status Quo Biases

Loss aversion, the endowment effect, and status quo bias are cognitive biases that significantly influence human decision-making, particularly in situations involving risk and uncertainty. These biases can be exploited in cybersecurity scenarios to manipulate attacker behavior. **Loss Aversion** refers to the tendency for individuals to strongly prefer avoiding losses over acquiring equivalent gains, meaning that the psychological pain of losing something is typically more intense than the pleasure of gaining something of equal value [24]. In a cybersecurity context, this bias could cause attackers to become overly cautious after gaining network access, fearing the loss of access more than they value the potential rewards of further infiltration.

The **Endowment Effect** takes this one step further, as it posits that people become attached to possessions or assets they currently have, making them more reluctant to give them up (Kahneman et al., 1990). Once attackers gain access to a valuable asset within a network, they may be reluctant to engage in risky behaviors that could jeopardize their current access, even if there are greater potential rewards elsewhere. Ownership of a network credential, for example, becomes a reference point, and the attacker is less willing to risk losing that access, even if the potential gain is significant.

Lastly, **Status Quo Bias** suggests that individuals prefer maintaining their current state over making changes that could introduce uncertainty or loss [33]. In cybersecurity, this could lead attackers to favor maintaining their current level of access and mimicking regular traffic patterns, rather than attempting riskier maneuvers such as privilege escalation. Attackers may choose to avoid actions that could alert defenders to their presence, instead opting for slow, methodical infiltration.

Cyber Implementation

In a cyber attack, these biases can lead an attacker to make suboptimal decisions, particularly when they are unsure about the risks involved in escalating privileges or moving laterally within a network. For instance, after gaining initial access, an attacker may prefer to maintain their foothold by mimicking regular traffic patterns to avoid detection, rather than aggressively pursuing higher-privilege accounts or sensitive data. Loss aversion comes into play when the attacker fears that any overt actions might lead to losing their current access, especially if there is no immediate urgency or deadline pushing them to act. A **deceptive prompt** from the system, such as a notification that an upgrade is imminent and passwords will be reset, can exacerbate these biases. Even without a specific timeline, the possibility of losing access could push the attacker into making premature or irrational decisions. For example, they may attempt a "grab and run" operation, in which they try to gather as much data as possible before the system upgrade occurs, exposing themselves to detection.

Vignette Design

The vignette described explores how cognitive biases, such as loss aversion and the endowment effect, could influence an attacker's behavior during a targeted attack on a power and telecom company. The primary goal of the attacker is to gather valuable information about the company's infrastructure resiliency, operational procedures during outages, documentation, redundancies, and potential vulnerabilities. This information could be crucial for planning future attacks or for leveraging the network to extract more sensitive data. However, the attacker faces significant risks, such as being discovered due to multiple failed login attempts or triggering anomalous traffic alerts. Additionally, there is a risk of not achieving the attack's goal if the attacker hesitates to escalate privileges or take bolder actions to access sensitive admin accounts. These cognitive biases come into play as the attacker may hold back for fear of discovery or loss of access, which could prevent them from achieving their ultimate goal. The relevant stages of the Cyber Kill Chain in this scenario are **Exploitation** and **Installation**, with techniques aligning with the MITRE ATT&CK framework's **Persistence**, **Credential Access**, and **Discovery** tactics, all of which require careful balancing of risk influenced by cognitive biases.

The bias trigger, manipulation, and intervention in this scenario involve priming the attacker to exhibit bias-driven behavior by emphasizing the difficulty of achieving initial infiltration. After investing significant time and effort to gain network access, the attacker may overvalue the access they currently have, which can lead to risk-averse behavior. Several factors amplify this effect. First, the attacker has already achieved successful infiltration after considerable effort, and the cost of losing this access becomes particularly significant due to loss aversion and the endowment effect. Second, there is a disparity in rewards, where admin-level information is more valuable than monitoring data, priming the attacker to prioritize certain information over others. Third, the network is highly regulated, with strict traffic monitoring and password lockout policies after three failed login attempts. This constant threat of discovery reinforces the attacker's cautious approach, heightening loss aversion. The introduction of a password reset notification (which might appear as a security patch, maintenance message, or system upgrade) exacerbates the bias further. Even without a specific deadline, the mere mention of a reset triggers fear of losing access, prompting irrational and hurried actions.

In terms of hypothesized behavioral manifestation, **rational behavior** in the absence of bias would involve the attacker maintaining regular traffic patterns, patiently awaiting an opportunity to escalate privileges under more favorable conditions or when a specific deadline necessitates action. However, under the influence of cognitive bias, **biased or irrational behavior** emerges. Loss aversion could cause the attacker to panic, fearing that they will lose access once the system upgrade occurs. This may prompt a "grab and run" strategy, where the attacker attempts to extract as much information as possible before the password reset, thereby exposing themselves to detection and potentially compromising their efforts entirely.

The activation of these biases can be observed through specific **bias sensors and observable network metrics**. For example, a sudden increase in attempts to access admin-level accounts following the password reset notification could indicate a shift toward riskier behavior driven by loss aversion. Additionally, changes in **traffic patterns**—such as deviations from normal traffic emulation or shifts in attack patterns—might signal panic or bias-driven decisions. Monitoring these shifts provides insight into how attackers respond to perceived risks and loss of access.

Several **confounding or moderating variables** could influence the strength of these biases. **Time spent emulating normal traffic** is one such factor. Attackers who have spent more time blending in with regular traffic may become more reluctant to take risks, which could intensify the endowment effect. **Situational framing** is another factor, as the wording of administrator messages or security alerts can shape how attackers interpret the risk of discovery or loss. Finally, individual differences in **cultural and socio-economic background** might lead to varying degrees of risk tolerance and susceptibility to cognitive biases, which could influence how different attackers respond to the same scenario.

To **validate** the influence of these biases, pre- and post-task surveys can be conducted to assess the attacker's reasoning and decision-making processes. These surveys would measure the extent to which cognitive biases such as loss aversion, the endowment effect, or status quo bias influenced their strategy throughout the attack.

A potential **CyphiD defense** mechanism involves the use of a password reset instruction as part of the network's routine operations. This serves as a bias trigger, pushing attackers toward irrational decisions—such as accelerating their attacks or prematurely attempting to escalate privileges. By closely monitoring traffic patterns and failed login attempts, defenders can detect when an attacker is likely acting under the influence of bias and take appropriate countermeasures. These might include directing the attacker toward honeypots or increasing monitoring. The advantage of this approach is that it has minimal impact on benign users, as the password reset notification would align with typical network security practices.

Hypothesized Cyber Behavior Impacts

Table 2 outlines the hypothesized impacts of cyber deception strategies on attacker behavior, focusing on key metrics related to detection and resource expenditure during an attack. The table breaks down three main areas: Decrease in Time Until Detection, Increase in Detectability of the Attacker, and Increase in Attack Resources Wasted. These areas are tracked using specific behavioral metrics and experimental measures, providing a structured way to quantify the effects of deception techniques.

(i) Decrease in Time Until Detection: This impact area focuses on reducing the time it takes for a cyber defense system to detect an attacker's presence. The reference behavioral metric is the time until the first alert is triggered, which indicates how quickly the system recognizes an anomaly or malicious activity. The instantiated metric—the amount of time spent monitoring network traffic—captures how long the attacker is able to remain undetected while blending in with regular traffic patterns. The experimental measures track this by comparing the ratio of time spent undetected versus detected both before and after a network update message is triggered (e.g., a password reset notification). The goal is to assess how effectively the notification accelerates detection, forcing the attacker to act rashly and making them easier to spot.

Table 2 Metrics for assessing the impact of cyber deception on attacker behavior

Cyber behavioral impact	Reference behavioral metric	Instantiated behavioral metric	Experimental measures
Decrease in time until detection	Time until first alert	Amount of time spent monitoring network traffic	Ratio of time spent undetected versus detected before update message/ratio of time spent undetected versus detected after update message
Increase in detectability of attacker	Ratio of true positive alerts	Number of "grab and run" operations	Number of attacks on admin accounts before update message/number of attacks on admin accounts after update message
Increase attack resource wasted	Number of attempts per task	Number of admin accounts burned because of "grab and go" tactics induced by the password reset alert	Number of admin accounts burned after network update message

(ii) Increase in Detectability of the Attacker: The second area examines how easily the attacker can be detected following a deception prompt, such as a system notification. The reference metric here is the ratio of true positive alerts, which measures how accurately the defense system identifies the attacker's behavior as malicious (as opposed to false positives). The instantiated metric is the number of "grab and run" operations the attacker initiates—instances where the attacker, fearing loss of access, aggressively attempts to extract data or escalate privileges. This behavior is contrasted by measuring the number of attacks on admin accounts before the update message and after the message. The experimental measure compares these attack frequencies, indicating how the prompt affects the attacker's behavior and makes them more detectable.

(iii) Increase in Attack Resource Wasted: This impact area focuses on how much effort and resources the attacker wastes due to cyber deception strategies. The reference metric is the number of attempts per task, capturing how many actions the attacker takes while trying to accomplish their goal (e.g., accessing admin accounts).

The instantiated metric focuses specifically on the number of admin accounts burned—admin accounts that the attacker tries to compromise but fails because they are decoys or lead to detection. The attacker may be driven to act hastily due to the password reset alert, causing them to burn more accounts in their haste. The experimental measure compares the number of admin accounts burned after the network update message to quantify the impact of the deception tactic on the attacker's wasted resources.

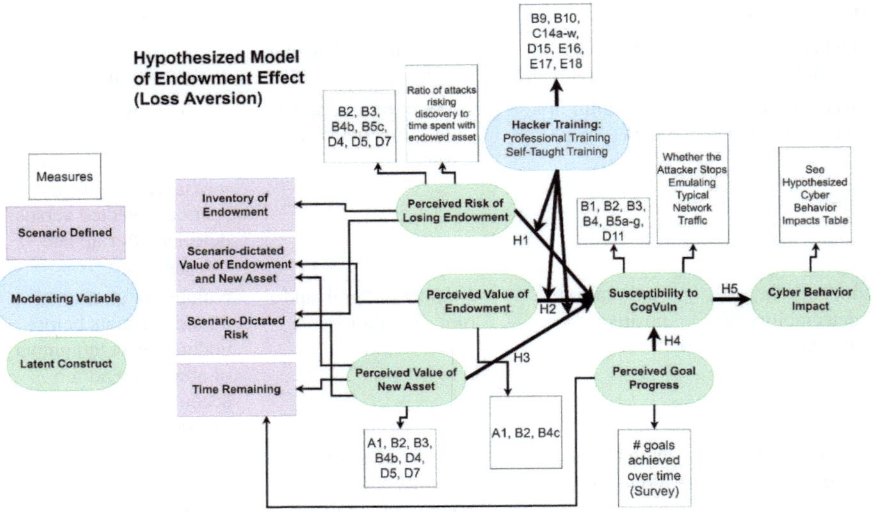

Fig. 4 Structural equation model (SEM) of attacker behavior influenced by loss aversion

Graphical Representation(s) of Hypothesized Relationships Between CogVulns, Behavioral Impacts, Bias Sensors and Bias Triggers (Hypothesized SEM)

This SEM (Fig. 4) illustrates the hypothesized relationships between various constructs and factors that influence attacker behavior, particularly focusing on **Loss Aversion**, the **Endowment Effect**, and **Status Quo Bias**. These cognitive biases are explored in the context of cyber deception, where attackers must decide whether to continue emulating normal network traffic to avoid detection or take riskier actions when presented with new assets or the potential loss of their current foothold in the network. The model organizes these decisions and behaviors into key constructs, such as moderating variables, cognitive biases, and observable cyber behavior impacts, and connects them through causal paths to explain how attackers may behave in response to different stimuli.

Measures (Left Side)

Scenario Defined encompasses the specific parameters set by the cyber attack scenario, including elements such as the network's structure and the complexity of the attack. These parameters shape the environment in which the attacker operates, dictating the challenges they face and the opportunities they perceive. **Moderating Variables** are factors that influence the attacker's behavior. In this model, the primary moderating variable is **Hacker Training**, which is subdivided into two categories: **Professional Training** and **Self-Taught Training**. These distinctions affect how attackers perceive risk, value their foothold in the network, and assess the potential for escalating their attack. More formally trained attackers might have a better understanding of the risks involved, while self-taught hackers may be more prone to taking impulsive actions based on incomplete information.

Latent Constructs are unobservable psychological factors that are inferred through the attacker's actions. In this case, they include the **Perceived Risk of Losing Endowment**, the **Perceived Value of the Endowment**, the **Perceived Value of a New Asset**, and **Perceived Goal Progress**. These latent constructs represent the attacker's internal assessment of their situation, guiding their decision-making process. For example, an attacker who overvalues their current foothold in the network (due to the endowment effect) may behave more cautiously to avoid losing it, while an attacker who perceives significant value in a new asset may take more risks to acquire it.

Inventory of Endowment and Risk (Center)

The **Inventory of Endowment** represents the assets or access points that the attacker currently controls within the network. These assets are subject to the **Endowment Effect**, meaning attackers are likely to overvalue what they already possess, making them more reluctant to take actions that could jeopardize their control. The **Scenario-Dictated Risk** refers to external factors, such as network monitoring or the potential for discovery, that influence how risky the attacker perceives their current position to be. The higher the perceived risk, the more cautious the attacker may become in their actions. **Time Remaining** captures how much time the attacker believes they have before the scenario concludes or before an event, such as a password reset, forces them to act. A limited amount of time may push the attacker to make riskier decisions, as they fear they won't have another opportunity to achieve their goals.

These factors together affect the **Perceived Risk of Losing the Endowment**, which triggers **Loss Aversion**—the fear of losing what is already possessed. This fear can drive attackers to act cautiously, or in some cases irrationally, in an attempt to hold onto their foothold in the network, even when it may not be strategically advantageous.

Perceived Value of Endowment and New Asset

The attacker weighs the **Perceived Value of their Endowment**—the access they already control—against the **Perceived Value of New Assets** they could target. When the new assets appear significantly more valuable than their current foothold, the attacker may decide to take action despite the risks. However, when their current access is perceived as highly valuable, they may hesitate to act, preferring to maintain the status quo due to loss aversion.

Attacker Susceptibility to Cognitive Vulnerabilities (CogVuln)

This construct measures the attacker's vulnerability to cognitive biases, such as the endowment effect and loss aversion. Attackers who are highly susceptible to these biases may be disproportionately influenced by the fear of losing access or by the value they place on their current foothold, leading them to act in predictable ways that defenders can exploit. For example, an attacker may delay escalation in order to avoid losing control of their current access, even when it would be strategically sound to move forward.

Cyber Behavior Impact

The **Cyber Behavior Impact** represents the observable consequences of the attacker's decisions and actions. These impacts are the culmination of the attacker's internal assessments and cognitive biases, and they manifest as measurable behaviors, such as the number of attacks on high-value targets or the time spent on specific activities. Metrics like the **Ratio of Attacks Risking Discovery to Time Spent with Endowed Asset** or **Whether the Attacker Stops Emulating Typical Network Traffic** provide defenders with data to quantify how biases influence attacker behavior. These metrics are crucial in determining whether the attacker's decision-making is being influenced by cognitive vulnerabilities like loss aversion.

Connections Between Constructs

The **Perceived Risk of Losing the Endowment** is directly linked to the **Susceptibility to Cognitive Vulnerabilities** and the **Perceived Value of the Endowment**. These connections explain how attackers balance the risks of losing their current foothold with the potential rewards of moving forward, as illustrated in Fig. 4. The higher the perceived risk or value of the endowment, the more likely attackers are to behave cautiously, avoiding actions that could jeopardize their current position.

Hacker Training acts as a moderating variable, shaping the relationship between these constructs and the attacker's behavior. Attackers with professional training may have a more refined understanding of the risks and rewards involved, allowing them to overcome some of the cognitive biases. In contrast, self-taught attackers may be more prone to acting on cognitive vulnerabilities, such as overvaluing their current position or underestimating the risks associated with taking action.

3.3 Summary of Two SEM

These two hypothesized implementations of structural equation modeling to understand cyber attackers' behavior and decision-making serve as an excellent example of how cognitive modeling techniques can apply to cyber security settings. Specifically, these models demonstrate how indicators of factors can be constituted by surveys or behavioral network measures stemming from network monitoring. Further, attacker behavior can be better understood using experimental methods, such as manipulating the nature of the network that attackers infiltrate, making those contextual features independent variables within the structural equation model. These examples target a model of cyber attackers' vulnerability to falling victim to various cognitive vulnerabilities (representativeness bias and loss aversion). Because of this research goal, the scenario described depicts networks with related characteristics (i.e., more than the average amount of admin accounts) that act as honey pots or decision points that the attacker could choose between a rational and irrational decision. These specific inflection points created by the network are the independent variable that kicks off the cause-and-effect structural equation model, which, in this case, is also temporal in nature. The example hypothesized structural equation models are temporal as they attempt to characterize the factors influencing their decision-making process before modeling their susceptibility to the cognitive vulnerability and the subsequent effect that susceptibility has on their attack's effectiveness. Displaying these examples of structural equation modeling experimentation applied to cyber security contexts and oppositional human factors enables such techniques to be more easily emulated across the field. These examples also further the argument that leveraging structural equation modeling human behavior and decision-making is incredibly useful and necessary to advance cybersecurity with new and innovative techniques continually.

4 Conclusion

The current chapter argues for using structural equation modeling in cybersecurity to enhance researchers' ability to model human behavior and decision-making effectively. This modeling of human behavior is especially important to effectively deploying innovative and novel cyber defenses, such as those that rely on exploiting cognitive biases and heuristics to identify, slow, and repel cyber attackers. From this argument, structural equation modeling is a holistic and highly useful modeling technique with applications to improve machine learning models' explainability and feature selection. Further, structural equation modeling has several advantages in analysis by simultaneously validating the measurement and structural model, which is showcased in the examples in the chapter. Specifically, these examples shed light on how an experiment may be designed to model what factors make an attacker susceptible to a cognitive vulnerability and what data may be necessary to make that determination, further increasing the precision of feature selection for eventual machine learning models to implement in real-time networks. In sum, the need to utilize advanced techniques to model human behavior in cyber security is necessary to continue pushing the boundary of cyber defense, as it is essential to remain one step ahead of attackers to protect networked systems.

References

1. Evan Perez, Zachary Cohen, and Alex Marquardt. 2021. First on CNN: US recovers millions in cryptocurrency paid to Colonial Pipeline ransomware hackers. *CNN, June* 8, (2021).
2. Kimberly J. Ferguson-Walter, Robert S. Gutzwiller, Dakota D. Scott, and Craig J. Johnson. 2021. Oppositional human factors in cybersecurity: A preliminary analysis of affective states. In *2021 36th IEEE/ACM International Conference on Automated Software Engineering Workshops (ASEW)*, 2021. IEEE, 153–158. Retrieved August 12, 2024 from https://ieeexplore.ieee.org/abstract/document/9680296/
3. Kimberly Ferguson-Walter, Temmie Shade, Andrew Rogers, Michael Christopher Stefan Trumbo, Kevin S. Nauer, Kristin Marie Divis, Aaron Jones, Angela Combs, and Robert G. Abbott. 2018. *The Tularosa Study: An Experimental Design and Implementation to Quantify the Effectiveness of Cyber Deception.* Sandia National Lab.(SNL-NM), Albuquerque, NM (United States). Retrieved August 12, 2024 from https://www.osti.gov/servlets/purl/1524844
4. Kimberly J. Ferguson-Walter, Maxine M. Major, Chelsea K. Johnson, and Daniel H. Muhleman. 2021. Examining the efficacy of decoy-based and psychological cyber deception. In *30th USENIX security symposium (USENIX Security 21)*, 2021. 1127–1144. Retrieved August 12, 2024 from https://www.usenix.org/conference/usenixsecurity21/presentation/ferguson-walter
5. Robert Gutzwiller, Kimberly Ferguson-Walter, Sunny Fugate, and Andrew Rogers. 2018. "Oh, Look, A Butterfly!" A Framework For Distracting Attackers To Improve Cyber Defense. *Proceedings of the Human Factors and Ergonomics Society Annual Meeting* 62, 1 (September 2018), 272–276. https://doi.org/10.1177/1541931218621063
6. Robert S. Gutzwiller, Sunny Fugate, Benjamin D. Sawyer, and P. A. Hancock. 2015. The Human Factors of Cyber Network Defense. *Proceedings of the Human Factors and Ergonomics Society Annual Meeting* 59, 1 (September 2015), 322–326. https://doi.org/10.1177/1541931215591067
7. Mohammed H. Almeshekah and Eugene H. Spafford. 2016. Cyber Security Deception. In Cyber Deception, Sushil Jajodia, V.S. Subrahmanian, Vipin Swarup and Cliff Wang (eds.). Springer International Publishing, Cham, 23–50. https://doi.org/10.1007/978-3-319-32699-3_2
8. Ehab Al-Shaer, Jinpeng Wei, Kevin W. Hamlen, and Cliff Wang (Eds.). 2019. *Autonomous Cyber Deception: Reasoning, Adaptive Planning, and Evaluation of HoneyThings*. Springer International Publishing, Cham. https://doi.org/10.1007/978-3-030-02110-8
9. Andrew Bushby. 2019. How deception can change cyber security defences. *Computer Fraud & Security* 2019, 1 (January 2019), 12–14. https://doi.org/10.1016/S1361-3723(19)30008-9
10. Kimberly J. Ferguson-Walter, Dana S. LaFon, and T. B. Shade. 2017. Friend or faux: deception for cyber defense. *Journal of Information Warfare* 16, 2 (2017), 28–42.
11. Kristin E. Heckman, Frank J. Stech, Roshan K. Thomas, Ben Schmoker, and Alexander W. Tsow. 2015. *Cyber Denial, Deception and Counter Deception: A Framework for Supporting Active Cyber Defense*. Springer International Publishing, Cham. https://doi.org/10.1007/978-3-319-25133-2
12. Zhuo Lu, Cliff Wang, and Shangqing Zhao. 2020. Cyber Deception for Computer and Network Security: Survey and Challenges. Retrieved October 11, 2024 from http://arxiv.org/abs/2007.14497
13. Niels Provos. 2004. A Virtual Honeypot Framework. In *USENIX Security Symposium*, 2004. 1–14. Retrieved October 11, 2024 from https://www.usenix.org/event/sec04/tech/full_papers/provos/provos_html
14. Kimberly J. Ferguson-Walter. 2024. An empirical assessment of the effectiveness of deception for cyber defense. (2024). Retrieved October 11, 2024 from https://scholarworks.umass.edu/items/7914473b-3742-4226-93fc-868b5a3b7a73
15. Kimberly J. Ferguson-Walter, Maxine M. Major, Chelsea K. Johnson, Craig J. Johnson, Dakota D. Scott, Robert S. Gutzwiller, and Temmie Shade. 2023. Cyber expert feedback: Experiences, expectations, and opinions about cyber deception. *Computers & Security* 130, (2023), 103268.

16. Robert S. Gutzwiller, Kimberly J. Ferguson-Walter, and Sunny J. Fugate. 2019. Are Cyber Attackers Thinking Fast and Slow? Exploratory Analysis Reveals Evidence of Decision-Making Biases in Red Teamers. *Proceedings of the Human Factors and Ergonomics Society Annual Meeting* 63, 1 (November 2019), 427–431. https://doi.org/10.1177/1071181319631096
17. Chelsea K. Johnson, Robert S. Gutzwiller, Kimberly J. Ferguson-Walter, and Sunny J. Fugate. 2020. A cyber-relevant table of decision making biases and their definitions. (2020). Retrieved October 11, 2024 from https://www.researchgate.net/profile/Chelsea-Johnson-11/publication/344106644_A_Cyber-Relevant_Table_of_Decision_Making_Biases_and_their_Definitions/links/5fc973c6299bf188d4f14630/A-Cyber-Relevant-Table-of-Decision-Making-Biases-and-their-Definitions.pdf
18. Natasha K. Bowen and Shenyang Guo. 2011. *Structural equation modeling*. Oxford University Press. Retrieved October 11, 2024 from https://books.google.com/books?hl=en&lr=&id=VN9oAgAAQBAJ&oi=fnd&pg=PP1&dq=Structural+Equation+Modeling+bowen&ots=bg8hntusJT&sig=W0vEyDqK_JZ_mzDNdC0iUnLwdNY
19. Herbert Alexander Simon. 1997. *Models of bounded rationality: Empirically grounded economic reason*. MIT press. Retrieved October 11, 2024 from https://books.google.com/books?hl=en&lr=&id=9CiwU28z6WQC&oi=fnd&pg=PA1&dq=Models+of+bounded+rationality:+empirically+grounded+economic+reason&ots=GMSRbnhJ3j&sig=uYjDaHMLETVXHNtIBMInZn0u-8Q
20. Amos Tversky and Daniel Kahneman. 1974. Judgment under Uncertainty: Heuristics and Biases: Biases in judgments reveal some heuristics of thinking under uncertainty. *Science* 185, 4157 (September 1974), 1124–1131. https://doi.org/10.1126/science.185.4157.1124
21. Daniel Kahneman. 2011. Thinking, fast and slow. *Farrar, Straus and Giroux* (2011). Retrieved October 11, 2024 from https://www.pdcnet.org/pdc/bvdb.nsf/showopenaccess?open&repid=852577BA0050DC0D&docid=2BE9C7FA6C507E4DC1257ADA0072A186&solarid=inquiryct_2012_0027_0002_0054_0057
22. Gerd Gigerenzer and Peter M. Todd. 1999. *Simple heuristics that make us smart*. Oxford University Press, USA.
23. Barry M. Staw. 1997. The escalation of commitment: An update and appraisal. *Organizational decision making* 191, (1997), 215.
24. Nathan Novemsky and Daniel Kahneman. 2005. The Boundaries of Loss Aversion. *Journal of Marketing Research* 42, 2 (May 2005), 119–128. https://doi.org/10.1509/jmkr.42.2.119.62292
25. Charles T. Clotfelter and Philip J. Cook. 1993. Notes: The "Gambler's Fallacy" in Lottery Play. *Management Science* 39, 12 (December 1993), 1521–1525. https://doi.org/10.1287/mnsc.39.12.1521
26. Amos Tversky and Daniel Kahneman. 1971. Belief in the law of small numbers. *Psychological bulletin* 76, 2 (1971), 105.
27. Norbert Schwarz, Herbert Bless, Fritz Strack, Gisela Klumpp, Helga Rittenauer-Schatka, and Annette Simons. 1991. Ease of retrieval as information: Another look at the availability heuristic. *Journal of Personality and Social psychology* 61, 2 (1991), 195.
28. Roger Tourangeau and Kenneth A. Rasinski. 1988. Cognitive processes underlying context effects in attitude measurement. *Psychological bulletin* 103, 3 (1988), 299.
29. Richard H. Thaler and Cass R. Sunstein. 2021. *Nudge: The final edition*. Yale University Press. Retrieved October 11, 2024 from https://books.google.com/books?hl=en&lr=&id=Wf1AEAAAQBAJ&oi=fnd&pg=PR11&dq=Nudge:+The+final+edition&ots=rJ-h2NnkwE&sig=XGB4g_PhHOY8tGUPMqZGE4PBbmo
30. Eric J. Johnson and Daniel G. Goldstein. 2004. Defaults and donation decisions. *Transplantation* 78, 12 (2004), 1713–1716.
31. Gerd Gigerenzer and Daniel G. Goldstein. 1999. Betting on one good reason: The take the best heuristic. In *Simple heuristics that make us smart*. Oxford University Press, 75–95. Retrieved October 11, 2024 from https://pure.mpg.de/rest/items/item_2102907/component/file_2102906/content

32. Amos Tversky and Daniel Kahneman. 1973. Availability: A heuristic for judging frequency and probability. *Cognitive psychology* 5, 2 (1973), 207–232.
33. Amos Tversky and Daniel Kahneman. 1992. Advances in prospect theory: Cumulative representation of uncertainty. *J Risk Uncertainty* 5, 4 (October 1992), 297–323. https://doi.org/10.1007/BF00122574
34. Victoria Savalei and Peter M. Bentler. 2006. Structural equation modeling. *The handbook of marketing research: Uses, misuses, and future advances* 330, (2006), 36.
35. Francesco Ricci, Lior Rokach, and Bracha Shapira (Eds.). 2015. *Recommender Systems Handbook*. Springer US, Boston, MA. https://doi.org/10.1007/978-1-4899-7637-6
36. Timothy A. Brown and Michael T. Moore. 2012. Confirmatory factor analysis. *Handbook of structural equation modeling* 361, (2012), 379.
37. Ralph O. Mueller and Gregory R. Hancock. 2018. Structural equation modeling. In *The reviewer's guide to quantitative methods in the social sciences*. Routledge, 445–456. Retrieved August 12, 2024 from https://www.taylorfrancis.com/chapters/edit/10.4324/9781315755649-33/structural-equation-modeling-ralph-mueller-gregory-hancock
38. Li-tze Hu and Peter M. Bentler. 1999. Cutoff criteria for fit indexes in covariance structure analysis: Conventional criteria versus new alternatives. *Structural Equation Modeling: A Multidisciplinary Journal* 6, 1 (January 1999), 1–55. https://doi.org/10.1080/10705519909540118
39. Bart Knijnenburg and Martijn Willemsen. 2015. Evaluating recommender systems with user experiments. In *Recommender Systems Handbook*. Springer US, Boston, MA, 309–352.
40. Jiarui Li, Tetsuo Sawaragi, and Yukio Horiguchi. 2021. Introduce structural equation modelling to machine learning problems for building an explainable and persuasive model. *SICE Journal of Control, Measurement, and System Integration* 14, 2 (June 2021), 67–79. https://doi.org/10.1080/18824889.2021.1894040
41. Siddharth Gulati, Sonia Sousa, and David Lamas. 2019. Design, development and evaluation of a human-computer trust scale. *Behaviour & Information Technology* 38, 10 (October 2019), 1004–1015. https://doi.org/10.1080/0144929X.2019.1656779
42. Gongmeng Chen, Kenneth A. Kim, John R. Nofsinger, and Oliver M. Rui. 2007. Trading performance, disposition effect, overconfidence, representativeness bias, and experience of emerging market investors. *Behavioral Decision Making* 20, 4 (October 2007), 425–451. https://doi.org/10.1002/bdm.561

Human Risks and Cognition-Inspired Adaptive Cyber Deception

Ya-Ting Yang, Yunfei Ge, and Quanyan Zhu

1 Human Cyber Risks

With the rapid growth of modern internet technology, cyber security has gained attention from a variety of communities, from researchers to industries, as cyber-attacks can lead to significant consequences [6] such as unauthorized access, stealing of information, operational disruptions, and financial losses. A cyber attack often finds its roots in the art of social engineering (SE)—a technique that exploits human vulnerabilities rather than technical ones [49], as humans also play an important role in the cyber-physical world (as illustrated in Fig. 1). Figure 1 is composed of three interconnected layers. The physical layer includes critical infrastructure that supports the cyber world; attackers may compromise or destroy components like base stations or cables to disrupt cyber operations and pursue their malicious objectives. The cyber layer comprises devices owned by individuals or organizations, all interconnected through networks. Here, attackers can exploit technical vulnerabilities to advance their goals. Social engineering (SE) typically operates within the human layer, where attackers manipulate individuals (the victims) into taking actions that serve the attacker's intent.

For example, in 2014, Sony fell victim to a series of sophisticated attacks that began with hackers sending malicious emails containing malware to employees. The breach by the employees led to the theft of over 100 terabytes of sensitive data, including newly released files, financial records, and customer information, with a financial impact of over 100 million [31]. In 2016, Belgium's Crelan Bank lost approximately 75.8 million due to a CEO fraud attack. The attack began with a

Y.-T. Yang (✉) · Y. Ge · Q. Zhu
New York University, New York, NY, USA
e-mail: yy4348@nyu.edu; yg2047@nyu.edu; qz494@nyu.edu

Q. Zhu et al. (eds.), *Foundations of Cyber Deception*, Advances in Information Security 90, https://doi.org/10.1007/978-3-031-93867-2_8

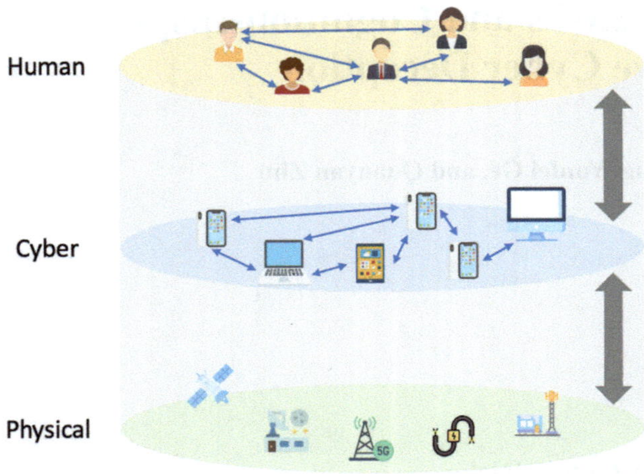

Fig. 1 An illustrative framework showing how humans are positioned in the cyber-physical world

phishing email impersonating the CEO, which instructed the finance department to wire funds to an account controlled by the criminals [32].

With the emergence of generative artificial intelligence (AI), social engineering tactics, such as phishing emails, deceptive phone calls, and fraudulent messages, have become more sophisticated, making it easier to trick users into inadvertently facilitating attacks [50]. ChatGPT's [45] capabilities in answering various questions, generating code, creating page layouts, and drafting high-quality messages enable it to replicate popular websites and produce realistic content, making it easier for attackers to quickly prepare materials for effective social engineering attacks [14]. For example, the attacker could use ChatGPT to generate a message that appears to come from a colleague or supervisor at the victim's workplace. Crafted with a professional tone and language, this message might request sensitive information or prompt a specific action, such as clicking a malicious link [16].

To mitigate such user cyber risks, various solutions have been proposed to detect and prevent malicious content from reaching their target victims [15, 38] such as the use of blacklists containing previously detected phishing URLs, addresses, or keywords, as well as the use of visual similarity and other features. In this context, machine learning (ML) techniques have shown promising results compared to conventional methods. In some cases, ML-based approaches can nearly eliminate zero-day cyber attacks and achieve very high true-positive detection rates [5]. However, practical challenges remain, including but not limited to effective training of ML-based detection systems and addressing adversarial ML usage.

More proactive viable approaches are through user phishing awareness training and the metric from penetration testing. Awareness training [33] aims to educate users on how to identify and appropriately respond to phishing emails. This can be achieved through dedicated courses or simulated phishing scenarios, often developed by an organization's security team. Such training intends to help users become more vigilant and better equipped to handle potential threats [18]. Additionally, penetration testing [42] involves conducting simulated cyber attacks to identify and address vulnerabilities in an organization's system. This proactive approach helps organizations strengthen their security measures by exposing weaknesses before malicious entities can exploit them. However, the absence of standardized benchmarks raises questions about the certainty of achieving user awareness, the interplay between knowledge and awareness, the definition of an ideal penetration test, and the human inclination to speculate about test outcomes. Hence, a profound understanding of human behavior becomes an essential focus to address these challenges.

To understand human behaviors better, the concept of Cyber Risk Belief (CRB) is proposed. CRB is the beliefs users form while navigating the virtual world that influence how much effort they put into processing information [55] and is a crucial element to consider during security awareness training or penetration test design. CRB states that people might believe that certain actions (opening PDFs instead of Word documents or favoring SMS text messages over online platforms like Facebook Messenger or WhatsApp) are at lower risk. However, the stark reality is that none of these actions can be considered entirely safe. Additionally, automatic responses driven by ingrained habits often obscure our judgment and reduce our sensitivity. For instance, an employee might click on a link in a seemingly urgent email from IT without much scrutiny due to the habit of quickly responding to IT-related requests, which potentially leads to a phishing attack.

2 Role of Cognitive Biases on Cyber Security

Human beings often serve as the initial entry points for cyberattacks, frequently through means like phishing emails. Thus, it becomes imperative to delve into the psychological facets of how individuals face cyber threats [43] and explore the field of cognitive security [26]. Conventional security strategies, unfortunately, contain vulnerabilities due to the influence of people's cognitive biases. These biases represent ingrained thinking patterns that can lead individuals to make irrational or sub-optimal decisions. For example, the study [29] utilizes the Hidden Markov Model (HMM) to capture human decision-making processes under normal conditionals as well as different cognitive vulnerabilities, as the two patterns shown in Fig. 2. The following will also discuss five illustrative examples of psychological phenomena closely related to cybersecurity.

We begin with the **illusion of invulnerability**, which refers to the optimism bias in cognitive biases where people mistakenly believe they are immune to harm or that adverse events will not happen to them [13]. This mindset can lead to overconfidence and risky behaviors (i.e., ignoring warnings or failing to take precautions) because those who possess it underestimate potential dangers and overestimate their ability to avoid harm. In the context of cybersecurity, a study

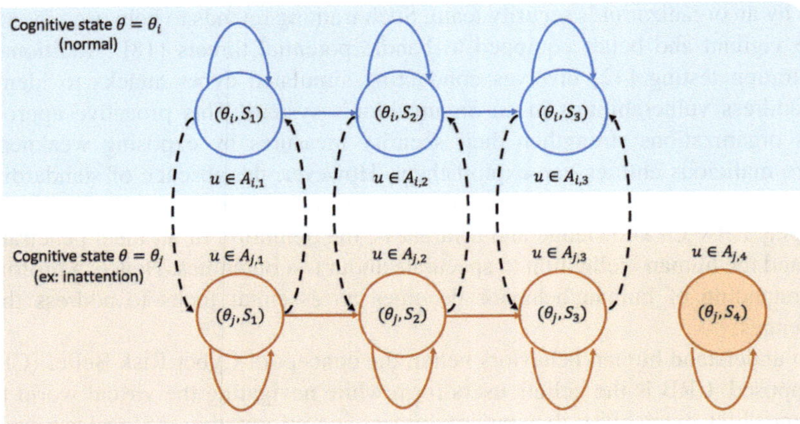

Fig. 2 The Hidden Markov Model (HMM) for different decision processes of human decision-makers under different cognitive vulnerabilities (states). The decision-maker can take actions (*blue and orange arrows*) to transition between stages S. Each colored box represents a series of decision-making processes under specific cognitive states. The transition between cognitive states (*black dotted arrows*) happens if and only if the human is exposed to a trigger

shows that Americans estimate others are 50% more likely than they are to respond as requested in a phishing scam [9]. That is, people often underestimate their roles in cybersecurity and might not be cautious enough when facing threats because they "feel" immune to potential consequences.

The second one is **base rate neglect**, a cognitive bias where people tend to underutilize or ignore general population-wised statistical information (base rates) of a particular event or characteristic when making decisions or judgments. Instead of considering the broader statistical context, people often focus too much on specific, vivid, or recent information when evaluating the probability or likelihood of an event. That is, most people are not using the information such as base rates they were informed previously, which means people are still likely to fall for cyber-attacks even if gone through awareness training. Experimental study [9] reveals that people tend to self-enhance when assessing risk, believing they are less likely than others (base rate) to engage in actions that threaten their cybersecurity. That is, people are more likely to "neglect base rates" when forecasting for themselves, which also demonstrates the previous "illusion of invulnerability" phenomenon.

The third cognitive bias is the **bandwagon bias**, also known as the bandwagon effect [19], where people adopt ways of thinking, working, and acting simply because others are doing it, regardless of their own beliefs or the underlying evidence or received information. The bandwagon effect is deeply rooted in human nature, driven by our inherent desire to conform and be part of a group. The tendency to follow the crowd can influence behaviors and decision-making, often leading to a herd mentality. The bandwagon effect can be seen in various contexts, such as politics, fashion, investing, social media trends, and cybersecurity, where the popularity of an idea or behavior increases as more people adopt it. Specifically, in the context of cybersecurity, bandwagon bias can manifest when organizations adopt certain security measures or defense technologies simply because other organizations are doing so, rather than based on a thorough assessment of their own needs and risks. Additionally, risks of bandwagon bias can also occur in the form of the pro-innovation bias which leads to the belief that an innovation or new technology should be adopted by society as a whole without sufficient evidence or consideration of its potential downsides [54]. It can then lead the organization to premature adoption of new technologies, unknown vulnerabilities, and ignorance of conventional reliable solutions.

The fourth one is the **confirmation bias** [34, 44], which is a well-known cognitive bias that leads people to favor information that confirms their pre-existing hypotheses or beliefs while disregarding or minimizing even the latest information that contradicts them. People often strengthen their existing beliefs by selectively gathering new evidence, interpreting information in a biased way, or recalling only supportive information from memory. For example, an analyst who believes they have identified a pattern in a series of failures may ignore other potential causes and focus solely on the evidence that supports their hypothesis [39]. Similarly, human users who have preconceived notions about the security of their information infrastructure may become overconfident, making them even more susceptible to cyber-attacks [47].

The fifth bias is **bounded rationality**, which suggests that the human mind has limited cognitive capacity [25] and cannot process or pay attention to all available information, leading to sub-optimal judgment and decision-making [58]. For example, when deciding which stock to invest in, individuals are often overwhelmed by information such as news, financial reports, company background, and metrics like earnings per share. As a result, they may simply follow the market index, which may not lead to the best outcome in the end. To characterize this, [51] proposes replacing the optimization problem of maximizing expected utility with a simpler decision criterion known as "satisficing." This means that humans will stop searching for the optimal strategy once they find one that meets or exceeds their aspiration level. In the context of cybersecurity, human users cannot process all the information related to potential cyber-attacks. Additionally, awareness and defense strategies often place extra cognitive loads on users, affecting their ability to process and prioritize information. This can impact both their performance on regular tasks as well as their accuracy in recognizing cyber attacks [7, 27]. For example, users may find it challenging to apply all learned skills from the awareness training due to cognitive overload; employees in security teams may focus on familiar types of attacks while underestimating new or complex threats due to limited information and cognitive resources.

Cybersecurity awareness training with ongoing and latest education (such as letting people be aware that they are also vulnerable to scams) can help individuals recognize and counteract the above-mentioned and other cognitive biases to some extent, leading to more informed and cautious behavior when dealing with cyber threats. Additionally, designing user-friendly security systems and interfaces [21], such as tagging the sender's email address to warn users, guide the users' attention to the right contents of the email [24], or using alert and attention management strategy that de-emphasizes some alerts triggered by feint attacks intended to overload human operators [23], can also improve their accuracy of phishing recognition as well as help to minimize the impact of cognitive biases in decision-making processes related to cybersecurity.

3 Adaptive Cognitive Model and Deception for Defense

Cyber deception defenses play a vital role against malicious attackers seeking to breach systems and compromise data [59]. The deception defense strategies and technologies are often carefully designed to misdirect cyber attackers, thus shielding valuable assets. In this context, defenders can construct a parallel reality with fabricated services for decoying purposes, such as Honeypots [12, 48] or fictitious documents in a network or system using cunning techniques, rendering the distinction between genuine data and fabricated assets exceptionally challenging for would-be intruders.

However, the current landscape of cyber deception in defense is far from perfect, as several critical issues still exist. First, the practical viability of deception strategies, such as decoying, is under scrutiny. While these tactics may seem promising in theory and simulation, their effectiveness in real-world scenarios remains questionable, particularly against human attackers [1]. Additionally, although these methods often perform well in controlled environments, their ability to withstand the unpredictable and dynamic nature of real-world attacks is still uncertain. This gap between simulated success and practical application raises concerns about their reliability in actual cyber defense. Furthermore, many deceptive techniques in cyber defense are inherently static, providing attackers with the opportunity to study and eventually bypass them. The lack of adaptive in these defenses allows attackers to spend time crafting sophisticated exploits. Once inside a network, attackers can persist undetected, exploiting the static nature of the defense to maintain a foothold and continuously pose a threat. Moreover, the implementation of deception techniques can also introduce additional complexity to a network's defense infrastructure, potentially leading to unforeseen vulnerabilities. The challenge lies in balancing the sophistication of deceptive measures with the simplicity and robustness needed to avoid creating new entry points for cyber attackers.

An illustrative example arises in the discrepancy between theoretically optimal masking defense strategies and random masking strategies in practical scenarios. Different from the controlled simulation environment, human attackers in practice tend to adapt their strategies based on risk aversion and cognitive biases [37], rendering the optimal defense approach less effective than originally anticipated [11]. To address these challenges, defenders must incorporate human cognitive biases when developing deceptive strategies. Using the model described in Fig. 2 as an illustrative example, if the defender can accurately assess (or predict) the

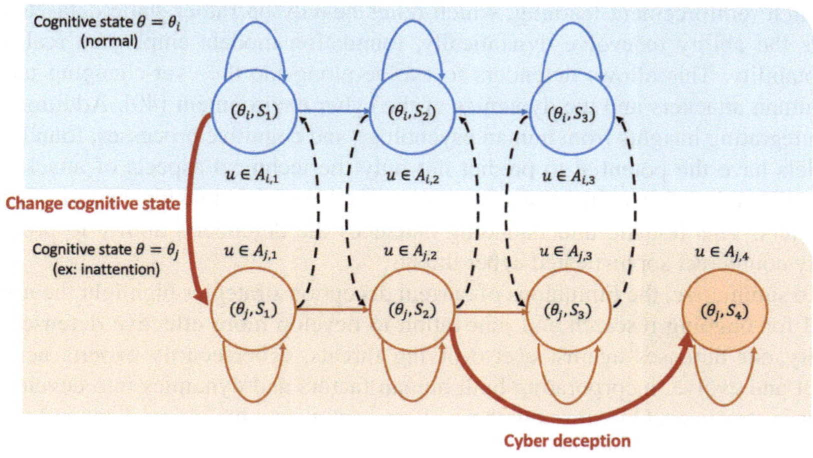

Fig. 3 An example illustrating how human (attacker's) cognitive states can be integrated into deceptive strategies to achieve the desired outcome set by the strategy designer (defender). The red arrow shows an example of intentionally triggering another cognitive state to create a mental environment where deception is possible

human attacker's current cognitive state, the defender can strategically influence it or intentionally trigger another state to create a mental environment where deception is not only possible but also most effective, leading the attacker's decision toward a defender-preferred outcome (see Fig. 3).

In the context of inducing a specific cognitive state and deceiving a human attacker, a viable approach is using behavioral game theory. With this in mind, signaling games provide a valuable framework for analyzing how human attackers make decisions when faced with deception [46]. The defender (sender) can transmit truthful or deceptive information (signals) to the attacker (receiver) to gain a strategic advantage such as triggering a specific mental state. Then, by constructing cognitive models that replicate the dynamic decision-making processes of human attackers, defenders can better anticipate and predict an attacker's behavior. This predictive capability enhances the effectiveness of game-theoretic and ML-based defense strategies. For instance, [10] proposes an instance-based learning (IBL) cognitive model, implemented within the Adaptive Control of Thought-Rational (ACT-R) cognitive architecture [3, 4], to explore how attackers make decisions under deceptive (signaling) conditions in cyber-attack scenarios.

Another promising approach is the application of foundation models, which excel in predictive capabilities that can forecast future scenarios and decipher strategies likely to be employed by human attackers [41], particularly those influenced by cognitive biases. Moreover, foundation models are especially valuable in the domain of predictive reinforcement learning [17], where they enable the continuous updating of defense policies based on the defender's forecasts of future outcomes and anticipated reactions of human attackers. Unlike conventional offline or batch reinforcement learning, which relies heavily on rather static datasets and lacks the ability to evolve dynamically, foundation models emphasize real-time adaptability. This allows defenders to evolve alongside the ever-changing tactics of human attackers and the dynamics of the cyber environment [40]. Additionally, by integrating insights from human psychology and cognitive processes, foundation models have the potential to predict not only the technical aspects of attacks but also the underlying motivations, reasoning, and decision-making patterns of the attackers. This holistic understanding enhances the defender's ability to preemptively counteract sophisticated cyber threats.

To summarize, the limitations of current deception strategies highlight the urgent need for ongoing research and innovation to develop more effective defenses. To fortify our defenses against ever-evolving threats, cybersecurity experts need to adapt and evolve, incorporating both human factors and dynamics into developing defense strategies. Only through these efforts can we maintain a resilient and robust defense in the face of an increasingly sophisticated cyber landscape.

4 Designing Human-Aware Cyber Deception

The concept of deception has long played a pivotal role in the context of warfare, dating back through the ages. As Sun Tzu once asserted, "All warfare is based on deception." However, when it comes to applying this principle to cybersecurity, many aspects remain a subject of ongoing discussion and exploration. We begin with the process of designing cyber deception for defense.

The conventional process of designing cyber deception involves several key steps, each critical to the overall strategy.

- Firstly, it necessitates a clear understanding and definition of the desired responses from the targeted system or adversary, which helps in shaping the deceptive environment. This step includes identifying the desired behaviors or decisions from the attacker, such as wasting their resources, altering their attack path, or revealing their intent as well as intelligence.
- Secondly, the formulation of a domain-specific language for deception design is essential. It provides a framework to communicate deceptive tactics and strategies effectively, allowing security professionals to specify how deception should unfold across different components of the system. It ensures consistency in applying deceptive methods and ensures that they align with the intended security goals.
- Thirdly, the incorporation of state-of-the-art deception techniques is a crucial step. These techniques may include honeypots, honey tokens, fake credentials, or more advanced methods like content generated by foundation models or behavioral manipulation. Choosing the right combination of these techniques, depending on the attack vectors and adversary profiles, ensures that the deception plan is both effective and adaptive to real-world attack scenarios.

- Lastly, the translation of the design into configuration data and scripts is vital for execution. This step involves executing the deception by programming the necessary scripts and configurations that will be deployed across the system. These may include network configurations, virtual machines, or software-defined environments designed to create a convincing deceptive environment that interacts with the attacker in real time.

Cyber deception often serves a variety of objectives, from conventional protection measures like obfuscation, noise generation, and decoy usage [12, 48], to more sophisticated strategies for confusing or extracting intelligence from adversaries. For example, through carefully crafted disinformation, deception may mislead human adversaries into believing they have found valuable data, however in reality, they are interacting with fabricated information. These objectives are not mutually exclusive and can be complementary, as a layered deception strategy may simultaneously protect assets while gathering critical intelligence about the attacker's methods and intentions.

There are various dimensions that requires careful consideration for designing effective cyber deception. First, we must determine the **depth and consistency** of deception coverage within a network-based system. Second, it is essential to decide which stages of the **cyber kill chain**, both external and internal, should be the focus of the deception efforts. Third, **deployment and infrastructure** considerations must also be integrated into the deception design process, as achieving the desired goals of cyber deception depends on careful planning.

In a broader sense, the success of cyber deception relies on the interplay of **techniques, humans, and metrics**, forming what we can call the cyber deception triad. During the design phase, several critical questions must be addressed within this triad.

- Techniques: It is crucial to evaluate the effectiveness of the chosen deception techniques, ensuring that they are not only technically sound but also capable of deceiving sophisticated attackers nowadays. Besides, gaining support from human users and stakeholders for the deployment of these techniques is equally important, as their cooperation, understanding, and feedback are often key to the success of deception strategies.
- Humans: The human element, such as biases mentioned in Sect. 2, requires careful consideration of the perspectives and behaviors of all parties involved in the deception. This includes the knowledge of how defenders can craft and implement deceptive measures while anticipating and countering the strategies and tactics of attackers. Recognizing the psychological and cognitive biases that influence human attackers, defenders and other parties involved plays a vital role in shaping effective deception strategies.
- Metrics: Selecting and applying appropriate metrics is essential for measuring the impact and success of cyber deception efforts. These metrics help to quantify the effectiveness of deception techniques, assess the reactions of attackers, and provide actionable insights for refining and enhancing future deception design.

Implementing cyber deception requires not only a solid technical foundation but also a well-thought-out plan of action. The threat models and supporting technologies are already in place. However, to put these technologies into operation effectively, we must carefully consider deployment and management systems. Additionally, testing the effectiveness of the deception design through the use of testbeds, prototypes, and rehearsals with feedback is essential for continual improvement. While definitive answers may not yet exist for all the questions surrounding cyber deception, these points serve as indispensable considerations in any discussion of the topic.

4.1 Dynamic, Multi-Layer, Multi-Stage, Cognition-Inspired Active Cyber Deception

The rapid advancement of computer techniques has led to a substantial increase in organizations' expenditure on cyber defense. This has given rise to what appears to be an asymmetric cyberwar between defenders and attackers. Attackers have the luxury of time to probe defenses, select targets from a vast pool, and only need to exploit one critical vulnerability to breach a system. Conversely, defenders are under immense pressure, with only seconds to respond to attacks. They often find themselves defending numerous legacy assets while striving to close all observable vulnerabilities.

Cyber deception emerges as a promising means to rectify this asymmetry. Various cyber deception techniques, such as honeynets, honeypots, honeywords, and fake document generation, have been implemented as defensive measures. To grasp the concept fully, it is crucial to clarify a common misconception—cyber deception should not be conflated with obscurity or obfuscation. Cyber deception aims to create a false sense of certainty for attackers, whereas obfuscation seeks to induce uncertainty. Additionally, cyber deception differs from moving target defense, as the latter involves changing tactics when deception is detected.

The objectives of cyber deception can be summarized as 4D [2]: Deflect, Distort, Deplete, and Discover. These four pillars provide approaches to misleading, exhausting, and ultimately uncovering adversarial actions and intentions.

- Deflect adversarial attention: This objective involves redirecting an adversary's attention away from valuable or vulnerable assets by presenting them with decoys or less critical targets. For example, a financial institution might create a decoy database filled with fake customer information. An attacker who breaches this decoy would waste their efforts on worthless data, while the real sensitive information remains protected.
- Distort adversarial beliefs: Distortion focuses on feeding adversaries false or misleading information to bias their understanding and decision-making processes. For instance, a network might present attackers with fake system configurations or erroneous security settings, leading them to believe they have

compromised the system when, in fact, they are interacting with a controlled environment. This tactic can cause attackers to miscalculate their next steps and waste time on false leads.

- Deplete adversarial resources: The goal of depletion is to drain the adversary's resources, such as time, computational power, energy consumption, or even financial assets. By creating complex and resource-intensive decoy environments, defenders can force attackers to expend significant effort on tasks that lead nowhere. For example, a company could set up a series of interconnected decoy servers that require substantial effort to breach, only to lead to more decoys. This approach not only delays the attacker but can also discourage them from continuing their efforts.
- Discover adversarial capabilities, motives, and Tactics, Techniques, and Procedures (TTP): Discovery is the proactive aspect of cyber deception, where the primary objective is to gather intelligence about the adversary. By engaging with attackers in a controlled and monitored environment, defenders can uncover critical information about the attacker's capabilities, motives, and Tactics, Techniques, and Procedures (TTP). For example, a decoy system might be designed to allow attackers to think they have gained access to a critical system, leading them to reveal their methods and tools in the process. The intelligence gathered can then be used to strengthen defenses, anticipate future attacks, and even identify the attackers.

To achieve these objectives, it is essential to understand that cyber deception is an interdisciplinary, data-driven science. The field of cyber deception and resilience draws from a wide range of disciplines, including game theory, economics, cognitive sciences, risk management, machine learning, and computer science, among others [36, 60]. The data-driven nature of cyber deception is rooted in the fact that all information about cyber attacks is essentially data. However, this data presents significant challenges, as it is often scarce, unlabeled, or lacks ground truth. While real network and system logs can provide insights into attacker activities, the absence of labeling makes it difficult to discern clear patterns or draw reliable conclusions. On the other hand, synthetic data, though rich in detail, may fail to accurately represent real-world attacks, thereby limiting its effectiveness. Traditional methods like honeypots or honeynets also come with limitations, as they are vulnerable to evasion tactics by sophisticated attackers and often provide limited interaction, reducing their ability to capture comprehensive attacker behavior.

The existing challenges of cyber deception can be summarized as 4A: Assimilation, Automation, Adaptation, and Assurance. Addressing these challenges requires a multifaceted approach. For instance, honey-patching and deceptive software version emulation are strategies that tackle the challenge of assimilation by offering attackers misleading or incomplete information, thus creating red herrings that divert their efforts. Automation in cyber deception is enhanced by embedding deceptive elements within software systems and utilizing pre-trained language models (PLMs) to generate convincing decoy data. This automation not only streamlines the deployment of deceptive tactics but also ensures that these tactics can be scaled to match the growing sophistication of cyber threats. Adaptation is another crucial aspect, where game theory and machine learning come into play to model and anticipate the dynamic behaviors of attackers. These adaptive strategies allow defenders to stay a step ahead by evolving their deceptive measures in response to changing threat landscapes. Finally, assurance, which is critical for validating the effectiveness of deception, can be strengthened through the use of big data synthesis. By employing human subject experiments and other empirical methods, researchers can evaluate the success of deception strategies and then refine them accordingly.

4.2 *Cyberpsychology and Cyber Deception*

The strategy for defending against cyber adversaries has evolved significantly, encompassing a broad spectrum of responses that range from traditional, reactive methods to more sophisticated and proactive approaches, as illustrated in Fig. 4. Defense strategies primarily relied on reactive measures, such as firewall denials, antivirus solutions, and intrusion detection systems, which focus on blocking or mitigating known threats after they are detected. However, the rapidly changing threat landscape and the increasing sophistication of cyber attackers have necessitated a shift towards more interactive defense mechanisms that include both passive and active deception techniques [22]. The ultimate goal of these advanced strategies is to transition from a defensive posture to a proactive one [20], where the engagement with adversaries is not only responding to attacks but also anticipating and preempting them. This proactive defense involves actively engaging with attackers, thwarting their efforts, and extracting valuable intelligence that can inform future defenses.

To achieve this level of proactive defense, organizations can leverage various opportunities. One of the most effective strategies is to implement deception directly within their production environments. This approach involves using advanced obfuscation techniques to deploy decoy systems, or "honeypots", generate high-fidelity alerts, and detect and respond to insider threats as well as other sophisticated attacks effectively. Another innovative approach is the concept of self-infection in a controlled environment. By deliberately exposing their networks to simulated attacks, organizations can study the behavior of advanced persistent threats (APTs) and gather valuable insights that can be used to strengthen their defenses.

For effective planning and execution of cyber deception, organizations can leverage established frameworks like MITRE ATT&CK and the MITRE Engage

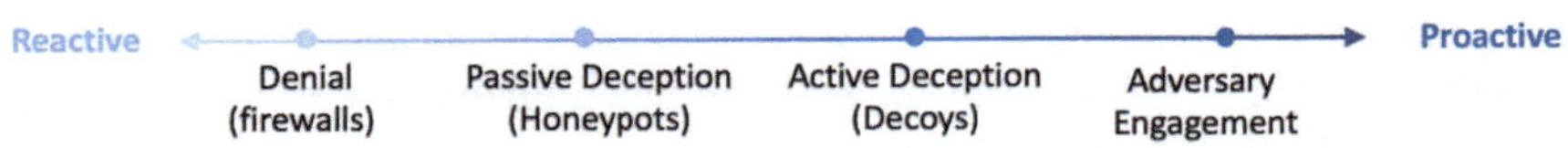

Fig. 4 Spectrum of response to adversaries in cyber security

framework [53]. The MITRE framework provides a structured approach to cyber deception, guiding organizations through three key stages: prepare, operate, and understand. In the preparation phase, organizations assess their knowledge of adversaries and their own objectives. They define deception goals, methods, and success criteria. Once an operation is executed, the focus shifts to understanding the consequences, translating raw data into actionable intelligence, and using feedback to analyze both successes and failures. Throughout the process, organizations can adjust the "ambiguity knob" to either reinforce (speed up) or challenge (slow down) their assumptions. This adaptability ensures that the deception framework remains responsive to the evolving threat landscape and is tailored to the specific needs and objectives of the organization.

In designing effective cyber deception strategies, it is also important to consider the role of cyberpsychology. Understanding the psychological factors that influence adversaries' decision-making processes can provide deeper insights into how and why certain attack paths are chosen. By analyzing cognitive biases, decision-making heuristics, and other psychological traits, defenders can predict which deceptive elements are most likely to mislead or deter attackers. This knowledge allows organizations to design deception strategies that not only protect their assets but also exploit the human limitations of their adversaries. Moreover, there is a growing recognition of the need for defenses that leverage attackers' inherent decision-making biases and cognitive vulnerabilities. These human limitations can be a critical factor in the success of cyber deception, as they often lead attackers to make predictable mistakes or take less secure paths when confronted with uncertainty. By incorporating these psychological insights into their defensive strategies, organizations can develop more resilient and effective deception techniques that are harder for attackers to bypass.

Several techniques can be used to incorporate psychological insights into cyber deception defense strategies [30]. One important field mentioned earlier in Sect. 2 is bounded rationality, which assists in explaining the rather irrational behavior and sub-optimal decision-making of both human users and human attackers. In the context of game-theoretic frameworks, elements in cyber security games as well as physical security games can then be modified and utilized to account for such human errors due to limited memory, attention, or reasoning capability. Additionally, Prospect theory [35] provides a valuable method for understanding how individuals perceive and react to potential losses versus gains, highlighting the concept of loss aversion in human decision-making. It recognizes that people tend to weigh losses more heavily than the equivalent utility of gains, leading to decisions that may deviate from rational behavior. By extending conventional risk-neutral decision-making models to account for risk aversion, Prospect theory allows organizations or defenders to better understand and predict the impact of cognitive biases on the attackers' decision-making processes. Another essential area to consider is the rational inattention [52] of humans, which can also be incorporated into decision-making models to reflect the limited cognitive capacity of individuals when making decisions. For example, an attention-constrained risk analysis model has been used to assess risks in interdependent networks [8].

In conclusion, the rapidly evolving landscape of cybersecurity demands a shift towards more proactive and adaptive [28] defense strategies that actively engage with adversaries. By leveraging opportunities such as deception in production environments, utilizing comprehensive frameworks like MITRE Engage, and integrating insights from cyberpsychology, organizations can enhance their cyber defenses. These strategies not only protect against current threats but also anticipate and mitigate future attacks, ensuring a more secure and resilient cyber infrastructure.

5 Challenges and Future Directions

5.1 Ways to Build Scalable Data Collection System for Security

Constructing a scalable data collection system for security presents several challenges that need to be carefully addressed. Firstly, many organizations are understandably hesitant to share their proprietary data due to concerns about privacy, security, and competitive advantage. Secondly, the absence of a universally ideal dataset in the field of security underscores the need to consider trade-offs when contemplating the sharing of proprietary information for research purposes. In response to these challenges, potential solutions emerge. One approach involves providing organizations with data collection tools that empower them to control and customize their data sharing, ensuring that sensitive information remains confidential.

Additionally, the utilization of generative AI technologies can be instrumental in creating synthetic datasets that closely mimic real-world data while safeguarding proprietary details. These solutions aim to navigate the complex landscape of data collection for security purposes, balancing the imperative for advancing research with the necessity of respecting organizations' concerns regarding their proprietary data. By offering adaptable and privacy-conscious options, a scalable data collection system for security can be designed to encourage collaboration and innovation within the field.

5.2 Change People's Habits

To effectively change a habit, it is essential to understand that habits are learned behaviors shaped by our interactions with the environment. To initiate a change in habits, we must first define the specific habit to be altered, including the desired behavior within a particular context and the environmental cues that trigger the habit. The following steps can help people cultivate new habits more effectively.

One effective approach is to implement rewards. By aligning desired behaviors with rewards, people can experience a sense of fulfillment upon achieving them, and the desired behaviors would gradually become habits. For instance, children might earn extra playtime as a reward for consistently washing their hands before meals. Besides, consistency is another crucial element in habit formation. Repeating the new behavior consistently until it becomes automatic is vital. For example, during the pandemic, wearing masks became a habit for many to protect themselves and others.

Modifying the environment to support the new habit is also paramount. Making engaging in the desired behavior easier while creating barriers to the old habit can accelerate habit change. For example, the quickest way to learn a new language is by immersing oneself in a country where that language is spoken, surrounded by native speakers. Last but not least, the power of group learning also plays an important role in habit cultivation. Joining a community or group with similar goals can provide invaluable support. Sharing experiences and feeling part of a collective effort can boost motivation and discipline. In the language-learning example, practicing with others in a group setting can be more effective than attempting it alone.

Ultimately, the journey to change habits is not solitary; it is a collective effort that can lead to lasting, positive transformations in people's daily lives.

5.3 Aspects to Consider Carefully Regarding Human Factors

One aspect to be mindful of is the presence of attacker biases. Predicting human behavior, especially that of cyber attackers, can be an intricate challenge due to individuals' inherent biases. These biases can lead to unexpected actions and unconventional strategies employed by attackers, which makes the previously optimal defending strategy less effective. Hence, defenders must consider attacker biases, maintain adaptability, and prepare for a wide range of potential attacker behaviors when developing security strategies. Another crucial one is insider threat, as attacks initiated by insiders can often be more impactful and challenging to detect than external ones. Therefore, the defenders need to understand user cyber risks and, at the same time, mitigate the risks by internal security measures, monitoring for unusual activities, and implementing strict access controls. Furthermore, it is essential to recognize the diversity among communities and organizations. Each community and organization possesses its unique characteristics and requirements. Consequently, what may be considered valuable or irrelevant information can vary significantly depending on the specific context. Thus, a tailored approach that considers each community or organization's distinct attributes and needs is indispensable when assessing the relevance of information for defending strategies.

5.4 Discussion on User Suspicion

The presence of conscious gaps, willful ignorance, and unconscious behaviors influence whether users become suspicious of the received information. This sense of unease can trigger a more detailed review of the content. With appropriate training, the scrutiny may lead to the detection of deceit. By evaluating suspicion along with these factors, organizations can develop a risk index to mitigate the most vulnerable link in their security [56]. Overall, suspicion, cognition, and automaticity collectively constitute the SCAM (Suspicion, Cognition, Automaticity Model) framework [57], which delves into why individuals fall victim to social engineering schemes, incorporating critical human behaviors. For example, SCAM suggests that automatic and impulsive usage of email (quickly skimming through an email and then responding) can prevent users from becoming suspicious about possible phishing emails, potentially resulting in falling into scams. By taking those human factors into account during the design of penetration tests, experiments show that the initial click rate of less than 1% can escalate to 22%. This amplifies the significance of awareness training and the cultivation of sound cybersecurity habits.

5.5 Adaptive Deception as Attackers Evolve

Deception strategies must adapt as attackers evolve. One approach involves embracing a data-driven perspective, wherein we continually update our deception methods and engagement tactics based on the evolving database of threat intelligence. This dynamic approach ensures that our deception efforts remain effective in countering emerging threats. Additionally, when developing prototypes, it becomes essential to concentrate on desired responses and fundamental principles, rather than assuming predictability in how they will function when confronted by attackers. Attackers' actions can be unpredictable, so focusing on these core elements allows for a more resilient and adaptable deception strategy that can effectively thwart their evolving tactics and techniques.

5.6 Adapt to the Misalignment of Goals Between the Defender and the Attacker

Adapting to the misalignment of goals between defenders and attackers, when the attacker's intentions differ from the defender's focus on a specific threat like ransomware, necessitates a flexible and comprehensive security strategy study. While extensive studies and real-world datasets in such scenarios may be limited, several adaptable methods can address this misalignment:

- Shift the focus from specific threats like ransomware to a broader, more holistic threat analysis. That is, assess the organization's overall cybersecurity posture instead of solely concentrating on one threat.
- Implement a defense-in-depth strategy to fortify defenses. By integrating multiple layers of security controls, defenders create a robust security infrastructure that can deter attackers with different objectives.
- Embrace adaptive technologies like artificial intelligence can empower defenders to identify and counter new attack patterns in real time, enhancing overall adaptability.
- Raise awareness and foster a security-conscious culture. Organizations can empower their human assets to identify and report suspicious activities and potential security incidents for more effective defense.

Overall, achieving realistic deception in cybersecurity presents a multifaceted challenge that demands a careful balance. One critical consideration is the trade-off between creating a deception that mirrors real-world scenarios and maintaining a safe environment. While mature technologies like testbeds exist, the core issue lies in justifying the use of deception without introducing unnecessary risks. Realistic deception must be designed to operate seamlessly alongside normal system functions, ensuring that regular users remain unaffected by its presence. However, an added layer of complexity arises when addressing the potential impact on internal attacks. Striking the right balance entails developing deception techniques that convincingly mimic real conditions without compromising the overall security posture. This delicate equilibrium not only enhances cybersecurity but also minimizes disruptions for legitimate users, ensuring that the implementation of realistic deception remains a viable and effective strategy within the evolving landscape of cyber threats.

References

1. Aggarwal, P., Venkatesan, S., Youzwak, J., Chadha, R., Gonzalez, C.: Discovering cognitive biases in cyber attackers' network exploitation activities: A case study (2024)
2. Al-Shaer, E., Wei, J., Kevin, W., Wang, C.: Autonomous cyber deception. Springer (2019)
3. Anderson, J.R., Bothell, D., Byrne, M.D., Douglass, S., Lebiere, C., Qin, Y.: An integrated theory of the mind. Psychological review **111**(4), 1036 (2004)
4. Anderson, J.R., Lebiere, C.J.: The atomic components of thought. Psychology Press (2014)
5. Basit, A., Zafar, M., Liu, X., Javed, A.R., Jalil, Z., Kifayat, K.: A comprehensive survey of ai-enabled phishing attacks detection techniques. Telecommunication Systems **76**, 139–154 (2021)
6. Center for Strategic and International Studies: Significant cyber incidents, https://www.csis.org/programs/strategic-technologies-program/significant-cyber-incidents
7. Ceric, A., Holland, P.: The role of cognitive biases in anticipating and responding to cyberattacks. Information Technology & People **32**(1), 171–188 (2019)
8. Chen, J., Zhu, Q.: Interdependent strategic security risk management with bounded rationality in the internet of things. IEEE Transactions on Information Forensics and Security **14**(11), 2958–2971 (2019)

9. Cox, E.B., Zhu, Q., Balcetis, E.: Stuck on a phishing lure: differential use of base rates in self and social judgments of susceptibility to cyber risk. Comprehensive Results in Social Psychology **4**(1), 25–52 (2020)
10. Cranford, E.A., Lebiere, C., Gonzalez, C., Cooney, S., Vayanos, P., Tambe, M.: Learning about cyber deception through simulations: Predictions of human decision making with deceptive signals in stackelberg security games. In: CogSci (2018)
11. Du, Y., Prébot, B., Xi, X., Gonzalez, C.: A cyber-war between bots: human-like attackers are more challenging for defenders than deterministic attackers (2023)
12. Franco, J., Aris, A., Canberk, B., Uluagac, A.S.: A survey of honeypots and honeynets for internet of things, industrial internet of things, and cyber-physical systems. IEEE Communications Surveys & Tutorials **23**(4), 2351–2383 (2021)
13. Grant, A.M., Hofmann, D.A.: It's not all about me: Motivating hand hygiene among health care professionals by focusing on patients. Psychological science **22**(12), 1494–1499 (2011)
14. Grbic, D.V., Dujlovic, I.: Social engineering with chatgpt. In: 2023 22nd International Symposium INFOTEH-JAHORINA (INFOTEH). pp. 1–5 (2023). https://doi.org/10.1109/INFOTEH57020.2023.10094141
15. Gupta, B.B., Tewari, A., Jain, A.K., Agrawal, D.P.: Fighting against phishing attacks: state of the art and future challenges. Neural Computing and Applications **28**, 3629–3654 (2017)
16. Gupta, M., Akiri, C., Aryal, K., Parker, E., Praharaj, L.: From chatgpt to threatgpt: Impact of generative ai in cybersecurity and privacy. IEEE Access **11**, 80218–80245 (2023). https://doi.org/10.1109/ACCESS.2023.3300381
17. Hammar, K., Li, T., Stadler, R., Zhu, Q.: Automated security response through online learning with adaptive conjectures. arXiv preprint arXiv:2402.12499 (2024)
18. Hillman, D., Harel, Y., Toch, E.: Evaluating organizational phishing awareness training on an enterprise scale. Computers & Security **132**, 103364 (2023). https://doi.org/https://doi.org/10.1016/j.cose.2023.103364, https://www.sciencedirect.com/science/article/pii/S0167404823002742
19. Hoffman, B.: Bandwagon effect: What it is and how to overcome it (May 26 2024), https://www.forbes.com/sites/brycehoffman/2024/05/26/bandwagon-effect-what-it-is-and-how-to-overcome-it/
20. Hu, Y., Zhu, Q.: Game of travesty: Decoy-based psychological cyber deception for proactive human agents. arXiv preprint arXiv:2309.13403 (2023)
21. Huang, L., Jia, S., Balcetis, E., Zhu, Q.: Advert: An adaptive and data-driven attention enhancement mechanism for phishing prevention. IEEE Transactions on Information Forensics and Security **17**, 2585–2597 (2022). https://doi.org/10.1109/TIFS.2022.3189530
22. Huang, L., Zhu, Q.: Strategic learning for active, adaptive, and autonomous cyber defense. Adaptive autonomous secure cyber systems pp. 205–230 (2020)
23. Huang, L., Zhu, Q.: Radams: Resilient and adaptive alert and attention management strategy against informational denial-of-service (idos) attacks. Computers & Security **121**, 102844 (2022)
24. Huang, L., Zhu, Q.: Advert: Defending against reactive attention attacks. In: Cognitive Security: A System-Scientific Approach, pp. 67–83. Springer (2023)
25. Huang, L., Zhu, Q.: Cognitive capacities for designing, operating, supervising, and securing complex systems. In: Cognitive Security: A System-Scientific Approach, pp. 41–48. Springer (2023)
26. Huang, L., Zhu, Q.: Cognitive security: A system-scientific approach. Springer Nature (2023)
27. Huang, L., Zhu, Q.: Review of system-scientific perspectives for analysis, exploitation, and mitigation of cognitive vulnerabilities. In: Cognitive Security: A System-Scientific Approach, pp. 49–65. Springer (2023)
28. Huang, L., Zhu, Q.: Zetar: Modeling and computational design of strategic and adaptive compliance policies. IEEE Transactions on Computational Social Systems (2023)
29. Huang, S., Zhu, Q.: Psyborg+: Cognitive modeling for triggering and detection of cognitive biases of advanced persistent threats. arXiv preprint arXiv:2408.01310 (2024)

30. Huang, Y., Chen, J., Huang, L., Zhu, Q.: Dynamic games for secure and resilient control system design. National Science Review **7**(7), 1125–1141 (2020)
31. INKY: 7 of the biggest phishing scams of all time (2021), https://www.inky.com/en/blog/7-of-the-biggest-phishing-scams-of-all-time-2021
32. Irwin, L.: The 5 biggest phishing scams of all time (October 22 2022), https://www.itgovernance.eu/blog/en/the-5-biggest-phishing-scams-of-all-time
33. Jampen, D., Gür, G., Sutter, T., Tellenbach, B.: Don't click: towards an effective anti-phishing training. a comparative literature review. Human-centric Computing and Information Sciences **10**(1), 33 (2020)
34. Jones, M., Sugden, R.: Positive confirmation bias in the acquisition of information. Theory and Decision **50**, 59–99 (2001)
35. Kahneman, D., Tversky, A.: Prospect theory: An analysis of decision under risk. In: Handbook of the fundamentals of financial decision making: Part I, pp. 99–127. World Scientific (2013)
36. Kamhoua, C.A., Kiekintveld, C.D., Fang, F., Zhu, Q.: Game theory and machine learning for cyber security. John Wiley & Sons (2021)
37. Katakwar, H., Gonzalez, C., Dutt, V.: Attackers have prior beliefs: Comprehending cognitive aspects of confirmation bias on adversarial decisions. In: International Conference on Frontiers in Computing and Systems. pp. 261–273. Springer (2023)
38. Khonji, M., Iraqi, Y., Jones, A.: Phishing detection: a literature survey. IEEE Communications Surveys & Tutorials **15**(4), 2091–2121 (2013)
39. Lewicka, M.: Confirmation bias: cognitive error or adaptive strategy of action control? In: Personal control in action: Cognitive and motivational mechanisms, pp. 233–258. Springer (1998)
40. Li, T., Hammar, K., Stadler, R., Zhu, Q.: Conjectural online learning with first-order beliefs in asymmetric information stochastic games. arXiv preprint arXiv:2402.18781 (2024)
41. Li, T., Zhu, Q.: Symbiotic game and foundation models for cyber deception operations in strategic cyber warfare. arXiv preprint arXiv:2403.10570 (2024)
42. Mughal, A.A.: Building and securing the modern security operations center (soc). International Journal of Business Intelligence and Big Data Analytics **5**(1), 1–15 (2022)
43. Network, G.C.S.: The role of human factors in cyber security: Addressing the weakest link (2023), https://globalcybersecuritynetwork.com/blog/human-factors-in-cyber-security/
44. Nickerson, R.S.: Confirmation bias: A ubiquitous phenomenon in many guises. Review of general psychology **2**(2), 175–220 (1998)
45. OpenAI: Introducing chatgpt (2023), https://www.openai.com/chatgpt
46. Pawlick, J., Colbert, E., Zhu, Q.: A game-theoretic taxonomy and survey of defensive deception for cybersecurity and privacy. ACM Computing Surveys (CSUR) **52**(4), 1–28 (2019)
47. Pfleeger, S.L., Caputo, D.D.: Leveraging behavioral science to mitigate cyber security risk. Computers & security **31**(4), 597–611 (2012)
48. Provos, N., Holz, T.: Virtual honeypots: from botnet tracking to intrusion detection. Pearson Education (2007)
49. Salahdine, F., Kaabouch, N.: Social engineering attacks: A survey. Future internet **11**(4), 89 (2019)
50. Schmitt, M., Flechais, I.: Digital deception: Generative artificial intelligence in social engineering and phishing (2023), https://arxiv.org/abs/2310.13715
51. Simon, H.A.: A behavioral model of rational choice. The quarterly journal of economics pp. 99–118 (1955)
52. Sims, C.A.: Implications of rational inattention. Journal of monetary Economics **50**(3), 665–690 (2003)
53. Strom, B.E., Applebaum, A., Miller, D.P., Nickels, K.C., Pennington, A.G., Thomas, C.B.: Mitre att&ck: Design and philosophy. In: Technical report. The MITRE Corporation (2018)
54. Ting, D.: Why cognitive biases and heuristics lead to an under-investment in cybersecurity (2022)
55. Vishwanath, A.: Unlock your cyber risk beliefs, https://www.arunvishwanath.us/cyber-risk/

56. Vishwanath, A.: The weakest link: How to diagnose, detect, and defend users from phishing. MIT Press (2022)
57. Vishwanath, A., Harrison, B., Ng, Y.J.: Suspicion, cognition, and automaticity model of phishing susceptibility. Communication research **45**(8), 1146–1166 (2018)
58. Yang, Y.T., Zhang, T., Zhu, Q.: A game-theoretic analysis of auditing differentially private algorithms with epistemically disparate herd. In: International Conference on Decision and Game Theory for Security. pp. 349–368. Springer (2023)
59. Zhang, L., Thing, V.L.: Three decades of deception techniques in active cyber defense-retrospect and outlook. Computers & Security **106**, 102288 (2021)
60. Zhu, Q.: Foundations of cyber resilience: The confluence of game, control, and learning theories. arXiv preprint arXiv:2404.01205 (2024)

Part III
Design and Integrations

Designing Deceptions for Protecting Industrial Control Systems

Neil C. Rowe

1 Introduction

Defensive deception is a powerful technique for defending computer systems and digital devices since it is often unexpected [1]. The subtype of cyber-physical systems (CPSs) called industrial control systems (ICSs) are particularly vulnerable targets of cyberattacks due to their predominant function as critical infrastructure, their frequent use of old software for compatibility with hardware, and the difficulty of updating them to fix vulnerabilities due to the need to keep them running continuously [2, 3]. ICSs thus greatly benefit from additional defense methods including cyberdeception since traditional access controls and intrusion detection are insufficient to defend them [4]. Deception can also be especially effective in defending ICSs because many have large networks of uncommon devices and sensors in which attackers can become confused, and their controls are designed for specialists familiar with the underlying physics or chemistry, unlike many attackers. Although they can use defensive deception methods common to other digital systems, ICSs thus present new opportunities for deception related to their processes that have no counterpart in traditional operating systems. This chapter will survey ICS deception planning opportunities in the context of an experimental network which we are developing.

N. C. Rowe (✉)
U.S. Naval Postgraduate School, Monterey, CA, USA
e-mail: ncrowe@nps.edu

Q. Zhu et al. (eds.), *Foundations of Cyber Deception*, Advances in Information Security 90, https://doi.org/10.1007/978-3-031-93867-2_9

2 Previous Work

A classic distinction is between defensive deception to encourage an attacker, as with honeypots trying to collect attack intelligence, and defensive deception to discourage an attacker, as with real ("production") systems trying to defend themselves [5]. Most previous work has used encouragement deceptions to collect data on attacks, but we will focus here on discouragement deceptions for production systems. Deceptions tend to be more convincing on production systems because they can show real rather than simulated activity. Nonetheless, honeypots can test useful encouragement ideas as well.

Franco et al. [6] surveyed previous work with honeypots for ICSs and Internet-of-Things (IoT) networks. IoT designs are related because they also use large numbers of networked processors. However, ICS devices often provide more complex services than IoT nodes, and require more processing.

Honeypots can be considerably more useful when they use deception, since attackers avoid known honeypots because attackers know honeypots collect their data and thwart exploitation attempts [7]. Previous work has examined ideas of building networks of honeypots (honeynets) for ICSs since honeypots can attract more attacks when they are present in large numbers ("honeypot farms"). Some relevant work is Urias et al. [8], Abe et al. [9], Cifranic et al. [10], and Dutta et al. [11]. Honeypots can be placed on broad networks, local networks, or in hardware [12]. Honeypot farms can use a wide range of deceptions to attract a broad range of attacks.

Our previous work has built and tested honeypot types and tactics for defending ICSs. We showed that honeypots are best implemented with cloud services [13] as supported in [14]. After preliminary experiments, we have focused on the IEC 104 protocol for ICSs, since it is increasingly popular, and the HTTP protocol, the most popular protocol with our attackers [15]. We have been using a design with a modified general-purpose honeypot Conpot as a front end to a GridPot electrical-grid honeypot on the back end [16], which was later hardened with a user-interface front end on a separate machine and a separate logging site [17]. Hardening was essential to collecting data on the more serious attacks since it prevented erasing the log or terminating the virtual machines used to run the honeypot. Further experiments showed we got similar traffic independent of where in the world the honeypot was situated, whether it was a virtual machine, and what details it claimed about its operations [17] .

Deception for discouragement is appropriate in defending real infrastructure including ICSs. Its goal is to convince an attacker that attacking a system will be costly and unlikely to succeed. Discouragement deceptions are not easy to test because they should involve real systems and real attacks to accurately measure effectiveness. Nonetheless, we can implement them and compare them to similar systems that are not using discouragement, if we are patient enough to get a representative sample of attacks.

3 Example Layered Deception Plan for a Sophisticated Adversary

Effective digital defensive deception requires advance planning, much like deceptions for defensive military operations [18]. We focus in this chapter on planning for protecting an ICS against a sophisticated adversary with many resources, such as a nation-state or "advanced persistent threat". We cannot stop such an attack indefinitely, given sufficient time and resources for an attacker to try many methods. However, it often suffices to delay them. Delays give defenders time to figure out the type, methods, sources, and targets of an attack, and that may suffice to divert or block the attack's most damaging aspects.

Military defenses often use multiple layers (or "lines") to delay attacks considerably, a concept called "defense in depth". Since ICSs are often analogous critical infrastructure, defensive ICS deception can also use multiple layers for "deception in depth" [19]. Each layer can use different deceptions, choosing them for the setting and from an ontology [20]. A layered deception permits testing different attacker skills at each level, providing valuable intelligence about the different methods they use. However, Clark and Mitchell [18] also suggests that intelligent adversaries are most effectively fooled by a consistent plausible "story", as for instance "the site is well hardened" or "the site is logging your activities". A useful plausible story for discouragement should be consistent through the levels of defense, reinforce prior attacker beliefs, and should encourage them to leave.

Consider an example of a layered deceptive defense to discourage an attacker of a real ICS network at a military facility. An initial line of defense could try to persuade adversaries that the ICS site is not worth attacking by mislabeling it as a less desirable target by its name and owner. An example would be labeling a water-treatment plant as a cistern system for collecting rainwater for gardening, something not critical to a military facility. However, the site must still run legitimate ICS protocols consistent with its cover story so that the adversary's network mapping can detect them. Legitimate users of the network would be told the correct resources to use.

A second line of defense could provide a confusing interface to the real network containing the ICSs. It could use cryptic descriptions of its resources with numbers and codewords to make it difficult for adversaries to recognize what is there. Legitimate users would be given a document to decipher these descriptions. Attackers could be quickly identified from their exploratory behavior.

A third line of defense could try to decoy adversaries from the legitimate targets another way, by providing files with explicitly false information like incorrect network maps, faulty instructions for using systems, and false data files allegedly obtained from the network. The more detailed a false story that is constructed, the more time that sophisticated adversaries will waste exploring the fakes. As a side benefit, the defender will obtain valuable information about adversary methods and goals from which to harden defenses.

A fourth line of defense could try to waste attacker time and prove attacker reconnaissance intentions by offering some minimal ICS network nodes that look promising but provide few services [10]. This idea goes back to Cohen [21] and is used in several commercial tools. It provides a quick way to identify reconnaissance. Its disadvantage is that network scanning tools like Nmap can quickly reveal minimal nodes.

A fifth line of defense could provide false error messages to discourage exploration, while legitimate users would be given a secret codeword to permit normal operation. False error messages have the advantage of working best against alert and sophisticated attackers that examine their interactions carefully, like advanced persistent threats. Many kinds of false error messages can be provided ([1], chapter 9). Since messages are verbal rather than architectural, they can deceive in a different way even if adversaries have figured out the others.

A sixth line of defense could be a confusing or obfuscating user interface to a device, as contrasted with the confusing interface to a network in the second line of defense. This can be a visual deception rather than a verbal or architectural one, and may have a renewed chance of working.

A seventh level of defense could transfer a persistent attacker to a safe "sandbox" environment simulating a device, and either feed them fake data about the state of the device or simulate fake states consistent with the adversary commands. The GridLab-D simulator of an electric grid from Pacific Northwest Laboratories is an example we have used in our honeypot research [22]. Even if an adversary could infer they have been transferred to a simulation, it will take them a while to recognize it, and in the meantime, they will provide useful data about their methods and goals.

4 Deception Planning

We now present a defensive deception strategy for ICSs. Rowe and Rrushi [1], Han et al. [23], and Pawlick et al. [24] provide taxonomies of broadly applicable deception methods for cyberspace on which we build here. ICSs can use most of these, but they have additional deception capabilities due to their mission of controlling devices. A few are specific to programmable logic controllers [25], but we can get some generality if we take a broader perspective. With ICSs, attackers generally want to set switches and dials to interfere with or stop normal operations. Deceptions can fool them into thinking that they have done this and achieved goals.

4.1 A Procedure for Deception Planning

Figure 1 shows our defensive-deception discouragement-planning procedure for local-area ICS networks and their systems.

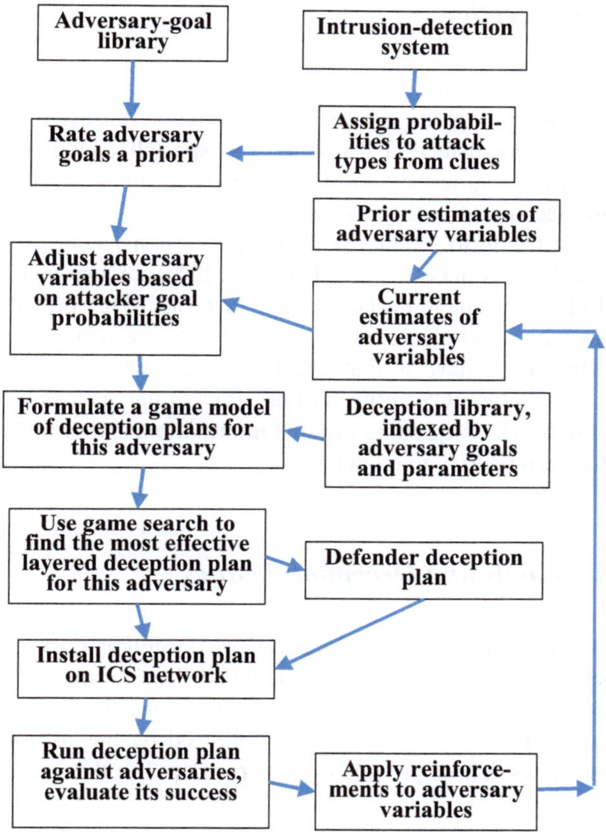

Fig. 1 Discouragement-deception planning flowchart for defending ICS systems

The overall procedure for ICS defensive deception planning can also be summarized as follows:

1. Use an attacker-goal library to rate possible attacker goals for those possible cyberattacks, including both physical and psychological goals.
2. Use an intrusion-detection system to identify cyberattacks in activity on the local-area network of the ICS [26].
3. Obtain estimates of adversary variables from prior values and recent network activity.
4. Modify adversarial variables based on conditional probabilities of goals.
5. Use a game model to propose and rate possible deception tactics for the defender based on a deception library.
6. Use game theory to build a good deception plan, and implement it in the local-area network.
7. Run the deception plan against attackers, and monitor the results.
8. Calculate reinforcements on adversary variables, and apply them.

4.2 Attacker Detection

Defenses must first distinguish normal traffic from attack traffic. Standard ways are access monitoring, log inspection, signature-based intrusion detection, and anomaly-based intrusion detection. These must be specialized to handle ICSs since ICS protocols differ significantly from those of other information systems. ICS attacks may provide specialized clues such as attempting to set device parameters to unusual values, trying to interact with devices in nonstandard ways, or trying to violate physical constraints [27, 28]. However, ICSs are also increasingly using Web (e.g., HTTP) and remote-desktop (e.g., SSH and RDP) protocols for easier network management, and also can be susceptible to the many attacks on them. An advantage that ICSs have is that attacks are easier to distinguish than with most digital systems since ICS traffic is often very regular, as attack traffic such as enumeration of networks, requesting unusual information, and setting of parameters to unusual values can be easy to recognize.

4.3 Attacker Goals and Deception Venues

A key issue is what attack activities on an ICS merit deception. Overuse of deception makes it easier to detect [1], so it is desirable to deceive sparingly and only at important steps in an attack. Tables 1 and 2 show, in the first two columns, a set of attacker goals for ICSs proposed in [2], followed by our assessment of their deception possibilities. These provide options for step 2 in the deception-planning procedure of Sect. 4.1.

4.4 Deception Architecture

Deception methods will be an overlay on existing systems and must cooperate with the operating system. An issue is where a deception should be implemented, for following step 5 of Sect. 4.1. Figure 2 shows a generic ICS architecture with eight numbered locations, extending the three of [29].

We assess the deception locations in as follows:

1. External interface: Can provide some broad deceptions such as fake networks.
2. User interface: Deceptions are relatively easy to implement here since they can imitate normal functions of the interface. On the other hand, most user interfaces are friendly, and deceptive behavior may be implausible.
3. Real and bait files: Useful as delaying tactics, though unlikely to help against advanced persistent threats that have time to study them.
4. Device table: Deceptive nodes are easy to implement if the table's device addresses include decoys or honeypots as well as regular devices. However,

Table 1 Evaluation of broad options for deception in ICS defense, part 1

Attack goal	Target	Attack difficulty	Possible deceptions	Deception difficulty	Deception desirability
Do reconnaissance	ICS network	Easy	Decoys, honeypots	Easy	High
Steal credentials	ICS network	Moderate	Fake traffic	Moderate	Moderate
Analyze packets to system to get intelligence	ICS network	Difficult	Fake traffic	Moderate	Moderate
Replay network traffic	ICS network	Moderate	Honeypots	Moderate	Moderate
Inject packets	ICS network	Difficult	Honeypots, false data	High	Moderate
Spoof packets	ICS network	Difficult	Honeynets	High	Moderate
Gain remote access	Controllers	Moderate	Honeynets	High	High
Modify data to/from controller	Controllers	Difficult	Honeynets	Moderate	Moderate
Modify configuration	Controllers	Difficult	Honeypots	High	Moderate
Modify control algorithms	Controllers	Difficult	Honeypots	High	Moderate
Modify data to affect control	Controllers	Moderate	Honeynets	Moderate	High
Modify controller firmware	Controllers	Difficult	False data	High	Moderate
Modify I/O data of controller	Controllers	Moderate	False data	Moderate	Moderate
Escalate privileges	Workstations	Difficult	Decoys, honeypots	Moderate	Moderate
Gain remote access	Workstations	Easy	Honeypots	High	Moderate
Copy sensitive data	Workstations	Moderate	Honeypots	Easy	Low
Modify data	Workstations	Difficult	Honeypots	Moderate	Moderate
Modify configuration	Workstations	Difficult	Decoys, honeypots	Moderate	Moderate
Send commands to controller	Workstations	Moderate	Honeypots	Moderate	Moderate
Maintain persistence	Workstations	Moderate	False data	Moderate	Moderate
Do denial of service	Workstations	Easy	Delays	Easy	Low

Table 2 Evaluation of broad options for deception in ICS defense, part 2

Attack goal	Target	Attack difficulty	Possible deceptions	Deception difficulty	Deception desirability
Escalate privileges	Application and SCADA servers	Difficult	Decoys, honeypots	High	Moderate
Gain remote access	Application and SCADA servers	Difficult	Honeynets	Moderate	Moderate
Copy sensitive data	Application and SCADA servers	Moderate	Honeypots	Easy	Low
Modify data	Application and SCADA servers	Difficult	Honeypots	Moderate	Moderate
Disrupt process communications	Application and SCADA servers	Moderate	False data	Hard	Moderate
Disrupt user interface	Application and SCADA servers	Moderate	False data	Hard	Moderate
Maintain persistence	Application and SCADA servers	Moderate	False data	Moderate	Moderate

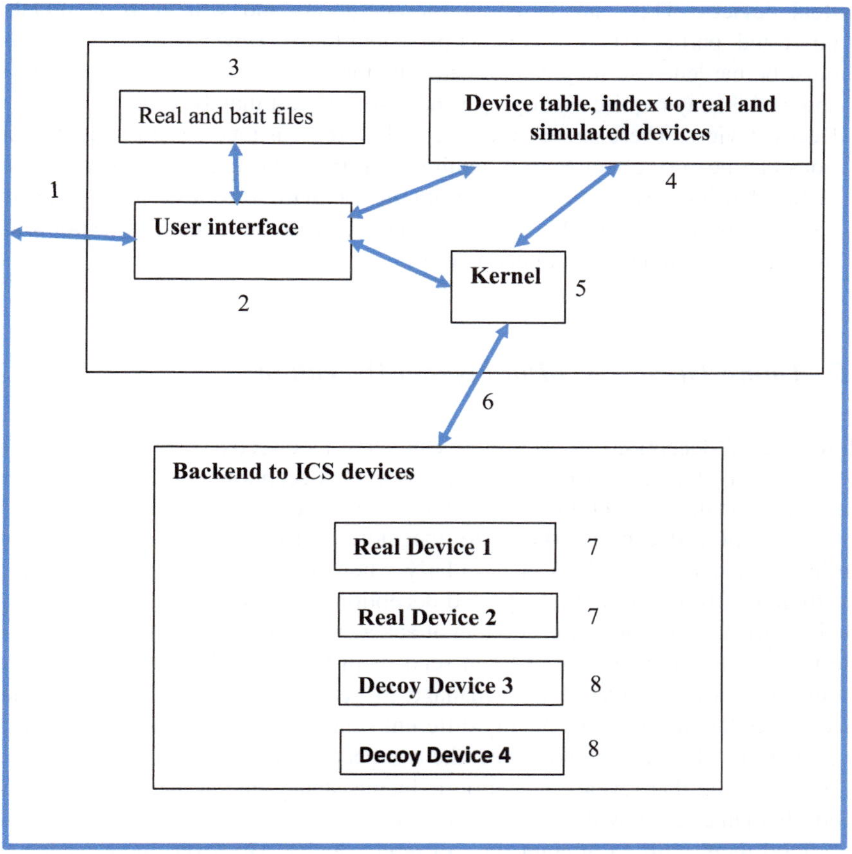

Fig. 2 Block diagram of a generic ICS with possible deception locations

honeypots must be installed for each simulated device, and this may require work since overly similar simulations will be easy to spot as deceptions.

5. Kernel: Besides sending users to decoys or honeypots, the driver can implement other tactics such as delays, unnecessary passwords requests, false error messages, or flooding of the user with information. These should not be overdone to remain plausible. This also requires modifying highly secure features of a system, and can only be done if planned at an early stage in designing a kernel. Since a kernel must be minimal, deception should be triggered by external decisions as in the user interface.
6. Interface to devices: Changing the software that interacts with backend ICSs requires modifying their drivers. This is simpler than modifying the operating system, but requires understanding of specialized software. Putting deceptions here does enable monitoring them to avoid overuse or underuse of deceptions.

7. Real devices: These are essential for operations and will keep an attacker interested, particularly an advanced persistent threat. However, the devices also must be hardened so they cannot cause major harm or easily spread an attack; and as this may require modifying vendor software, it may be difficult.
8. Decoy devices: These should simulate real systems as much as possible. Deceptions can be very effective, but require work in the design and implementation to be plausible. This may not be difficult for many devices, since some like thermostats are simple. However, timing (such as the speed of response) is important to simulate accurately as well.

4.5 Game Theory for Multilayered Deception

Multi-layered deceptions as in Sect. 3 can serve as effective obstacles to attacks by persistent attackers, particularly where each deception provides a different challenge, and the attacker must solve all the challenges to gain access. The tradeoff is that the more deceptions there are, the more easily they can be detected and the less effective they will be, particularly when they are similar. It will help to use significantly varied and unexpected deceptions that are hard to connect to one another. So if for instance we flood an attacker with information through the user interface to slow their attack, we can send them to decoy simulations of devices through the device driver if they manage to get there in a later phase of their attack. Simulations are conceptually different from information displays, so it may be difficult for the attacker to connect the two deceptions.

Another clue that reveals deception is inconsistency on similar tasks. So if we flood a human attacker with information on one attempt to query a device, we should also flood them with an attempt on a different device. However, inconsistency is not much noticed by automated attacks, or even a human controller reviewing their output. It will help to identify in advance the activities by the defender that most require consistency. Otherwise, maximally different responses to similar situations may prevent attackers from seeing them as an overall deception strategy.

The tradeoffs with deceptions are best planned with game theory (step 6 in Sect. 4.1) using the conditional probability of detection of each deception given the detection of previous deceptions [30]. These conditional probabilities can be based on observations of human subjects, including non-attackers.

5 Adversary Goals

Planning of discouragement deceptions can benefit from knowledge of the adversary's goals. We identify here the possible material and psychological goals, and discuss how they can be modeled.

5.1 Material Goals

Material goals aim to change the physical state of an ICS. For power plants, most material goals will be based on the physics of electromagnetism; for a chemical plant, most will be based on chemistry. Some more specific material goals for ICSs than those of Tables 1 and 2 are:

- Disabling the ICS hardware. This could be the overall goal of nation-state adversaries, consistent with the primary warfare objective of disabling a nation-state's ability to wage war. However, it is difficult to achieve because ICSs have many safeguards to keep them running. But successful damage can have a long-term effect much like that of munitions.
- Disabling the ICS software. This could be done by modifying software executables or possibly input data. It could have the same effect as disabling the hardware while being easier for the adversary. Operations could be restored by the defender from backup copies of software or data, although it could take time.
- Denial of service of the ICS software. This could slow operations considerably while not disabling anything. This could be useful for adversaries who want to send a political signal.
- Modifying the ICS functionality, as by changing switch settings or installing malware in controllers. For instance, the Industroyer2 attacks on Ukraine in April 2022 apparently attempted this with the IEC 104 protocol [31]. Modifications could be targeted, or it could be random to create confusion.
- Changing control parameters in the ICS. For instance, decrease power output of a generator. Effective changes require specialized knowledge of the physics or chemistry of the ICS.
- Reprogramming the ICS software to change its operation. This is difficult because it would require access to the management system, which is usually more protected than the ICS itself. It also likely requires exploiting non-ICS vulnerabilities, which are likely to be better protected than ICS vulnerabilities because of the more networks they could affect.
- Thorough reconnaissance of the ICS to enable later attacks. This could involve sending crafted packets to test responses, or systematically modifying settings to see what they do. Most of what we saw on our ICS honeypots [17] was packet traffic of this type.
- Making money. Ransomware can do this; since ICSs are often critical infrastructure, holding them hostage can be very effective. Also, some information-warfare organizations pay bounties to employees to attack sites of adversaries.

Since material goals often seek a change of a physical or chemical system, actions to accomplish them can be seen as "derivative changers", changes to the rate of some parameter, analogous to Newton's Second Law which implies that forces are velocity changers. For instance, Stuxnet attempted to increase the speed of centrifuges, and Industroyer 2 attempted to change switch states while enumerating them. The appearance of more or stronger derivative-changing commands than normal on a system, as by data injection, is suspicious and can be detected by deviations from normal behavior [32]. "Second-derivative" commands that alternate first derivatives of opposite directions, such as in turning on and off power repeatedly, can damage equipment by creating strong stresses. They can be mounted by injecting a quickly varying signal into an ICS.

While predicting the effect of derivative changes in unfamiliar domains may seem daunting, simplified models of ICS processes may suffice for deception planning. This has been called "naïve physics" for physical processes [33], and "naïve chemistry" for chemical processes [34]. So for instance, causing centrifuges to run much faster than normal, or flooding a chemical reaction with petrochemicals, will likely do something bad even if an attacker does not know exactly what. That is because they considerably exceed normal parameters and measures for which the processes are designed. Five subcases of "derivative attacks" can be identified:

- First-derivative attacks: These increase or decrease numeric parameters such as the applied power from correct settings to interfere with an ongoing process. An example is reducing the power on a generator so it is not supplying its required level of power, or increasing the heat in a chemical reactor. As [34] points out, modifying a chemical process can damage more than the equipment, possibly the chemicals produced or the output compliance conditions about safety or pollution, and such damage can be done by changing the first derivative of a parameter at critical times.
- Second-derivative attacks: These increase or decrease a numeric parameter and then shortly thereafter change it in the opposite direction to stress a system. An example is repeatedly heating and cooling a chemical reactor to create unwanted chemicals.
- First-derivative attack with boundary condition: These increase or decrease a numeric parameter until it exceeds a safe value, such as by increasing the power supplied to a transformer until it catches fire.
- Second-derivative attack with boundary condition: These alternate increasing and decreasing a parameter until the change exceeds safety constraints, as with rapidly changing the direction of a rotating shaft until it breaks. These attacks require identification of safety limits for first derivatives.
- Transit attacks: These change directions of flow within the ICSs, such as opening valves normally kept closed in a water-treatment plant [35] or supplying electric current to an unusual location.

5.2 Psychological Goals

Psychological goals satisfy personal and emotional needs of the attacker. These are more important with amateur attackers than paid professionals, but all attackers have them and they can often be exploited. Possible psychological goals are:

- Accomplishment of a job. Information-warfare operatives may enjoy attacking adversary countries and feel it is patriotic.
- Confidence and self-worth. Attackers like to feel they know what they are doing and can achieve results reliably and efficiently.
- Social rewards: Attackers may work in teams and enjoy the praise of their colleagues.
- Obedience to authority. Attackers may enjoy satisfying their bosses as a means of gaining self-worth or material benefits.
- Revenge for perceived slights. Terrorists are often motivated this way.
- Fantasies of power and control. Adolescents often have such needs, and entertain fantasies of controlling people as well as engaging in pointless exhibitions like petty vandalism.
- Stress reduction. If an attacker becomes frustrated with a system, they may feel better if they go away and do something else.

Psychological goals can be inferred from what is attacked and how. Some work has attempted automated inference of such goals [36]. Psychological goals do not necessarily make sense, as terrorists may be motivated by unreasonable hatreds.

5.3 Adversary Mental States Relevant to Discouragement

Defenders can affect adversary mental goals and goal-directed behavior by influencing their emotions and inducing mental states. Some mental states defenders should consider encouraging are

- Disappointment: Defenders want adversaries to feel disappointed after interacting with them, so they will be less likely to return. But if they are too disappointed, they may take it as a challenge and want to return with more sophisticated attacks.
- Unhappiness: Defenders want adversaries to feel unhappy when they cannot fully compromise our systems, as this will discourage them from continuing and encourage them to find easier targets. But as with disappointment, we do not want to make them so unhappy that they take that as a challenge.
- Trust/mistrust: Defenders want adversaries to trust them so adversaries are more likely to believe their deceptions. For instance, we may want adversaries to think that a resource is unavailable even when it is not. However, it may also be useful to encourage distrust in impatient adversaries looking for easy targets, who may abandon an attack site once they see evidence of deception.
- Irritation and anger: Defenders may want to irritate adversaries, as with false error messages, to show that interacting with them will be unpleasant. However, if defenders make them too irritated, they can become angry and retaliate vigorously.
- Frustration: A good way to create irritation and anger is to create unexpected obstacles in attempting to achieve an apparently easy goal. For instance, getting

onto an ICS and implanting exploits is often easy with today's infrequently updated and vulnerable ICSs. Then if an attacker meets unexpected obstacles, they can become frustrated. Frustration is particularly useful to encourage in attackers as it will both discourage them from continuing and encourage them to stay away.
- Betrayal: Advanced persistent threats are expecting deception and are not fazed by it. However, many amateur attackers recognizing deception against them feel betrayed. This may cause an unpredictable range of behaviors, including terminating interactions abruptly, publicizing the deception, and redoubling attack efforts. Because of this unpredictability, encouraging feelings of betrayal is not very useful against most adversaries.
- Superiority: Many adversaries have high opinions of themselves, and it may be useful to encourage this. Then they may underestimate defenders, and be fooled by a complex multi-layered deception.
- Fear: Unlikely to be induced because many adversaries have high opinions of themselves and their skills.
- Sanguinity: Not useful for discouragement because we generally want attackers to feel unhappy, but it could be useful for an encouraging honeypot.

5.4 Psychological Adversary Variables

Mental states of adversaries can be inferred by their actions. For instance, if the adversary can elevate privileges of an account or change switch settings, they have high confidence in their abilities and low frustration; if they log out after a short session, they have low confidence and high frustration; or if they have ten times opened fake files and discovered only gibberish, they have a high threshold for frustration and may be professionals of an intelligence-gathering organization that requires them to search exhaustively. Hidden Markov models and reinforcement learning are classic machine-learning models for inferring mental states, and a variety of neural-network architectures can be trained to infer them as well.

Although Sects. 5.1 and 5.2 listed a variety of attacker goals, the number of mental states relevant to achieving them is more limited. We have thus argued [19] that they can be modeled by a small set of "adversary variables" representing key aspects of the mental state of an adversary that affect their actions, and these variables can be used to plan the deceptions most likely to succeed against them. Table 3 shows our proposed adversary variables. These are used at steps 3, 4, and 5 of the deception-planning procedure of Sect. 4.1. The rightmost column represents possible predictions when the deceivee measures high on the adversary variable. However, predicting the actual outcome requires estimating costs of the options for the deceivee such as time wasted on fruitless tasks, and using a decision tree to estimate the weighted cost of options. The table should apply to automated attacks as well, since after finding a rare vulnerability in a system, human judgment is necessary to decide what to do next, and then the variables apply to that human.

Table 3 Adversary variables useful for predicting mental states of an adversary

Name of adversary variable	How inferred	Correlations to other variables	Predictive use
Sophistication of the adversary	Ratio of advanced actions to basic actions	Lack of surprise	Superiority
Confidence of the adversary in their methods	Consistency in following a plan without digressions	Sophistication	Trust
Interest more in intelligence gathering than sabotage	Ratio of sabotage-related actions	None	Rate of attempts to modify the system
Adversary estimate of reliability of the target system	Number of anomalous events observed by user	Sophistication, alertness	Acceptance of deceptions as unreliability
Trust in information shown about the attack target	One minus ratio of redundant confirming actions to normal actions	Sophistication, alertness	Likelihood of ending the interaction
Alertness of adversary to the target	Whether they notice obvious inconsistencies	Sophistication	Ineffectiveness of deceptions
Surprise of the adversary at the target	Increase in idle time	Lack of sophistication and confidence	Likelihood of ending the interaction
Adaptability of adversary to the target	How well they find alternatives to obstacles created by deceptions	Sophistication, alertness	Ineffectiveness of deceptions
Impatience of the adversary	Count of steps after encountering obstacles	Frustration, lack of confidence, desire to disconnect	Likelihood of ending the interaction
Desire of adversary to disconnect without achieving their goals	Fraction of connections ended without achieving goals	Impatience	Choice of deceptions
Frustration level of the adversary	Ratio of unnecessary sabotage to normal actions	Lack of trust	Increased length of interaction
Interest of the adversary in financial gain	Ratio of sabotage to normal actions, and sending ransom notes	Confidence, sophistication	Length of reconnaissance

6 Deceptive Tactics for Foiling Adversary Goals

Rowe and Rrushi ([1], chapter 4) lists a range of defensive deceptions against general cyberattacks. The options for ICSs can be rated differently since the ICS environment usually tries to maintain ongoing processes rather than do new things. Some good tactics for ICSs for accomplishing steps 5–7 of the deception planning in Sect. 4.1, roughly in order of decreasing usefulness, are:

- T1, false displays of system state: If an attacker tries to do something dangerous, it can be a useful deception for the defender to merely simulate what happens. For instance, increasing the power in many processes could cause overheating, which can be simulated with increases on a thermostat icon. Most industrial processes have a "digital twin" simulation for testing and analysis, and a display of the twin could deceive the attacker. False displays can be effective for ICSs because their specialized nature ([1], chapter 11) means inconsistencies in a simulation are more likely to be missed by most attackers. A particularly useful false display is for a target system to imitate an obvious honeypot, since attacks try to avoid honeypots [37].
- T2, fake controls: Attackers want to control systems, so an interface they can manipulate as in [38] is appealing. It can look like the controls of a real ICS, with knobs and switches that appear to change the ICS, though they do not. They can also log what the attacker does for future analysis.
- T3, fake resources ("decoys"): These include useless nodes, processes, and files to waste attacker time. ICSs tend to have many nodes and features, and it is easy to make some extra ones. Fake resources can also be generated dynamically to answer attacker interests, as a more active defense [39]. Files can be made more realistic by simulating plausible resource use [40].
- T4, false error messages: These can be used as excuses not to do something dangerous. Attackers can take error messages seriously, particularly for an unfamiliar and specialized system like an ICS, since they may mean goals are unachievable ([1], chapter 9). False error messages can also thwart automated attacks because they cause unexpected interruptions, made worse if followed by requests to do new things for which the automated attack is unprepared.
- T5, fake crises: These can be triggered by defenders by interjecting messages that an intruder has been detected, or reporting that the ICS is out of control. This is useful in fooling intended saboteurs, but is too dramatic to be used routinely.
- T6, flooding the adversary with data: This is denial of service in reverse. It can be done by generating fake data or using historical data with dates changed. It is useful against sophisticated attackers who may waste time trying to understand the data.
- T7, obfuscatory controls: An interface can be made hard to understand so that the attacker cannot usefully control it. Controls can be poorly labeled with code names and numbers, so an attacker has few clues about how to proceed. Real systems designed for a limited set of specialized users often lack adequate

labeling, and many ICSs require specialized technical knowledge to understand, so incomprehensible interfaces are plausible. The interface can also require confusing preconditions before anything happens.
- T8, misleading controls: A deception unique to ICSs is to have the knobs and switches do something different from expected. A knob labeled "power" could decrease power if turned clockwise, contrary to the usual expectation, or switches labeled "on/off" could be inconsistent in which direction is "on".
- T9, process interruptions and delays: The system can stop responding for random periods of time for no obvious reason, or can respond very slowly as in "tarpits". This will confuse the attacker or encourage them to think they have disabled the system.
- T10, decoy financial records: These encourage adversaries who seek monetary gain.

These deceptions work best when tied to high-priority adversary goals. Some examples:

- Adversaries want a feeling of control, and many want to disable things. So simulate disablement events that the attackers likely want. An example would be to simulate the turning off an entire power plant by terminating all protocols connecting to it. It could be made further convincing if preceded by dramatic fluctuations of the dials and lights of the display.
- Adversaries want to do reconnaissance, and they may get bounties for the nodes that they find. So simulate an ICS network with so many nodes that it will take a long time to explore, perhaps even an unbounded time if nodes are generated whenever an adversary queries a new address. Most nodes can be decoys to confuse the adversary; this might seem suspicious, but will not impede an automated attack.
- To frustrate adversaries who need to feel in control and having achieved persistence on systems, simulate an unreliable system with inconsistent behavior to give them a sense of failure to control things. For instance, terminate access to resources randomly, and ask for passwords repeatedly.
- Similarly, to frustrate adversaries who need to feel in control, provide complex visual displays that are difficult to decipher and waste their time. Use ambiguous labels and abbreviations to require adversaries to use considerable trial and error to accomplish anything.

Another consideration in choosing deceptions is their compatibility with high and low values of the adversary variables. Table 4 summarizes the compatibility of these deception tactics to the adversary variables in Table 3.

7 Reinforcement Learning of Adversary Variables

Choosing among these options can try to optimize defender benefits by assigning costs and benefits to both attacker and defender tactics, and then using decision theory (if the attack plan is fixed), game theory [30, 41], or stochastic modeling [42]

Table 4 Compatibility of deception tactics with high and low values of the adversary variables

Adversary variable	Deception tactics for high values of this variable	Deception tactics for low values of this variable
Sophistication of the adversary	T6, T7, T8, T9	T1, T2, T3, T4, T5
Confidence of the adversary in their methods	T1, T2, T3, T4, T8	T5, T6, T7
Interest of adversary in intelligence gathering versus sabotage	T3, T6, T10	T4, T5, T7, T8
Adversary estimate of reliability of the target system	T1, T2, T3, T4	T8, T9
Trust in information shown about the attack target	T1, T2, T3, T4, T5, T6	T8, T9
Alertness of adversary to the target	T6, T7, T8, T9	T1, T2, T3, T4, T5
Surprise of the adversary at the target	T3, T4, T6	T1, T2, T3, T4, T10
Adaptability of adversary to the target	T6, T7, T8, T9, T10	T1, T2, T3, T4, T5
Impatience of the adversary	T4, T5, T6, T7, T8, T9	T1, T2, T3
Desire of adversary to disconnect without achieving their goals	T4, T5, T6, T7, T8, T9	T1, T2, T3
Frustration level of the adversary	T4, T5, T6, T7, T8, T9	T1, T2,T3
Interest of the adversary in financial gain	T3, T10	

to determine the best tactics. Deception methods are also just one kind of active-defense method; alternative methods to consider are moving-target defenses that modify configurations and software [43] and active searching for attackers [44].

Our experience with real ICS honeypots has been that most malicious activity is exploratory [38], and can be deceived by simple methods like random error messages. Defensive planning is primarily useful against the rarer sophisticated adversary who has time to make a plan specific for the target site, and can adjust to our attempts to deceive. For such adversaries, reinforcement learning is a simple way to dynamically find their weaknesses (as step 8 in the deception plan of Sect. 4.1). For instance, many Chinese attacks attempt espionage; so to deceive them, offer them plenty of what looks like valid intelligence, and see if they like it by looking for more. Many Russian attacks attempt to sabotage; so to deceive them, give them plenty of evidence of suddenly crashed processes after malicious-appearing adversary commands, and see if they try to do more.

After deceptions, reinforcements can also update the estimates of the adversary variables based on adversary choices and deception success or failure. Reinforcement learning also has the advantage that it is self-correcting. After a false error message for instance, we could decrease the estimated perception by the adversary of the reliability of the system, and increase the estimated frustration of the adversary. It simplifies matters to treat adversary variables as probabilities on a range of 0 to 1. To keep variables in that range, we can ignore increments that would force them outside the range. Alternatively, a common method is to set the probability of choice p to $c_D * \mathrm{p}$ for a decrease and to $\mathrm{p} + c_D * (1 - \mathrm{p})$ for an increase, where p is the value of the adversary variable, D is a particular deception or system response, and c_D is the reinforcement constant specific to deception D.

For ICSs and a deception plan focused on discouragement, a high rating should be given to deceptions that caused an attack to stop. Lesser but positive ratings should be given to deceptions that cause an attack to waste time, as by retrieving bait files or visiting decoy network nodes, with the rating proportional to the time wasted [45]. Negative ratings should be given to deceptions which the attacker ignored. From these ratings we should subtract the values to the attacker of achieving partial goals, such as legitimate nodes they have found, legitimate documents they have stolen, and how much they have disrupted actual operations. Data to estimate these values can be collected from intrusion-detection systems, log files, and packet captures.

Reinforcements can be applied with attenuation to deceptions earlier in the attacker's session. For instance, if the adversary disconnected after a second error message about network availability, this should reinforce the decision to issue a first error message about it, so that the first error message should be issued more often by the defender in similar situations in the future. However, it is usual that the reinforcement should be attenuated by multiplying by it by a fraction for each step backward since earlier actions are less related to outcomes. Multiple reinforcements to the same action can be averaged, so that if at one time the defender's deception worked well and at one time it worked badly, the average will assign a more neutral effect to the deception. Reinforcements can be averaged over all attacks so very different attacks will still generate separate reinforcements for the deceptions that worked with them.

Data for reinforcement learning can be enhanced with "data farming". This means generating synthetic data based on real data and training with it. [46] tried this method by generating new variants of ICS attacks for Log4j and IEC 104 permutation attacks using an evolutionary algorithm. To implement this in a more general way, we need a simulation of the attacker-defender game that we can run many times to generate automated outcomes. We need some starting data of attacker behavior from which to enumerate a set of attacker actions. We then create sequences of those actions that we have not seen previously, choose random sets of defender actions, and rate the outcomes based on the achievement of defender goals minus the achievement of attacker goals. This then creates new data for reinforcement learning.

A secondary issue affecting planning of multilayer deceptions is how often deceptions should be used. Adversaries that are high on the sophistication parameter such as advanced persistent threats will be expecting obstacles including deceptions, so we can use as many deceptions as we like without expecting them to react differently, since they are low on the "trust" parameter concerning us. But amateur attackers may experience a major change to the trust variable when they realize we are deceiving them, and they may redouble their efforts or seek revenge against us. We should try to avoid this situation because it may lead to new circumstances against which we are unprepared to defend, so we may not want to use multilayered deceptions against such attackers.

8 Case Study: Experiments with Building Maintenance Systems

8.1 The Equipment

We have recently been exploring these ideas in the context of heating, ventilation, and air-conditioning (HVAC) systems for buildings, a type of ICS underestimated for security vulnerabilities even though its manipulation can make a building uninhabitable and disable its computer systems. We have been working with our Facilities Management department to learn about their controls. They have centralized control over all the buildings on our campus, using the BACnet protocol for the lower levels of device control.

To foil attacks on facilities, a honeypot designed for discouragement is appropriate. We are currently experimenting with an Automated Logic fan-coil unit [47], obtained as excess hardware from Facilities Management, which exemplifies their hardware and software. The unit contains an actuator, a fan motor, a temperature sensor, and a thermostat. It is controlled by a Web-based graphical user interface

WEBCTRL [47] that shows the state of the equipment, and it reports data to a centralized collection point using the BACnet-over-IP protocol.

We could block all unauthorized attempts to control the fan, but this would give an attacker quick feedback and enable them to switch their targeting to a more vulnerable device. A better way to control attackers would be to simulate cooperation with attacks by false representations in the graphical user interface. For instance, if an attacker tries to turn off a running fan, we should just simulate turning it off by substitution of a visualization of a nonrotating fan in the interface, while keeping the fan actually on [48]. Similarly, if an attacker tries a second-derivative attack by turning on and off the fan repeatedly to try to damage it, we can simulate it stopping and no longer responding to commands. Appearing to cooperate with user sabotage first plays to their sense of power as discussed in Sect. 5.2, and then increases their frustration if they discover later that their actions actually failed. People are unlikely to question what graphics shows them, and are more likely to blame themselves for failures.

Similar honeypot ploys can be used for heating and air-conditioning units where attackers will have similar goals such as increasing the heat or cooling rate. We can use naïve-physics models [33] to simulate the temperature change when following attacker commands; all we need for deception is a temperature gauge showing the simulated temperature, while in reality the temperature remains the same.

8.2 *Example Reinforcement-Learning Scenario*

Figure 3 shows part of the state diagram for an attacker-defender game on the equipment described in the last section, assuming the attacker has access to the controller machine which displays a table of devices and their associated measures. We assume there is a fan, a temperature gauge, and a thermostat.

For a demonstration, we will use only the adversary variables given in Table 5, chosen from the variables in Table 3, with some example initial assignments.

We can update these values using a table of reinforcements applied to the adversary model, giving increments to parameters due to events (Table 6). The increment should be ignored if it makes the probability greater than 1 or less than 0. We have used plausible increments here, but they can be fit to data from real adversaries.

As a demonstration of how reinforcement works, Table 7 gives an example interaction with deceptions based on Fig. 3, showing how its steps affect the adversary variables.

Observing the last row of the table, the overall effect of this sequence of events is to leave the attacker frustrated and thinking they have been deceived, less confident of themselves, but still thinking they are sophisticated because they did provide a good test of the system. If we see the attacker's IP address again, or an address in the same subnetwork, it will be good to avoid deceptions involving fakes (T1, T2, T3, T4, and T5 of Sect. 6) since we inferred that this attacker is aware of

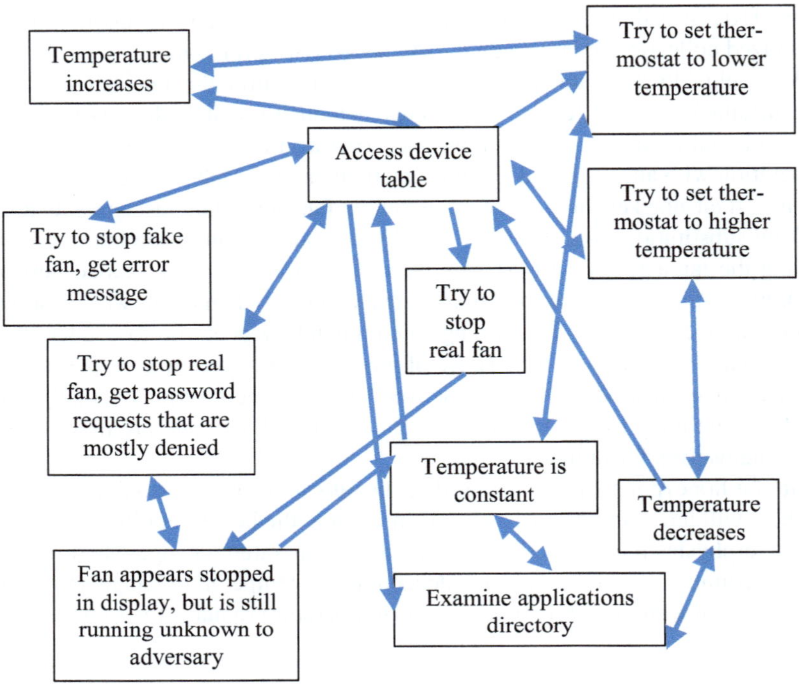

Fig. 3 State diagram for some deceptive interactions with a fan, thermostat, and temperature gauge in an HVAC (heating, ventilation, and air-conditioning) system

Table 5 Parameters in the HVAC example with demonstration initial values

Symbol	Parameter	Initial value for Table 6
p_d	Probability that adversary disconnects without achieving their goals	0.02
p_c	Probability that adversary tries to confirm display data	0.01
p_t	Probability adversary trusts data shown	0.05
p_s	Probability adversary is sophisticated	0.30
p_k	Probability adversary is confident about their methods	0.50
p_a	Probability that adversary is alert	0.30
p_r	Probability that adversary thinks the system is reliable	0.50
p_f	Probability that adversary is frustrated	0.01

deception and may tell colleagues in their organization. Instead, we could prefer tactics of flooding the attacker with data, obfuscatory controls, misleading controls, and process interruptions (T6, T7, T8, and T9).

Table 6 Proposed reinforcements to adversary variables based on adversary events

Event	p_d	p_c	p_t	p_s	p_k	p_a	p_r	p_f
Get error message	0.01	0.05	0.01	0.00	−0.10	0.10	0.00	0.03
Command fails	0.03	0.05	0.02	0.00	−0.10	0.05	−0.05	0.10
Command had opposite effect of expected	0.07	0.10	0.05	0.00	−0.10	0.05	−0.05	0.05
Nothing unusual found in examining display	0.00	0.00	0.02	0.02	0.00	0.03	0.02	0.00
Something unusual found in examining display	0.10	0.00	0.02	0.05	0.00	0.03	−0.05	0.00
Unusual response delay	0.10	0.00	−0.05	0.00	−0.05	0.00	−0.02	0.05
"Suspicious behavior" noted by system	0.10	0.00	−0.10	0.00	−0.10	0.05	−0.05	0.10
Adversary leaves	0.10	−0.05	0.00	0.00	−0.20	0.00	0.00	0.10

Table 7 Modifications to adversary variables for an example sequence of adversary actions with some defensive deceptions

Attacker event and result	p_d	p_c	p_t	p_s	p_k	p_a	p_r	p_f
Start	0.02	0.01	0.05	0.30	0.50	0.30	0.50	0.01
Attacker views the device table, sees nothing interesting	0.02	0.01	0.07	0.32	0.50	0.33	0.52	0.01
Attacker sets the thermostat to a higher temperature; temperature decreases in device table, an unexpected result	0.09	0.11	0.12	0.32	0.60	0.38	0.47	0.06
Adversary tries to stop the fan; no effect in the display	0.12	0.16	0.14	0.32	0.50	0.43	0.42	0.16
Adversary tries to stop the fan a second time, gets long delay	0.22	0.16	0.09	0.32	0.45	0.43	0.35	0.21
Adversary gets password requests, system notes "suspicious behavior"	0.32	0.16	0.00	0.32	0.35	0.48	0.32	0.31
Attacker leaves	0.42	0.11	0.00	0.32	0.15	0.48	0.32	0.41

9 Conclusions

The cybersecurity problems of industrial control systems differ in important ways from those of most information systems. This means their defensive tactics should be different, including their deceptive defenses, which should be especially sensitive to the environment in which they occur. We have identified a range of tactics in this chapter for better design of multilayered defensive deception methods for industrial control systems. These methods infer a set of "adversary variables" from adversary actions, which can be used to predict subsequent adversary activity. These can be dynamically modified by using reinforcement learning from attacker behavior over an extended period of interactions with a range of attackers. We have provided a variety of design tools that can provide interesting and varied deceptions for a range of attackers. Testing these tools is our next step, but testing is difficult since attackers are deliberately uncooperative, and testing against known attacks does not capture the dynamics of real attack campaigns. Nonetheless, much as when artificial neural networks receive repeated feedback to improve their weights, and they can converge to surprisingly powerful consensus models, we expect our multiple methods of feedback can allow us to craft powerful defensive campaigns from repeated exposure to attacks.

Acknowledgements This work was supported by the U.S. Department of Energy and the Defense Intelligence Agency. Thuy D. Nguyen, Julian L. Rrushi, Scott D. Colvin, and Angela Tan contributed ideas. Opinions expressed are those of the author and do not represent those of the U.S. Government.

References

1. Rowe N, Rrushi J (2016) Introduction to cyberdeception. Berlin: Springer International Publishing.
2. Ackerman P (2017) Industrial cybersecurity. Birmingham, UK, Packt.
3. Kayan H, Nunes M, Rana O, Burnap P, Perera C (2022, September) Cybersecurity of industrial cyber-physical systems: A review. ACM Computing Surveys, 54(11s), Article 229
4. Sohl E, Fielding C, Hanlon T, Rrushi J, Farhangi H, Carmichael K., Dabell J (2015, October) A field study of digital forensics of intrusions in the electrical power grid. Proc. First ACM Workshop on Cyber-Physical Systems-Security and/or Privacy
5. Rowe N (2024) Cyber deception. Chapter in Encyclopedia of Cryptography, Security, and Privacy, 3rd edition, ed. Jagodia S, Samarati P, Young M, Springer Berlin, Heidelberg. https://doi.org/10.1007/978-3-642-27739-9_1766-1
6. Franco J, Aris A, Canberk B, Selcuk A (2021) A survey of honeypots and honeynets for Internet of Things, industrial Internet of Things, and cyber-physical systems. IEEE Communication Surveys and Tutorials.
7. Rowe N (2019) Honeypot deception tactics. Chapter 3 in Al-Shaer E, Wei J, Hamlen K, Wang C (Eds.), Autonomous Cyber Deception: Reasoning, Adaptive Planning, and Evaluation of HoneyThings, Springer, Chaum, Switzerland, 35-45
8. Urias V, Stout W, Van Leeuwen B (2018, October) On the feasibility of generating deception environments for industrial control systems. Proc. 2018 IEEE International Symposium on Technologies for Homeland Security, Woburn, MA, US
9. Abe S, Tanaka Y, Uchida Y, Horata S (2018, July) Developing deception network systems with traceback honeypot in ICS network. ISCE Journal of Control, Measurement, and System Integration, 11(4): 372-379
10. Cifranic N, Romero-Mariana J, Souza B, Hallman R (2020) Decepti-SCADA: A framework for actively defending networked critical infrastructures. Proc. 5th International Conference on Internet of Things, Big Data and Security - Volume 1: IoTBDS, 69-77
11. Dutta N, Jadav N, Dutiya N, Joshi D (2020) Using honeypots for ICD threats evaluation. In E. Pricop et al., (eds.), Recent Developments on Industrial Control Systems Resilience, Studies in Systems, Decision, and Control 255, Springer Nature, 175-196.
12. You J, Lv S, Zhao L, Niu M, Shi Z, Sun L (2020, November) A scalable high-interaction physical honeypot framework for programmable logic controller. Proc. IEEE 92nd Vehicular Technology Conference, Victoria, BC CA
13. Atadika M, Burke K, Rowe N (2019, August) Critical risk management practices to mitigate cloud migration misconfigurations. Proc. Intl. Conf. on Computational Science and Computational Intelligence, Las Vegas, NV, USA

14. Dodson M, Beresford A, Vingaard M (2020) Using global honeypot networks to detect targeted ICS attacks. Proc. 12th International Conference on Cyber Conflict.
15. Foley B, Rowe N, Nguyen T (2022, December) Analyzing attacks on client-side honeypots from representative malicious Web sites. Proc. International Conference on Computational Science and Computational Intelligence
16. Rowe N, Nguyen T, Kendrick M, Rucker Z, Hyun D, Brown J (2020, January) Creating effective industrial-control-systems honeypots. Proc. Hawaii Intl. Conf. on Systems Sciences, Wailea, HI
17. Meier J, Nguyen T, Rowe N (2023, January) Hardening honeypots for industrial control systems. Proc. Hawaii Intl. Conf. on Systems Sciences, Maui, HI.
18. Clark R, Mitchell W (2019) Deception: counterdeception and counterintelligence. Sage Publishing.
19. Landsborough J, Nguyen T, Rowe N (2024, January) Retrospectively using multilayer deception in depth against advanced persistent threats. Proc. Hawaii Intl. Conf. on System Sciences, Hawaii, HI
20. Basan A, Basan E, Korchalovsky S, Bikhailova V, Ivannikova T, Shulika M (2022, November) The concept of the knowledge base of threats to cyber-physical systems based on the ontological approach. Proc. IEEE International Multi-Conference on Engineering, Computer, and Information Sciences, Novosibirsk-Yekaterinburg, RU.
21. Cohen F (1999) A mathematical structure of simple defensive network deceptions. all.net/journal/deception/mathdeception/mathdeception.html, accessed 15 Jan 2016.
22. Rowe N, Nguyen T, Dougherty J, Bieker J, Pilkington D (2021, September) Identifying anomalous industrial-control-system network flow activity using cloud honeypots. Springer Lecture Notes, Proc. National Cyber Summit, Huntsville, Alabama.
23. Han X, Kheir N, Balzarotti D (2018, July) Deception techniques in computer security: a research perspective. ACM Computing Surveys, 51(4) article 80.
24. Pawlick J, Colbert E, Zhu Q (2019, August) A game-theoretic taxonomy and survey of defensive deception for cybersecurity and privacy. ACM Computing Surveys, 52(4), Article 82
25. Morales E, Rubio-Medarno C, Doupe A, Shoshitsishvili Y, Wang R, Bao T, Ahn GJ (2020, October) HoneyPLC: a next-generation honeypot for industrial control systems. Proc. ACM SIGSAC Conf. on Computer and Communications Security, 279-291
26. Qassim Q, Jamil N, Mahdi M, Rahim A (2020, August) Towards SCADA threat intelligence based on intrusion detection systems – A short review. Proc. 8th Intl. Conf. on Information Technology and Multimedia, Selangor, Malaysia, 144-149.
27. Rrushi J (2022, May) Physics-driven page fault handling for customized deception against CPS malware. ACM Transactions on Embedded Computing Systems, 21(3), 1-36
28. Yahya M, Sharaf N, Rrushi J, Tay H, Liu B, and Xu K (2020, December) Physics reasoning for intrusion detection in industrial networks. Proc. IEEE International Conference on Trust, Privacy and Security in Intelligent Systems, and Applications.
29. Lin H, Alemzadeh H, Chen D, Kalbarczyk Z, Iyer R (2016, April) Safety-critical cyber-physical attacks: Analysis, detection, and mitigation. Proc. Symposium on the Science of Security, Pittsburgh, PA, US
30. Rowe N, Green J, Benn A, Drew S, Heinen C, Bixler R, Tan A, and Barton A (2024) Game-based testing for active cyberdefense and cyberdeception. Chapter in Cybersecurity – Cyber Defense, Privacy and Cyberwarfare, ed. Dimitoglou A, Deligiannidis L, Arabnia, H, Berlin, DE: De Gruyter
31. Zafra D, Leong R, Sistrunk C, Proska K, Hildebrandt C, Lunden K, Brubaker N (2022, April 25) Industroyer.V2: Old malware learns new tricks. https://www.mandiant.com/resources/blog/industroyer-v2-old-malware-new-tricks
32. Miao P, Dong L (2021, July) Attack effect observer-based security control for cyber-physical systems subjected to false data injection attack. Proc. 40th Chinese Control Conference, Shanghai, CN

33. Smith B, Casati R (1994) Naive physics: An essay in ontology. Philosophical Psychology, 7(2) 225–244. https://doi.org/10.1080/09515089408573121.
34. Gollmann D, Gurikov P, Isakov A, Krotofil M, Larsen J, Winnicki A (2015, April) Cyber-physical systems security – experimental analysis of a vinyl acetate monomer plant. CPSS '15: Proceedings of the 1st ACM Workshop on Cyber-Physical System Security, Singapore, SP
35. Lucchese M, Lupia F, Merro M, Paci F, Zannone N, Furfaro A (2023, August) HoneyICS: A high-interaction physics-aware honeynet for industrial control systems. Proc. 18th Intl. Conf. on Availability, Reliability, and Security, Benevento, IT, Article 113.
36. Shinde A, Doshi P, Setayeshfar O (2021, May) Cyber attack intent recognition and active deception using factored interactive POMDPs. Proc. Intl. Conf. on Autonomous Agents and Multiagent Systems.
37. Maesschalck S, Fantom W, Giotsas V, Race, N (2024, June). These are not the PLCs you are looking for: Obfuscating PLCs to mimic honeypots. IEEE Transactions on Network and Service Management, 21(3), 3623-3635.
38. Ramirez R, Nguyen T, Rowe N, Meier J (2022, December) Classifying RDP remote attacks on user interfaces to industrial control systems. Proc. Intl. Conf. on Computational Science and Computational Intelligence, Research Track on Cyber Warfare, Cyber Defense, and Cyber Security.
39. Yang D, Mashima D, Lin W, Zhou J (2020, October) DecIED: Scalable k-anonymous deception for IEC61850-compliant smart grid systems. Proc. CPSS, Taipei, Taiwan.
40. Sutton A, Tahiri S, Bond B, Rrushi J (2019, December) Countering malware via decoy processes with improved resource utilization consistency. Proc. IEEE International Conference on Trust, Privacy and Security in Intelligent Systems, and Applications
41. La Q, Quek T, Lee J, Jin S, Zhu H (2016, December) Deceptive attack and defense game in honeypot-enable-networks for the Internet of Things. IEEE Internet of Things Journal, 3(6)
42. Betancourt J, Gonzalex GP, Gonzalex SR, Cuellar , Gomez, C, Mariotti F, Montecchi L, Lollini P (2022, November) Modeling attacker behavior in cyber-physical-systems. Proc. Latin-American Symposium on Dependable Computing, Fortaleza/CE, BR
43. Ma D, Tang Z, Sun X, Guo L, Wang L, Chang K (2022, November) Game theory approaches for evaluating the deception-based moving target defense. Proc. 9th Workshop on Moving Target Defense, Los Angeles, US
44. Ajmal A, Alam M, Khaliq A, Khan S, Qadir Z, Mahmu M (2021, September) Last line of defense: reliability through inducing cyber threat hunting with deception in SCADA networks. IEEE Access, 9.
45. Reti D, Elzer K, Fraunholz D, Schneider D, Schotten H (2022, November) Evaluating deception and moving target defense with network attack simulation. Proc. Workshop on Moving Target Defense, Los Angeles, CA, US
46. Haynes N, Nguyen T, Rowe, N (2023, January) Creating synthetic attacks with evolutionary algorithms for proactive defense of industrial control systems. Proc. Hawaii Intl. Conf. on Systems Sciences, Maui, HI, US.
47. Automated Logic (2019, May 9) WebCTRL V7.0. https://www.mindmeister.com/generic_files/get_file/10093951?filetype=attachment_file
48. Colvin S (2023, December) Implementing a high-interaction hybrid honeypot for facility automation systems. M.S. thesis, U.S. Naval Postgraduate School.

MaxPro: Strengthening UAV Network Security with Proactive Dynamic Routing Against Inference Attacks

Shangqing Zhao, Zhengping Luo, and Zhuo Lu

1 Introduction

Unmanned Aerial Vehicles (UAVs), commonly known as drones, have emerged as versatile platforms with the potential to revolutionize various industries and applications, including surveillance, monitoring, disaster management, and communication [19]. UAV networks refer to the interconnected system of these drones, working together to achieve specific objectives. For example, UAVs can be deployed efficiently to provide high quality of service for Internet of Things [57]. These networks are characterized by their ability to operate autonomously, communicate with each other, and collaborate to accomplish complex tasks efficiently. UAV networks, while offering numerous benefits and applications, are also vulnerable to various security threats that can compromise their operations and data integrity. Securing UAV networks is crucial to ensure safe and reliable operation, protect sensitive information, and mitigate the risks posed by malicious actors [31].

Wireless eavesdropping attacks pose a significant threat within UAV networks, as attackers observing the network can gather critical information. One of the significant information in the UAV network includes network flow information, which covers sensitive data such as the data rates between source and destination pairs across end-to-end paths. Should this information fall into the wrong hands,

S. Zhao (✉)
University of Oklahoma, Tulsa, OK, USA
e-mail: shangqing@ou.edu

Z. Luo
Rider University, Ewing, NJ, USA
e-mail: zluo@rider.edu

Z. Lu
University of South Florida, Tampa, FL, USA
e-mail: zhuolu@usf.edu

Q. Zhu et al. (eds.), *Foundations of Cyber Deception*, Advances in Information Security 90, https://doi.org/10.1007/978-3-031-93867-2_10

it enables malicious parties to deduce communication patterns, setting the stage for sophisticated attacks. For instance, by accessing this data, attackers can profile UAVs based on their activity, improving their chances of successfully targeting specific devices or crafting convincing phishing schemes [20, 58].

In many wireless networks, including UAV networks, directly accessing end-to-end flow information is often impractical or restricted due to privacy issues, legal constraints, or technical challenges[7, 25, 32, 35, 51, 54, 60, 66]. UAV communication networks, in particular, present a unique difficulty for monitoring because UAVs establish direct links with each other, creating a self-organizing network without relying on a centralized infrastructure. This decentralized nature complicates the task of direct observation.

Network inference, or network tomography, emerges as a technique to indirectly deduce sensitive flow information by analyzing readily available link metrics within a UAV network [2, 28, 39, 52]. This method leverages the relationships between end-to-end flow rates and individual link rates, which are influenced by routing protocols and the network's topology, to infer critical data [2, 14, 16, 23, 29, 34, 36, 40, 42, 43, 56, 59].

However, this indirect approach to gathering network insights presents a vulnerability. Malicious entities can utilize network inference to extract flow information from seemingly benign link metrics, circumventing the need for direct access to the network's sensitive data [11, 12, 24, 37, 38, 61, 63]. Such exploitation introduces significant security and privacy risks, as attackers can gain insights into the network's operations without breaching its defenses directly.

The effectiveness of traditional reactive defenses against inference attacks in UAV networks is less effective. Such methods are primarily based on the principle of detecting an attack once it has already started, leading to a critical period during which the initial stages of the attack could remain undetected, allowing sensitive information to be at risk of exposure. This inherent delay in the detection process provides attackers with a valuable opportunity to collect crucial data. Recognizing this gap, we notice that the inherent dynamism of UAV networks presents a promising opportunity for a more proactive approach to security. Given the absence of a static infrastructure and the perpetual motion of UAVs, we can continuously change the data transmission routes. This makes it hard for attackers to keep up and accurately map out the network's routing patterns. Applying to the inference attack, proactively altering how data travels can create a mismatch between what an attacker observes and the actual operational patterns of the network, making it difficult for them to draw precise conclusions from what they see. This approach significantly challenges an attacker's capacity to accurately analyze and infer sensitive information from link metrics, thereby providing a robust defense mechanism against inference attacks.

In our preliminary research [10, 62], we conducted an analysis and comparison of various existing random routing protocols. However, these protocols were not tested in a real-world wireless network setting to assess their effectiveness in mitigating inference attacks. Moreover, while many of these routing protocols were initially crafted to protect anonymous information, i.e., to secure the identities of the communication endpoints, their effectiveness in obscuring flow information remains unexplored.

In this chapter, we notice that the inference error is closely related to the likelihood of discrepancies arising between the flow patterns, i.e., represented by a randomly observed by attackers, and the genuine template operational within the network. Motivated by this observation, we introduce a proactive defense strategy designed to counter inference attacks, called MaxPro. This approach involves the use of a dynamic routing protocol for UAV networks, which continuously alters the routing pattern. The goal is to maximize the probability that the routing pattern observed by attackers will not match the actual routing pattern used within the network, thereby increasing the inference error. We carried out extensive theoretical and empirical analyses to show that our proposed method, MaxPro, is capable of achieving an inference error that is proportional to the number of UAVs within the UAV network.

The main contributions of our chapter could be summarized as follows:

- We introduce a novel dynamic routing protocol, named as MaxPro, specifically designed to enhance resilience against network inference attacks in UAV networks.
- We provide a detailed theoretical analysis of MaxPro's performance against inference attacks, considering inference errors and the protocol's cost (delay).
- We conduct comprehensive simulations to demonstrate the performance and cost of MaxPro, confirming the validity of our theoretical analysis.

The whole structure of the chapter is organized as follows: We briefly introduce background information on UAV networks and related network inferences, attack modeling, and design motivation in Sect. 2. The mathematical model of the routing protocol and the theoretical results are detailed in Sect. 3, followed by simulations in Sect. 4 to verify our findings. Finally, we discuss related work in Sect. 5 and conclude the chapter in Sect. 6.

2 UAV Network Modelling and Prerequisites

In this section, we outline the architecture of UAV networks and the necessary background information for network inference. Subsequently, we define the research problems addressed in this chapter. Throughout this chapter, uppercase bold denotes a matrix, lowercase bold denotes a vector, and calligraphy font denotes a set, unless otherwise specified.

We introduce several notations to facilitate our discussion. $\mathbf{X}^T$ denotes the transpose of matrix $\mathbf{X}$, while $\mathbf{X}^{-1}$ signifies the inverse of matrix $\mathbf{X}$. The $\mathcal{L}$-p norm of vector $\mathbf{x} = [x_1, x_2, \cdots, x_n]^T$ is represented as $|\mathbf{x}|_p$. For functions $f(n)$ and $g(n)$, $f(n) = O(g(n))$ or equivalently $g(n) = \Omega(f(n))$ indicates that there exists a constant c and a threshold n_0 such that $f(n) \leq cg(n)$ for all $n > n_0$. When we say $f(n) = \Theta(g(n))$, it means that $f(n) = O(g(n))$ and simultaneously

$f(n) = \Omega(g(n))$. The cardinality of a set $\mathcal{F}$ is denoted by $|\mathcal{F}|$. The trace of matrix $\mathbf{X}$ is indicated by $\mathbf{trX}$. Finally, the floor function of a scalar x, which rounds x down to the nearest integer, is represented by $\lfloor x \rfloor$.

2.1 UAE Network Architecture

UAV networks are intricate systems that comprise multiple interconnected UAVs collaborating to achieve diverse objectives [19]. The architecture of UAV networks is meticulously designed to enable efficient communication, coordination, and control of UAVs, allowing them to execute tasks autonomously and efficiently.

The communication infrastructure lies at the heart of UAV network architecture, enabling UAVs to exchange data and information among themselves and with ground stations. This infrastructure typically encompasses wireless communication technologies like Wi-Fi, Bluetooth, and cellular networks, enabling UAVs to communicate over both short and long distances [31, 57]. Figure 1 illustrates a detailed communication architecture of UAVs. It includes an air-based network interconnected through UAVs and a ground-based network employing radio communication via cellular, Wi-Fi, Internet, or other communication networks. UAVs are typically managed by ground stations through radios.

The flexibility and advantages of UAVs allow UAV networks to extend their reach to remote rural areas, providing network services for emergency communication requirements. For instance, UAV networks can be deployed to assist cellular mobile systems in achieving better coverage [5].

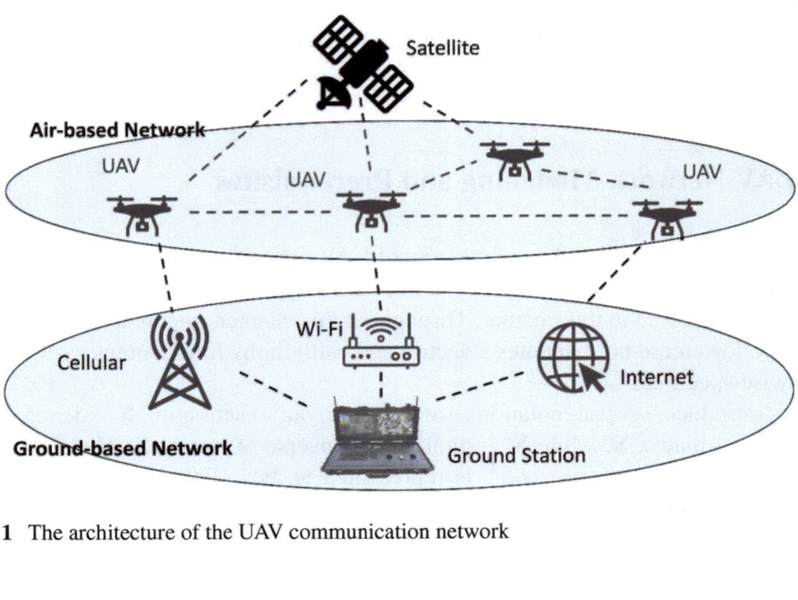

Fig. 1 The architecture of the UAV communication network

Safety is a paramount concern in UAV networks, as they operate in shared airspace and interact with manned aircraft and ground vehicles. The design and implementation of UAV networks present several challenges, including communication and coordination among UAVs, efficient task allocation, energy management, and ensuring safe and reliable operation [31]. Communication is a critical aspect of UAV networks, enabling UAVs to share information, coordinate their actions, and relay data to ground stations or other UAVs. The use of wireless communication technologies, such as Wi-Fi, Bluetooth, and cellular networks, plays a crucial role in enabling seamless communication among UAVs and between UAVs and ground stations.

2.2 UAV Network Model

In an UAV communication network, if we have a malicious attacker in the air-based network, usually through an manipulated UAV or multiple UAVs, or directly through traffic sniffing, could obtain the information of the network, then there will have a lot of consequences the attacker could bring to the network, such as inference attacks [2, 28, 39, 52].

In this work, we model the topology of an air-based network within UAV communication network as a random geometric graph (RGG), a common approach for modeling distributed wireless networks [13]. The network is represented as $\mathcal{G} = (\mathcal{V}, \mathcal{L})$, where $\mathcal{V}$ is the set of UAVs and $\mathcal{L}$ is the set of undirected links. Let $N = |\mathcal{V}|$ and $L = |\mathcal{L}|$ denote the total number of UAVs and links, respectively. In this model, each UAV corresponds to an RF front end, and the UAVs are randomly distributed in a region $\Omega = [0, \sqrt{N/\lambda}]^2$, where λ is the UAV density. We assume λ is sufficiently large such that the entire network is connected asymptotically almost surely [13]. The transmission range of each UAV is denoted by r, and two UAVs are considered connected if they are within each other's transmission range. The network model is shown in Fig. 2.

In the UAV network model, packets are exchanged between different UAVs, resulting in multiple end-to-end data flows. We denote the set of end-to-end flows as $\mathcal{F}$, representing potential flows for each UAV pair. Therefore, there are at most $|\mathcal{F}| = N(N-1)/2$ flows in the network model, corresponding to the total number of UAV pairs. Let x_i represent the data rate of flow $f_i \in \mathcal{F}$. We define the flow rate

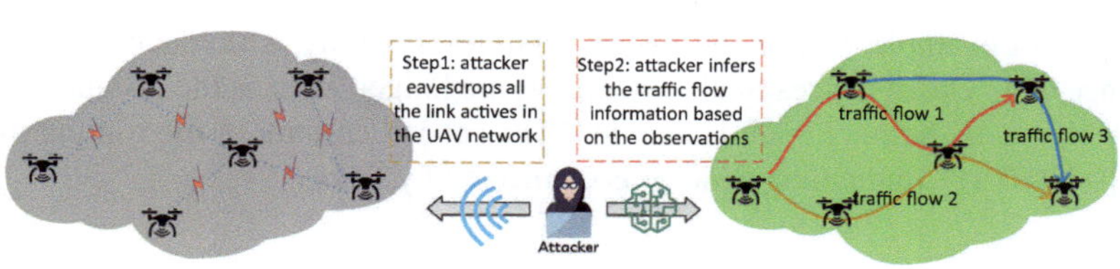

Fig. 2 Inference attacks in UAV networks

vector $\mathbf{x} = [x_i]_{i \in [1, |\mathcal{F}|]}$, where $x_i = 0$ if flow f_i does not exist (i.e., there is no communication).

By analyzing the flow rate vector **x**, we can determine the communication relationships and data rates between UAVs in the network. However, disclosing such information is often undesirable or prohibited in many practical scenarios, such as military and civil applications [3, 27, 30].

2.3 Inference Attack Model

In our study, we focus on the flow rate vector **x**, which contains critical network information. Malicious adversaries can leverage this information to launch potent attacks against a network. Therefore, we define the attacker's objective as acquiring the flow rate vector **x**. It is important to note that while each link is wirelessly connected with a broadcast nature, the flow rate vector **x** is typically not directly measurable by attackers. This is because flow information is typically indicated at the network or higher layers, with data encrypted at the physical or link layers [1]. Consequently, attackers must infer this information indirectly from physical and link-layer activities, a process known as network inference.

Mathematically, we denote the measured link rate vector as $\mathbf{y}=[y_1, y_2, \cdots, y_L]^T$, where y_i represents the rate of link l_i. In network inference, we model the relationship between the link rate vector **y** and the flow rate vector **x** as a linear system:

$$\mathbf{y} = \mathbf{R}\mathbf{x}, \tag{1}$$

where **R** is the routing matrix with size $L \times |\mathcal{F}|$. The entry r_{ij} of **R** is defined as:

$$r_{ij} = \begin{cases} 1, & \text{if link } l_i \text{ is present on a path of flow } f_j \text{ ;} \\ 0, & \text{otherwise.} \end{cases} \tag{2}$$

The routing matrix **R** in Fig. 3 demonstrates an example on how flows are constructed by links based on the shortest-path routing protocol in a network consisting of 5 UAVs, 5 links, and 6 flows. Here, the link set is denoted as $\mathcal{L} = l_1, \cdots, l_5$ and the flow set as $\mathcal{F} = f_1, \cdots, f_6$. In a UAV network using the shortest-path protocol, each flow selects the shortest path for routing packets based on the number of hops. For example, flow f_2 will go through links l_5 only, which have the shortest distance of 1. The distances of all other paths are longer, such as the distance of path $u_2 \to u_5 \to u_3$ being 2, so it is avoided. The second column of the routing matrix **R** is $[0\ 0\ 0\ 0\ 1]^T$, indicating flow f_2 is connected by links l_5.

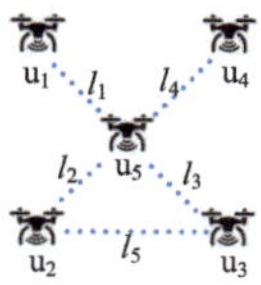

(a) Network topology.

Flow No.	f_1	f_2	f_3	f_4	f_5	f_6
Source	u_1	u_2	u_1	u_1	u_2	u_3
Destination	u_3	u_3	u_2	u_4	u_4	u_4

(b) Traffic flow information

	f_1	f_2	f_3	f_4	f_5	f_6
l_1	1	0	1	1	0	0
l_2	0	0	1	0	1	0
l_3	1	0	0	0	0	1
l_4	0	0	0	1	1	1
l_5	0	1	0	0	0	0

(c) A routing matrix **R**.

Fig. 3 An illustrative example of a UAV network including 5 UAVs (UAVs $u_1 \cdots u_5$), 5 links (links $l_1 \cdots l_5$) as shown in (**a**). There are 6 traffic flows in this network (flows $f_1 \cdots f_6$) as shown in (**b**). Given the flow information and topology, we have the routing matrix **R** built based on the shortest-path routing protocol, as shown in (**c**)

We assume a powerful attacker with comprehensive knowledge of the network topology and routing protocol. The attacker aims to minimize the inference error ϵ in obtaining an inferred flow rate vector $\hat{\mathbf{x}}$, given the link rate vector $\mathbf{y}$, the network topology $\mathcal{G}$, and the routing protocol T.

$$\epsilon = \|\hat{\mathbf{x}} - \mathbf{x}\|_2. \tag{3}$$

The attacker's objective is to minimize the inference error ϵ in obtaining an inferred flow rate vector $\hat{\mathbf{x}}$, given the link rate vector $\mathbf{y}$, the network topology $\mathcal{G}$, and the routing protocol T, i.e.,

$$\begin{aligned} \text{Objective} : \hat{\mathbf{x}} &= \arg\min \epsilon \\ \text{Given} : \mathbf{y},\ &\mathcal{G},\ T. \end{aligned} \tag{4}$$

In a UAV network, obtaining the link rate vector $\mathbf{y}$ through eavesdropping is straightforward. The routing matrix $\mathbf{R}$ is determined by the network topology and routing protocol. Since the number of flows $|\mathcal{F}|$ is usually larger than the number of links L in a UAV network, the linear system denoted by Equation (1) is under-determined. This allows the attacker to leverage any optimization algorithms to minimize the inference error ϵ.

For the example shown in Fig. 3, we fix the routing path of each traffic flow onto the one with the shortest distance. Then, if the flow rate of f_4 is 10 bps and other flows have no data exchange, i.e., $\mathbf{y} = [0\ 0\ 0\ 10\ 0\ 0]$, and given the routing matrix $\mathbf{R}$, the attacker can determine that the rate of links l_1 and l_4 are 10 bps, i.e., $\mathbf{x} = [\ 10\ 0\ 0\ 10\ 0\ 0]$ based on an optimization algorithm. We assume the optimization algorithm used by the attacker is unknown to us, as knowing it would enable us to provide a more specific defense strategy.

3 The Design of MaxPro in UAV Networks

In this section, we'll first provide the motivation of our proposed proactively defensive method, MaxPro and the design details of the defense method.

3.1 Motivation

From Equation (1), we can observe that the inference error is influenced by two main factors: the routing matrix $\mathbf{R}$ and the eavesdropped link rate vector $\mathbf{y}$. Since the transmission medium in UAV networks is often open, the malicious attackers can acquire an accurate link rate vector $\mathbf{y}$ through various spectrum sniffing tools [50, 64]. Therefore, our attention is on studying how the routing matrix $\mathbf{R}$ affects the attacker's ability to infer and obtain the flow rate in UAV networks.

While the routing matrix $\mathbf{R}$ may not be directly available to the attacker in some UAV network scenarios, the malicious attacker can re-construct it based on the routing protocol T and network topology $\mathcal{G}$. Let $\hat{\mathbf{R}}$ denote the constructed routing matrix by the attacker. Assuming the optimization algorithm used by the attacker to construct the network topology is precise enough, the inference error ϵ will be primarily determined by the mismatch between the re-constructed routing matrix $\hat{\mathbf{R}}$ and the actual matrix $\mathbf{R}$ used by the UAV network.

In the scenario of static routing networks, for example, the shortest-path protocol, the routing matrix $\mathbf{R}$ is often uniquely determined by the routing protocol and remains fixed for all the following communication traffic. Even if the routing protocol is not directly ready, the attacker can still access it through sensing or sniffing. Therefore, the attacker can re-construct the exact routing matrix with high probability, i.e., $\hat{\mathbf{R}} = \mathbf{R}$, resulting in an precise inference of the flow rate vector $\hat{\mathbf{x}}$.

On the other hand, under a dynamic routing protocol, the routing path of each network flow will change for each connection. Provided the routing protocol and topology $\mathcal{G}$, the routing matrix $\mathbf{R}$ will be very difficult to be determined accurately, making it extremely difficult for the attacker to construct an accurate routing matrix. This leads to more inference errors for the attacker compared to deterministic routing protocols. Besides, in UAV communication networks, usually each UAV is changing its position constantly, which means that the topology of the network is changing constantly. Further the network traffic will be changed dynamically even using the same routing strategy. Previous work [62] analyzed the performance of many existing dynamic routing protocols without proposing new protocols. However, we noticed that most existing dynamic protocols prioritize security objectives over defending against network inference, thereby hindering resilience performance. Therefore, in this work, we design a routing protocol specifically aimed at improving resilience against network inference attacks in UAV networks.

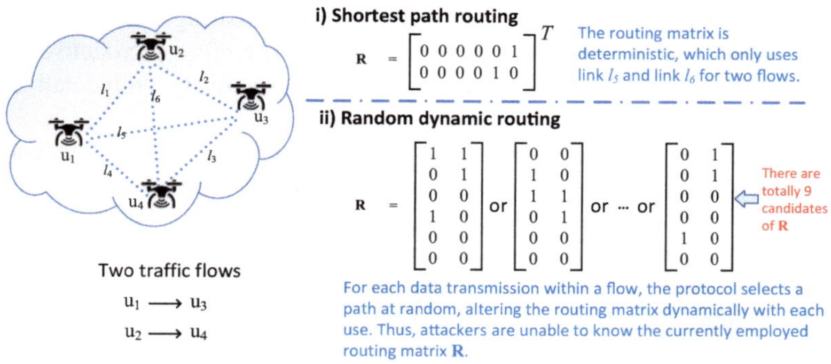

Fig. 4 Example of the difference between static routing, such as the shortest-path strategy, and a random routing in terms of the routing matrix **R**

In Fig. 4, we present an illustrative example showcasing how the routing matrix **R** is constructed in a 4-UAV, 6-link network based on two routing strategies: (i) shortest-path and (ii) random dynamic routing. In this example, there are two traffic flows: flow 1 from UAV u_1 to u_3 and flow 2 from UAV u_2 to u_4, each with three potential paths. Flow 1 may use path $l_1 \to l_2$, $l_4 \to l_2$, or l_5, while flow 2 may use path $l_1 \to l_4$, $l_2 \to l_3$, or l_6.

For the shortest-path protocol, the routing matrix can be uniquely determined. Flow 1 exclusively uses link l_5, and flow 2 utilizes link l_6, resulting in only one candidate **R** for the routing matrix. With the shortest-path protocol, the attacker can effortlessly construct a routing matrix $\hat{\mathbf{R}}$ such that $\hat{\mathbf{R}} = \mathbf{R}$, facilitating an accurate derivation of the flow rate vector.

However, for the random dynamic routing strategy, the routing matrix can be randomly selected from $3 \times 3 = 9$ candidates (3 paths for flow 1 and 3 paths for flow 2) at each transmission round. As the routing matrix selection is random and unpredictable, even with knowledge of the routing protocol, the attacker cannot gain an advantage in selecting the current routing matrix. The probability that $\hat{\mathbf{R}} = \mathbf{R}$ is $1/9$. Therefore, the random selection of the routing matrix introduces additional errors, which helps protect the network against inference attacks.

Figure 4 illustrates the basic concept of how dynamic routing can safeguard networks against inference attacks by introducing additional errors. This chapter aims to propose a dynamic routing protocol T that maximizes the inference error ϵ.

3.2 *The Design of MaxPro*

From a network defender's perspective, designing a routing strategy that minimizes the information malicious attackers can infer from UAV communication networks is crucial. However, achieving this goal is challenging. Attackers can perform network inference through passive observation or overhearing, making it difficult for the network to definitively identify their presence. Therefore, a proactive defense approach is necessary, where the network is always actively online rather than passively waiting for malicious attacks.

To systematically develop a proactive defense strategy against inference attackers, it is essential to analyze the network inference process. Attackers infer network flow information based on collected data flow information. Therefore, from a defender's perspective, it is practical for each UAV to maximize the mismatch probability between the paths it actually uses the path inferred by the attacker. A natural solution is for each flow, the UAV network will randomly choose one path among all the feasible paths. This would make it very difficult for a malicious attacker to infer the right path used in the network for a specific flow. However, it would be costly for the UAVs to store all the available paths for a given network traffic flow. Therefore, we adopt a localized solution to address this problem, in which each UAV will randomly choose an adjacent UAV among all the UAVs that could lead to the destination. Thus, this becomes a local decision for each UAV, rather than an end-to-end style centralized decision. What's more, as every time we're choosing among all the UAVs that could lead to the destination, thus we maximized the choosing space. Therefore the mismatch probability of the attacker's guess compared to the actual network flow will be maximised. We termed this strategy as *Max*imum discrepancy *Pro*bability (MaxPro) routing. Therefore, it becomes significantly more challenging for attackers to obtain network flow information, thus decreasing the success probability of the attack.

Let's use an example to explain the logic. In a static UAV network routing environment, as illustrated in Fig. 5a, given a traffic flow and the routing algorithm, usually the path taken by the network will be fixed. Attackers can easily determine the flow information of the targeted network through network inference. However, if a decentralised dynamic routing strategy is deployed, as shown in Fig. 5b, each UAV will pick one path randomly among all the feasible paths stored in its system. In this example, it is path a, b, c, d, e, f. UAVs employ a dynamic routing strategy to deliver the packets and thus significantly decreasing the success probability of network inference attacks. In our example, the success probability turns to $\frac{1}{6}$. By adopting a proactive strategy where the network randomly chooses available flows to transmit messages, the probability of the mismatch between the actual routing path and the inferred network path by the attacker will be maximized.

There are two key points are worth to be noted here. To defend against network inference attacks, UAV networks should focus proactively on two aspects:

- Increase redundant information: introduce redundant information into the UAV network to confuse attackers, further decrease the attack success probability. Through picking the path randomly, as shown in Fig. 5b, the network can include more redundant information for the attacker to infer, making it much more difficult for attackers to infer network traffic.
- Change routing paths dynamically: mislead attackers by dynamically changing the routing path. Adopt a strategy to dynamically change the route so that even

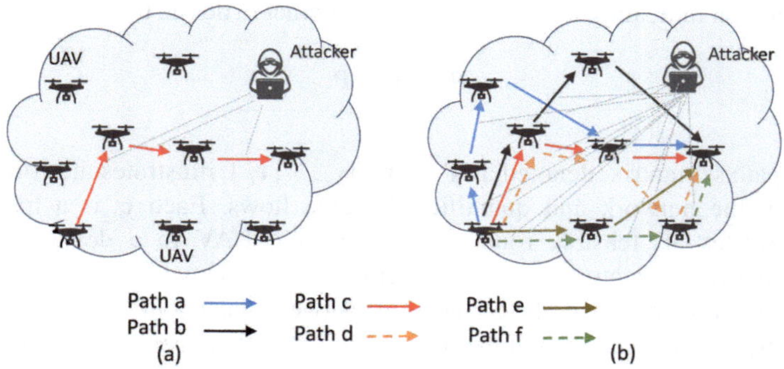

Fig. 5 Illustrative examples of strategies for proactive dynamic routing through maximizing mismatch probability: (**a**) normal network routing; (**b**) dynamic routing through maximizing mismatch probability

if the attacker figures out one flow, they will still not be able to get complete routing information, which makes the attack a probabilistic event.

The above two aspects could be summarized as a strategy maximizing the mismatch probability. Inspired by these ideas, we propose the theoretical model and strategy of proMax in the following subsections in detail.

3.3 Theoretical Modelling of MaxPro

In this part, we introduce a mathematical model for our newly proposed MaxPro routing protocol within the UAV network framework. Following this, we present theoretical analyses.

In Fig. 4, we demonstrate that each traffic flow in a UAV network can include multiple paths, and the routing protocol determines which path is selected. For example, in the figure, there are two traffic flows, and each flow includes three paths, resulting in a total of 9 combinations. From Fig. 4, it is evident that the formation of the routing matrix is mainly influenced by two elements: the overall network structure and the routing protocol itself. The complete network layout delineates the number of interconnected nodes and the potential paths that can be established among them, while the routing protocol determines the specific paths selected for data transmission. Thus, to better comprehend the security advantages provided by the routing strategy, we have the following routing decomposition model for construction the relationship among the routing matrix with the topology and routing strategy.

Model 1 (Routing Matrix Decomposition) In a network, we break down the routing matrix into two components: the topology matrix, denoted as **T**, and the routing protocol matrix, denoted as **P**. This leads to the following formulation of the relationship on indicating how these matrices interact to define the routing structure.

$$\mathbf{R} = \mathbf{T} \times \mathbf{P}. \tag{5}$$

- The path set matrix, denoted as $\mathbf{T} = [\mathbf{t}_1, \mathbf{t}_2, \ldots, \mathbf{t}_F]$, illustrates the connectivity within the network and quantifies the data flows. Each $\mathbf{t}_i$ is a matrix that enumerates all feasible routes from a source UAV to a destination UAV. This matrix's structure is uniquely defined by the network topology; once the topology is established, the connections between each node can be established, thereby determining the number of possible paths between any pair of nodes.
- The protocol matrix $\mathbf{P} = \text{diag}(\mathbf{p}_1, \mathbf{p}_2, \ldots, \mathbf{p}_F)$ consists of the routing protocol's strategy by choosing a specific path for each UAV communication flow in operation. Each $\mathbf{p}_i$ is a column vector, the length of which matches the total number of possible paths for that flow, and it is characterized by a singular entry marked as 1 (indicating the chosen path) while the rest are set to 0. In conventional routing protocols, given the static nature of network topology and prioritization of efficiency, this $\mathbf{p}_i$ remains constant, reflecting a fixed routing decision. Conversely, within the MaxPro framework, $\mathbf{p}_i$ dynamically adjusts with each data transmission, accommodating changes due to the mobility of the UAV network or alterations in the routing strategy.

Based on Model 1, and considering the operational focus of routing protocols on selecting specific paths for data transmission, we can mathematically define the routing protocol as a function

$$M : \mathbf{T} \mapsto \mathbf{P}. \tag{6}$$

This means the routing protocol accepts the routing topology matrix $\mathbf{T}$ as input and generates the protocol matrix $\mathbf{P}$ as its output.

Figure 6 illustrates an example of how the decomposition of the routing matrix and the function of the routing protocol operate. In this scenario, there are two active data flows, hence $\mathbf{T} = [\mathbf{t}_1, \mathbf{t}_2]$. If we assume that the last path is chosen for flow 1 and the first path is chosen for flow 2, then there would be an entry marked as 1 in the first column of $\mathbf{p}_1$ and another entry marked as 1 in the last column of $\mathbf{p}_2$. Following the routing protocol function, we obtain $[\mathbf{p}_1, \mathbf{p}_2] = M([\mathbf{t}_1, \mathbf{t}_2])$, indicating the protocol matrix $\mathbf{P}$ is derived by applying the routing function M to the topology matrix $\mathbf{T}$.

Remark 1 Model 1 indicates the formation of the routing matrix $\mathbf{R}$ as a process influenced by two distinct elements: the topology matrix $\mathbf{T}$ and the protocol matrix $\mathbf{P}$. The function M showcases the methodology for deriving $\mathbf{P}$ from $\mathbf{T}$. In traditional network setups, $\mathbf{T}$ remains constant, and $\mathbf{P}$ is generated through a deterministic mapping from $\mathbf{T}$. Conversely, our approach allows for a dynamic $\mathbf{T}$, accommodating the UAV network's mobility, which in turn leads to variable instances of $\mathbf{P}$. Moreover, the routing protocol function does not establish a direct one-to-one correlation; instead, for a given topology, it may present multiple potential paths and

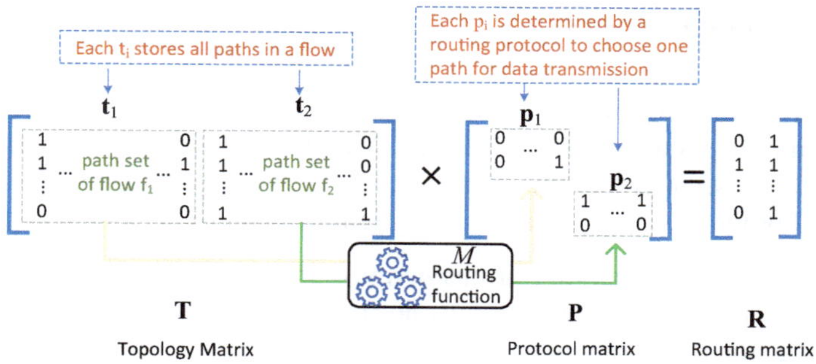

Fig. 6 Example of how the routing matrix **R** can be decomposed into the topology matrix **T** and the routing protocol matrix **P**

select one at random for data transmission. This introduces a probabilistic mapping, resulting in a routing mechanism that inherently supports random path selection.

Leveraging the framework established by Model 1 and the routing protocol function M, we are now ready to formalize our MaxPro strategy. The essence of MaxPro is to optimizing the likelihood that $\hat{\mathbf{R}} \neq \mathbf{R}$, where $\hat{\mathbf{R}}$ represents the routing matrix reconstructed through network observation or eavesdropping, typically mirroring the routing paths utilized in the preceding time slot. Our approach involves devising a routing strategy, encapsulated by the function M, aimed at achieving this goal. Consequently, we define the objective function for this attack strategy as follows.

$$\text{MaxPro Objective:} \quad M_{\text{MaxPro}} = \arg\max \Pr\{\mathbf{T} \times M(\mathbf{T}) \neq \hat{\mathbf{R}}\} \tag{7}$$

According to (3), the inference error is directly related to the difference between $\hat{\mathbf{R}}$ and $\mathbf{R}$, denoted by $|\hat{\mathbf{R}} - \mathbf{R}|$. This magnitude represents the extent of discrepancy between the observed or eavesdropped routing matrix and the actual routing matrix used by the network. The objective of maximizing the probability that $\hat{\mathbf{R}} \neq \mathbf{R}$ is intrinsically linked to increasing this discrepancy. In essence, a larger difference implies a greater deviation from the expected or intercepted routing configuration, thereby enhancing the effectiveness of the MaxPro strategy. This correlation suggests that by aiming to maximize the likelihood of $\hat{\mathbf{R}} \neq \mathbf{R}$, we inherently increase the absolute discrepancy $|\hat{\mathbf{R}} - \mathbf{R}|$ between the actual routing matrix and its observed or eavesdropped counterpart, thus directly contributing to the security of the communication within the UAV network.

3.4 Theoretical Results

In this part, we investigate the theoretical advantages brought forth by the MaxPro strategy and the associated costs it incurs. We also examine the balance between the heightened security benefits provided by the protocol and the consequential expenses. For the theoretical analysis, two significant challenges must be tackled:

- An attacker might employ various optimization algorithms to deduce the flow rate vector, and our approach does not presuppose knowledge of the specific optimization algorithm used;
- The capability of UAVs to traverse any location results in both $\mathbf{T}$ and M being indeterminate, complicating the assessment of the discrepancy probability.

In the subsequent sections, we address these challenges head-on before presenting our theoretical findings.

For challenge 1, we employ the concept of the genie bound as a solution. This approach is derived from robust statistical methods [6] and involves a few key steps. Initially, we refine the flow rate vector $\mathbf{x}_g$ by excluding zero entries with the assistance of a hypothetical genie, thus obtaining a condensed routing matrix $\mathbf{R}_g$ corresponding to $\mathbf{x}_g$. The system is effectively simplified to $\mathbf{y} = \mathbf{R}_g\mathbf{x}_g$. Subsequently, the least squares method is utilized to estimate $\mathbf{x}_g$, resulting in $\hat{\mathbf{x}}_g = (\mathbf{R}_g^T\mathbf{R}_g)^{-1}\mathbf{R}_g^T\mathbf{y}$. The genie bound is then quantified as the mean square error between $\hat{\mathbf{x}}_g$ and $\mathbf{x}_g$, offering a lower error bound that remains valid irrespective of the inference method applied.

The methodology effectively transforms an under-determined system into a determined one by excluding flows that do not exist, ensuring that the inference error ϵ is computed solely based on actual traffic flows. This process renders the inference approach irrelevant in determining the genie bound. Then the inference error can be give by $\epsilon_g = \mathbb{E}\left(\|\hat{\mathbf{x}}_g - \mathbf{x}_g\|_2^2|\right)$.

To address challenge 2, our strategy is to shift this uncertainty to the routing protocol function M. This approach simplifies the problem by reducing it to a single variable that needs to be determined. The rationale behind this method is that while UAVs can move and change positions, the number of flows, i.e., $\mathbf{t}_i$, remains constant because it is determined by the specific instances when and which UAVs need to transmit data, not by their locations. The variability, then, primarily lies in the size of each $\mathbf{t}_i$, which is the number of possible paths that could be taken between any two UAVs.

To manage this, we propose the creation of an expansive topology matrix $\mathbf{T}$ that encompasses not just the paths currently feasible given the existing UAV topology but also potential connections that might be established in the future. This comprehensive $\mathbf{T}$ allows us to focus solely on optimizing the routing protocol function M. This approach effectively reduces the complexity of dealing with the dynamic nature of UAV networks and allows for a more focused analysis on how best to leverage the routing protocol function M for enhanced network performance and security.

Inference Error and Delay With the groundwork laid for addressing the challenges and modeling our approach, we can now proceed to outline our theoretical results for the network $\mathcal{G}$, characterized by N UAVs and F traffic flows. We posit that each flow rate x_i within the refined flow rate vector $\mathbf{x}_g$ is a random variable, governed by a statistical distribution with mean μ and variance σ^2. This assumption allows us to model the behavior of traffic flows within the network in a probabilistic manner, reflecting the inherent variability and unpredictability of data transmission rates in dynamic UAV networks. It should be noted that the reasoning behind the proofs presented in this section draws partially from the methodologies described in [10].

Theorem 1 (Inference Error) *Given the UVA network model by $\mathcal{G}$, the genie bound interference error incurred by the proposed MaxPro strategy can be bounded by*

$$\Theta\left(\frac{F^2\mu^2(N-1)^2}{N^2(\sqrt{(N)}+F)}\right) \le \epsilon_g \le \Theta\left(\frac{2F^2(\mu^2+\sigma^2)}{N/(N-1)}\right). \tag{8}$$

Proof Denoted by $\hat{\mathbf{P}}$ the protocol matrix used by the attacker. Based on Model 1 and genie bound, from the attacker's perspective, (1) can be expressed by $\mathbf{y} = \mathbf{T}\hat{\mathbf{P}}\mathbf{x}_g$. By applying the linear programming, the inferred flow rate vector $\hat{\mathbf{x}}$ is

$$\hat{\mathbf{x}}_g = [(\mathbf{T}\hat{\mathbf{P}})^T\mathbf{T}\hat{\mathbf{P}}]^{-1}(\mathbf{T}\hat{\mathbf{P}})^T\mathbf{y}. \tag{9}$$

Applying the genie bound, we have

$$\begin{aligned} G(\mathbf{x}_g) &= \mathbb{E}\left(\|\hat{\mathbf{x}}_g - \mathbf{x}_g\|_2^2\right) \\ &= \mathbb{E}\left(\|\mathbf{U}\mathbf{D}\mathbf{x}_g\|_2^2\right), \end{aligned} \tag{10}$$

where $\mathbf{U} = [(\mathbf{T}\hat{\mathbf{P}})^T\mathbf{T}\hat{\mathbf{P}}]^{-1}\mathbf{T}\hat{\mathbf{P}}^T$, and $\mathbf{D} = \mathbf{T}\mathbf{P} - \mathbf{T}\hat{\mathbf{P}}$. The $\mathbf{D}$ indicates the difference between the routing matrix observed by the attackers and the real routing matrix. According to [10], we have

$$\lambda_{\min}(\mathbf{U}^T\mathbf{U})\|\mathbf{D}\mathbf{x}_g\|_2^2 \le \|\mathbf{U}\mathbf{D}\mathbf{x}_g\|_2^2 \le \lambda_{\max}(\mathbf{U}^T\mathbf{U})\|\mathbf{D}\mathbf{x}_g\|_2^2, \tag{11}$$

where $\lambda_{\min}(\mathbf{U}^T\mathbf{U})$ and $\lambda_{\max}(\mathbf{U}^T\mathbf{U})$ are minimum and maximum eigenvalues of $\mathbf{U}^T\mathbf{U}$. According to [62], $\lambda_{\min}(\mathbf{U}^T\mathbf{U}) = \lambda_{\max}^{-1}(\mathbf{T}\hat{\mathbf{P}}(\mathbf{T}\hat{\mathbf{P}})^T)$ and $\lambda_{\max}(\mathbf{U}^T\mathbf{U}) = \lambda_{\min}^{-1}(\mathbf{T}\hat{\mathbf{P}}(\mathbf{T}\hat{\mathbf{P}})^T)$. In addition, we have that $\lambda_{\min}(\mathbf{T}\hat{\mathbf{P}}(\mathbf{T}\hat{\mathbf{P}})^T) = \Theta(\tau(N))$ and $\lambda_{\max}(\mathbf{T}\hat{\mathbf{P}}(\mathbf{T}\hat{\mathbf{P}})^T) \le \Theta\left(\tau(N) + F\tau^2(N)/N\right)$. Then the above equation on the inference error can be rewritten as the following asymptotically expression

$$\frac{\mathbb{E}\|\Delta \mathbf{x}_g\|_2^2}{\Theta\left(\tau(N)+\frac{F\tau^2(N)}{N}\right)} \leq \epsilon_g \leq \frac{\mathbb{E}\|\Delta \mathbf{x}_g\|_2^2}{\Theta(\tau(N))}. \tag{12}$$

According to [37], we have $\mathbb{E}\|\Delta \mathbf{x}_g\|_2^2 = \Theta\left(\frac{2F^2(N-1)(\mu^2+\sigma^2)\tau(N)}{N}\right)$. Then replace $\mathbb{E}\|\Delta \mathbf{x}_g\|_2^2$ into the above equation, we can complete the proof. □

Remark 2 Results showing in the Theorem 1 suggest that the inference error correlates with the network's number of data flows, F. Increasing the data flows to intensify and complicate the communication landscape within the network results in a quadratic rise in the inference error. In addition, traffic characterized by higher data rates contributes to a greater inference error compared to traffic at lower rates.

Compared to the shortest-path protocol, the proposed MaxPro protocol incurs a large inference error since packets are not always routed through the shortest route. In evaluating the cost associated with the proposed MaxPro strategy, we employ the metric of delay, denoted by τ, defined as the number of hops required for data to travel from the source node to its destination. This metric serves as a measure of the strategy's efficiency, reflecting the operational cost in terms of time and resource utilization within the UAV network.

Theorem 2 (Delay) *Within the given network framework, the expected asymptotic delay associated with the proposed MaxPro strategy can be expressed as follows.*

$$\tau = \Theta(\sqrt{N}). \tag{13}$$

Proof We first calculate the delay for one path. Define the distance of any flow k as h_k. The distance is defined based on the number of hops in the shortest path. It has been shown that, in a wireless network model by RGG, the number of path for any flow is $\Theta(N)$. Then we have $\tau_k = h_k + \frac{1}{uN}\sum_j c_{kj}$, where u is an arbitrary positive factor. and c_{kj} is the difference between two path j and k.

Then, for the entire network, we have

$$\tau = \frac{1}{F}\sum_{i=1}^{F} h_i + \frac{1}{FuN}\sum_{i=1}^{F}\sum_{j=1}^{uN} c_{ij}. \tag{14}$$

Therefore two terms in (14), according to [10], the first term approaches to $\Theta(\sqrt{N})$ and the second term approaches to $\Theta(1)$. Therefore, we can complete the proof. □

Remark 3 Theorem 2 reveals that the average delay experienced within the network follows an order of magnitude of $\sqrt{N}$, mirroring the performance of conventional shortest-path routing protocols. This observation implies that, in comparison to shortest-path routing, the MaxPro routing protocol does not lead to a notable escalation in delay. However, it substantially bolsters security against inference attacks, thus offering a significant improvement in safeguarding network communications without compromising on efficiency.

4 Experimental Validation and Analysis

In this section, we provided the experimental results and the analysis of the proposed method, MaxPro, in terms of the inference error and the induced delay. We also compared it with the Tor network.

4.1 Experimental Configuration

We first give the experiment settings in this section.

UAV Network Topology and Parameters

In the experiments, we model the ad-hoc based UAV network using a RGG with varying numbers of UAVs, ranging from 100 to 1000. The UAVs are randomly placed in a region of size $[0, \sqrt{N/\lambda}]^2$, where $\lambda = 5$ represents the UAV density, indicating an expected number of 5 neighbors for each UAV. The default communication range of each UAV is set to $r = 1.5$. This setup allows us to create a realistic UAV network scenario with varying densities and numbers of UAVs, reflecting different deployment scenarios and network scales.

The theoretical results from Theorem 8 suggest that the inference error is linked to the number of flows F. To explore this relationship in our experiments, we consider three distinct traffic scenarios:

- Limited Traffic: $F = \lfloor \sqrt{N} \rfloor$. In this scenario, only a few UAVs are engaged in communication.
- Normal Traffic: $F = N$. Here, almost all UAVs are active in at least one traffic flow.
- Intensive Traffic: $F = N^2$. In this scenario, most UAVs are involved in multiple concurrent traffic flows.

For each flow, we model the data rate x_i as a random variable following a Gaussian distribution. Unless otherwise specified, we set the default mean and variance of x_i to $\mu = 0.2$ and $\sigma^2 = 0.2$, respectively.

Metrics

In our experiments, we assume a worst-case scenario where the inference algorithm is unknown. To assess inference errors, we apply the genie bound approach. Additionally, we calculate the delay by averaging the hop count across all network flows.

Our strategy is related to the random routing or anonymous networking. For comparative analysis with results from prior work [62], we also include a popular Tor network as a benchmark to evaluate existing routing protocols.

4.2 Inference Error Evaluation

We begin by evaluating the inference error of our MaxPro protocol in this section.

Inference Error Under Different Values of Parameters

Theoretical analysis in Theorem 8 indicates that the inference error increases quadratically with the number of UAVs. We compare the results for the three different traffic scenarios mentioned above in Fig. 7. It is evident that as we increase the number of UAVs N, the difference in inference errors among the three traffic scenarios becomes more pronounced. This is because under normal traffic conditions, the attacker needs to guess more paths, making it increasingly difficult for the attacker to correctly guess the routing matrix.

The communication range r plays a crucial role in determining the inference error of MaxPro. In our validation, we maintained a normal traffic pattern and varied the communication range r. We experimented with five different values of r, specifically $r = 0.5$, $r = 1.0$, $r = 1.5$, $r = 2.0$, and $r = 2.5$. The experimental results in Fig. 8 clearly indicate that the inference error increases significantly as

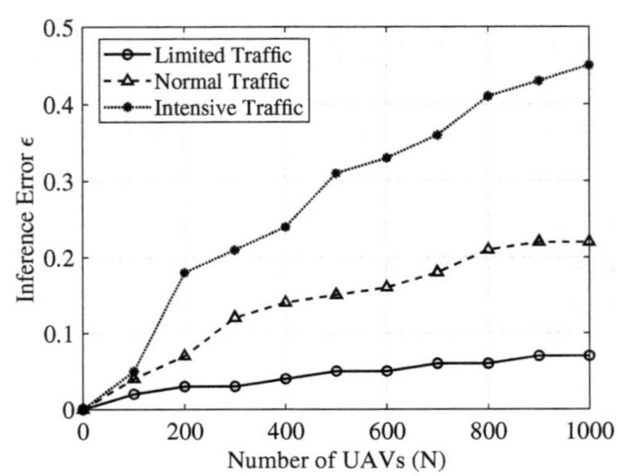

Fig. 7 Comparison of the inference error under 3 different traffic patterns: (a) limited traffic; (b) normal traffic; (c) intensive traffic; with different number of nodes from 20 to 1000

Fig. 8 Inference error comparison when changing the communication range r

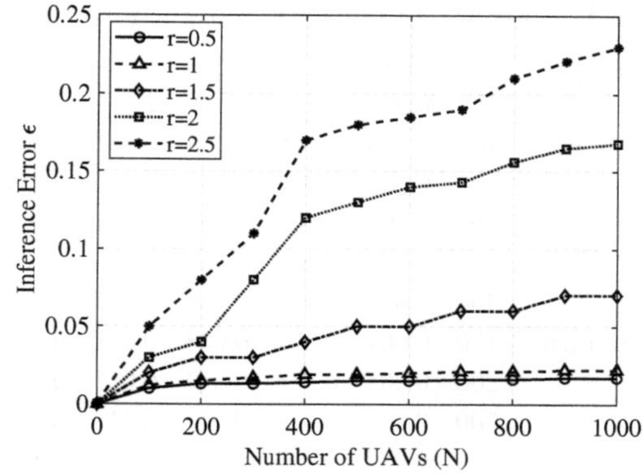

Fig. 9 Comparison of the inference error when vary the mean value of traffic from 0.1 to 0.4

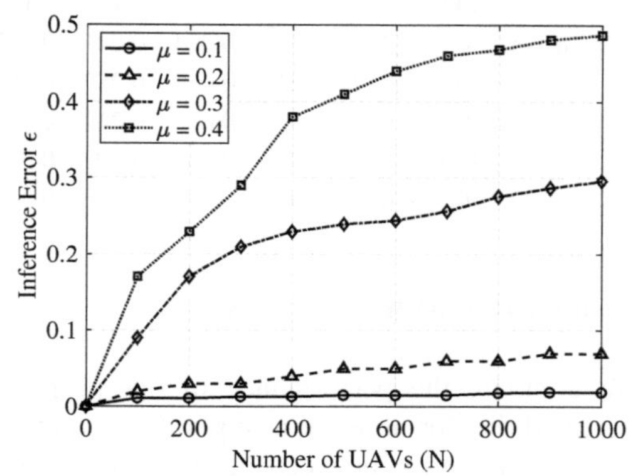

the value of r grows. For example, the inference error goes up from 0.051 to 0.235 when we increase the number of nodes from 100 to 1000. In addition, we observed that when the communication range of each UAV is less than 1.5, there is a slow increase in inference error. This phenomenon occurs because, under such conditions, the communication range is too narrow, leading to a scenario where the network might not be entirely connected. As a result, the number of available paths for each data flow is constrained. Consequently, despite the ability to select a path from the entire available set of paths, the limited size of this path set restricts the potential to increase inference errors.

The inference error is also influenced by the mean value μ of the flow rate. Figure 9 illustrates the comparative results of the inference error under different values of μ. As the value of μ increases from 0.1 to 0.4, the inference error increases significantly. This observation further supports our Theorem 1, stating that the inference error increases quadratically with the mean traffic values. Additionally, when the mean traffic rate $\mu = 0.4$, the inference error can rise to 0.489.

Table 1 Comparison of inference error between MaxPro and Tor

Traffic	r	MaxPro					Tor				
	N	0.5	1	1.5	2	2.5	0.5	1	1.5	2	2.5
Limited	100	0.006	0.008	0.009	0.012	0.013	0.00	0.004	0.009	0.011	0.012
	200	0.007	0.008	0.019	0.031	0.059	0.007	0.009	0.011	0.018	0.052
	300	0.007	0.007	0.028	0.087	0.123	0.006	0.009	0.026	0.058	0.092
	400	0.010	0.008	0.041	0.118	0.158	0.011	0.013	0.033	0.086	0.124
	500	0.011	0.018	0.048	0.127	0.174	0.018	0.027	0.089	0.134	0.145
Normal	100	0.004	0.021	0.025	0.032	0.053	0.005	0.007	0.008	0.021	0.029
	200	0.005	0.018	0.032	0.043	0.078	0.008	0.009	0.022	0.034	0.047
	300	0.005	0.016	0.047	0.117	0.131	0.008	0.022	0.064	0.102	0.114
	400	0.007	0.018	0.057	0.127	0.176	0.009	0.024	0.081	0.112	0.137
	500	0.019	0.022	0.058	0.154	0.187	0.011	0.034	0.084	0.134	0.151
Intensive	100	0.006	0.017	0.024	0.041	0.063	0.005	0.005	0.006	0.017	0.019
	200	0.019	0.021	0.052	0.059	0.081	0.006	0.009	0.018	0.042	0.057
	300	0.017	0.017	0.062	0.212	0.278	0.008	0.012	0.029	0.123	0.154
	400	0.021	0.032	0.164	0.308	0.314	0.011	0.024	0.030	0.207	0.234
	500	0.028	0.032	0.281	0.313	0.344	0.013	0.024	0.043	0.219	0.284

Comparison with Tor Network

To compare the performance of our proposed method with existing work, we selected the Tor network as a point of comparison. Table 1 presents the difference in inference error between our proposed MaxPro and Tor. The results show that the inference error of MaxPro is slightly higher than that of the Tor network when varying the values of r and N. This difference can be attributed to Tor's requirement for paths to pass through selected relays, which reduces the search space for selecting a path. Consequently, the size of the path set for arbitrary flows in Tor is a subset of that in MaxPro, leading to a lower inference error in Tor compared to MaxPro.

4.3 Delay Evaluation

Network Delay When Varying the Values of Parameters

According to Theorem 2, the delay is related to the number of UAVs N in the network. To verify this, we conducted experiments and observed the relationship between network delay and the number of UAVs N. Figure 10 illustrates the evaluation results, indicating that the delay increases with the number of UAVs N. Interestingly, there is no significant difference in delay between the two traffic scenarios, suggesting that the number of flows has little impact on the delay.

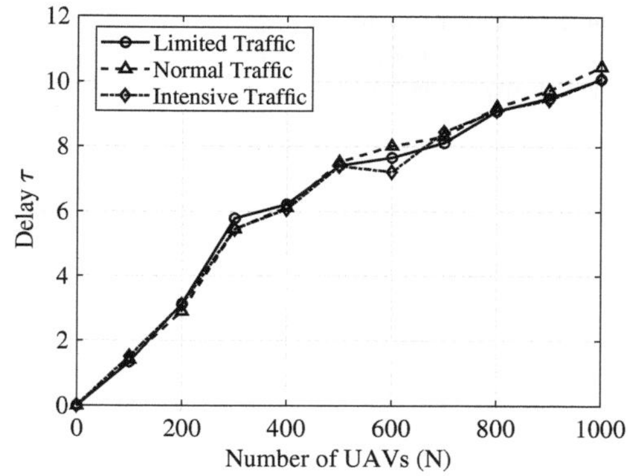

Fig. 10 Comparison of network delay when varying the number of UAVs under three different traffic scenarios: (a) limited traffic; (b) normal traffic; (c) intensive traffic

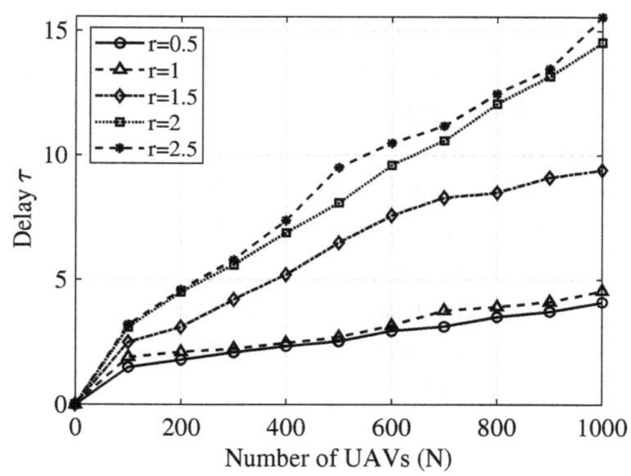

Fig. 11 Comparison of network belay when varying the communication range r

Secondly, we compared the network delay of MaxPro under different values of the communication range r and the number of UAVs. The experimental results are shown in Fig. 11. It can be observed that when the number of nodes is fixed, the larger the range r, the longer the network delay. Likewise, with a communication range below 1.5, the network is prone to not fully connected, resulting in shorter path distances. Consequently, even with an increase in the number of UAVs, the delay experiences a minimal rise. In contrast, when the communication range is extended to 2 or 2.5, the delay demonstrates an almost linear increase in response to the number of UAVs.

Comparison with Tor Network

We also conducted a comparative experiment of MaxPro and Tor in terms of network delay under different numbers of UAVs. Figure 12 shows the difference between MaxPro and Tor in terms of network delay. We can observe from the results that MaxPro has a slightly longer delay than the Tor network if the numbers of UAVs is small. For instance, when there are 100 UAVs, the delay encountered by MaxPro

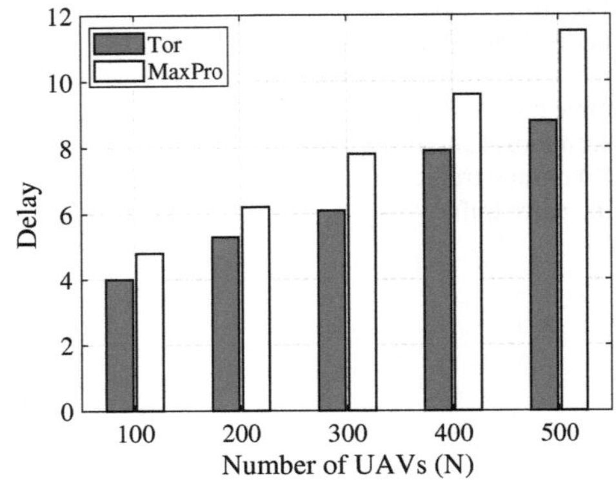

Fig. 12 Comparison of network delay between MaxPro and Tor network

and Tor is quite comparable, with Tor experiencing a delay of 4.01 and MaxPro a slightly higher delay of 4.81. As the number of UAVs escalates, the disparity in delay between the two also widens. This is because with a limited number of UAVs, the available paths for a data flow are also restricted. Consequently, MaxPro likely to select paths with shorter delays. Conversely, the minimum delay of Tor is 3, indicating that it consistently involves three relay points. Nevertheless, as the UAV population increases, MaxPro's delay accelerates at a quicker pace compared to Tor. This acceleration is due to MaxPro having access to a broader array of path options than Tor as the number of UAVs expands.

5 Related Work

Here in this section we give our related work of UAV network security and network inference attacks.

5.1 UAV Communication Network Security

UAVs have become integral to numerous civilian and military applications, ranging from surveillance and reconnaissance to package delivery and disaster management [22, 45, 49]. However, the widespread deployment of UAVs has brought to the forefront the critical issue of securing their communication networks. Unlike traditional wireless networks, UAV communication networks are characterized by their dynamic topology, limited energy resources, and vulnerability to various security threats. Addressing these challenges is paramount to ensuring the safe and reliable operation of UAVs in diverse environments [21, 48].

One of the primary security concerns in UAV communication networks is unauthorized access, where malicious entities attempt to gain control over the UAVs or eavesdrop on their communication channels [18]. Such unauthorized access can lead to a range of detrimental consequences, including data breaches, privacy violations, and even the hijacking of UAVs for malicious purposes. Additionally, UAVs are susceptible to jamming attacks, where adversaries disrupt communication links by transmitting interference signals [48]. These attacks can severely impact the ability of UAVs to perform critical missions, such as surveillance or search and rescue operations.

Another significant security challenge in UAV communication networks is data integrity and confidentiality [17]. UAVs often collect and transmit sensitive information, such as images, videos, and sensor data, which must be protected from unauthorized tampering or interception. Ensuring the integrity and confidentiality of this data is essential to maintaining the trustworthiness of UAV operations and safeguarding the privacy of individuals and organizations involved.

Furthermore, UAV communication networks are vulnerable to network-based attacks, such as denial-of-service (DoS) attacks, which aim to disrupt communication by overwhelming the network with excessive traffic, and network inference attacks, which aim to compromise the network by first collecting network information [45]. These attacks can render UAVs inoperable and compromise their ability to fulfill their intended functions. Additionally, UAVs are susceptible to physical attacks, where adversaries attempt to physically damage or destroy the UAVs or their communication equipment, further highlighting the need for robust security measures.

In light of these challenges, there is a critical need for comprehensive security solutions tailored to the unique characteristics of UAV communication networks [18, 33, 53]. These solutions should encompass a combination of encryption, authentication, intrusion detection, and resilience mechanisms to protect UAVs and their communication channels from a wide range of security threats. By addressing these challenges, we can ensure the secure and reliable operation of UAVs in various applications, paving the way for their continued integration into our daily lives.

In this work, we introduce a proactive defense strategy designed to counter network inference attacks, called MaxPro. This approach involves the use of a dynamic routing protocol for UAV networks, which continuously alters the routing pattern. The goal is to maximize the probability that the routing pattern observed by attackers will not match the actual routing pattern used within the network, thereby increasing the inference error.

5.2 Network Tomography and Inference

Network tomography and inference have become essential techniques in network monitoring and analysis [28, 52]. Network inference involves estimating flow information by eavesdropping on wireless link activities, leveraging the broadcast nature of the wireless medium [24, 37, 38, 64]. Many existing works on network inference and tomography focus on optimizing inference accuracy [2, 14, 16, 34, 40, 43, 56].

However, the applicability of network inference is often constrained by strong assumptions, such as known network topology. To address this limitation, machine learning techniques can be employed to predict unknown parameters [26, 27, 41, 46]. For instance, in [41], deep neural networks are used to predict unmeasured network attributes and reconstruct network topology. Similarly, in [46], machine learning is applied to facilitate network inference with limited topology information.

From a security perspective, network inference enables attackers to obtain internal network information without direct access. For instance, in [61, 63], a data poisoning attack is proposed to mislead network operators. Additionally, in [11, 12], the limitations of a stealthy attacker in degrading end-to-end communication performance without being detected are analyzed.

Regarding defense, proactive strategies can intentionally reduce inference performance [24, 37, 38]. For example, in [38], the relationship between inference error and artificial noise added to measurements is analyzed. In [24], machine learning techniques are used to obfuscate the network topology from attackers. In contrast, our work in [62] focuses on the resilience of dynamic routing protocols against inference attacks, as most existing protocols prioritize security over defending against network inferences. This chapter investigates the causes of inference errors and designs a dynamic routing protocol to enhance network resilience against inference attacks in wireless networks.

The concept of network inference and topology enables the reconstruction of network properties, such as link delays, packet loss rates, and traffic volumes, which are typically hidden from direct observation. Various approaches, including active probing and passive monitoring, have been developed to gather the necessary measurement data. Concurrently, network inference techniques leverage statistical models and machine learning algorithms to deduce network states and attributes based on the collected data. These methods play a crucial role in diagnosing network issues, optimizing resource allocation, and enhancing overall network performance. As the complexity of modern networks continues to grow, advancements in network tomography and inference remain pivotal for maintaining robust and efficient communication infrastructures.

5.3 Dynamic Routing

Dynamic and random routing strategies are becoming increasingly popular in wireless networks due to their adaptability to the constantly changing and unpredictable nature of wireless environments [9, 15]. Dynamic routing adjusts data transmission paths in real-time based on factors such as signal strength [44, 55, 65], traffic load [47], channel interference [4, 8], and changes in network topology [65]. For instance, in [55], relay selection is based on instantaneous Received Signal Strength Indicator (RSSI) and Link Quality Indicator (LQI) values to adapt to the wireless environment.

The introduction of dynamic routing can bolster security by adding variability to network traffic patterns, making it more difficult for attackers to deduce network information. Prior studies [38, 62] have demonstrated that random routing can introduce inaccuracies in the inference process. However, the extent to which existing dynamic routing protocols effectively introduce enough randomness to thwart network inference attacks remains uncertain. In this chapter, we highlight the relationship between inference error and the probability of discrepancy between the flow template observed by attackers and the actual template used in the network. Motivated by this observation, we propose MaxPro, a strategy that aims to maximize this discrepancy probability and thereby increase the inference error.

This adaptability enhances network efficiency and reliability, ensuring that data is routed through the most optimal paths. On the other hand, random routing strategies introduce an element of stochasticity by allowing packets to be forwarded along random paths. While seemingly counterintuitive, this randomness can help balance network load and mitigate congestion by distributing traffic across different routes. Furthermore, such approaches are inherently resilient to UAV failures and can lead to better load balancing in heterogeneous wireless networks. The interplay between dynamic and random routing mechanisms presents a fertile ground for research aimed at achieving robust, efficient, and scalable wireless communication, particularly in scenarios where traditional static routing falls short due to the dynamic and uncertain nature of wireless channels.

6 Conclusion

UAV communication networks plays an important role in many real world tasks where it is challenging for human beings. However, the security of UAV networks has not been studied intensively. Network inference attacks pose a substantial threat to network security, enabling attackers to gain insight into sensitive flow information without direct access. This information can be leveraged to launch potent attacks against UAV networks. Dynamic routing in UAV communication networks can enhance security and privacy by introducing variability in traffic patterns, thus increasing the inference error. In this chapter, we present MaxPro, a proactive defense strategy against inference attacks in UAV networks. MaxPro utilizes a dynamic routing protocol that continuously changes the routing pattern, aiming to increase the likelihood that attackers' observed routing patterns do not align with the actual network routing. This proactive approach enhances the inference error, thereby improving network security. Our research includes comprehensive theoretical and empirical analyses, demonstrating that MaxPro achieves an inference error proportional to the number of UAVs in the network.

References

1. (2013) Wireless LAN medium access control (MAC) and physical layer (PHY) specifications. IEEE Std 80211
2. Bartolini N, He T, Arrigoni V, Massini A, Trombetti F, Khamfroush H (2020) On fundamental bounds on failure identifiability by boolean network tomography. IEEE/ACM Transactions on Networking 28(2):588–601
3. Bekmezci I, Sahingoz OK, Temel Ş (2013) Flying ad-hoc networks (fanets): A survey. Ad Hoc Networks 11(3):1254–1270
4. Biswas S, Morris R (2004) Opportunistic routing in multi-hop wireless networks. ACM SIGCOMM Computer Communication Review 34(1):69–74
5. Bor-Yaliniz I, Yanikomeroglu H (2016) The new frontier in ran heterogeneity: Multi-tier drone-cells. IEEE Communications Magazine 54(11):48–55
6. Candès EJ, Romberg J, Tao T (2006) Robust uncertainty principles: Exact signal reconstruction from highly incomplete frequency information. IEEE Trans Inf Theory 52
7. Castro R, Coates M, Liang G, Nowak R, Yu B (2004) Network tomography: Recent developments. Statistical Science
8. Chachulski S, Jennings M, Katti S, Katabi D (2007) Trading structure for randomness in wireless opportunistic routing. ACM SIGCOMM Computer Communication Review 37(4):169–180
9. Chakchouk N (2015) A survey on opportunistic routing in wireless communication networks. IEEE Communications Surveys & Tutorials 17(4):2214–2241
10. Chen J, Luo ZJ, Liu Y, Zhao S (2023) Mmp: A dynamic routing protocol design to proactively defend against wireless network inference attacks. In: Proceedings of the 10th ACM Workshop on Moving Target Defense, pp 1–11
11. Chiu CC, He T (2021) Stealthy dgos attack against network tomography: The role of active measurements. IEEE Transactions on Network Science and Engineering 8(2):1745–1758
12. Chiu CC, He T (2021) Stealthy dgos attack: Degrading of service under the watch of network tomography. IEEE/ACM Transactions on Networking 29(3):1294–1307
13. Dall J, Christensen M (2002) Random geometric graphs. Physical review E 66(1):016121
14. Fan X, Li X (2017) Network tomography via sparse bayesian learning. IEEE Communications Letters 21(4):781–784
15. Fan X, Cai W, Lin J (2017) A survey of routing protocols for highly dynamic mobile ad hoc networks. In: 2017 IEEE 17th International Conference on Communication Technology (ICCT), IEEE, pp 1412–1417
16. Firooz MH, Roy S (2014) Link delay estimation via expander graphs. IEEE Trans Commun 62:170–180
17. Fotohi R, Nazemi E, Aliee FS (2020) An agent-based self-protective method to secure communication between uavs in unmanned aerial vehicle networks. Vehicular Communications 26:100267
18. Fotouhi A, Qiang H, Ding M, Hassan M, Giordano LG, Garcia-Rodriguez A, Yuan J (2019) Survey on uav cellular communications: Practical aspects, standardization advancements, regulation, and security challenges. IEEE Communications surveys & tutorials 21(4):3417–3442
19. Gupta L, Jain R, Vaszkun G (2015) Survey of important issues in uav communication networks. IEEE communications surveys & tutorials 18(2):1123–1152
20. Hanawal MK, Nguyen DN, Krunz M (2016) Jamming attack on in-band full-duplex communications: Detection and countermeasures. In: IEEE INFOCOM
21. Haque MS, Chowdhury MU (2018) A new cyber security framework towards secure data communication for unmanned aerial vehicle (uav). In: Security and Privacy in Communication Networks: SecureComm 2017 International Workshops, ATCS and SePrIoT, Niagara Falls, ON, Canada, October 22–25, 2017, Proceedings 13, Springer, pp 113–122

22. He D, Chan S, Guizani M (2016) Communication security of unmanned aerial vehicles. IEEE Wireless Communications 24(4):134–139
23. He T (2018) Distributed link anomaly detection via partial network tomography
24. Hou T, Qu Z, Wang T, Lu Z, Liu Y (2020) Proto: Proactive topology obfuscation against adversarial network topology inference. In: IEEE INFOCOM 2020-IEEE Conference on Computer Communications, IEEE, pp 1598–1607
25. Huang Y, Feamster N, Teixeira R (2008) Practical issues with using network tomography for fault diagnosis. ACM SIGCOMM Computer Communication Review 38(5):53–58
26. Ibraheem A, Sheng Z, Parisis G, Tian D (2021) Neural network based partial tomography for in-vehicle network monitoring. In: 2021 IEEE International Conference on Communications Workshops (ICC Workshops), IEEE, pp 1–6
27. Ibraheem A, Sheng Z, Parisis G, Zhou J, Tian D (2022) Internal network monitoring with dnn and network tomography for in-vehicle networks. In: 2022 IEEE International Conference on Unmanned Systems (ICUS), IEEE, pp 928–933
28. Kakkavas G, Gkatzioura D, Karyotis V, Papavassiliou S (2020) A review of advanced algebraic approaches enabling network tomography for future network infrastructures. Future Internet 12(2):20
29. Kasai H, Kellerer W, Kleinsteuber M (2016) Network volume anomaly detection and identification in large-scale networks based on online time-structured traffic tensor tracking. IEEE Trans Netw Service Manag 13
30. Lakew DS, Sa'ad U, Dao NN, Na W, Cho S (2020) Routing in flying ad hoc networks: A comprehensive survey. IEEE Communications Surveys & Tutorials 22(2):1071–1120
31. Li B, Fei Z, Zhang Y, Guizani M (2019) Secure uav communication networks over 5g. IEEE Wireless Communications 26(5):114–120
32. Li F, Ren P, Yang G, Sun Y, Wang Y, Wang Y, Li S, Zhou H (2021) An efficient anonymous communication scheme to protect the privacy of the source node location in the internet of things. Security and Communication Networks 2021:1–16
33. Li T, Zhang J, Obaidat MS, Lin C, Lin Y, Shen Y, Ma J (2021) Energy-efficient and secure communication toward uav networks. IEEE Internet of Things Journal 9(12):10061–10076
34. Li Y, Liang Y (2018) Compressed sensing in multi-hop large-scale wireless sensor networks based on routing topology tomography. IEEE Access 6:27637–27650
35. Li Y, Cai W, Tian G, Wang W (2007) Loss tomography in wireless sensor network using gibbs sampling. In: Wireless Sensor Networks: 4th European Conference, EWSN 2007, Delft, The Netherlands, January 29–31, 2007. Proceedings 4, Springer, pp 150–162
36. Liu Y, Zhang R, Shi J, Zhang Y (2010) Traffic inference in anonymous manets. In: IEEE SECON
37. Lu Z, Wang C (2015) Network anti-inference: A fundamental perspective on proactive strategies to counter flow inference. In: IEEE INFOCOM
38. Lu Z, Wang C (2016) Enabling network anti-inference via proactive strategies: A fundamental perspective. IEEE/ACM Transactions on Networking 25(1):43–55
39. Ma L, He T, Leung KK, Swami A, Towsley D (2013) Identifiability of link metrics based on end-to-end path measurements. In: ACM IMC
40. Ma L, He T, Leung KK, Towsley D, Swami A (2013) Efficient identification of additive link metrics via network tomography. In: 2013 IEEE 33rd International Conference on Distributed Computing Systems, IEEE, pp 581–590
41. Ma L, Zhang Z, Srivatsa M (2020) Neural network tomography. arXiv preprint arXiv:200102942
42. Mardani M, Giannakis GB (2016) Estimating traffic and anomaly maps via network tomography. IEEE/ACM Trans Netw 24
43. Matsuda T, Nagahara M, Hayashi K (2011) Link quality classifier with compressed sensing based on\ell_1-\ell_2 optimization. IEEE Communications Letters 15(10):1117–1119
44. Mei-Hsuan L, Peter S, Tsuhan C (2009) Design, implementation and evaluation of an efficient opportunistic retransmission protocol. Proc Of IEEE MobiCom, Beijing, China

45. Pandey GK, Gurjar DS, Nguyen HH, Yadav S (2022) Security threats and mitigation techniques in uav communications: A comprehensive survey. IEEE Access 10:112858–112897
46. Sartzetakis I, Varvarigos E (2022) Machine learning network tomography with partial topology knowledge and dynamic routing. In: GLOBECOM 2022–2022 IEEE Global Communications Conference, IEEE, pp 4922–4927
47. Shah RC, Wietholter S, Wolisz A (2005) Modeling and analysis of opportunistic routing in low traffic scenarios. In: Third International Symposium on Modeling and Optimization in Mobile, Ad Hoc, and Wireless Networks (WiOpt'05), IEEE, pp 294–304
48. Sharma A, Vanjani P, Paliwal N, Basnayaka CMW, Jayakody DNK, Wang HC, Muthuchidambaranathan P (2020) Communication and networking technologies for uavs: A survey. Journal of Network and Computer Applications 168:102739
49. Sharma J, Mehra PS (2023) Secure communication in iot-based uav networks: A systematic survey. Internet of Things p 100883
50. Singh R, Kumar S (2018) A comparative study of various wireless network monitoring tools. In: 2018 First International Conference on Secure Cyber Computing and Communication (ICSCCC), IEEE, pp 379–384
51. Syverson P, Dingledine R, Mathewson N (2004) Tor: The secondgeneration onion router. In: USENIX Security
52. Vardi Y (1996) Network tomography: Estimating source-destination traffic intensities from link data. Journal of the American statistical association 91(433):365–377
53. Wang J, Wang X, Gao R, Lei C, Feng W, Ge N, Jin S, Quek TQ (2021) Physical layer security for uav communications in 5g and beyond networks. arXiv preprint arXiv:210511332
54. Wang W, Wang H, Wang B, Wang Y, Wang J (2013) Energy-aware and self-adaptive anomaly detection scheme based on network tomography in mobile ad hoc networks. Information Sciences 220:580–602
55. Wang Z, Chen Y, Li C (2012) Corman: A novel cooperative opportunistic routing scheme in mobile ad hoc networks. IEEE journal on selected areas in communications 30(2):289–296
56. Yu CK, Chen KC, Cheng SM (2010) Cognitive radio network tomography. IEEE Trans Veh Technol 59
57. Zhang Q, Jiang M, Feng Z, Li W, Zhang W, Pan M (2019) Iot enabled uav: Network architecture and routing algorithm. IEEE Internet of Things Journal 6(2):3727–3742
58. Zhang Z, Mukherjee A (2016) Friendly channel-oblivious jamming with error amplification for wireless networks. In: IEEE INFOCOM
59. Zhang Z, Mara O, Argyraki K (2014) Network neutrality inference. In: ACM SIGCOMM
60. Zhao J, Govindan R, Estrin D (2002) Sensor network tomography: Monitoring wireless sensor networks. ACM SIGCOMM Computer Communication Review 32(1):64–64
61. Zhao S, Lu Z, Wang C (2017) When seeing isn't believing: On feasibility and detectability of scapegoating in network tomography. In: IEEE ICDCS
62. Zhao S, Lu Z, Wang C (2020) How can randomized routing protocols hide flow information in wireless networks? IEEE Transactions on Wireless Communications 19(11):7224–7236
63. Zhao S, Lu Z, Wang C (Nov. 2021) Measurement integrity attacks against network tomography: Feasibility and defense. IEEE Transactions on Dependable and Secure Computing 18:2617–2630
64. Zhao Z, Huangfu W, Sun L (2012) Nssn: A network monitoring and packet sniffing tool for wireless sensor networks. In: 2012 8th International Wireless Communications and Mobile Computing Conference (IWCMC), IEEE, pp 537–542
65. Zhao Z, Rosário D, Braun T, Cerqueira E, Xu H, Huang L (2013) Topology and link quality-aware geographical opportunistic routing in wireless ad-hoc networks. In: 2013 9th international wireless communications and mobile computing conference (IWCMC), IEEE, pp 1522–1527
66. Zhuo L, Li Y, Deng J, Wang H (2020) An anonymous communication method for wireless sensor networks based on bilinear pairings. In: 2020 IEEE 2nd International Conference on Civil Aviation Safety and Information Technology (ICCASIT, IEEE, pp 517–525

Proactive Deception for Enterprise Networks with Dynamic Views and Conversation-Based Synthetic Traffic, Enabled by P4 Switches

Alex Poylisher, Latha Kant, and Ritu Chadha

1 Introduction

In this chapter, we describe a recently developed approach to ambiguity-increasing (A-type) cyber deception against *passive* reconnaissance by advanced persistent threat (APT) adversaries via network traffic observation. The approach targets organizations that own their switching fabric and gives the defender control over the statistics of attacker-observable traffic and the volume of generated deceptive traffic, with quantifiable fidelity. The approach is made practical by next-generation multi-layer switch architectures programmable with P4 [1]. As an expected side effect, it also enables a rich environment to operate future misleading (M-type) deception mechanisms.

An APT is commonly defined as "a stealthy cyber-attack in which a person or group gains unauthorized access to a network and remains undetected for an extended period" [2]. At the time of writing, every major business sector has recorded instances of attacks by APTs with specific goals seeking to steal, spy, and disrupt, or non-specific goals of maintaining presence in support of future specific goals.

Figure 1 shows a notional APT cyber kill chain for the specific goal of information stealing, but all such kill chains, regardless of the ultimate goal, start with *reconnaissance*. APT actors can spend months on *initial reconnaissance* efforts against high-value targets, and conduct *continuous reconnaissance* after penetration to both maintain and *extend* their foothold (via lateral movement). Hence, disrupting/delaying/degrading the quality of the attacker reconnaissance is of general interest to all defenders. Cyber deception has been proposed and, to

A. Poylisher (✉) · L. Kant · R. Chadha
Peraton Labs, Basking Ridge, NJ, USA
e-mail: apoylisher@peratonlabs.com; lkant@peratonlabs.com; rchadha@peratonlabs.com

Q. Zhu et al. (eds.), *Foundations of Cyber Deception*, Advances in Information Security 90, https://doi.org/10.1007/978-3-031-93867-2_11

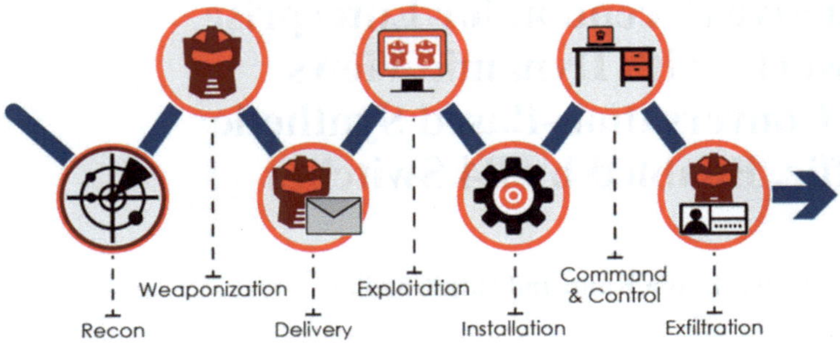

Fig. 1 A notional APT cyber kill chain

an extent, used as an approach to support these defensive objectives. Effective deception imposes multiple costs on the attacker: the cost of detecting the lies, the cost of incorrect action, or the cost of exposed presence/intent [3]. Against reconnaissance, the defender enjoys an inherent asymmetric advantage of having the potential to observe and know the entire defended network.

A seminal study of military deception [4] identified two major branches of deception to achieve these aims: "Ambiguity increasing" deception, or "A-type," and "Misleading" deception, or "M-Type," deception. A-type deception signals the presence of a large number of attractive targets and thus *statistically* raises the cost of reconnaissance and increases the attacker's uncertainty in the accuracy of information obtained by reconnaissance.

In contrast, M-type deception attempts to lead the attacker to specific conclusions, both within and *outside* the cyber domain, by planting *specific* misinformation for the attacker to discover. "Of the two types, A-type deception seems to be the "low hanging fruit." It has a broad deception target because it aims to frustrate the adversarial operators, not planners. It doesn't require the same level of coordination for the deception story as the M-type since the story only aims to complicate the environment. Moreover, the A-Type, once more developed, would offer the defender the greatest agility in response" [5].

Use of deception to deter/degrade attacker reconnaissance is a powerful defense mechanism. Ranging from honeypot (end host)-based deception to creating entire honeynets, several deception-based defenses have been proposed [3, 6–8]. However, developing believable deception that is cost-effective at scale continues to be a significant challenge.

To date, proactive A-type deception, including our prior work, has mostly been targeted against *active* reconnaissance wherein the attacker sends packets to discover potential targets and estimate their value, e.g. [9, 10]. However, well-resourced and patient APT actors with multiple points of presence both within and outside of the target network would be able to largely avoid active reconnaissance and obtain useful recon data from passive observation. For instance, honeypot-based deception is vulnerable to passive reconnaissance *unless* the honeypots appear to be genuinely interacting with other hosts seen in the network. While there are efforts to create realistic honeynets via "digital twinning" of production networks [6], this is expensive at scale.

Other prior work on A-type network deception [11–14] has looked at obfuscating and rapidly changing network addresses in real packets to thwart the attacker's ability to identify candidate targets via their network addresses. However, this type of deception is vulnerable to statistical analysis of passively collected traffic, whereby the attacker can identify endpoints with high confidence regardless of network addresses, by only observing endpoint *traffic behavior*.

In particular, the attacker can periodically construct a conversation graph (CG) from the headers of the packets collected over an epoch. A CG is a weighted directed graph where nodes represent apparent end hosts (identified by a network addresses from packet headers), and there is an edge between two nodes if any traffic has been observed between the two. Edges are assigned weights that reflect distributions of flow characteristics (e.g., packet size, inter-arrival time). Armed with a sequence of successive CGs, the attacker can compute similarity of each node's properties (degree, flow density) over the sequence, cluster highly similar nodes, label each cluster with a new identifier, and use that identifier instead of the network address.

To counter the afore-mentioned vulnerability, complementary prior work [9, 15] has looked into injecting deceptive traffic without emulating endpoints at all. The approach in [9] is to replay packets captured in the past, with modified addresses, ports and timestamps in the headers and payloads. This guarantees high fidelity of deception, but does not allow the defender to control either the fundamental statistics of the observed traffic or scale its volume to match available resources. The approach in [15] relies on intimate knowledge of a restricted set of protocols in a constrained environment. Generation of believable fake traffic in less constrained environments remains a hard problem.

We focus on proactive deception against passive reconnaissance in wired enterprise networks, and assume a switching fabric built partially or wholly on top of P4-programmable multi-layer switches and defender's complete control over the switching fabric. P4 compiler backends [16] exist for expensive high-end switches, lower performance and lower cost NICs and FPGAs, and efficient software pipelines (e.g., eBPF, uBPF, and tc), which enables a variety of possible deployments with minimal implementation changes.

Without loss of generality, we restrict the study to: (a) the traffic that flows entirely within the defended network (intranet), (b) IPv6 network layer only, and (c) Linux-based clients and servers. With these assumptions, we design a complete deception system architecture, prototype and evaluate its key components, discuss the limitations of the current prototype, and indicate directions for future work.

The rest of the chapter is structured as follows. In Sect. 2, we describe the threat, network and defender models. In Sect. 3, we discuss the high-level approach and system architecture. Section 4 discusses deceptive view construction approach, design alternatives and algorithms. Section 5 describes the implementation of dynamic view enforcement and change at run-time. Section 6 presents experimental evaluation design and results. We conclude with discussion of possible future work in Sect. 7.

2 Threat, Network and Defender Models

In this section, we briefly describe the network, threat and defender models under consideration.

Network Model The networks under consideration leverage the programmability and speed of modern P4-programmable multi-layer switching fabrics (PMLSFs). The networks appear to the users as multi-hop, routed L3 (Layer 3) networks. The default operating mode of the PMLSF is to restrict the visibility of unicast traffic to the two communicating parties, and support link-layer broadcast only for a small set of known services. The PMLSF control plane is completely isolated from the data plane of the defended network. We assume a mixture of physical and virtual machine/container-based hosts in the defended network.

Threat Model We assume that attackers may have taken over one or more nodes on the defended network, but not the PMLSF. Nodes on the defended network are heterogeneous and have different capabilities of some value to the attackers, so we assume attackers would be interested in lateral movement from the infected to the uninfected nodes to improve their attack posture. Attackers generally do not know the exact capabilities and vulnerabilities of all the nodes of interest, so the attackers' lateral movement would be preceded by reconnaissance.

We assume that the attackers are able to observe all activity on the infected nodes, including the L3 traffic visible from the infected nodes (passive reconnaissance), and to actively probe reachable, but not yet infected nodes (active reconnaissance), via an apparent L3 network. We assume that even the most patient attackers would be compelled to act at some point; an action can be either active probing or an actual attack to exploit one or more vulnerabilities. We assume that the attackers will choose a target, *identified by an address, a protocol and a port*, based both on the L3/L4 (Layer 4) headers *and* the statistical properties of the observed flows (e.g., to estimate an exploit's success, the attackers need to guess the target's OS and other software.

Defender Model The defender is in full control of the PMLSF, so the defender determines what data traffic is visible at each switch port (or VLAN tag when using VLANs), and can inject fake traffic at any switch at will and mutate L3/L4 headers of both real and fake packets in flight. The network operator determines the per-PMLSF switch bandwidth budget (mean packet rate) available for fake traffic injection to the defender. Additionally, the defender can enforce opaqueness of the L4 payload (e.g., *pretending* that any unicast traffic not destined for a particular observation point is encrypted).

The defender can also program the PMLSF to quickly detect packets matching particular sources/destinations, protocols, ports, and notify the controller. Furthermore, the defender can program the PMLSF to produce custom responses to detected packets (e.g., delay TCP connection establishment). The defender is also in control of some/all the kernels/hypervisors on the physical machines or VM/container hosts.

3 Deception System Approach and Architecture

Leveraging the programmability and speed of modern PMLSFs, we provide proactive defense and deter reconnaissance by employing deception as follows. We build upon the port isolation support in the switches to create, maintain and dynamically change *individual* deceptive views of the defended network *for each observation endpoint* (connected L3 interface) in the data plane. More specifically, leveraging the port isolation capabilities, we ensure, by configuration, that any endpoint, connected via a switch port, will be able to observe only the network traffic that the defender allows it to observe.

Defining a *deceptive view* as a collection of information wherein some *part of the information is real*, and *some part is intentionally fake*, we construct and play fake conversations (packet exchanges) to be observed at each endpoint, to complement the real conversations in the network, resulting in a *per-endpoint* deceptive view. The information is limited to that in: (a) L3 packets in flight (promiscuously captured at the observation point), (b) the observation point's own L3 address, and (c) responses to a small set of defender-permitted network discovery probes (ICMP). To obviate the need for transport and application layer content generation in the fake traffic, we do not generate any actual payloads for the fake Layer 3 (L3) unicast packets with exceptions for the selected well-known auxiliary networking protocols. Instead, we fill the L3 payloads of such packets with random noise, so the attacker cannot tell whether it is encrypted with a cipher that ensures indistinguishability [17], or truly random.

From the defender point of view, it is convenient to decompose a deceptive view into two planes: (a) network (L3) that captures the topology (i.e., who is connected to who) and (b) conversation (L4) that captures who talks to who. Figure 2 provides a schematic of the individual deceptive views of the same underlying network as seen by two different endpoints (N1 and N9), in each of the two planes, with real entities shown in blue and fake entities in green.

As shown in Fig. 2, the conversations that can be observed at an endpoint will be composed of both real (blue) and fake (green) conversations. By making information in a fake conversation statistically indistinguishable from that in a real conversation, the probability of an attacker interacting with a fake endpoint (probing or attacking) becomes a function of the quantity of the fake endpoints. We ensure the prevalence of fake conversations among all observable at any endpoint to increase the probability of an attacker interacting with a fake endpoint. We inject the traffic

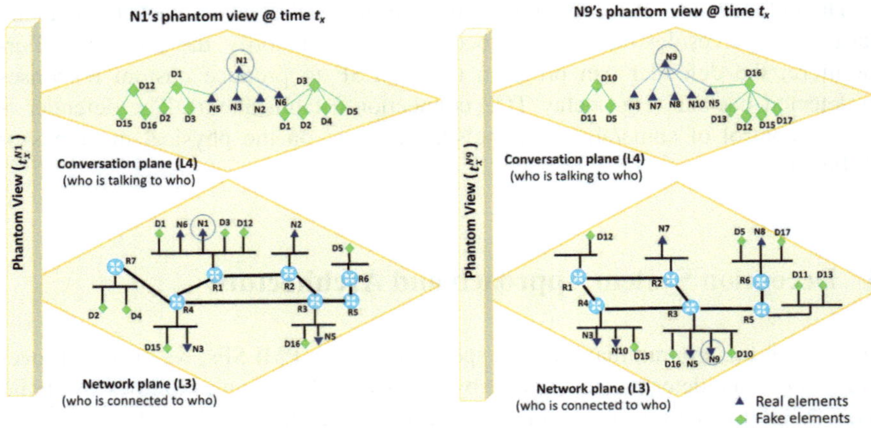

Fig. 2 Deceptive views at two different endpoints: N1, *left* and N9, *right*

representing fake conversations into each programmable switch and selectively forward it to specific switch ports (i.e., real endpoints) for observation.

Since adversarial reconnaissance takes place in deceptive views, we change the deceptive view content frequently and substantially, to reduce the time an attacker has to collect traffic statistics and make inferences from the observables. We expect an attacker to quickly become aware of an unusual nature of the defended network and persist with their effort.

We construct the per-endpoint deceptive views in the conversation and network planes, ensuring that: (a) the inter-plane constraints are not violated (e.g., if endpoint Y is unreachable from endpoint X, there could be no link between the endpoints in the conversation plane), and (b) an endpoint present in multiple views behaves identically in each view. The latter is necessary if the adversary can fuse information from multiple points of presence in the defended network. All real endpoints observable from X have to be present in X's deceptive view, but we have considerable freedom in the type and number of fake elements, limited only by the available resources.

We employ an intuitive construction approach that automatically preserves the above inter-view and inter-plane constraints as follows. We start with the global view of the real network that is available to the defender, augment it with fake endpoints and conversations to create a *master deceptive view*. Armed with the master deceptive view, we then carve out a deceptive view *for each endpoint*. Figure 3 shows a schematic of the master and individual deceptive views for the conversation and network planes, with real elements shown in blue and fake in green.

Section 4 provides details of the algorithms and the implementation of deceptive view construction' in each of the two planes.

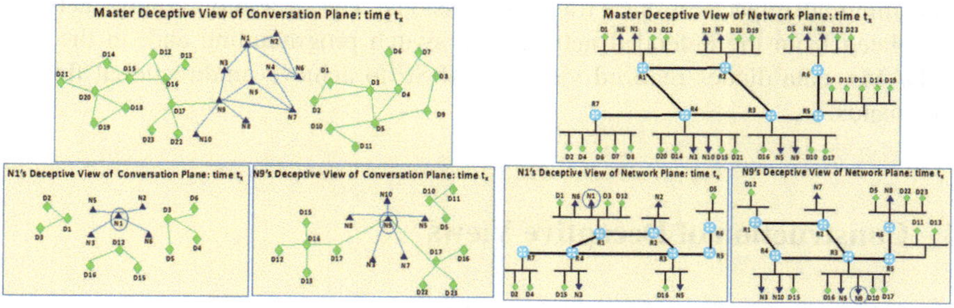

Fig. 3 Sample master deceptive views (*top*) and individual end-point deceptive views (*bottom*) of the conversation plane (*left*) and network plane (*right*)

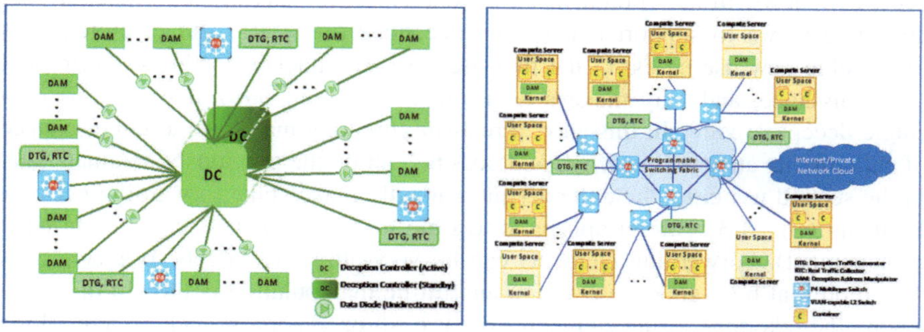

Fig. 4 Schematic of the deception control system (*left*) and a representative network employing the deception control system (*right*)

Figure 4 shows a high-level architecture of our deception system embedded in a P4-programmable multi-layer switching fabric (PMLSF) with the deception components in green.

The *defended network* carries the user data and control packets, both real and fake. Real traffic is produced by the communicating processes on compute servers. In the *deception control network*, a deception controller (DC), backed by a hot standby, continuously constructs sets of deceptive views for its domain of control, based on the information from the real traffic collectors (RTCs), (as summarized in Sect. 4) and instructs the programmable switches, deception traffic generators (DTGs) which generate traffic based on the algorithms discussed in Sect. 4, and deception address manipulators (DAMs) (whose operations are described in Sect. 5) to start enforcing a particular set. The programmable switches implement view isolation, packet forwarding and address translation between. The DTGs inject fake traffic in the user plane, to represent fake conversations.

The fake endpoints are observable only via the control and data traffic they generate; there is no target that can be interacted with behind a fake endpoints. On deceptive view changes, the DAMs modify the L3 addresses on interfaces and existing L4 protocol endpoints (e.g., TCP), to enable seamless transition with minimal impact on open transport sessions. The deception control network is isolated from the defended network via switch programming and, in the case of DAMs, data diodes realized via the PMLSF to achieve unidirectional flow of commands.

4 Construction of Deceptive Views

As outlined in Sect. 3, deceptive views for individual endpoints in the network and conversation planes are carved out from the master deceptive views for the respective planes. This section describes the algorithms used to construct the master deceptive views. In our approach, we generate *realistic* network topologies for the deceptive views to support two known deceptive use cases, and in anticipation of possible new use cases. In the first use case, an attacker conducts intermittent reconnaissance, and may make a decision to act based on offline analysis of a single deceptive view. In this case, a realistic topology may have a higher chance of enticing the attacker to revisit, and possibly act on the previously obtained data. In the second use case, the defender intentionally makes fake forwarding network elements (e.g., L3 routers) appear accessible as L3 endpoints (e.g., for in-band management). Forwarding elements can be very attractive targets to attackers as they represent both good observation and traffic manipulation points. In this case, having the fake forwarding elements appear positioned appropriately in a topology would help nudge the attacker towards them.

All real networks are built with one or more use cases in mind. Such use cases can be broad (e.g., provide Internet access to a collection of computers), or very specific (e.g., process credit card payments via a finical network). The use cases, available technology and compliance standards impose a structure on the topology of the target network. Network standards, such as [18] and data protection standards, such as [19, 20], impose traffic isolation requirements that force endpoints within the network to be clustered and isolated in particular ways. Technology recommendations from vendors, such as [21, 22], may impose constraints on how traffic is aggregated, which in turn create restrictions on where endpoints may be placed. Thus, the layout of any actively used network is rarely random.

This property of network topologies creates a trade-off between believability and ease of construction when generating topologies. On one extreme, one can simply generate random graphs and name the endpoints with IP addresses. Assuming one enforces constrains on reachability, this will produce a viable network that can forward traffic. However, it is highly unlikely to convince a hypothetical attacker that this network is real. In the other extreme we can strictly adhere to a compliance standard, but this has some difficulties. One issue is that these standards lack the specificity to build an actual network. However, if such specificity were present, the resulting network would again fail to convince an attacker by being too compliant. A generated network needs to have some random elements, but not too many.

One major drawback of the parameterized random generation methods is that they generate purely random graphs. The generated graphs never capture any of the real-world constraints that shape graphs such as standards compliance or hardware constraints. To incorporate these constraints, we employ an alternative method that uses an existing real-world topology as a starting point, and then adds a tunable amount of randomness to the graph.

This alternative strategy uses graph replication methods such as degree-based replication [23] or spectral replication [24] to produce topology graphs that are similar to the source graph. The replication methods can be tuned to preserve the graph properties directly. For example, spectral replication uses the eigenvalues of the graph Laplacian to preserve the clique structures and can be tuned by controlling the number of eigenvectors used to construct the replica. Degree replication preserves edge statistics by replicating subgraphs that contain specific edge structures and can be tuned by fixing the size of the subgraphs that are replicated. This approach naturally incorporates the real-world constraints via the source graph.

While the replication approach is more desirable because it captures real-world constraints, the approach has a significant limitation. If the source graph is too simple, the replication will end up being simple. On one extreme, if the replication parameters are set too low, the replication simply produces a star topology or something equally simple (e.g., a transit-stub graph in Fig. 5; we assume that the source graph is a single connected component and ensure that the replication preserves this property). In the other extreme, setting the parameters too high will simply result in copying the source topology. The source graph needs to be complex enough for there to be room for random variation. If we have a source graph that is too simple, we can mitigate the issue by using parameterized random generation. There is a potential for hybrid approaches where a portion of the network is randomly generated, and replicas are subsequently grafted on this generated graph.

To effectively model the traffic observed at an endpoint, we define the notion of a conversation graph (CG). We then describe how traffic collection provides the data analyzed to produce a conversation graph that represents the current state of real conversations, and consider how to generate new conversations that are statically similar to real conversations. Finally, we describe how the observed distributions on real traffic are used to produce fake traffic injection schedules provided to the deceptive traffic generators (DTGs). The DTGs follow the schedules while an appropriate deceptive view is active. At the observation endpoint, an attacker will see traffic from real and fake elements in the network that are statistically indistinguishable.

Properties of Conversation Graphs We consider a conversation between two endpoints to be identified by the four tuples of (source L3 address, destination L3 address, L4 protocol, L4 port). While multiple application layer protocols can be overlaid on the existing IP network, it is rarely the case that all endpoints within the network exchange packets using any particular protocol.

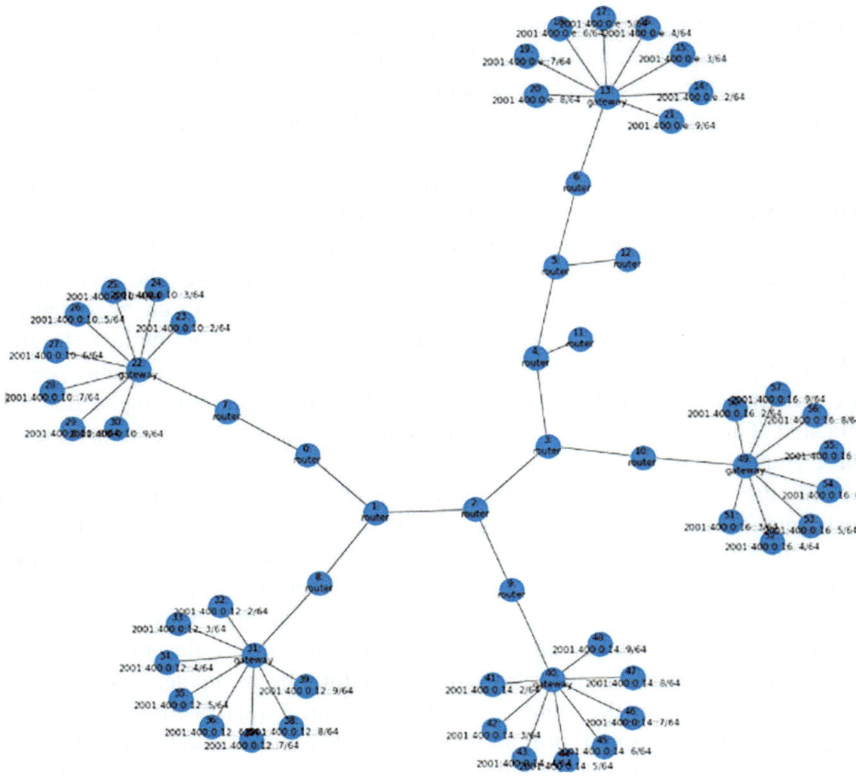

Fig. 5 A generated Transit-Stub Graph

A conversation graph tracks which endpoints within the network exchange packets, over some time window. Since the conversations over different protocols are largely independent, we create one graph per (protocol, port) pair (e.g., FTP in Fig. 6). Each edge within the graph is weighted by the traffic metric distribution parameters (as a vector) of the conversations, e.g., the location (mean μ) and scale (standard deviation σ) parameters of bytes exchanged. Since most conversations are asymmetric, there will be different distributions for each direction between a pair of endpoints. Since forwarding elements are transparent in the conversation at L4, forwarding elements only show up in the conversation graphs when they are the end point of a conversation, e.g., using the web interface to configure a router.

The key component of a conversation graph is the edge weights that consist of traffic metric distribution parameters for each direction of traffic. To compute these weights, an RTC is connected to each programmable switch in the PMLSF, and the switch is configured to mirror all passing traffic to the RTC port. The updates to the distributions are done iteratively as new data arrives. This results in some lag in the possible rate of change for generated traffic but can be tuned by

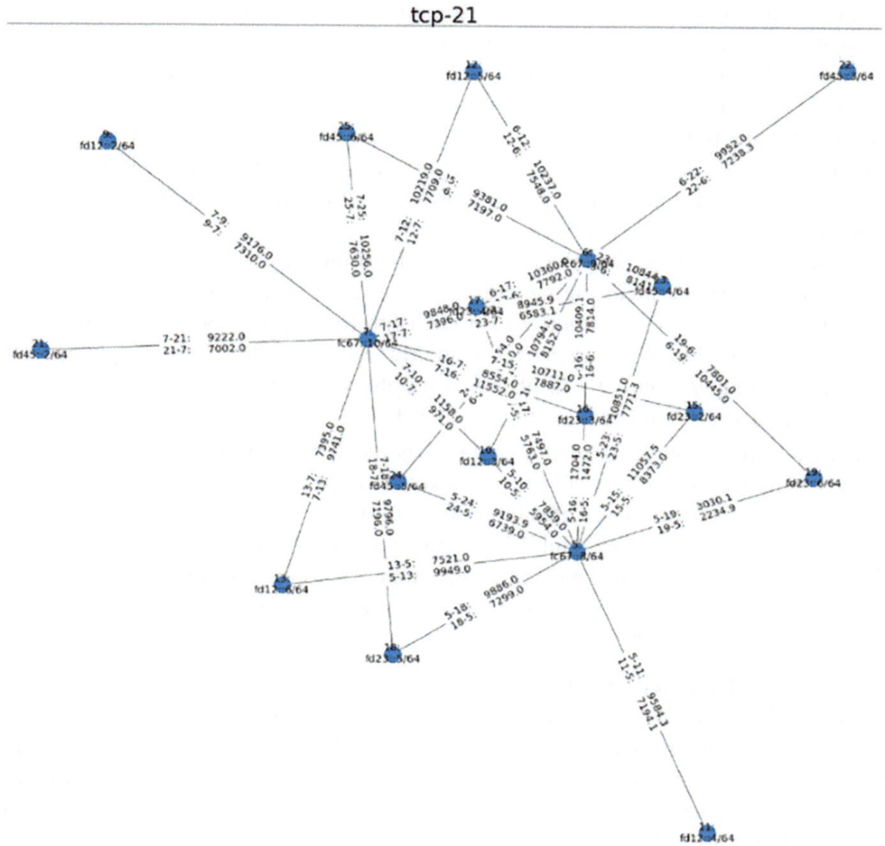

Fig. 6 Observed conversation graph for TCP port 21 showing the location parameter of the distribution on bytes sent

adjusting the size of the observation window. Further optimizations are possible, including sampling traffic data from representative nodes. Sampling would require grouping conversation endpoints by their traffic profiles and collecting data for only one member of the group. This would require us to collect all session establishment/termination packets and all data packets at the beginning/end of a session, but sampling the rest. Additionally, we can use the packet counting and windowed statistical analysis capability in the PMLSF switches.

Mapping of Real and Fake Endpoints to the Generated Topology To generate the conversation plane of a deceptive view, we first need to map both real and fake endpoints to the generated network topology. We use the same process for real and fake endpoints.

To maintain a topology agnostic to the naming of endpoints, we first assign a unique identifier to each real IP address. Because services (e.g., DNS) and access controls often enforce isolation along subnet boundaries, it is important that any mapping preserve the subnet relationships. To this end, we cluster the unique identifiers by subnet. We then map each subnet in the real topology to a subnet in the generated topology which was pre-populated with enough subnets to enable a one-to-one mapping. Within each subnet, each real IP address is mapped to at least two IP addresses in the target topology (one for itself and at least one for a fake counterpart). Each unique pair of IP addresses within the real conversation graph has one or more twins in the generated topology.

Within each view, all the fake endpoints will mimic the conversations of their real counterparts. To complete the generated conversation graph, we sample from the observed traffic metric distributions for each (protocol, port, source IP, destination IP) tuple to produce the target traffic metric values in the generated view. For example, if real IP_1 and IP_2 in observed topology are map to fake IP_1^1 and IP_2^1 in view 1, and IP_1 and IP_2 exchange ~1024 bytes over TCP port 80, then IP_1^1 and IP_2^1 will exchange $1024 \pm \epsilon$ bytes, whereϵ is the observed variation, when view 1 is active. When this occurs, if packets from the exchange between IP_1 and IP_2 were observed on a specific interface within the network, then packets from the exchange between IP_1^1 and IP_2^1 would also be observable on that interface. This conversation mapping will preserve subnet relationships and traffic loads on forwarding fabric ingress points (e.g., if there was a lot of inter-subnet traffic in the original conversation graph, this property is preserved).

Generation of Packet Injection Schedules In the deception architecture, DTGs are located next to each PMLSF switch. Each DTG is provided with a schedule of packets to generate for each (source IP, destination IP, protocol, port) tuple that will be observed by each target endpoint (all connected to the same PMLSF switch). Each view will have its own set of schedules as each view may have different observabilities and IP address spaces.

The injection schedules are identified by the set of observed endpoints that the generated traffic will be mimicking, i.e., via the unique identifier assigned to a real endpoint above. The generated conversation graph has the sampled traffic metrics values that the schedule must adhere to (e.g., bytes sent between endpoint pairs within an observation window). Send schedules can be pre-computed because the parameters are known before the view is active. For example, if a generated endpoint pair must exchange 1024 bytes over a 350-s window, we can pre-compute the payload lengths and packet inter-arrival times to meet this target. At the DTG, each send schedule is identified by the (source IP, destination IP, protocol, port) tuple that it will use to form the packet header. When the view is active, the only operation the DTG performs is to form packets with the appropriate header and packet characteristics, and inject them at the correct intervals.

5 Implementation of Deceptive Views

This section describes the implementation of the deceptive views and is organized as follows. We begin with a description of the Deception Controller (DC) that is responsible for generating deceptive views (using the fake conversations as described in Sect. 4), and instructing the P4 switches which views to use. The actual address manipulation is performed by the Deceptive Address Manipulator (DAM) which is explained later in this section.

The **Deception Controller** (DC) takes as input a machine-readable description of deceptive views constructed as described in Sect. 4. The DC is responsible for translating those view descriptions into P4 programs, P4 runtime instructions, runtime instructions for the DAMs, and DTG packet injection schedules. For the PMLSF switches, the DC sends P4 programs and runtime instructions over a dedicated deception control plane as described in Sect. 3. The DC sends DAM runtime instructions through that same deception control plane to the individual hosts that have the DAM Loadable Kernel Module installed inside their kernels. These control messages all flow in one direction and are suitable for protection with data diodes.

The P4 switches that comprise the PMLSF are responsible for performing packet forwarding and address translation for all packets that traverse the PMLSF data plane. When implementation of a deceptive view requires address manipulation on the host level, the DAM is responsible for modifying kernel data structures so source address, destination address, or both may be changed without disruption to active connection-oriented protocol sessions. In our implementation we demonstrate the ability to change both source and destination addresses of TCP sockets without disruption to established connections.

At an implementation level we define the view of a particular port on a particular switch to be the address transformation function and the view key. The transformation function and view key are constructed by the DC so that IP addresses in the headers of packets entering and exiting the PMLSF are manipulated by that transform function according to the specified key to be consistent with the addresses in a switch port's deceptive view. In our initial implementation, we implement the transformation function as a set of lookup tables to map between a host's canonical address and the host's assigned address in a deceptive view, and use a view identifier as the key, to select an appropriate lookup table.

At the DC, during the mapping phase described in Sect. 4, the lookup tables for each element of the PMLSF are generated based on what portion of the master view they observe. These tables are forwarded to respective DAMs via the deception control plane. In our implementation the lookup tables were sent as three-column tab-delimited text file where the column values were view number, observed IP, generated IP. After schedules were generated for each observer according to the procedure described in Sect. 4, each generator was sent a five-line text file that contained the header and schedule information. The first four lines were the values of the identifying tuple (source IP, destination IP, protocol, port). The last line was

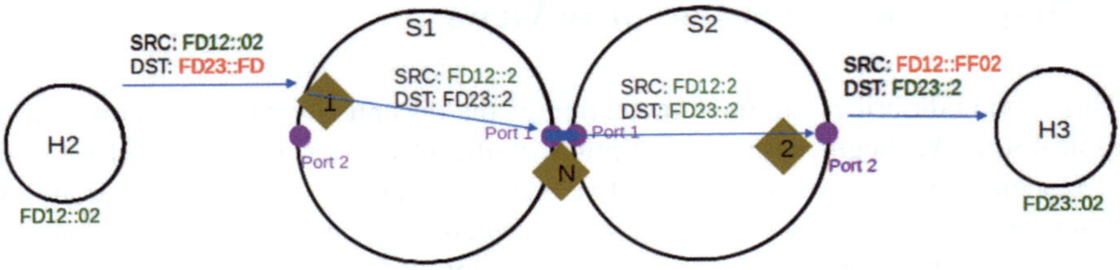

Fig. 7 Illustration of IP address translation between 2 deceptive views

a list of real number values which were the wait times between packet send events in seconds. Future implementations of this system would also include additional packet characteristics such as payload length, and header flags.

Figure 7 shows an illustrative example of a P4 switch-based address transformation. Host *H2* has address *fd12::2*, Host H3 has address fd23::2. H2 is connected to Switch S1. The port on S1 to which H2 is connected to is in View 1. The port on S2 to which H3 is connected is in View 2. The hosts are labeled with their addresses in green. These canonical addresses are used by the switching network for forwarding.

Because H2 is in View 1, it sees H3's address as fd23::fd. When H2's packet enters the switching network, S1 looks up the canonical address for H3 (fd23::2). When that packet exits the switching network, S2 uses the view key to transform the source address to H3's view (fd12:ff02). When the DC orders a view change for those ports, it sends P4 runtime messages to S1 and S2 to change the view keys on those ports.

The reader will notice that when the view at H2's port changes it must now use a different address to reach H3. All traffic within the switching fabric uses canonical IP addresses. For this reason the DNS server does not need to do anything special to support deceptive views. When H2 requests H3's address after a view change, the DNS server will respond with H3's canonical address, which S1 will transform to the correct address for H2's new view.

P4 switches typically manipulate the headers and not the contents of higher layer protocols such as DNS. In P4, however, the concept of what constitutes a header is flexible. The switches in our system treat DNS response packets as an additional header above the UDP header. The location of the IP addresses in the DNS response is determined as the packet is parsed, and the address is transformed in the ingress phase of the switch's pipeline. At this point there is a complication: changing the body of a UDP packet requires updating the UDP header checksum. We implemented the incremental internet checksum algorithm from Eq. 3 in [25] in the egress processing element of the switch pipeline.

Deceptive Address Manipulator (DAM) Our deception system allows existing TCP connections to proceed without interruption during view changes. This requires modification of the data structures in the Linux kernel associated with the source and destination addresses of the open socket. This is the function of the DAM Loadable Kernel Module (LKM), as explained below.

It would be possible for an LKM to intercept all incoming and outgoing packets and apply a transformation to the addresses in the packets, however this would add latency and increase processing cost on that host for the duration of the TCP session. Instead, the DAM modifies the addresses in the TCP socket structures obviating the need for continuing address transformation. The DAM supports changing the foreign IP address, the local IP address, or both simultaneously.

When the DAM is loaded it uses *ftrace* to hook several kernel functions including *tcp_sendmsg()*, *__inet6_lookup_established()* and *tcp_v6_early_demux()*. The name of the DAM functions that hook those kernel functions are *decep_tcp_sendmsg()*, *decep__inet6_lookup_established()* and *decep_tcp_v6_early_demux()*. The DAM exposes a *sysfs* attribute for adding view addresses and for changing the current view. A simple UDP server implemented in Python writes the desired to the attribute. The DC sends its view change instructions to this UDP server.

Sending When a view change instruction is received by a host that is sending a tcpv6 packet the next call to *tcp_sendmsg()* is intercepted by the *ftrace* hook and control is passed to *decep_tcp_sendmsg()* which is shown as State 1 in Fig. 8. If the view change has already been completed the state machine transitions to State 3 which passes control back to the kernel where it completes the real *tcp_sendmsg()*. If the view change has not been completed the machine enters State 2 which the source and destination addresses in the packet according to the transformation for

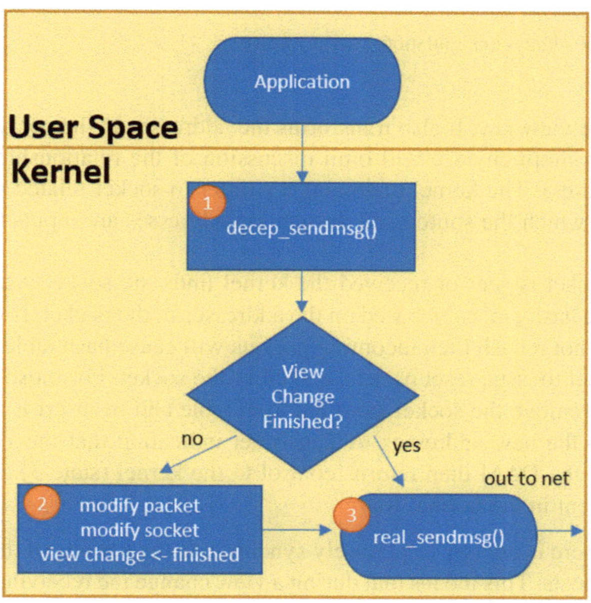

Fig. 8 Deceptive address manipulation: packet send

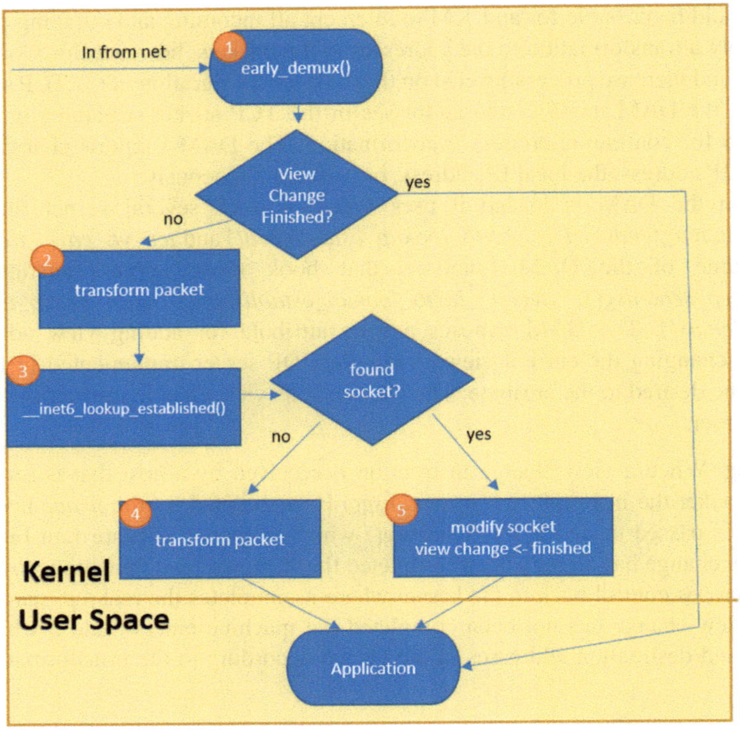

Fig. 9 Deceptive address manipulation: packet receive

the appropriate view key. It also transforms the addresses in the socket related data structures (for simplicity we will omit discussion of the relationship between the various structures). The kernel maintains a pointer to socket related structures in a hash table for which the source and destination addresses are inputs to the hashing function.

When a packet is sent or received the kernel finds the socket data structure by looking for the hash table slot based on the addresses in the packet. If we modify the socket and do not rehash then incoming packets will cause hash table misses which cause the kernel to issue reset packets and close the socket. For those reasons while in State 2 we remove the socket from the hash table and re-insert it at the position appropriate to the new addresses. A flag is set indicating that the view change is complete, and the DAM then returns control to the kernel (state 3) and from there the packet is sent in the normal way.

Receiving There is no way to precisely synchronize the kernels of the sending and the receiving hosts. This means that during a view change the receiving host may get packets with the addresses from the previous view or its new view. Figure 9 shows the DAM state machine to handle this.

When a packet arrives it is intercepted in *tcp_v6_early_demux()* (State 1). If the flag is set that indicates the view change is complete then control is returned to the kernel which will deliver it to the application in the normal way.

If the view change was not already complete the machine transitions into State 2. In State 2 the packet's addresses are transformed with the new view key. Note that only the packet is altered, not the socket. At this early stage in the receiving process it is not yet possible to lookup the socket associated with this connection. State 2 therefore returns control to the kernel which performs the next several steps of packet processing. At some point in the processing of that packet the kernel will need to get the socket that corresponds to the packet. This occurs in *__inet6_lookup_established()* which is State 3.

Recall that the packet's addresses were transformed in the previous step. That means that if the packet was originally using the old addresses, it will now have the new addresses and vice versa. If the original packet was for the old addresses, a look-up at this point will not find it, because it is looking for a not-yet-changed socket at the addresses used by the new view. When the socket is not found in the lookup by the new addresses, the packet's addresses are transformed back to those of the previous view, the socket is looked up correctly, and the kernel will automatically ACK the packet and copy it into userland for access by the application.

If the original packet was for the *new* addresses on the other hand at this point (Step 3) the addresses will have been transformed to the addresses from the previous view. This time when the lookup happens it will find the socket under the old address. This tells the LKM that the sender has completed its view change and the receiver should complete its as well. It transforms the addresses of the packet back (so it will now be using the new addresses again). It then maintains a pointer to the socket while removing it from the hash table, transforms the addresses in the socket data structures, and inserts it into the hash table at the new correct position. At this point the packet and the socket are both using the new addresses. The view change is now complete and the appropriate flag is set. Control is returned to the regular kernel which automatically sends an ACK using the new addresses and copies the packet into userland for access by the application.

6 Experimental Evaluation

Based on the assumptions outlined in Sect. 1, we evaluate the deception system prototype in a small-scale enterprise environment with a realistic traffic mix.

Scenario Description Figure 10 shows the layout of the experimental network. Three client subnets (Client 1, 2 and 3, with 5 hosts in each) and a single server subnet (Servers, 9 hosts) are connected by the PMLSF in the data plane. In the control plane, the DC is connected to P4-programmable multi-layer switches, the DAMs in each server/client host, and the DTG hosts. Both planes use IPv6 ULA addressing; the addresses shown in the figure are the statically-assigned baseline

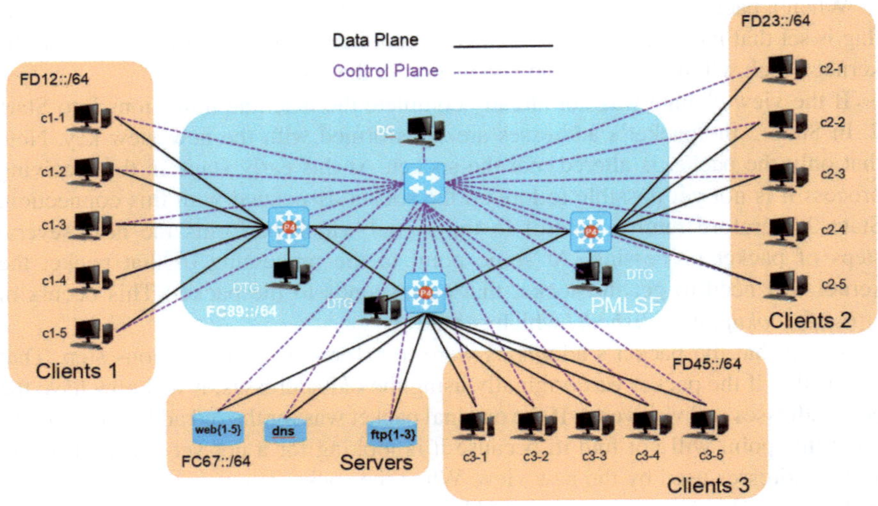

Fig. 10 Scenario network layout

addresses (independent of deception). In the network layer of the data plane, the P4-programmable switches act as conventional IPv6 routers.

Users on the client hosts interact with Web and FTP servers in the Servers subnet, via Web browsers and FTP clients (TCP-based). IPv6 neighbor discovery and router advertisement (ICMP), DNS (UDP), etc. are exercised as needed to support user activity. User activity represents mid-day enterprise interactions.

Scenario Implementation The scenario is implemented in hybrid network emulation on a CyberVAN testbed [26], with 1 Gbps Ethernet links, P4-programmable switches and the dumb L2 switch modeled in ns-3. The Ethernet link and dumb L2 switch models are standard ns-3 code. The P4-programmable ns-3 switch model is based on the P4 reference switch implementation [27], which we ported to ns-3 as part of prototyping.

All hosts, including clients, servers, the DC and the DTGs, have been modeled as x86 QEMU/KVM virtual machines (VMs) and run Ubuntu 16.04.6 with the 4.4.0-137-generic kernel (modified for DAM as described in Sect. 5). The client hosts ran the *fluxbox* window manager, Firefox 75 and the command-line FTP client. The Web servers run *apache,* the FTP servers run *vsftpd,* and the name server runs *dnsmasq*, all from the standard Ubuntu 16.04.6 repositories.

The website content (a mix of text and images) has been made to refer only to the URL within the same set of five Web servers. The FTP content is a mix of binary files (software packages, video clips), with file sizes generally orders of magnitude larger than Web pages.

We modeled user activity with ConsoleUser [28], a Markov transition matrix-based synthetic user of real applications (the Firefox web browser and the command-line FTP traffic) that interact with the Web or FTP servers. ConsoleUser uses multiple levels of transition matrices to decide on what activity to choose (Web browsing, FTP, etc.), and what to do within each activity (type the URL, choose a link, read the page, etc.)). The transition probabilities are derived from earlier studies done with ConsoleUser.

Experiments and Results We describe two experiments designed to demonstrate deception system feasibility.

Experiment 1: No Harm As discussed in the earlier sections, a major constraint on our deception system is that view changes are accomplished with minimal disruption to the operation of the network. This goal requires view changes to not cause connection-based protocols active during the view change to fail. In this section we will consider the experiments that we performed that demonstrate the DAM LKM does not cause interruption of TCP traffic.

We performed no specific tests of the stability of the LKM in terms of possible kernel crashes, but throughout all our tests of latency and throughput we observed no kernel malfunction or crashes. We ran these tests on the CyberVAN testbed, a testbed for executing virtual machines (VMs) connected to networks whose implementation is a network simulator. Our tests executed using version CyberVAN 4.1 on one of the internal Perspecta Labs instances. The network simulator is the ns-3.27 simulator distributed with CyberVAN 4.1, including the functionality to simulate P4 switches within ns-3. In our DAM experiments, we used Ubuntu 16.04.5 LTS VMs running a 4.4.0-137-generic kernel that we modified to always use 0 as the seed for the socket related hashtables. The VMs were running on a Dell R430 server with an Intel Xeon E5-2640 v3 processor rated at 2.60GHz and144 GiB of RAM. Each VM was allocated a single processor and 1 GiB of RAM. The simulation ran on a server with similar specification.

In each experiment, we used the Multi-Generator (MGEN) flow generation tool to send 1024-byte messages 15,000 times a second (a nominal rate of 123 Mb/s) for 120 s from endpoint c1-1 to endpoint c2-1. We then processed the MGEN [29] receive logs using TRPR [30] in summary mode to compute both latency and throughput. We ran three experiments: the base case to measure the expected behavior of the system (base), the base case with the DAM LKM loaded but no view changes (lkm_p4), and an experiment that cycles among four views every 15 s (lkm_p4_vc). We ran each experiment ten times. In all cases, the measured latency was within the bounds of the accuracy of the clocks indicating that view changes do not adversely affect the latency of the flows. As shown in Fig. 11, there is no significant difference in throughput between the experiments in any of the runs.

Experiment 2: Fake/Real Endpoint Discrimination Under Deception In this experiment, we consider an attacker deciding which endpoint to probe/attack. Since any interaction with a fake endpoint is potentially fatal for the attacker, the attacker's first step is to attempt to eliminate suspected fake endpoints, based on observed traffic metric values. For ease of presentation of the experiment results we use a single metric, bytes exchanged within the observation window, as a digestible

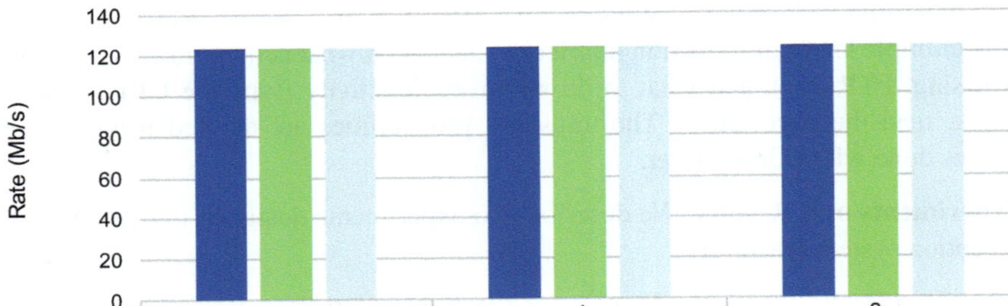

	0	1	2
base	123866	124090	124091
lkm_p4	124040	124056	124112
lkm_p4_vc	124112	124036	123985

Experiment Run

Fig. 11 Results for experiment 1

example of the metrics that could be considered. A full implementation of the system would need to consider several metrics at the same time and solve a multivariate optimization problem to determine a compromise between metric values that ensures believability.

Next, we examine the set of choices and the distribution on metric values that an attacker observes after reconnaissance. We compare the conversations present on an interface within the observed network when no deceptive view is active versus when active deception is present. For simplicity, we consider a single view and a fixed observation window of approximately 350 s. In normal operation, the views will cycle according to schedule which balances view change overhead and useful lifetime of the passively observed information.

In the network described above, we consider two observation endpoints, the client c1-1 and the server web1. We compare the observed conversations and traffic metrics distributions when deception is active versus inactive. When the deception is active, the endpoints will also observe traffic between the endpoints within the generated topology shown in Fig. 12. Generated traffic within this deceptive view will pass through the PMLSF and will be mapped to the appropriate address space for the observer. This generated traffic will obey the schedules described in Sect. 4. For each observing endpoint, we run a packet capture active for the observation window and then extract a conversation graph from that capture in both the deceptive and non-deceptive cases.

First, we consider the observations at web1. When deception is not active, this endpoint observes many conversations as it is a server connected to the service end of the switching fabric. Many conversations are occurring, not only to this server, but all of it neighbors which are also servers. When deception is not active, there is a single densely connected component that reflects a large set of real conversations. When deception is active, the conversation graph has two disjoint components. One

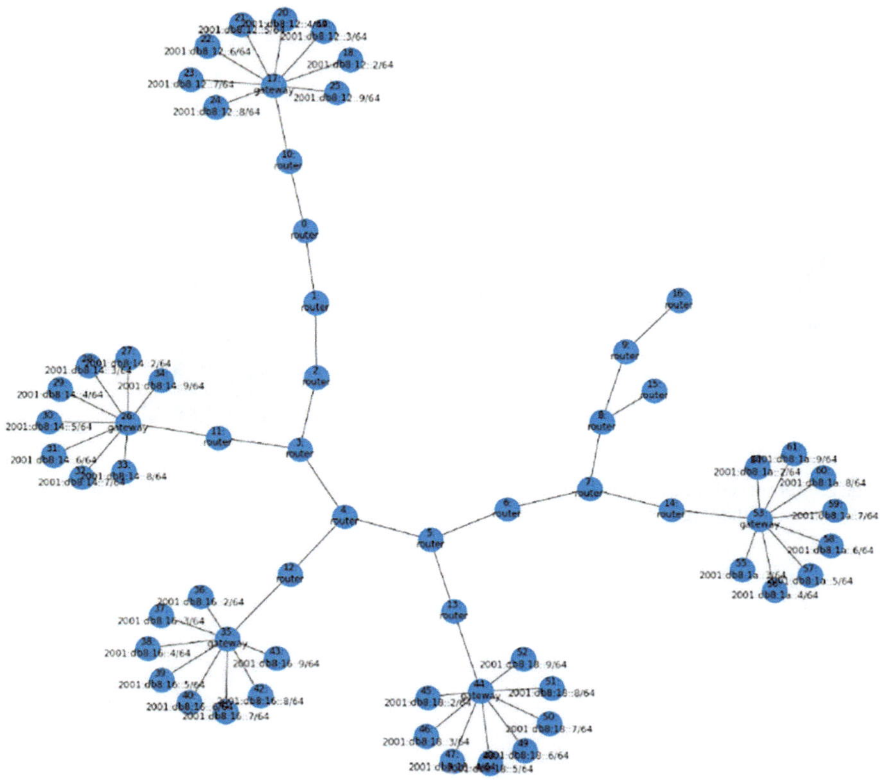

Fig. 12 Generated topology for view 1

component corresponds to the real conversations, and the other corresponds to the deceptive conversations among entirely fake endpoints within the same IP space.

An attacker observing these conversations will try discern the real traffic from the fake traffic by looking at the observable metrics. Since the flow of most web requests is asymmetric, an observer will notice a pattern where the bytes sent from the client to server are significantly smaller than the bytes sent in the other direction. An attacker can potentially identify which endpoint of a conversation is the server by checking which endpoint sends more bytes.

In Fig. 13, the left plot shows the relative frequency of observing a specific byte metric value, and we observe the split for both cases where deception is active and inactive. We observer that the distribution parameters for both cases are very similar. In the right plot, we show two sampled normal distributions parameterized by the parameters for the higher byte count that were observed in both cases. The key observation here is that these distributions show significant overlap. If an attacker were to formulate a hypothesis test based on these distributions, the attacker would have a very difficult time telling the cases apart.

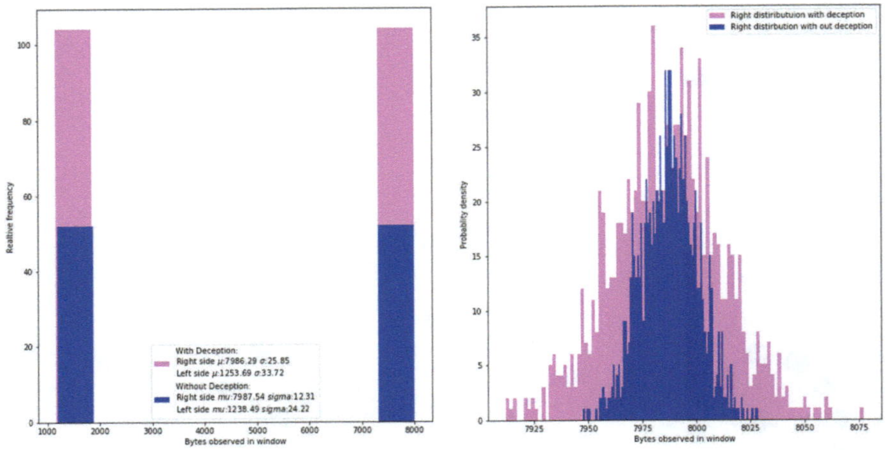

Fig. 13 Observed metric distributions at web1: bytes exchanged in each conversation (*left*), the distribution of the larger byte counts (*right*)

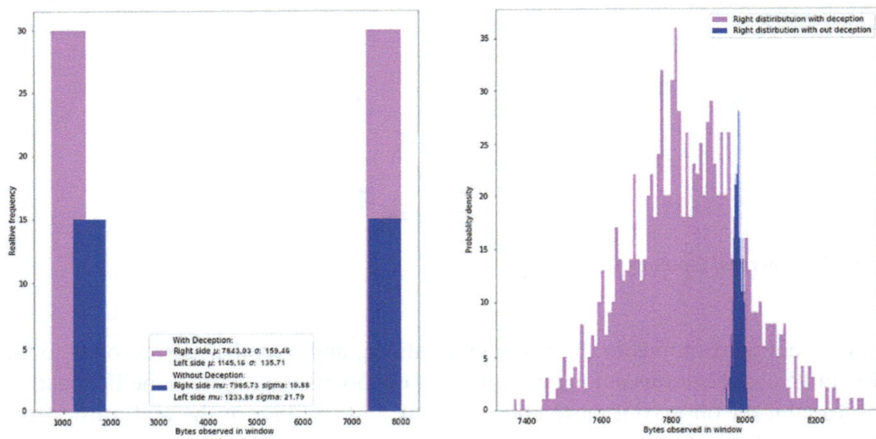

Fig. 14 Observed metrics at c1-1: bytes exchanged in each conversation (*left*), the distribution of the larger byte counts (*right*)

When considering the client c1-1, the results are largely similar. Since this endpoint is a client, it has a more restricted view of the network and observes fewer conversations. When deception is not active, the conversation graph has a single component which corresponds to conversations between real endpoints in the network. With deception active, there are two disjoint components.

In Fig. 14, we again see the same separation of metric values. In the right plot of the sampled distributions of the higher byte counts show that the deceptive distribution fully encompasses the real distribution. Since the parameters of the deceptive traffic are entirely under the defenders control, the defender has the ability to modify the traffic patterns to realize any desired metric distribution. In this particular case the generated traffic used a fixed packet length of ~1300 Bytes.

Since the interactions with the web servers were likely to use significantly smaller packet lengths, we observe a larger variation of byte counts in the from the generated traffic versus the real traffic within the observation window. This behavior is configurable and can be adjusted to influence the hypothesis tests the attacker must ultimately preform. This capability can be leveraged to steer an attacker towards a specific target.

7 Summary and Future Work

In the work presented in this chapter, we investigated proactive deception against passive reconnaissance in wired enterprise networks, based on the new capabilities of a switching fabric built partially or wholly on top of P4-programmable multi-layer switches. We designed a complete deception system architecture, prototyped its key components, and evaluated them in small-scale realistic experiments.

We conclude that the proposed system (a) is practically feasible with next-generation programmable switches, regardless of the hardware backend, (b) would not significantly interfere with real operations, and (c) is capable of achieving the stated purpose of indistinguishability of fake and real conversations within isolated views for each observation endpoint.

This investigation has opened up multiple extensions for future work. Near-term improvements include (i) extending the DAM to handle initiation and termination of TCP sessions and support other protocols in addition to TCP (e.g., UDP, ICMP, etc.), (ii) removing the kernel security bypass for the Linux DAM, (iii) implementing DAM for MS Windows, (iv) supporting realistic latency for both fake and real conversations and handling of network discovery recovery requests (e.g., traceroutes on deceptive topologies), and (v) investigating performing real traffic probability distribution analysis entirely on the P4 switches.

Longer term extensions include: (i) incorporating the notions of value of target to an attacker and known attacker cognitive biases while generating fake conversation graphs, to skew the probability of an attacker touching a fake entity in favor of the defender, (ii) incorporating ML to learn attacker behavior and prevent advanced adversaries on multiple colluding hosts by skewing our traffic distributions, and (iii) scaling to thousands of endpoints. The latter would involve: (a) extending the deception controller (DC) to work in a hierarchical manner, and (b) design of compact "deceptive view change functions" to provide information about new L3 addresses when the deceptive views are being changed, in place of a table-lookup as currently implemented.

References

1. The P4 Project: P4 Open Source Programming Language. https://p4.org (2022). Accessed 27 Jan 2025
2. Maloney, S.: What is an Advanced Persistent Threat (APT)? https://www.cybereason.com/blog/advanced-persistent-threat-apt (2017). Accessed 27 Jan 2025
3. Provos, N.: A virtual honeypot framework. Paper presented at USENIX Security Symposium, 2004
4. Daniel, D., Herbig, K., Reese, W., Heuer, R., Sarbin, T., Moose, P., Sherwin, R.: Multidisciplinary Perspectives on Military Deception. Naval Postgraduate School, Monterrey, CA (1980)
5. Calder, S. R.: A Case for Deception in the Defense. Military Cyber Affairs. Vol. 2, Iss. 1, Article 4 (2016)
6. Activo Networks: Deception Visibility. https://attivonetworks.com/documentation/Attivo_Networks-Deception_Visibility.pdf (2017). Accessed 27 Jan 2025
7. Spitzner, L.: The honeynet project: trapping the hackers. IEEE Security and Privacy. March/April (2003)
8. Spitzner, L.: Honeypots: Tracking Hackers. Addison-Wesley (2002)
9. Bowen, B., Kemerlis, V., Prabhu, P., Keromytis, A., Stolfo, S.: A system for generating and injecting indistinguishable network decoys. Journal of Computer Security. 20. 199-221 (2012)
10. Han, X., Kheir, N., Balzarotti, D.: Deception Techniques in Computer Security: A Research Perspective". ACM Comput. Surv. 51, 4, Article 80 (2018)
11. Chiang, C.-Y., Gottlieb, Y., Sugrim, S., Chadha, R., Serban, C., Poylisher, A., Marvel, L., Santos, J.: ACyDS: An adaptive cyber deception system. Paper presented at the IEEE Military Communications Conference, 2016
12. Chiang, J. C.-Y., Venkatesan, S., Sugrim, S., Youzwak, J., Chadha, R., Colbert, E.I., Cam, H., Albanese, M.: On Defensive Cyber Deception: A Case Study using SDN. Paper presented at the IEEE Military Communications Conference, 2018
13. Robertson, S., Alexander, S., Micallef, J., Pucci, J., Tanis, J., Macera, A.: CINDAM: Customized Information Networks for Deception and Attack Mitigation. Paper presented at the IEEE 9th International Conference on Self-Adaptive and Self-Organizing Systems Workshops, 2015
14. Trassare, S.T., Beverly, R., Alderson, D.: A technique for network topology deception. Paper presented at the IEEE Military Communications Conference, 2013
15. Lin, H., Dunlap, S., Rice, M., Mullins, B.: Generating honeypot traffic for industrial control systems. Paper presented at the 11th International Conference on Critical Infrastructure Protection (ICCIP) (2017)
16. The P4 Project: P4 Compiler backends. https://github.com/p4lang/p4c/tree/main/backends (2025). Accessed 27 Jan 2025
17. Bernstein, D.J., Hamburg, M., Krasnova, A., Lange, T.: Elligator: Elliptic-curve points indistinguishable from uniform random strings. Paper presented at the ACM SIGSAC Conference on Computer & Communications, Security, 2013
18. Karn, P.R., Touch, J.D., Mahdavi, J., Bormann, C., Montenegro, G., Grossman, D.B., Reiner, L., Fairhurst, G., Wood, L.: RFC 3819. Advice for Internet Subnetwork Designers. https://datatracker.ietf.org/doc/html/rfc3819 (2004). Accessed 27 Jan 2025
19. The Payment Card Industry Security Standards Council. Payment Card Industry Data Security Standard (PCI DSS), Version 4.01. https://docs-prv.pcisecuritystandards.org/PCI%20DSS/Standard/PCI-DSS-v4_0_1.pdf (2024). Accessed 27 Jan 2025
20. U.S. Department of Health and Human Services: Summary of the HIPAA Security Rule. https://www.hhs.gov/hipaa/for-professionals/security/laws-regulations/index.html (2024). Accessed 27 Jan 2025
21. Cisco Systems: Connecting Networks Companion Guide: Hierarchical Network Design. https://www.ciscopress.com/articles/article.asp?p=2202410 (2014). Accessed 27 Jan 2025

22. Cisco Systems: Medium Enterprise Design Profile (MEDP) - LAN Design. https://www.cisco.com/c/dam/en/us/td/docs/solutions/Enterprise/Medium_Enterprise_Design_Profile/chap2sba.pdf (2017). Accessed 27 Jan 2025.
23. Mahadevan, P., Krioukov, D., Fall, K., Vahdat, A.: Systematic topology analysis and generation using degree correlations. ACM SIGCOMM Computer Communication Review 36.4 (2006)
24. Baldesi, L., Markopoulou, A., Buttsc, C.T.: Spectral Graph Forge: A Framework for Generating Synthetic Graphs With a Target Modularity. IEEE/ACM Transactions on Networking 27.5 (2019)
25. Rijsinghani, A.: RFC 1624. Computation of the Internet Checksum via Incremental Update. https://datatracker.ietf.org/doc/html/rfc1624 (1994). Accessed 27 Jan 2025
26. The CyberVAN team: CyberVAN publications. https://cybervan.perspectalabs.com:9000/publications (2024). Accessed 27 Jan 2025
27. The P4 Project: Behavioral Model (bmv2). https://github.com/p4lang/behavioral-model (2024). Accessed 27 Jan 2025
28. Skaion Corporation: Skaion ConsoleUser 2.0 Documentation. https://skaion.com/cu/api (2024). Accessed 27 Jan 2025
29. U.S. Naval Research Laboratory (NRL): Multi Generator (MGEN) traffic generation tool. https://www.nrl.navy.mil/itd/ncs/products/mgen (2024). Accessed 27 Jan 2025
30. U.S. Naval Research Laboratory (NRL): Tcpdump Rate Plot Real Time (TRPR). https://www.nrl.navy.mil/itd/ncs/products/protean_tools (2022). Accessed 27 Jan 2025

Part IV
Future Directions

Visions and Considerations for Next-Generation Holistic Cyber Deception

Jason H. Li, Gregory Briskin, J. Sukarno Mertoguno, Nicholas Evancich, and Kyung Kwak

1 Introduction

Over the past decade, cyber deception, as a research topic in the science and technology community or an essential component of organizing cyber operations in the modern cyber landscape, has attracted much attention from researchers and practitioners alike [1]. There are a good number of publications or some commercial products touching upon various aspects of cyber deception, being technology or human factor-focused, or network or host or content-focused. However, a relatively holistic consideration of the overall cyber deception landscape is largely missing. This situation may hinder the understanding, research, development and deployment of current and future cyber deception techniques and tools. The authors aim to serve the community with our attempt to help rectify this situation. It is our hope that our work could trigger further holistic, critical thinking in the research and practitioner community.

To set the stage, we consider a typical enterprise as the representative environment with typical network and host assets including firewalls, routers, switches, servers, hosts, file systems with content, etc. Essentially, the main purpose of cyber deception for defense is to waste the attacker's resources. Deception is fundamentally achieved by the defender via strategically responding to the attacker's queries and movements. Such responses can be largely categorized as either network or host protocol messages (such as ICMP or TCP responses) or data content (such

J. H. Li (✉) · G. Briskin · N. Evancich · K. Kwak
Trusted Science and Technology Inc., Rockville, MD, USA
e-mail: jason@trustedst.com; greg@trustedst.com; nick@trustedst.com; kj@trustedst.com

J. S. Mertoguno
School of Cybersecurity and Privacy, Georgia Institute of Technology, Atlanta, Georgia
e-mail: karno@gatech.edu

Q. Zhu et al. (eds.), *Foundations of Cyber Deception*, Advances in Information Security 90, https://doi.org/10.1007/978-3-031-93867-2_12

as fake OS banners or rogue documents). With this generic setup, this chapter will include the following features focusing largely on the holistic design.

First, we discuss the major aspects in developing cyber deception technologies: modeling/analysis, design methods, human elements, and their interactions. We will include the following key points: (1) The role of modeling, analysis results and verification, how modeling may lead to sensible designs, and common pitfalls in modeling and analysis. (2) Design methods and considerations will be the central aspect for this chapter, which include a multitude of factors such as positioning, purpose, assumptions, views at different levels across various user groups, management of views, ways of deception (e.g., hide the truth, tell the lie, half-truth with half-lie), various network and host responses, various kinds of fake data, etc. For example, attackers may be led to focus on the decoy view, rather than the actual view (being networking assets, hosts, or data). Or attackers may obtain complex and incomplete data, causing further confusion. When deception is carefully crafted to mimic the natural enterprise landscape, this artificially-presented view can alter the decision-making process of an attacker and deter future attacks. We will also discuss the interaction between modeling and human factors. (3) The anticipated roles and responsibilities of human elements in our setup, and a cursory discussion on the effectiveness and interactions related to design and implementation. We will identify gaps and recommended direction, including how modeling may overcome its inherent shortcoming to guide the design, various design recommendations, and how the envisioned research ideas may bear tangible fruits. These insights and recommendations for future approaches come directly from the authors' extensive experience and lessons learned in visioning and developing cyber deception technologies [2, 3]. (4) We present the "Cyber Deception Triad", namely the triad of Technology, Metrics, and Humans. While this may seem to overlap with the previous part, here we focus on the importance of metrics, which is an inherently difficult topic, but now has become worse with the notion of deception and human involvement in the picture. Authors plan to describe the aspects to consider among these, with recommendation for cyber deception for defense, such as example metrics with justification.

While the concept that defensive deception relies on "the fog of war" is a familiar one, the authors believe that legitimate cyber deception will need to possess concrete, measurable evidence for deployment consideration. Therefore, along the line of measuring cyber deception effectiveness, authors will emphasize the importance of believability and the critical need for a repeatable, high-fidelity test and evaluation (T&E) environment. We will identify different ways of achieving believable deception, putting consideration in the context of the enterprise network providing deceptive messages or data, attack and defense goals, as well as not affecting the normal enterprise operation. For repeatable test and evaluation, authors will describe the gaps in current simulation and emulation practice for cyber deception research, and recommend novel paradigms and approaches for cyber deception T&E, with suggested methodology for experimentation, measurement and analysis.

Finally, this chapter will include discussions on how recent advances in Artificial Intelligence (AI), machine learning (ML), and particularly large language models (LLM) and ChatGPT may play a role in the landscape of cyber deception. While it may seem natural to apply AI/ML/LLM to cyber deception, the authors will provide some cautionary notes and recommendations on what the next generation of cyber deception may look like.

2 Enterprise Environment

In this section, we will outline the typical environment found within enterprise setups. Traditionally, Computer Network Defense (CND) relies on reactive mechanisms such as signature-based detection, lists that either permit or deny access, and systems designed for intrusion detection and protection. However, as cyber deception starts to gain traction as available tools for system administrators, it offers a means to mislead or divert attackers into believing in a non-existent version of the network and hosts being targeted. This strategic misdirection requires a meticulously planned environment beyond the traditional enterprise IT infrastructure.

To illustrate, let us visualize a standard enterprise environment, which includes the usual network components and computing resources such as firewalls, routers, switches, servers, and various hosts along with their file systems. At its core, the strategic use of cyber deception is intended to exhaust an attacker's resources by presenting the attacker with a misleading representation of the enterprise's IT infrastructure. Today, the most commonly understood deception technique is the use of honeypots to understand adversary trends, explore botnet command and control networks, and collect malware and exploits for analysis. This practice aims to collect early indicators of adverse actions, not necessarily to defend the organization to fully realize the potential of cyber deception.

Researchers may speculate that deception defenses have not caught on in mainstream cyber defense as much as expected due to a handful of drawbacks: (1) Having fake IT resources on the network can confuse the IT team, let alone the regular users; (2) The legal team may feel that active measures such as deception could be a potential liability; and (3) For deception to be most effective, it needs to be customized and unique; this may require a significant workload which most organizations are reluctant to invest in.

To realize cyber deception to its potential, the enterprise network & host configurations and behaviors must reflect what an attacker expects to encounter. Any deviation from the expectation may alert the attackers that they are engaging with decoys. The network and host behaviors must be sufficiently convincing, leading them to exhaust their efforts on a simulated landscape. Consequently, this puts an extra burden on system administrators and cyber defenders in that they must strike the intricate balance of distinguishing between genuine and decoy network and host elements, ensuring their time is not squandered on a fabricated environment and end users are not affected by the deployed deception modalities. Standard-compliant IT policies and rules should be applied for regular users (i.e., business as usual)—genuine network traffic is encrypted, multi-factor authentication is mandated, and unauthorized devices are barred, etc. In contrast, these stringent measures can be relaxed in the decoy network, creating a seemingly less restrictive and more vulnerable environment.

Deception strategies benefit from the advancements in virtualization technology, which facilitates the creation of network traffic and host/user behaviors that mimic legitimate activity, using methods such as replaying mouse and keyboard actions or employing traffic generators. A deceptive enterprise must present the illusion of having standard defensive tools such as virus scanners and firewalls in place. It is crucial that the decoy mirrors the targeted enterprise in appearance to the attacker.

In a way, cyber deception is about crafting the defender's calculated responses to the attacker's inquiries and actions. These responses are categorized as network or host messages, such as ICMP or TCP responses, or data content (e.g., falsified OS banners or misleading documents). For example, effective deception should force the attacker to spend resources on the false view of the network, therefore standard request shall be met with legitimate (but false) responses. The main challenge is to make everything false yet believable. With the recent advent of sophisticated technologies such as Large Language Models (LLMs) and ChatGPT, the creation of diverse and believable decoy network environments has become significantly more straightforward. These tools enable the generation of multiple, reusable deceptive scenarios to convincingly engage attackers.

Deception plays a critical role in the early detection of adversaries conducting reconnaissance on the enterprise to find their target assets or credentials required to conduct the attack. When defenders identify adversarial reconnaissance, credential harvesting, or lateral movement efforts, they can unearth a set of behavior patterns, identify malicious actions, and understand how the adversary traverses the network. Misleading the adversary's conclusions about the organization's vulnerabilities and defense posture will influence what technology the adversary uses to conduct the attack, which fundamentally helps defend against the malicious payload.

3 Modeling, Design, and Human Elements

Cyber defenders can use cyber deception as an effective means for protecting cyber assets and ensuring enterprise mission success, through deceiving and diverting adversaries during the course of planning and execution of cyber operations and missions. To enable effective integration of cyber deception, it would be necessary to create a systematic design process for building a robust and sustainable deception system with extensible deception capabilities.

In a previous book chapter [2], the authors discussed various design aspects of designing cyber deception systems that meet a wide range of cyber operational requirements. These design aspects included general deception goals, deception design taxonomy, trade-off analysis, deception design process, design considera-

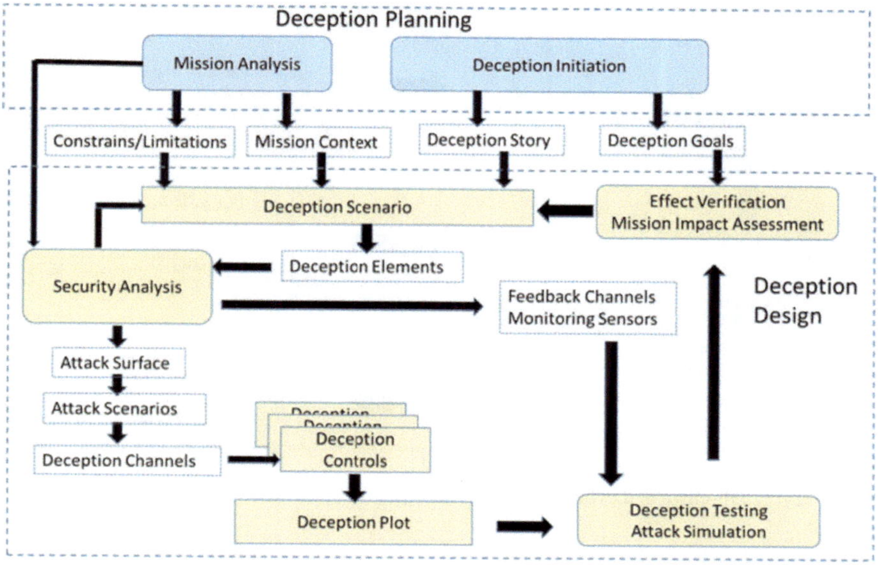

Fig. 1 Cyber deception design and planning [2]

tions such as modularity, interfaces and effect to cyber defenders, interoperability with current tools, deception scenarios, adversary engagement, roles of deception in cyber kill chains [16], and metrics such as adversary work factor. Figure 1 shows an overview of cyber deception design and planning, and Fig. 2 illustrates the cyber security kill-chain and the cyber deception focus, respectively. These figures are included here to provide an overview and general context for subsequent discussions. For more details of deception design considerations, please see reference [2].

3.1 Modeling: Roles and Common Pitfalls

Modeling is essential to every scientific and engineering enterprise. For both scientists and engineers, the "thing being modeled" (referred to as *target*) is typically an object, process, or system in the physical world. A "model" of a target is any description of the target that is not Kant's *thing-in-itself*. For example, mechanical engineers use Newton's laws as models for how a system will react to forces. Computer engineers model digital circuits as instruction set architectures (ISAs), programs as executions in an ISA, and applications as networks of program fragments [4]. Each of these models rests on a modeling paradigm. For example, a source code is a model of what a machine should do when it executes the program, but the source code is not what is actually run on a machine. The Java programming language, for example, is just such a modeling paradigm.

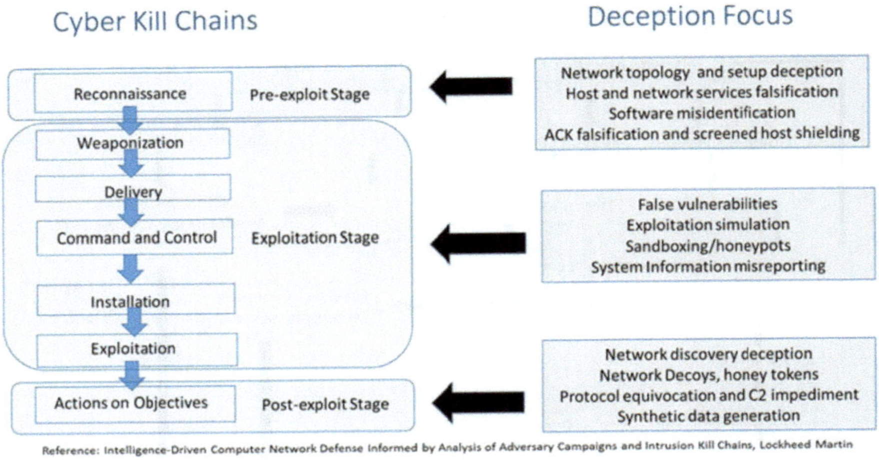

Fig. 2 Cyber kill-chain and cyber deception focus [2]

When the target is a physical object, process, or system, model fidelity is never perfect. But as stated in reference [5], "essentially, all models are wrong, but some are useful". As highlighted in reference [4], in science the value of a model lies in how well its properties match those of the target, whereas in engineering the value of the target lies in how well its properties match those of the model. A scientist constructs models to help understand the target. An engineer constructs targets to emulate the properties of a model, since for an engineer a model represents a design and the target is the implementation. These two uses of models are complementary.

For modeling in cyber deception, therefore, it is critical to always keep a clear mind in terms of the *thing*, the *model*, the *purpose* of the model, and the *interactions* between the thing and the model in either a science or engineering context. This is further complicated by the human factor nascent in cyber deception. Below, we describe some common roles and pitfalls of modeling in this context.

- *Environment modeling* generally entails capturing and emulating the enterprise, individual nodes in the enterprise, or the system stack of such nodes. This helps define the surroundings, such as the baseline defense posture (e.g., firewalls), where the deception participants (e.g., techniques, offensive and defensive actors) may interact. Various modeling and analysis methods exist, and while worthwhile, it is necessary to assert the appropriate fidelity for the purpose of cyber deception research and development, especially with respect to the practicality of the cyber deception techniques (Sect. 2). Where possible, it is prudent to expound why the models are useful for (guiding) practical measurements in real-world test and evaluation environments.
- *Deception techniques modeling* should be used rarely and carefully, since they should be *realized* in some believable way in the above environment as part of the defense mechanisms. For example, honeypots should look like regular

hosts, and software-defined networking (SDN)-based creation of artificial hosts and traffic (e.g., ballooning up) should mimic realistic host and traffic behaviors. Caution must be taken when relying on techniques modeling to make arguments about deception effectiveness.

- *Adversary modeling* falls into two categories. The first category is the traditional threat modeling, which is relatively straightforward and should follow the widely-accepted wisdom with realistic assumptions, scopes, weakness/vulnerabilities, and realizable attack vectors. The second category relates to deceiving the adversaries, which is a lot more involved and will be discussed separately in Sect. 3.3. In short, we position cyber deception as part of the defense mechanisms, and our model of the "mental state" of adversaries (e.g., deceived or not) is only as good as our own trust in the model without confirmation from the actual adversaries in real-world attack-defense settings.
- *Deception effectiveness* should be captured in the most measurable and realistic ways possible. Without knowing the mental state of the adversary, the practical way is to observe attack-related activities and characterize the *stage-of-engagement* in the context of both the realistic environment and the cyber kill-chain (Fig. 2). Toward this end, abstract metrics with only analysis results tend to be less convincing. Rather, relevant and practical metrics should be defined in appropriate places in the environment, with necessary instrumentation for timely measurement and collection of metrics data to enable effectiveness analysis, again in the context of the realistic environment and the cyber kill-chain, see Sect. 4.
- *Modeling the cyber deception process* combines some of the above modeling aspects and aims to provide analytical results. Examples include Markov decision process (MDP)-based or game theory-based modeling, and the results typically include some form of optimized defense decisions or course-of-actions. While these are worthy efforts with respectable goals that may help boost our understanding, they suffer the modeling drawbacks as mentioned above. Furthermore, such process modeling usually involves some (implicit) unrealistic assumptions which make it hard for practical design, development, implementation and assessment. For example, MDP-based modeling typically suffers from incomplete state information, partially observable MDP (POMDP) methods may lead to state explosion, and game theory-based results tend to be impractical at tactical levels including concrete actions since we cannot assume that the adversaries will play our game as configured in the model.

In summary, special care must be taken to inspect and justify models with respect to assumptions, context, purpose and usefulness of the modeling and analysis results. As researchers and practitioners, we cannot simply fit the problem into our own models for convenience. This naturally leads to the following questions: (1) how to sensibly design deception technologies? (2) how to appropriately capture human elements? and (3) how to carry out verification of modeling and design in a repeatable way for cyber deception solutions? The following sections describe these in details.

3.2 Design Methods and Considerations

Based on the technology-focused design considerations in reference [2], this section expands our thoughts on deception strategies and tactics in the context of recent technology advances.

At the heart of crafting a successful deception strategy is the design process, a complex challenge that the authors will explore, along with identifying potential areas for continued research. The primary goal of a deception strategy is to deplete an attacker's resources. This requires defenders to carefully balance how believable the deception is with the effort it takes to set it up, a balancing act that underscores the complexity of design. The components of deception design are wide-ranging, including the story it tells (narrative), its aims (objectives), the intricacies (complexity), and its weak points (vulnerability).

In terms of deception strategy, the deception story that is presented to the adversary is of the utmost importance [2]. It involves the creation of wholly fictitious environments and the placement of tantalizing traps to capture an attacker's interest. The design of this narrative requires a nuanced understanding of how it will be perceived by an attacker. A common strategy is to interweave a mix of fake and real assets, creating a web of confusion. Or, designers may choose to create compelling lures, such as seemingly confidential folders or exclusive data repositories, to capture an attacker's attention.

The intricacy of the deception design is crucial as it determines how thoroughly the defense strategy will outmaneuver an adversary. This intricacy splits into two main areas: host-based and network-based deception. Network deception is about creating phantom network hosts and traffic to give false impressions of the enterprise environment's scale and operations, such as using DNS redirection to construct a maze of false paths. Host deception, on the other hand, can involve elementary tricks such as mislabeling system types to more elaborate traps (e.g., honeypots), which entice attackers to waste resources on targets that do not exist.

In the sophisticated "chess game" of cyber security, a deeper layer of deception works in harmony with the narrative strategy. Designers craft an engrossing story, forming an ecosystem of non-existent assets and alluring decoys. The goal is to construct a narrative so compelling that it not only confuses attackers but also irresistibly lures them into the trap. Through meticulously designed false realities, complete with bait and counterfeit repositories, defenders lay out an elaborate facade.

Choosing this narrative sets the stage for a deception strategy that is streamlined for deployment, sharpens situational awareness, and offers insights into the attacker's tactics. The effectiveness of the ruse depends on distinguishing between authentic and deceptive elements, ensuring a clear view of the network's actual state. The illusion must be potent enough to captivate the attacker, leading them to invest their efforts in a mirage rather than the true network fabric.

The interplay of narrative depth and design is critical in steering attacker behavior. By altering perceptions with a complexly engineered environment filled with network and host deceptions, defenders not only safeguard assets but also harvest intelligence on the employed attack vectors, enhancing their defensive posture. This strategic application of deception, considering human elements in both offense and defense, is key to staying a step ahead in the dynamic threat landscape.

The essence of design depth is how profoundly defenders choose to ensnare the attacker. It splits into two paths: host and network deception. Network deception crafts illusory network hosts and traffic to mislead about the number of devices or the nature of traffic, such as using DNS redirections to create a web of false paths. Host deception ranges from simple masquerades, such as misidentifying an operating system, to more intricate traps such as honeypots that draw attackers into wasting their efforts on phantom targets.

After establishing a narrative, the strategy moves to its implementation phase. The goals here are straightforward: ensure the strategy is simple to deploy, enhance awareness of the operational environment, keep attackers engaged longer, and gain insights into their tactics. The simplicity of rolling out deceptive measures is essential, especially when certain enterprise assets are equipped for quick implementation of such strategies. Crucial to the success of these operations is the ability to distinguish between the real and the fabricated, maintaining a clear understanding of the true network situation.

To realize the deception strategies, it is crucial to dissect the strategic thinking and considerations that constitute the foundation of deception tactics. It involves a spectrum of factors such as the tactical deployment of resources, the intended tactical goals, inherent assumptions, managing the perceptions of different user groups, and the tactics of deception activities which involve masking the truth, spreading falsehoods, or mixing fact with fiction. These factors contribute to the responses of both network and hosts, as well as the creation of fake data. For example, attackers may be lured to focus on a decoy network, steering them away from real assets and data. This tactic is crucial in executing a successful deception by directing adversaries from the true nature of the network toward a thoughtfully crafted mirage.

Draining an attacker's resources hinges on their engagement with the deception. The illusion should be crafted to encourage the attacker to commit more time and resources, influenced by what they perceive and measure. Equally vital is understanding how an intrusion unfolds, as this information is priceless. In cyber security the foremost goal is to safeguard assets, and deception acts as a conduit to achieve this. For example, by diverting attackers to interact with decoy systems rather than the actual network infrastructure, they are left dealing with false or partial information, leading to misdirection. A deception that blends indistinguishably with the genuine enterprise environment can sway an attacker's strategic choices and foil potential attacks. The nuanced interplay of deception tactics, behavioral modeling, and human psychology is also critical and warrants further exploration to perfect the craft of cyber deception.

Command and control in deception revolve around managing this intricate web [2]. In the realm of incident detection and response, timing and context are critical. Traditional detection methods that only react post-compromise or provide incomplete data hamper effective response. Thus, a *command and control interface* is needed, one that adapts the presented reality as defenders learn more about the attacker's capabilities, creating a dynamic feedback loop. As attackers typically start with probing tools before escalating, the deception must evolve to reveal these initial attempts as futile, enticing the attacker further into the web of deceit. Interoperating with detection systems, cyber deception distinguishes itself by providing dependable alerts. Defenders create a web of bogus reconnaissance resources that should only attract attackers. Shielding these elements from legitimate users diminishes false alarms and strengthens the trust in the detection system, allowing defense teams to treat these alerts as definite signs of hostile activity. This is a side benefit cyber deception techniques (and some moving target defense techniques for that matter) can provide to current cyber defense tools.

A potential weakness in applying cyber deception is its fragility in the sense that sophisticated tools depend on a finite set of techniques. The same weakness exists in moving target defense (MTD)—there are only so many ways of randomizing things (e.g., software or protocol message exchanges), hence special care must be taken to guarantee sufficient randomness (e.g., entropy) and resulting security strength. To advance, cyber deception tools must address a broader attack surface with sufficient "deception power" and become more automated, user-friendly, compatible & interoperable, and adaptable across enterprise environments. In addition, similar to the MTD case, sensible management of when, what, and how much cyber deception to deploy will take a critical role in delivering effective solutions for cyber defense.

The recent advances in AI/ML and particularly LLM may provide additional tools to help automating the process of creating deception artifacts. For example, emerging research is harnessing LLMs such as ChatGPT to create increasingly realistic fake assets. Such capabilities enable organizations to not only divert attackers but also to gather critical insights into attack methodologies, reinforcing the overall cyber defense framework. However, special care must be taken when applying any AI/ML/LLM in cyber security for various reasons. These methods, despite the media attention of successes (which are often hype), largely speed up the exploration in the search space (which is of great value), and they do not provide any semantics at a fundamental level. Caution must be taken before putting any trust in their outcomes. Largely speaking, the real reason that such methods may work well lies in the domain expertise, manifested either by salient features via feature-engineering, clearly-defined rules for success and failure, and accumulated knowledge base (e.g., the tremendous amount of games stored for Go), with search expedited by unprecedented level of computing power (see Sect. 6 for further discussions). That said, prudent application of AI/ML/LLM may help automation, bringing about new research opportunities. The key, again, is to justify that the application of such methods is appropriate (blindly using a model is not appropriate, for example) and the outcomes are relevant for the subject domain, in this case automating cyber deception.

3.3 Human Elements: Roles and Common Pitfalls

Traditional cyber defense techniques and tools, such as firewalls or SDN-based traffic monitoring and filtering technologies, typically do not need to include human elements in the process of modeling, design, and evaluation. Even the closely related area of moving target defense usually has the luxury of leaving out human elements due to their technology-centric nature, such as randomization at the software or network levels. Cyber deception, however, inherently involves human elements as part of the overall modeling, design, and evaluation process. After all, technologies aiming to achieve deception without considering human elements are merely obfuscation, with moving target defense as a prominent example.

Generally speaking, we categorize two classes of human elements in the context of cyber deception: defenders of the enterprise, and adversaries aiming to attack and compromise the enterprise. The cyber deception technologies serve as part of the defense mechanisms managed by the defenders, who usually have a more complete view of and access to the enterprise. It is therefore fairly straightforward to capture the defenders' mindset as part of the technology design process. In fact, most cyber security technologies explicitly or implicitly take this approach.

Characterizing the adversaries poses more challenges. As mentioned in Sect. 3.1, while it is natural to carry out threat modeling, it is a lot more involved to characterize the "deception state" of adversaries, such as whether or not they are deceived to act based on defenders' models and analyses. The authors offer the following thoughts on this matter, based on the extensive experience in designing, evaluating, and deploying moving target defense and cyber deception technologies.

- *Roles of modeling adversaries:* When designing and evaluating cyber deception technologies, it is critical to remember that our adversary models are only reflecting *what we think* the adversaries may behave in the setup we provide. Such models are convenient tools for ourselves to formulate the problem aiming for analysis results or design recommendations; they do not represent reality without a meaningful validation. We will be fooling ourselves if failing to realize such.
- *Practicality of models and assumptions:* Further, even with the roles clearly in mind, it is still important to bear in mind that the results are only as good as the assumptions, and adversaries will unlikely behave as we expect in our modeling and analysis process. For example, adversaries may not behave rationally, which is a common assumption in game theory-based formulation, and they will not play the game set up by researchers. Hence, while game theory-based models considering adversary behaviors are useful in high, strategic-level critical thinking, it is unwise to rely on such models for dictating low, tactical level actions. Unfortunately, a plethora of research work exists doing just that.
- *Cognitive Task Analysis (CTA)* is a family of psychological research methods for uncovering and representing what people know and how they think. CTA is a necessary tool to include in the overall process of characterizing adversary behaviors, and the past decade has seen initial effort and advancement toward

this goal. However, such efforts tend to focus mostly on the CTA aspects in some generic cyber deception set up, with only loose connection with realistic deception technologies and enterprise environment.

- *Capturing stage of engagement:* In contrast to CTA, the authors recommend capturing adversary behaviors in the context of cyber deception via pinpointing concrete actions as *stage of engagement* relative to the cyber kill-chain. This is a pragmatic approach focusing on measuring observable adversary actions, as opposed to uncovering what an adversary may know or think. This needs to be performed in a realistic enterprise set up with implemented cyber deception technologies performing expected behaviors, and simulated or actual human adversarial actions engaging the enterprise. Simply resorting to modeling will not do. This is the state-of-the-art approach without relying on knowing what people may know or think; but this approach takes significant expertise and computing as well as human (e.g., serving as adversaries) resources.
- *Combined CTA and engagement approach:* It now seems natural to combine the above two approaches to both capture what adversaries may know and think and pinpoint (and thus corroborate) concrete actions as stage of engagement in the cyber kill-chain. While tempting and something the community should make progress for, special care needs to be taken to sensibly tie these two with sufficient semantics going both directions in a realistic enterprise and deception implementation set up. The authors believe that this is the way to go to further realize the potential of cyber deception, in technological, evaluation, management and operational terms.

With the thoughts described in Sects. 3.1–3.3, we are ready to delve into the cyber deception triad, which comes next.

4 Cyber Deception Triad

The "cyber Deception Triad" comprises Techniques, Humans, and Metrics. Each is important in its own way, and their interactions are particularly critical in the context of cyber deception (Fig. 3). *Techniques* refer to technical aspects of the overall technology portfolios (Sects. 3.1–3.2), *Humans* refer to the human elements

Fig. 3 Cyber deception triad

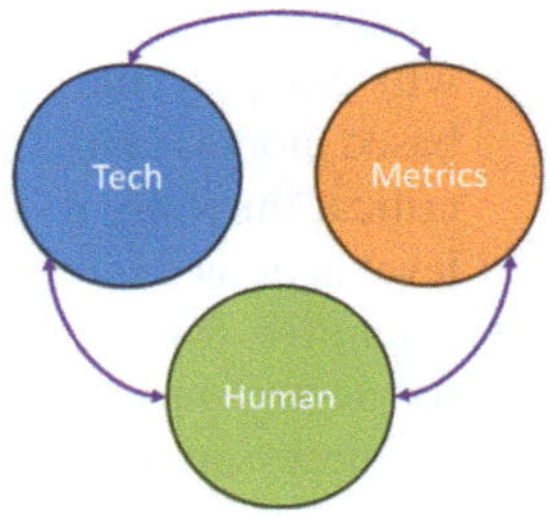

as described in Sect. 3.3, and *Metrics* refer to what to measure to gauge deception effectiveness.

In general, as defined by the National Institute of Standards and Technology (NIST), metrics are tools that are designed to facilitate decision-making and improve performance and accountability through collection, analysis, and reporting of relevant performance-related data. Security metrics can be considered as a standard or system used for quantitatively measuring the security strength or posture of an enterprise. Security metrics are essential to understand, manage, and improve enterprise security. The past two decades have seen a good amount of research publications on security metrics [6–11]. Particularly, the authors have investigated defining and using appropriate security metrics for cyber situational awareness [12, 13], where the enterprise network setup is similar to what we expect for cyber deception. However, most prior work did not tackle the interactions of techniques, metrics, and human elements, as we aim to describe here in the cyber deception context.

Focusing on techniques and looking at the interactions with metrics and human elements, the following research questions beg for answers.

- *Techniques Question (TQ) 1: How to measure deception effectiveness without considering human aspects of the adversary?* Depending on the particular techniques, examples include entropy (e.g., for software diversification) and ratio of fake vs. real hosts (e.g., for host-ballooning). These can be related to increased work factor, which is a typical argument point from a technical point of view not considering the human aspects.
- *TQ2: How to measure deception effectiveness considering the human aspects of the adversary?* This invariably involves some level of adversary modeling or CTA, which was discussed in Sect. 3.3. Naturally, researchers working on tools and techniques tend to focus more on the technical aspects, often times paying less attention to the human aspects resulting in less convincing effectiveness evidence.
- *TQ3: How to convince human users for deployment?* Typically, researchers focus on developing the tools and techniques. When it comes to why and how users may use their tools, the answers tend to miss the main point. Examples from our first-hand experience include arguments such as: “the solution significantly increases the enterprise security”, “our results outperform the previous works”, or “the benefits are significant”, etc. They may make good sense from the technical point of view, but are usually not the type of answers users are looking for.

Focusing on humans and looking at the interactions with techniques and metrics, the following questions need to be answered for the potential users, such as defenders (e.g., system administrators) of the enterprise environment.

- *Defender question (DQ) 1: What assumptions are made about the target environment?* Good researchers and developers usually include some environment assumptions in their work, including the general enterprise network set up (e.g., routers and switches), typical security measures (e.g., firewalls), and representative hosts (e.g., operating systems and applications such as browsers). These assumptions, while largely valid in research and development, typically lack real-world validation. This is expected and most common, but a point to remember during technology maturation and pilot installation.

- *DQ2: What are the requirements for users in the environment?* This is a similar case as the above, only more involved. Users may include system administrators with privileged access or normal users with limited access. Researchers and developers may assume that administrators are motivated and knowledgeable enough to deploy new, exciting technologies, which is far from the truth based on our first-hand experience trying to pilot-deploy advanced cyber security technologies. Administrators are mostly knowledgeable in the IT training they obtained, tend to follow industry-standard practices, and are largely conservative and reluctant to adopt disruptive technologies such as moving target defense, let alone cyber deception which sounds confusing and a tall order to administer. Normal users usually do not care, so long as their normal workflow is not disrupted.
- *DQ3: How to help defenders measure deception effectiveness and added value?* Good cyber deception research should include some metrics, measured results and effective analysis, albeit they are sometimes mainly for convenience and not relevant in an actual enterprise. The effectiveness metrics should go beyond the necessary improved security strength or speculative increased work factor of the adversary, for example. Focusing on humans, the key here is to help defenders do the measurement and make the value proposition, which necessitates human engagement through questionnaire or discussions.
- *DQ4: What are the anticipated impact on enterprise operations?* Good research should discuss potential benefits to enterprise operations, but in-depth discussions of the overall impact are usually lacking, which is not surprising. Holistic impact analysis should go beyond technical aspects (e.g., increased security) and cover aspects such as compatibility with existing tools, added administration burden, anticipated interoperability model with current configuration, perceived workflow changes, impact on business and user workflow, just to name a few.

Similarly, the following questions need to be addressed related to (modeling) the adversaries.

- *Adversary question (AQ) 1: What are the assumptions about adversaries?* There are various ways of capturing adversary behaviors, from the lower, activity level (e.g., cracking a password) to the higher, strategic goals level (e.g., compromising a database server via any possible means). In research and development, behaviors are usually represented in a way that can be reasoned upon, such as an action set (e.g., escalating a privilege). As indicated in Sect. 3.1, threat models need to be clearly delineated, and adversary behaviors need to be relevant and practical.

- *AQ2: Are those assumptions realistic/justifiable?* This is a common pitfall in most research and development effort in that researchers are eager to accept their own assumptions without a reasonable amount of effort to justify the assumptions in some realistic set up. This is not to require that research effort has to be totally practical; only a request to at least spend some effort and justify the assumptions. This exercise will be beneficial for both techniques- and humans-focused research.
- *AQ3: What is the correct way of capturing technical artifacts in CTA-focused research?* Similar to how tool developers treat human elements, CTA-focused research (maybe justifiably so) tends to spend some superficial level of effort on the verity and realism of technical artifacts. Examples include a sentence describing an activity (e.g., a response is received) in a questionnaire, or a representation (e.g, action *a*) to be included in some analysis. While reasonable, it is prudent to connect such representations with the real-world via consulting subject matter experts or extracting from realistic test and evaluation for realism and relevance.
- *AQ4: To what extent researchers can trust CTA results for cyber deception?* This question means to trigger controversies. On one hand, CTA is a mature field with most respectable tools and processes, providing a solid base for trust-worthiness. On the other hand, the complicated nature of cyber deception (e.g., the interactions in the Triad) exposes some drawbacks of traditional CTA, which was not designed to handle complications involving complex environment, sophisticated attacks, multi-stage nature of engagement, and the uncertainty of human behaviors. For example, CTA results indicate that a human participant (acting as an adversary) seems to be deceived, but what does this really mean for cyber deception research and development? Can this result be validated in real-world? Can this provide guidelines for design or operation? This situation brings about both challenges and opportunities: we need to consider CTA results in context (e.g., environment, assumptions, purpose of CTA, applicability, etc.), and ample opportunities exist to enhance CTA research and practice in cyber deception, for both defenders and adversaries. For example, we may connect and compare CTA results with concrete measurements of adversary actions in simulated or actual enterprise operations. This also ties with repeatable deception evaluation, see Sect. 5.

Finally, focusing on metrics and looking at the interactions with techniques and human elements, the following metrics questions emerge, related to techniques and humans, respectively.

- *Metrics question (MQ) 1: On techniques, what are the metrics?* This is a loaded question, and research efforts abound spanning from abstract properties (e.g., based on set theory for consistency) to artifact-specific calculations (e.g., entropy or fake/real ratio) . For cyber deception, we focus on metrics that relate to techniques (e.g., providing a customized view), assets (e.g., hosts and software stack), and operations (e.g., mission or business logic) in the enterprise. These metrics should be clearly defined, potentially at different levels (e.g., stack, messages, hosts, etc.), and are amenable to measurement and analysis. Metrics that are not readily measurable serve no practical use. In addition to technique-specific metrics, some system or enterprise level metrics are also needed, such as improved security, resilience, and performance cost.

- *MQ2: On techniques, where and how to measure the identified metrics?* While many research efforts have the luxury of largely ignoring this question via readily gathering metrics data from modeling and simulation, this is rather critical and involved in a realistic enterprise set up. Care must be taken to appropriately place measurement points at different levels across various locations of the enterprise, sometimes with necessary instrumentation. This ties closely with repeatable deception evaluation (Sect. 5).
- *MQ3: On techniques, what are the analyses and actions?* For modeling and analysis, the obvious answer is to better inform and provide some level of predictive power to users, such as trend analysis or captured malicious activities (serving as sensors). For cyber deception, this needs to go further. Particularly, analyses should put situations in context relative to the cyber kill-chain and the relevance in the enterprise environment. Further, analyses should inform course-of-actions as part of defensive counter-measures in the overall enterprise context.
- *MQ4: On human defenders, what are the proper metrics to enable adoption?* For both engaging discussions or collecting feedback via questionnaires, metrics proper to both the enterprise environment and the cyber deception techniques need to be defined, and they need to be relevant and meaningful (e.g., metrics embedded in a question that relates to the user) for human defenders. Prior work tends to be techniques-oriented; this has to be improved for cyber deception, emphasizing both enterprise and human relevance.
- *MQ5: On human adversaries, what are the proper metrics to gauge effectiveness?* A readily available (technical) answer is the anticipated increase in work factor for adversaries, which is typically related to the level of additional effort to access or compromise assets (e.g., scanning potential hosts, lateral movement, etc.). A perception answer is always hard to find, and the state-of-the-art typically adopts CTA in some (hopefully) realistic experimental setup. As previously mentioned, this approach lacks the sufficient level of connection with realistic cyber security and deception flavors.
- *MQ6: On humans in general, what improvement is needed for CTA?* In addition to enhancing the overall process for embracing cyber deception CTA, an important aspect is related to additional or improved metrics that can better connect with both the deception techniques and human elements. This is a new and interesting research area.

Careful readers may have noticed the overlapping flavor among some questions, which is natural due to the interactions in the Triad. The key point, however, is that different starting points and focuses will have different perspectives and priorities, which lead to different ways of emphasizing some aspects and paying less attention to others. This is expected. The purpose here is not to criticize ignorance or to demand completeness; capturing all aspects in equally high fidelity is neither wise principle nor good practice. Nonetheless, researchers should keep good awareness of the holistic picture, and make justifiable and relevant assumptions in modeling, design, and analysis. This is particularly important for cyber deception research, where human elements play critical roles and involve extensive interactions with techniques and metrics. Finally, given the potentially large number of interactions and cyber deception use cases, it is highly desirable to be able to perform repeatable deception evaluation and exercise different deception techniques under various levels of management and control in a representative enterprise environment.

5 Repeatable Deception Evaluation

In our experience, the evaluation of defense-based deception solution implementations had not yet reached a point of providing an acceptable degree of assurance of its efficacy and practicality. *First*, most cyber deception experiments lack (relatively) rigorous experimental control for reproducing a range of operational conditions and correlating the outcomes. *Second*, the assumed adversary models only reflect the defender's perception of adversary behaviors in the provided setup. It is challenging for a validation of such solution to be free of a prevailing bias. Moreover, various modeling-based approaches, such as dynamic Bayesian attack graphs, Markov decision process (MDP)-based or game theory-based modeling, do not scale very well as they lead to state explosion, partly because of the depth and amount of resources needed to maintain coherent and consistent fictitious views. *Third*, most existing, advanced cyber ranges are not yet tailored toward validating cyber deception solutions, since they aim at experimenting with the mainstream cyber-defense capabilities. *Fourth*, there is a lack of specific methodologies and metrics for cyber deception evaluation. In this chapter, we attempt to close some of these gaps.

5.1 Distributed Live, Virtual, and Constructive (LVC) Testing

The first step for deception evaluation is developing an environment which captures the complex, dynamic and stochastic nature of networks and computers. The evaluation platforms must be scalable, repeatable, and accessible. Most cyber-testing environments offer either a simulation, emulation, or live systems. The live systems approach offers realistic scenarios (including real tools, traffic, services, etc.). However, it is limited in experimentation and scale. Emulation [15] involves mapping a desired experimental network topology and software configuration onto the physical infrastructure. The emulation approach supports high fidelity testing, but it requires a higher cost since a significant amount of resources is required to emulate large networks. Even with the use of virtualization, its scalability is lower compared to simulation. The simulation approach [17] models the real world of interacting components and uses instrumentation to measure performance. Simulation has higher scalability but lower fidelity compared to emulation.

Our approach is to build a *hybrid* evaluation framework with integrated live, emulation and simulation capabilities and real hardware to balance large scale and high-fidelity requirements for evaluation. The hardware equipment is connected to the virtual (emulation) network. The emulation part of the evaluation framework is designed to faithfully emulate various constructs relevant to network operations with realistic constraints, superimposed through addition of the deception elements and injection of adversarial activity within each representative network segment. We then use the combined emulation results for extrapolation onto simulation behaviors for higher scale. In addition, we develop integrated analytical and visualization capabilities to quantitatively and qualitatively evaluate the monitored and captured outcomes against the metrics selected for such evaluations. Specifically, we develop the "what-if" analytical engine to model (through the use of emulation/simulation) operational effects of applying deception and effects of injecting cyber attack activities into the deception-fortified network and host environment. Our implementation features a layered scenario generation method to sequentially add deception infrastructure with associated network traffic and an orchestrated injection of adversarial effects into the emulation and simulation engines, respectively. This allows for separate testing to assess the deception impact on blue and red forces, respectively. The conceptual view of this approach is shown in Fig. 4.

The emulation platform integrates the software-in-the-loop (SIL) network stacks and software systems to reproduce wired and wireless data transmission environment with a high level of fidelity. We integrate full-stack containers with Common Open Research Emulator (CORE) and Extendable Mobile Ad-hoc Network Emulator (EMANE). CORE focuses on emulating layers 3 and above (network, transport, application) while EMANE is mostly concerned with layers 1 and 2 (physical and data link). Together, they provide an interface for designing and configuring virtual networks, consisting of lightweight virtual machines interconnected with pluggable MAC and PHY layer models. Our simulation-based evaluation features ns-3, a discrete-event network simulator supporting large-scale and complex network simulations, and OMNeT++ which uses a modular and component-based architecture with parallelization support. We split the system-under-evaluation using parallel domain decomposition techniques so that the segmented analysis can be used for evaluating the separated workflows for better scalability. In addition, we aggregate non-relevant aspects of node and network behaviors to further enhance scalability.

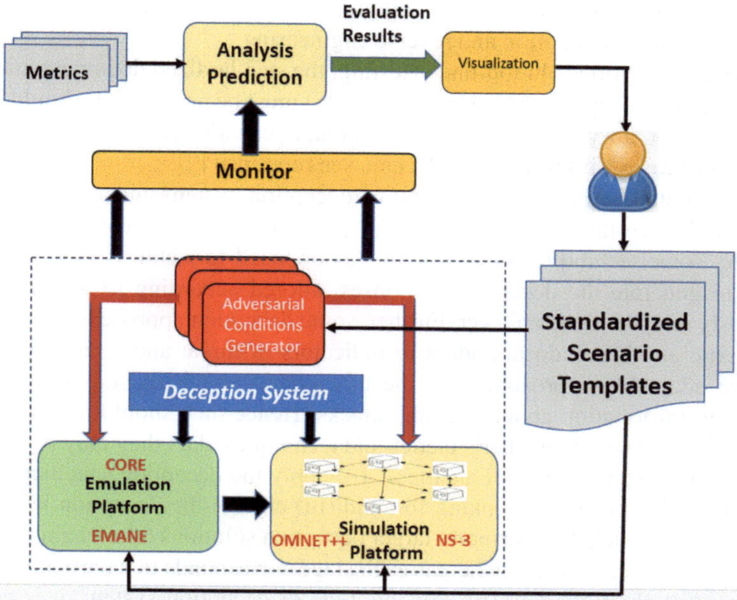

Fig. 4 Conceptual cyber-deception evaluation framework design

5.2 *Normalization of Evaluation Methodology*

The design of the deception evaluation framework must support standardization of the deception testing. We will examine several design factors for the deception evaluation framework that would contribute toward repeatability and comparability of testing deception operation scenarios.

The evaluation framework must support an ability to generate network traffic by using traffic generators and have playback capabilities based on the provided scenarios. For realistic scenario generation, and to reproduce operational enterprise environments, the deception testbed for the enterprise environment is expected to include (i) LAN/WAN enterprise equipment, (ii) data-centers, for example servers, clusters, (iii) end-user environments, for example desktops, printers, etc. In addition, they may also include telecommunications equipment, some VoIP infrastructure, IoT devices, etc.

The cyber-testing environment for deception testing must simulate the mechanics of computer and network attacks and allow for configuring and baselining of a range of automated attack scenarios, as well as new scenario developments, aimed at reproduceability, monitoring and performance measurements. The red team components must be standardized as automated probing and penetration tool kits with the well-defined (versioned) capabilities. This would allow for application of relative metrics to compare different deception solutions. This red team component of the evaluation framework must include automated tools for network reconnaissance, network and host penetration and reverse engineering.

For each deception solution-under-testing, the standardized documentation input in the form of concept of operations (CONOPS) must be provided. It should include (i) a deception story, (ii) supported operational scenario, (iii) types of supported network use cases, (iv) threat models, etc., see reference [2].

It is essential to note that the type of deception system-under-evaluation will heavily influence the selection of attacking scenarios and evaluation metrics. For example, some techniques offer stateful (as opposed to stateless) deception—the ability to generate the deception responses tailored according to the information previously relayed to the attacker. Further, some deception approaches are designed to be static and hence do not adapt to indicators of threat and compromises. The dynamic adaptable approaches, on the other hand, are based on observing and reacting to information about ongoing attacks. Hence they should be evaluated by their ability to (i) infer attacker's tactics and techniques, data they may be searching for, and sophistication level of an attack, (ii) apply the deception specifically to the information the attacker is looking for, and (iii) change the deception level before and during the attack. Furthermore, larger deception solutions offer chains of (multi-stage) deception capabilities whereas each stage corresponds to a particular stage in the cyber-kill chain model [16]. For this type of deception system, it is essential to perform an attacker movement tracking to create a dynamic feedback loop for a defender. Such system is expected to prepare and implement predictive defensive strategies or to react to detected suspicious activity without human intervention.

We distinguish several steps in the deception evaluation process (Fig. 5):

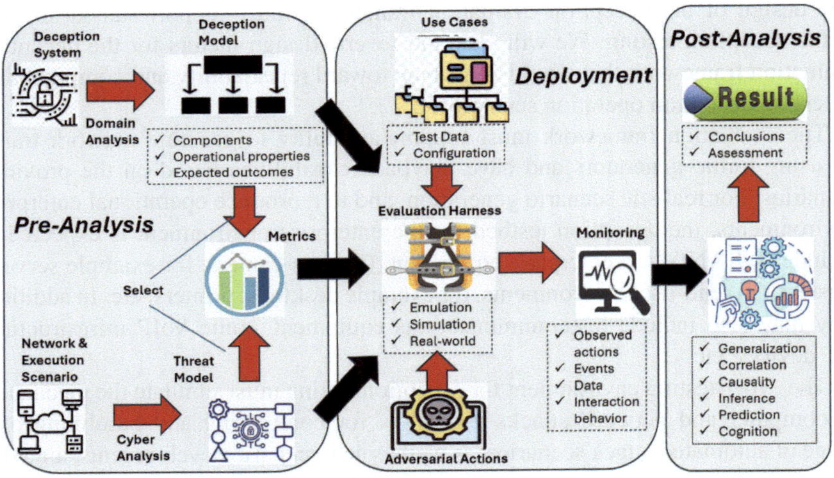

Fig. 5 Deception evaluation process

- The cyber analysis must be undertaken before the deception experiment testing, to correlate a given network use case with the provided threat model and with selected attack scenarios to verify consistency and applicability.
- The solution's domain analysis must be performed to infer main components and operational properties of the deception system-under-testing. This is necessary for a selection of proper evaluation metrics and for defining the expected outcome. For example, the solution may feature honeypots and decoys. The main purpose of a honeypot is to draw an attacker away from the true network and to gather information about the attacker and the plausible threats. The high-fidelity honeypots take time and resources to build. Decoy systems, on the other hand, tend to be embedded within the true network and are used to obfuscate the true network assets and confuse the attacker about the true network topology. Decoy-based systems are relatively static, low fidelity defensive measures which limit their long term utility against persistent or knowledgeable attackers. However, decoys implanted in the real sub-net increase the attacker's work factor since the attacker has to differentiate each asset as real or fake and to take extra precautions not to trigger an alert. A deception system is also expected to have sensor capabilities—collection of information to detect adversarial activity (network scanning, logon attempts, use of stolen passwords, etc.). The evaluation framework should determine the capabilities of a given solution for taking automated or directed action on a network/host (i.e.,updating or creating new decoys, configuration changes, modifying service banners, etc.) in response to detected suspicious activity (probing, intrusion alerts, etc.).
- Perform actual deception evaluation tests which include applying the test configuration based on selected network scenarios, starting the network scenario in emulation, simulation and hybrid environments, deploying deception solution-under-evaluation, injecting adversarial activities, and performing event monitoring and data collection.
- Conduct post-analysis to evaluate results of the tests based on the selected metrics in the context of the provided use cases. The analysis should use generalization, correlation, causal and prediction techniques based on the ground truth provided as a test input, observed actions and captured events/data. The evaluation system should provide usable interfaces to display the collected data and evaluation conclusions based on inferences and the selected metrics.
- Cognitive post-analysis focuses on human (network users, defenders, and attackers) cognition and behavior inferred based on collected data about the human interactions with the target environment. For example, the inferred network user behavior might look different between the benign user and the malicious interactions. Another example is that the attacker's realization of a presence of active deception can cause increased delays, confusion and surprise [14]. Further, cognitive biases are prevalent in cyber attacker behaviors and hence can be intensified to disrupt cyber attacks. By analyzing the collected data, it is possible to determine if a particular bias was triggered as a result of the deception activity and also to identify the technique(s) which caused the triggering effect.

There are a number of generic metrics that can be used to evaluate a deception solution-under-test:

- The solution efficacy is to be evaluated based on given test scenarios, captured outcomes and effects. The efficacy metrics may include (i) wasting attackers' resources (deny/delay) on probing/penetrating a given system, or on trying to deduce fictitious states/systems, (ii) revealing attackers' capabilities (strengths, weaknesses and intentions), and (iii) directing the adversary to a particular pattern of behavior. For example, the metric of delaying attackers rather than denying them access to a target system or networks is applicable for a scenario whereas an attacker already has a foothold on the network.
- Projected lifetime of a given deception solution.
- Potential adverse impact on a defended network, its services and missions.
- Depth of deception can be framed in relaying the deception story through multiple probing channels. The deception system must show story consistency in direct and indirect deceptive network responses on different network layers, protocols, nodes and networking boundaries.
- Believably—provable ability to frustrate, delay and confuse adversaries. The metrics may include collected statistics such as time spent by attacker, amount of network traffic (packets, bytes, connections, etc.), and intrusion detection alerts per (i) a single decoy, (ii) honeypot/honey-net, (iii) real host, and (iv) the number of detected exploit attempts against decoys/honeypots, etc.
- Presence of built-in capabilities to track and measure observable adversary actions. This may include ability to capture the states of engagements—pinpointing specific adversary behaviors in the form of concrete actions relative to the cyber kill-chain and corresponding deception chains [16].
- Deception configuration control—management capabilities to implement the Monitor, Analyze, Plan, Execute (MAPE) control-loop paradigm for agile, active, and adaptive deception.
- Deployment costs associated with performance overhead, path criticality for network operations, and a cost-benefit analysis. For example, configuring a high-fidelity honeypot often requires a similar amount of effort in configuring a true server while creating lightweight low-interaction decoys requires significantly less efforts and resources.

6 Recent Technology Advances and Cyber Deception

Intruder-defender interaction research, including deception topics areas, often emphasizes on understanding the adversary's objective and behavioral pattern. The defender's understanding of intruder/adversary is approximate at best, with ground truth rarely available. Furthermore, the intruder's objective can be dynamic and may change (unpredictably) due to the intruder's own strategy and conditions, which may be outside of the defender's purview.

In a deceptive enterprise environment, defenders' understanding of themselves and their environment are critical, and consistent presentation of the enterprise assets and environment is of the utmost importance for presenting a coherent landscape for the intruders to comprehend. This is particularly important for the case with multiple coordinating and colluding intruders.

In traditional cyber security where detection is imperfect, imprecise and often difficult, the asymmetry of advantage generally goes against the defenders who need to perform detection and analysis. In the case of cyber deception, however, it is the intruders that need to bear the burden to distinguish real versus virtual assets, real versus virtual/fake events, etc. Understanding of intruders' objectives will help with positioning and presentation of deceptive assets, e.g., network topology, device configuration (e.g., firewall), traffic monitoring and control (e.g., SDN-based controller configuration), deceptive documents, and other software or informational assets. However, this is not to substitute defenders' understanding of themselves, which enable the presentation of consistent and coherent views to intruders.

Deception (for enhancing defense) has historically been a resource-intensive process that required significant effort to create a convincing fictitious view or facade for attackers. Deception may experience state explosion with the depth and amount of resources needed to maintain coherent and consistent fictitious views. If the facade was not coherent and consistent, attackers would simply ignore it, rendering the resources used to create the facade wasteful.

Deception processes are manual, scripted, or recorded. Regardless, deception operations require assets, data, and events to be carefully generated, curated, and presented, in order to deliver coherent (e.g., making sense), consistent (with the environment), and corroborative deception views and capabilities.

The manual process involves creating deception elements by hand, such as changing host responses, inventing non-existent employees, and presenting false enterprise resources. Manual deception processes require extensive effort from defenders, who must create each deception asset from scratch and place it properly to present the deception view. A major disadvantage is that all of this must be done *a priori*, which means that the deception resources must be deployed before the attack happens, the deception view must be up and running all of the time, and it becomes very difficult to alter the deception view. Moreover, the view the attacker receives is more or less static and cannot adapt to attack actions.

Scripting takes the steps that defenders would do manually, but turn them into scripts. Scripts allow for defenders to stand up deception resources when needed, such as receiving attack alerts. Multiple deception strategies and tactics can be scripted and launched on-demand, enabling dynamic deception views based on awareness of the attack and security posture as well as business logic needs. Similar to the manual case, such scripting must be created *a priori*.

Modern gaming infrastructure may contribute to rendering the dynamics of deception mechanisms, for example by using multi-player gaming engines to serve and coordinate deception resources. One or more intruders who fall into the deception environment essentially play a multi-player game controlled by the defender's (role playing) gaming engine serving misleading assets (e.g., responses, data, documents, sequence of events, etc.). In this case, the defender needs to prepare a story line for the game, with all possible story paths and objects/assets within the game. The story line presented in the deception game needs to present a virtual but realistic world. The intruders will be forced to play within this world. Any intruders' action that may lead to 'escape' from this virtual world needs to be carefully responded and steered back into the deceptive game's world. This response needs to be viable and consistent with the deceptive game's world.

It is important to note that the intruders generally do not have direct physical access to the targeted network and devices. Hence, the intruder's understanding of targeted systems and the environment is based on accessing and querying targeted systems' software stacks. This fact enables the defender to optimize resources and response to the intruder's action on-demand. Without access to factual information, attackers cannot verify deception against ground truth, but can check against previous/historical exposure/experience from the environment. Multiple colluding intruders may also cross check each other's views of the environment and assets. Hence, coherent and consistent deception presentations across intruders are paramount.

In addition, defenders can also record network traffic and user interactions with enterprise elements, and play the recording back to the intruder overlaid on the deception elements to present a view that appears to be more accurate of the enterprise. Generative machine learning [18] can be used to further expand and diversify said recorded enterprise activity and traffic and store it in a database, for later retrieval and deployment at the advent of an attack. This traffic artifact gives the appearance of a standard workflow for the enterprise, except that all of these elements are fictitious. It is important to carefully splice traffic sequences to present a seamless and convincing enterprise traffic background. It is also important to synchronize the background traffic with the deception story presented to the intruders.

As mentioned in Sect. 3.2, human knowledge can be captured in deception assets and events, and artificial intelligence (AI)/machine learning (ML) can be utilized to pre-generate a rich set of traffic or other data to be later deployed in deception game sessions. Generative AI, such as large language model (LLM) [19, 20] and the popular Chat Generative Pre-trained Transformer (ChatGPT) [21], can be used for suggesting potential assets, data and events for supporting deception sessions. For example, large language models have created opportunities for rapid, automated generation of various kinds of data, which could be leveraged for deception purposes such as fake source code [22, 23], etc. Tools such as ChatGPT can create lots of simulated users with believable content in the enterprise efficiently, which will naturally push the attackers to expend more resources to understand and identify targets. Similarly, synthetic and realistic traffic can be generated in the environment, which can be used to confuse or trap the attackers in the deception deployment. All these will be executed in the context of the enterprise network environment and the various aspects discussed in this chapter.

However, before (blindly and hoping for the best) applying such tools, the understanding of appropriate positions, roles and potential pitfalls in the context of above aspects is critical; new technologies do not naturally fit in well in the current landscape. These assets, data, and events are integral parts of the deception story, and they need to be generated in a way that is coherent by themselves and consistent with the deception story line and the enterprise environment.

It is important to remember that, as much as great progress has been made in past decades and given all the media coverage, AI/ML by itself does not provide any semantic wisdom in the problem domain, including generic cyber security and the subject at hand, cyber deception. AI/ML methods may expedite the search process in finding/suggesting assets, data, or events based on human knowledge or repeated games, they cannot be relied upon in terms of the overall deception strategies, scenarios, or even the story line. As in many other problem domains, knowledge is the key to success, with AI/ML playing supporting (yet important) roles to make up for human weakness (e.g., humans are bad in performing labor-intensive, repetitive tasks). Moreover, LLM and ChatGPT (and technologies alike) tend to hallucinate resulting in nonsensical outputs, which if used for cyber deception means non-coherent and non-consistent suggestions. Special care must be taken to verify and validate such outcomes, understanding and controlling the quality and use of such assets, data, and events generated utilizing AI/ML or LLM/ChatGPT. A hybrid approach of human knowledge augmented by AI/ML/LLM has the best potential to achieve success.

References

1. Heckman et al (2015), Cyber Denial, Deception and Counter Deception A Framework for Supporting Active Cyber Defense, Springer, 2015.
2. Briskin et al (2016), Design Considerations for Building Cyber Deception Systems, in Cyber Deception. Building the Scientific Foundation (editors: Sushil Jajodia, V.S. Subrahmanian, Vipin Swarup, Cliff Wang), Springer, 2016. Invited book chapter.
3. Ahn et al (2018), NetShifter: A Comprehensive Multi-Dimensional Network Obfuscation and Deception Solution, in Autonomous Cyber Deception, Reasoning, Adaptive Planning, and Evaluation of Honeythings (editors: Ehab Al-Shaer, Jingpeng Wei, Kevin W. Hamlen, Cliff Wang), Springer, 2018. Invited book chapter.
4. Lee EA (2016) Fundamental Limits of Cyber-Physical Systems Modeling. ACM Trans. on Cyber-Physical Systems:1–26. https://dl.acm.org/doi/10.1145/2912149
5. Box GEP, Draper NR (1987) Empirical Model-Building and Response Surfaces, Wiley, New York
6. Fracker, M. (1991a). Measures of situation awareness: Review and future directions (Report No. AL-TR-1991-0128). Wright-Patterson Air Force Base, OH: Armstrong Laboratories.
7. Fracker, M. (1991b). Measures of situation awareness: An experimental evaluation (Report No. AL-TR-1991-0127). Wright-Patterson Air Force Base, OH: Armstrong Laboratories.
8. Hecker, A. (2008). On System Security Metrics and the Definition Approaches. the 2nd International Conference on Emerging Security Information, Systems and Technologies.
9. Heyman T., et al. (2008). Using security patterns to combine security metrics. the 3rd International Conference on Availability, Reliability and Security.

10. Jansen, W. (2009). Directions in Security Metrics Research. National Institute of Standards and Technology, Computer Security Division.
11. Manadhata P. and Wing J. (2011). An Attack Surface Metric. Software Engineering, IEEE Transactions on, vol. 37, no. 3, pp. 371–386.
12. Sun et al (2011) Automatic security analysis using security metrics. 1207–1212. 10.1109/MILCOM.2011.6127465.
13. Cheng et al (2014), "Metrics of Security", in Cyber Defense and Situational Awareness (editors: Alexander Kott, Cliff Wang, Robert F. Erbacher), Springer 2014. Invited book chapter.
14. Kimberly J. Ferguson-Walter, (2020) "An Empirical Assessment of the Effectiveness of Deception for Cyber Defense" University of Massachusetts, Amherst.
15. Jaime C. Acosta1 et al, (2017) "Cybersecurity Deception Experimentation System" CCDC Army Research Laboratory, El Paso, TX, USA. Department of Computer Science, University of Texas at El Paso, TX, USA
16. Geoff Hancock (2020) "CYBER DECEPTION: HOW TO BUILD A PROGRAM", Whitepaper, Attivo Networks, www.attivonetworks.com https://www.thinkers360.com/tl/assets/images/publication/file20220116030119.pdf
17. Edward A. Cranford et al, (2017) "Learning about Cyber Deception through Simulations: Predictions of Human Decision Making with Deceptive Signals in Stackelberg Security Games" Carnegie Mellon University, 5000 Forbes Avenue Pittsburgh, PA 15213 USA
18. "Generative Models". OpenAI. June 16, 2016
19. "Better Language Models and Their Implications". OpenAI. 2019-02-14. Archived from the original on 2020-12-19. Retrieved 2019-08-25.
20. Bowman, Samuel R. (2023). "Eight Things to Know about Large Language Models". arXiv:2304.00612
21. https://openai.com/index/chatgpt/
22. R. Lowe and J. Leike, "Aligning language models to follow instructions," 2022 27 January. [Online]. Available: https://openai.com/research/instruction-following.
23. J. Wei, X. Wang, D. Schuurmans, et. Al., "Chain-of-Thought Prompting Elicits Reasoning in Large Language Models," In Proceedings of 35th Advances in Neural Information Processing Systems, 2022.

MIX
Papier aus verantwortungsvollen Quellen
Paper from responsible sources
FSC® C105338

If you have any concerns about our products,
you can contact us on
ProductSafety@springernature.com

In case Publisher is established outside the EU,
the EU authorized representative is:
Springer Nature Customer Service Center GmbH
Europaplatz 3, 69115 Heidelberg, Germany

Printed by Libri Plureos GmbH
in Hamburg, Germany